*"This is the way I cook at home –
a wander around the garden to find the flavours for
our evening meal. Even if it's just a bunch of mint or parsley,
our everyday dinners get a fresh, vibrant lift."*

eat fresh

COOKING THROUGH THE SEASONS

annabel langbein

Photography
Aaron McLean

annabel langbein books

For my family, both past and present, with all my thanks for nurturing a deep respect for nature and nourishing my love of cooking and the pleasures of the table.

AN ANNABEL LANGBEIN BOOK

First published in September 2007 by Annabel Langbein Books.
An imprint of The International Culinary Institute Press Ltd,
PO Box 99068 Newmarket, Auckland, New Zealand
Reprinted December 2007

ISBN 978-0-9582029-7-8

© Text copyright Annabel Langbein 2007
© Photography copyright Aaron McLean 2007, except where listed in the photography credits on page 240
© Design and layout copyright The International Culinary Institute Press Ltd
All rights reserved. No part of this book may be reproduced in any form, except for brief reviews, without written permission of the publisher.

The right of Annabel Langbein and Aaron McLean to be identified as the author and photographer of this work has been asserted by them in accordance with the Copyright Act, 1994.

FOOD AND STYLING Annabel Langbein
DESIGN Inhouse Design
COPY EDITORS Sally Butters and Jane Turner
TYPESETTING & PRODUCTION Natalie Keys for ICIP
Printed in China, through Colorcraft Ltd., Hong Kong

www.annabel-langbein.com
www.annabel-cooking.com

Contents

Spring	Savoury	12-55
	Sweet	56-67
Summer	Savoury	68-111
	Sweet	112-123
Autumn	Savoury	124-167
	Sweet	168-179
Winter	Savoury	180-225
	Sweet	226-233
Glossary		234-235
Index		236-240

'I was lucky to grow up in a family where fresh garden harvests marked the seasons and home-cooked meals made with those harvests were a pleasurable ritual that punctuated our daily lives.'

Introduction

Like many New Zealanders, my roots are deeply tethered in the earth in a satisfying cycle of growing, harvesting, cooking and sharing around the table.

My father Fred, who worked in a downtown city office, would come home each night to tend his vegetable garden and his bees. His washed and trimmed vegetable offerings would arrive at the back door, ready for the creation of a delicious dinner. My mother Anne was a natural cook and a home science university graduate. Her well-honed cooking skills and astute relationship with Cyril the butcher, coupled with Father's prodigious garden efforts, provided us with a nutritious and interesting diet. Coming out of the Second World War, my parents were thrifty and resourceful. Nothing was wasted, but ours was no dour, mean-spirited table. Like many mothers of her era, mine chose to stay at home and she fed and clothed us with care.

Entering my teens in the 1970s as a fully-fledged hippy and feminist, I could not believe my mother's house-bound existence. To me, her life seemed akin to slavery. Although I loved to cook, I railed against domesticity, consumerism and the urban world in general, leaving school and home when I was just 16.

My mother took me to Europe, no doubt in the hope of convincing me that the real world had merit, but on my return I promptly moved up the Whanganui River with some friends to an alternative lifestyle growing vegetables, cooking over a fire and living off the land.

For several years I hunted and fished for much of my own food; caught eels, ran trap lines and jumped out of helicopters for live-deer recovery as a means of making a living. What I caught I cooked, experimenting endlessly in a learning process that drew where it could from what I had seen in my mother's kitchen. For the most part, my learning was unfettered by tradition or the rules of any particular school. Some things worked, others failed. I kept cooking. I never formally learnt to cook (aside from a couple of residential courses at the Culinary Institute of America in upstate New York later in my career), choosing instead to study horticulture at Lincoln University. Understanding how plants grow is incredibly useful when it comes to cooking.

We all know it's easier to serve a ready-made meal or takeaways than it is to cook a meal from the beginning. But it's not at all hard to cook a delicious meal from scratch and the results will not only taste better but chances are will be a lot better for you.

True, there will likely be an extra 20 or 30 minutes required in preparation, but who said that was all you could do? Cooking is not something that requires your full focus. You can chat with the kids while they do their homework or share a glass of wine with your partner. The kitchen is the hub of a home, where everyone naturally gravitates.

They say you go back to your roots as you age. In the recall of those simple childhood traditions we find ways to enjoy our own lives and families. Eating home-grown, home-cooked food is part of the way we live as a family today. It connects us, even if only in a small way, to the rhythms of nature. Wandering around my garden at the end of a busy day to find something to eat for our evening meal is incredibly satisfying. So, too, is the daily ritual of setting the table, lighting some candles and sitting down together to enjoy simple, freshly cooked food. I hope my own kids will take these rituals into their own future lives. They are small things, yet immensely nourishing.

Annabel Langbein, 2007

Look for this symbol - ⓥ - throughout the book and go on-line to www.annabel-langbein.com to access free cooking lessons with Annabel.

Spring

The promise of spring is unveiled in fat fruit buds and fragrant blossom. Soldier-like spears of asparagus emerge from the bare, cold earth while seeds that have lain dormant and seemingly lifeless for months spring to life, banishing winter in a flush of soft green growth. It's hard not to feel some sense of wonder. How does a lettuce become a lettuce and not a tomato or a bean? The magic within each seed, in a carefully coded blueprint, has evolved over millennia for survival and success. Emerging from the cocoon of winter, we savour the first delicate tastes of the new season in food that is light, fresh and revitalising.

'Learning to cook is a bit like learning to play music. Once you have a few chords up your sleeve you can start to improvise. Before you know it you are composing tunes and creating your own dishes.'

The spring palate

Fresh in spring

apricots
asparagus
broad beans
carrots
cherries
fennel
globe artichokes
lemons and limes
miner's lettuce
new potatoes
peaches
peas, snowpeas and sugar snaps
rhubarb
salad leaves - lettuces, mesclun
spinach, rocket
strawberries
tangelos and late oranges
watercress
zucchini

Flavours

bay
chervil
coriander
garlic chives
lemon grass
mint
thyme

The calendar tells us it's time and it feels as if spring is in the air, but the pleasure of new-season tastes has yet to be revealed. It takes a good few weeks before any of those luscious spring harvests are actually ready to pick. Early spring can be a time of lean pickings, but in the meantime, we are well over winter's stodge. A welcome interlude comes via Asian-style stir-fries, noodle bowls and soups that utilise brassicas, lemons and limes and the zesty tastes of hardy coriander, chives and mint. These bright zingy flavours revive palates jaded from months of hearty soups and stews.

The first early harvests – asparagus, snow peas or salad greens – have a soft green freshness and a sweetness that comes not from the sun but from the earth and their own inherent essence. Accent their fresh tastes with lemons and limes and soft aromatic herbs.

With such freshness at hand it's easy to banish winter from our minds. Menus shift to lighter meals that bring out the best in the new season's harvests.

As the days lengthen and grow warm, the choice of pickings gains momentum, bringing the cook treats such as new potatoes, the first peas and zucchini, tender carrots, snow peas and salad greens. Whatever your preferences, these fresh flavours of spring reinvigorate our appetites.

1. Apple mint
   Mentha rotundifolia
2. Purple basil
   and sweet-leaf basil
   Ocimum basilicum
3. Lemon grass
   Cymbopogon
4. Garlic chives
   Allium tuberosum
5. Winter mint
   Mentha cordifolia
6. Coriander
   Coriandrum sativum

'Pesto is a useful flavouring for lots of different dishes. Stuff under the skin of chicken before roasting, thin with oil for a dressing for roasted vegetables or greens, or toss through pasta with lightly cooked peas.'

Spring pestos

Tamari-almond & basil pesto
Prep   2 minutes

Place ½ cup tamari-roasted almonds (page 138), ¼ packed cup torn basil leaves and ½ cup extra virgin olive oil in a food processor and pulse a few times until mixture just forms a coarse, oily crumb. Keeps in the fridge for 2-3 days.
Makes 1 cup

Ligurian bean pesto
Prep   10 minutes
Cook   2 minutes

Drop 500g freshly podded or frozen broad beans into a pot of boiling water and cook for 2 minutes. Drain. Slip beans out of their outer greyish skins by grasping each one and squeezing gently. Discard skins.
Place 2 chopped cloves garlic, 16 fresh mint leaves, 4 anchovy fillets, ¼ cup grated pecorino or parmesan cheese and ½ cup extra virgin olive oil in a food processor and purée until smooth. Add the beans and pulse the mixture a few times so the beans just break up to a coarse purée. Season to taste. Spoon into a bowl and drizzle with a little extra virgin olive oil.
Mixture will keep for several days in the fridge or can be frozen. Serve as a dip or toss through cooked pasta or potato with diced crispy bacon.
Makes 2 cups, serves 6

Asian pesto
Prep   5 minutes

Remove stems from a big handful of fresh coriander and a big handful of mint (1 packed cup leaves each). Place leaves in a sieve and pour over boiling water to wilt then place under cold running water to cool. Drain and purée in a food processor with 1 cup oil, 1 tsp salt, 1 small hot red chilli, the finely grated zest of 2 limes and 1 cup roasted cashews. Mix until smooth. Keeps in the fridge for up to 2 weeks.
Makes 2 cups

ROCKET PESTO
Pour boiling water over 2 large handfuls (140g bunch) fresh rocket leaves. Drain at once and rinse under cold water. (This sets the colour so the pesto does not turn brown so quickly.) Squeeze out water and place in a food processor with 1 clove peeled garlic, ¾ cup toasted almonds, ½ cup extra virgin olive oil, ½ tsp salt and grinds of pepper. Purée until smooth.
Spoon mixture into a jar and pour a little oil over to cover the surface. Mixture will keep in the fridge for up to a week or can be frozen in ice-cube trays.
Makes 1¼ cups
Serving suggestion: Yummy stirred through pasta with fresh tomatoes.

Pictured right: Bruschetta with rocket, Ligurian bean pesto, avocado, prosciutto and tamari-almond and basil pesto.

'At the first hint of spring, invite a bunch of friends over to enjoy a nice bottle of wine and a platter of spring tastes. I can't think of a better way to herald in the new season and celebrate winter's end.'

A platter of spring tastes

There is something appealingly informal about serving a platter of food for people to help themselves to. Often if I am having people over, instead of serving a first course I will assemble a platter and open a bottle of wine for us to enjoy in the kitchen before we sit down at the table. Here I've served a dish of fresh, peeled broad beans and shaved pecorino drizzled with the best olive oil along with a dish of roasted asparagus wraps (page 32) and the Ligurian bean pesto from the previous page. Some crisp bruschetta bases or crusty bread are all that are needed to complete the plate.

Other dishes to serve on a spring platter include asparagus & goat's cheese tart (page 32) and new potatoes topped with tamari-almond & basil pesto (page 18) or mint & caper sauce (page 77).

You might also like to serve a platter of new season's baby vegetables – radishes, fennel or spring carrots with pesto, or a big bowl of lightly cooked asparagus with salsa verde (page 53).

HERBS AS GARNISH

I prefer to grow and use flat-leaf parsley rather than the curly variety as it's easier to chop and looks better on the plate. Finely chopped and sprinkled over a cooked dish, parsley adds a sweet freshness, particularly to Mediterranean-style dishes.

Coriander can be used in the same way to garnish dishes with Asian, Mexican or Middle Eastern tones. Some people find the taste of coriander rank. This is thought to be due to a genetic trait that produces an enzyme that affects their perception of the taste. Heat quickly diminishes the taste of coriander so it should be added just before serving. Chervil is a lovely herb to use with fish, chicken and salads – it has a gentle aniseed flavour. And mint is a must-have, especially for Asian food. Combinations of mint and coriander or mint and basil bring noodles, salads and sauces alive.

'If you don't have a garden, grow seeds of spring greens in small planters on the window sill or plant in wine tubs on the back deck. Water daily and in a few weeks tender greens will be ready to harvest.'

Enjoy raw flavours

Fresh beets with coriander seeds
Prep 5 minutes

Peel 1 large fresh beetroot and coarsely grate it into a bowl. Mix through 2 tbsp chopped mint, 1 tbsp best-quality extra virgin olive oil, 2 tsp lime juice, 1 tsp honey, ½ tsp ground allspice and 1 tsp toasted and coarsely crushed coriander seeds. Season with a little salt and pepper.
Serves 2

Fresh broad beans with parmesan & olive oil
Prep 5 minutes

Choose beans that are young and fresh. Once they get big the skins get leathery and the beans need peeling.
Pod 250g broad beans into a serving bowl. Shave over 30g parmesan or pecorino, drizzle with a little extra virgin olive oil and season with salt and pepper to taste.
Makes 4 small servings

Fresh asparagus & cashew slaw
Prep 5 minutes

Raw asparagus has a wonderfully fresh pea-like flavour.
Halve 250g fresh trimmed asparagus spears lengthways then chop finely. Toss with 1 spring onion, finely chopped, 1 small carrot, grated, ½ cup chopped toasted cashews, 1 tbsp rice vinegar, 1 tbsp flavourless oil, eg grapeseed, ½ tsp sesame oil and 2 tbsp toasted sesame seeds. Season with salt and pepper to taste.
Serves 4

Radishes with mint & chive cream
Prep 5 minutes

Wash, trim and halve 6 fresh radishes lengthways. Mix ¼ cup cream cheese with the finely grated zest of 1 lemon, 2 tbsp chopped mint and 2 tbsp chopped chives. Season to taste with salt and pepper. Spread each cut radish surface with 1 tsp of the mixture.
Serves 4-6 as a nibble

AVOCADOS
Persea Americana

Avocados will not ripen while they are attached to the tree so need to be harvested any time from 9-12 months after the fruit has set. Once picked they must be kept at room temperature until they are ripe or the flesh will go brown. Once ripe they can be chilled for a couple of days to prevent over-ripening.

Judging ripeness is the trickiest part of handling avocados – the fruit is ripe when the flesh separates from the seed, not when it is squishy. Aside from Hass, which changes colour as it ripens, all other varieties stay green. For these the best way to judge ripeness is by pressing gently on the stem where it meets the fruit – if there is some give the fruit will be ready. When Hass changes from bright green to olive green, it's just two days away from being ready to eat. When it changes from olive green to a greenish woody brown, it's ready to eat. Once it reaches black it is usually over-ripe and the flesh is likely to be starting to brown and become tainted.

Once cut the fruit browns quickly so add to salads at the last minute. Lemon or lime juice or vinegar help reduce browning as, for some odd reason, do tomatillos.

'A wander around the garden to find something to pick for dinner is my favourite way to unwind after a busy day. Even if it's just a bunch of mint, there's a sense of satisfaction and connection in the process.'

Seafood starters

Prawn-stuffed snowpeas
Prep 10 minutes

100g snow peas (about 30)
150g cooked sweet prawn meat, finely diced (or cooked chicken)
3 tbsp good-quality mayonnaise
finely grated zest of ½ lemon
1 tsp lemon juice
¼ tsp smoked paprika (don't overdo it)
salt and grinds of pepper

Pour boiling water over snowpeas to cover. Drain and cool at once under cold water. Split open on one side. Combine prawn meat, mayonnaise, lemon zest and juice and paprika. Season to taste.
Spoon mixture into snowpeas to form small boats. Chill until ready to serve. Prepared snowpeas will keep for several hours covered in the fridge.
Makes 30

Vegetarian spiced-egg snowpeas

Blanch and split 30 snowpeas as above, and stuff with the following spicy egg mixture instead of prawns.
Mash 3 hard-boiled eggs finely with a fork and combine with 2 tablespoons mayonnaise, 2 tablespoons chopped coriander, 1 teaspoon each curry powder and garam masala and salt and pepper to taste.
Makes 30

Gravlax crêpe rolls
Prep 10 minutes

200g cream cheese
2 tbsp capers, chopped
1 lemon, juice and finely grated zest
salt and grinds of pepper
8 savoury crêpes or pancakes
16 thin slices gravlax or smoked salmon
8 asparagus spears or green beans, lightly cooked and cooled
16-24 rocket leaves

Keep cooked crêpes or pancakes in the freezer to assemble rolls like this when impromptu visitors arrive.
Mix cream cheese with capers, lemon juice and zest. Season to taste. Spread a heaped tablespoon evenly over each crêpe (warm crêpes slightly if they are chilled to prevent splitting). Top with 2 slices of gravlax or smoked salmon, a cooked asparagus spear or green bean and 2-3 rocket leaves. Roll up firmly, sealing edges with a little of the cream cheese. Cover and chill until ready to serve (up to 8 hours). Cut each roll into 4. Stand upright like sushi on a serving plate.
Makes 32 rolls

My father kept a fantastic vegetable garden in the city, along with a couple of honey-producing hives. Although he lavished the garden with love and seaweed, his garage was an arsenal of every bug-killing chemical known to mankind. Lethal sprays and sacks of synthetic fertilisers left little room for the car. DDT and lindane are smells I can unfortunately still recognise. As a budding young hippy aged about 15 with every concern for the world's wellbeing, I challenged him to a red-onion-growing competition. He could grow his onions as he always had and I would grow mine organically, using my own home-brew of organic compost, horse dung and seaweed. As the weeks went by my onions overtook his in size and health, until at the due date of harvest they were virtually double his in weight – heavy and fat with a sweet, tangy flavour. My efforts did not go to waste as Dad installed a large compost bin to recycle all the household scraps.

'I operate on a cut-and-come-again salad policy: pick just the leaves you need and your salad greens will keep growing. From the same plant you can extract harvests for several weeks.'

Salad dressings

Riviera dressing
Prep 10 minutes

Make this up in advance. Kept refrigerated it will store for 4-5 days and makes a delicious dressing for any combination of seafood and vegetables.

Blend 8 anchovy fillets, 3 cloves garlic, 10 big basil leaves, ¼ cup pine nuts, 2 tbsp capers, 5 pitted green olives and 2 egg yolks to a purée in a food processor. Add ¼ cup spiced or rice vinegar and 1 cup neutral oil and blend until mixture is thick and creamy.
Makes 1½ cups

Raspberry balsamic dressing
Prep 5 minutes

Purée together in a food processor ¼ cup fresh or thawed frozen raspberries, ¾ cup neutral oil, 3 tbsp balsamic vinegar, 1 tsp honey, 1 tsp Dijon mustard, salt and grinds of pepper. (If you don't have a food processor, mash raspberries well and whisk in all other ingredients.) Store dressing in the fridge until ready to use – it will keep for 2-3 weeks. If desired, the dressing can be thinned with a little water or strained to remove the raspberry pips.
Makes scant 1 cup

Chilli citrus dressing
Prep 5 minutes

Make this dressing in bulk for a zingy, fat-free flavour boost for salads, seafood and noodles. It will keep in the fridge for up to a week.

In a screw-top jar shake together ¼ cup each fresh lemon and orange juice, ¼ cup Thai sweet chilli sauce, 2 tbsp each fresh lime juice, rice vinegar and fish sauce and 1 teaspoon minced fresh ginger. Chill until ready to serve. (Dressing tastes best after standing for 24 hours.) At serving time mix in 2 tbsp freshly chopped coriander and 1 tbsp very finely chopped spring onion or shallot.
Makes 1 cup

CREATING A TOSSED SALAD

Allow a small handful of salad greens per person for a side salad and a large handful for a light meal. (See page 140 for different types of salad greens.) Toss greens with dressing of your choice just before serving. You don't need much dressing, just enough to coat the leaves. Add other ingredients to give texture and flavour.

Here are some nice combinations:

Salad greens tossed with honey mustard dressing (page 84), cherry tomatoes, cucumber, olives and avocado

Salad greens tossed with raspberry balsamic dressing, avocado, fresh peas, tamari-roasted almonds and lightly cooked asparagus (pictured)

Salad greens tossed with chilli citrus dressing, lightly cooked prawns or scallops, avocado, spring onions, snowpeas and celery

Salad greens tossed with Riviera dressing, cooked chicken, capers, olives, cherry tomatoes and spring onions

For more dressings see page 84

'Whichever corner of the globe you find yourself in, there is always a special spot to discover and a wonderful picnic to be had. Portable food tastes great outdoors and even better in good company.'

Light spring plates

Spanish broad beans with eggs & ham

Prep   15 minutes
Cook   20 minutes

2 tbsp olive oil
2 red onions, thinly sliced
500g podded fresh broad beans, peeled if preferred
250g ham, cut into 2-3cm chunks
finely grated zest of 1 lemon
½ tsp salt and grinds of pepper
5 hard-boiled eggs, chopped
½ cup chopped parsley
To serve: lemon wedges

If the beans are large, shell them out of their grey pods. You could also make this dish with frozen broad beans or soy beans.

Heat oil in a deep, heavy pan and cook onions over medium-low heat until softened and just starting to brown, about 15 minutes. Add broad beans, ham, zest and about half a cup of water. Cook, stirring occasionally, until beans are cooked through, about 10 minutes. Season to taste with salt and pepper. Mix through chopped eggs and parsley. Accompany with lemon wedges for squeezing.
Serves 2 as a main course or 4 as a side dish, pictured left and on page13

Spring vegetable frittata cakes

Prep   10 minutes
Cook   15-25 minutes

2 tbsp olive oil
2 zucchini (about 300g), cut into 2cm chunks
1 cup shelled broad beans, fresh or frozen
140g baby spinach or sliced silverbeet
1 fat clove garlic, crushed
6 eggs
1 tsp salt and grinds of pepper
¼ tsp ground nutmeg
50g crumbled feta

Great for brunch or lunch. Vary the flavourings depending on the season.

Preheat oven to 180°C. Fully line 6 large muffin pans with baking paper.
Heat oil over medium heat and fry zucchini, broad beans, spinach and garlic until softened, 2-3 minutes. Remove from heat. In a mixing bowl lightly whisk eggs with salt, pepper and nutmeg. Stir in cooked vegetables and feta. Pour mixture into muffin pans and bake until set and golden, about 15 minutes. Alternatively, cook the mixture in a well-greased 23cm shallow baking dish for about 25 minutes. Accompany with a green salad or salsa.
Serves 6

Variation: In summer, I make this frittata with 1 cup corn kernels, 1 red capsicum, diced, and 3 rashers streaky bacon, diced, in place of the broad beans and spinach.

BROAD BEANS
Vicia faba
People who turn up their noses at broad beans (or favas, as they are known in Italy) just don't know what they're missing. It's often not until they have tried them peeled (without that grey outer husk) that they fall for them. Simply remove beans from pods, boil for 5 minutes in lightly salted water then drain, cool in cold water and slip off the grey outer skins. If the beans are young they taste good without being peeled.
A kilo of whole beans in the pod yields about a cup of shelled beans.
Broad beans freeze well too. Drop them into a big pot of boiling water for a minute then drain and plunge into ice-cold water to halt the cooking process. Drain thoroughly before freezing.
In my South Island garden, which is less prone to blight than the Auckland one, I can keep harvesting broad beans until late autumn. If you keep picking them the plants will keep flowering and producing more beans.

'Confidence is probably the most important element you can bring to cooking. Things can and do go wrong – it's not an exact science. When you try something new, read the recipe carefully before you start.'

An airy savoury soufflé

Double-baked goat's cheese soufflés

Prep 10 minutes
Cook 20 minutes

60g butter, plus extra to butter ramekins
½ cup flour
2 cups milk
¼ teaspoon freshly grated nutmeg
salt and grinds of pepper
5 egg yolks
200g goat's feta or chèvre, finely crumbled
1 teaspoon fresh thyme leaves
2 tablespoons chopped parsley
6 egg whites
To reheat: ¾ cup cream

There's no fleeting moment of glory with these delicious soufflés. Make them ahead and chill them until you're ready to serve. With a quick blast of heat in a hot oven they puff right back up.

Preheat oven to 175°C. Generously butter 8 medium ramekins or cups or 10 small (½-cup) ramekins. Melt butter in a large pot, add flour and stir over heat for a minute. Whisk in milk, nutmeg, salt and pepper, stirring constantly until sauce simmers and thickens.
Remove from heat and stir in egg yolks, one at a time. Mix in cheese and herbs. In a clean dry bowl, beat egg whites until stiff. Add a quarter of the egg whites to sauce and fold in until thoroughly mixed. Add rest of egg whites and fold together as lightly as possible.
Fill ramekins to top and smooth across. Run your thumb around edge of each dish so soufflés don't stick as they rise. Set ramekins in a deep roasting dish. Pour in boiling water to come halfway up their sides. Bake immediately until soufflés are puffed, browned and just set in the centre, 15-20 minutes.
If not serving at once, take out of water bath and leave to cool – the soufflés will shrink. Unmould them into an ovenproof dish and keep covered in the fridge for up to 24 hours. To reheat, drizzle cream evenly over soufflés. Bake at 220°C until browned and slightly puffed, 8 minutes.
Serves 8-10

PEA PLEASURES
Pisum sativum

It's fiddly to pod a bowl of peas but the taste is a special one. For a simple **pea side dish** place shelled peas in a pot with ½ cup water, a pinch of salt, a sprig of fresh mint and a slug of olive oil and cook until the water has reduced to nothing.

Make a great **pea, bacon and rocket pasta** for 2 people. Chop 4 rashers bacon and fry until crispy. Add 2 cloves crushed garlic and 3 cups peas and cook for a few minutes until peas have changed colour. Mash roughly to break up a bit. Add a couple of handfuls chopped rocket and ½ cup cream. Bring to a simmer, season well and toss through 400g cooked pasta with 1 cup grated parmesan.

Make a **pea and potato mash** with 4 cooked potatoes, 2 cups cooked peas, 2 cloves crushed garlic and ½ cup grated parmesan. Heat together and mash finely with a little butter or cream, seasoning with salt and pepper.

For a brilliant **green pea dip**, purée 2 cups cooked peas with 1 tsp salt, 1 tsp ground cumin, 2-3 drops Tabasco sauce, ¼ cup neutral oil and ½ cup coriander.

For more information on peas see page 46.

'Most of what we eat starts out as a seed or spore, taking weeks, sometimes even years, to grow. Nature's extraordinary efforts require our nurture and our appreciation.'

Asparagus pleasures

Roasted asparagus wraps

Prep 10 minutes
Cook 12-15 minutes

12 spears fresh asparagus
about 6 thin slices prosciutto or bacon, rind removed
2 tbsp olive oil
12 tbsp water
salt and grinds of pepper
finely peeled zest of ½ lemon

For everyday dining, roast asparagus without the prosciutto, using just lemon zest and olive oil – it is one of the best ways I know to cook it.

Preheat oven to 200°C. Snap off and discard tough ends of asparagus and trim spears to a neat edge. Cut prosciutto slices in half lengthways to create 12 long, thin strips. Wrap a strip of prosciutto in a tight twirl around each piece of asparagus.
Place rolls in a single layer in a shallow roasting dish with oil and water, carefully turning to coat. Season with salt and pepper and scatter over the lemon zest.
Roast until all the water has evaporated and asparagus spears are just tender and starting to brown around the tips, 12-15 minutes. Season and serve hot or at room temperature.
Serves 3-4

Asparagus & goat's cheese tart

Prep 10 minutes
Cook 35 minutes

100g goat's feta
100g cream cheese
2 eggs
½ cup cream
finely grated zest of ½ lemon
2 tbsp chopped chervil or parsley
½ tsp salt and grinds of pepper
12-14 trimmed asparagus spears
25cm pre-cooked savoury shortcrust pastry shell

Preheat oven to 170°C. Place feta and cream cheese in a bowl and beat with a wooden spoon to soften, then whisk in eggs, cream, lemon zest, herbs and seasonings until smooth. Arrange asparagus spears in a single layer in cooked pastry crust. Pour over cheese and cream mixture. Bake until set, about 35 minutes.
Serves 4-6

Variation: In summer, use sweet corn and red capsicums in place of asparagus. Spinach is also delicious – use 2-3 handfuls chopped leaves and a little chervil in place of asparagus.

ASPARAGUS

Asparagus officinalis
Asparagus is such a fleeting seasonal pleasure – a harvest of spring and no more. Immerse yourself in its flavour and commit the taste to memory.
It takes at least 2 years for an asparagus bed to get established to the point where you can start to harvest the spears.
If you start too early the corms from which the asparagus emerges do not get the chance to establish properly.
The first spears are the fattest and often the sweetest. For the first few seasons of harvest it's best to let the plants go to seed quite early to regenerate the corm, rather than picking through to the very last.
For information on handling asparagus see page 46

PRE-COOKING A PASTRY CRUST

Line a baking tin with pastry to cover base and sides. Cover with baking paper and sprinkle with dried beans or baking beans to weigh down. Bake at 180°C for 12-15 minutes until set and not sticky, then remove cover, reduce temperature to 170°C and cook a further 12-15 minutes until lightly golden and crisp.

'The surreptitious practice of taking the first small, tender tubers from under the nose of the potato plant without damaging it is called bandicooting. These stolen harvests always taste the sweetest.'

With new potatoes

Kerala potato salad

Prep   10 minutes
Cook 15 minutes

1kg small new waxy potatoes
1 tsp butter
2 stalks celery, thinly sliced
2 spring onions, diced
1 recipe kerala curry dressing (see right)
½ cup roasted peanuts, cashews or almonds
2 tbsp chopped mint or coriander
salt and grinds of pepper

Scrub potatoes and cut up any big ones so they are all roughly the same size. Bring to a simmer in lightly salted water with the butter. Cook over lowest heat until potatoes are just tender when pierced with a knife, about 15-20 minutes. Drain and place in a mixing bowl with all other ingredients. Toss to combine, adding salt and pepper to taste.
Serves 4-6

Kerala potato & avocado salad

Prepare the salad above and add 2 just-ripe avocados, diced, and 1 red capsicum, diced, just before serving.

Potato salad with gherkins & eggs

Prep   10 minutes
Cook 15-20 minutes

1kg small new waxy potatoes
1 tsp butter
4 hard-boiled eggs, peeled and cut into eighths
2 spring onions, finely sliced
½ cup finely chopped gherkins and ½ cup of their bottling liquid
4 tbsp chopped mint leaves
½ cup olive oil
2 tbsp lemon juice
1 tsp salt and grinds of pepper

Scrub potatoes and cut up any big ones so they are all roughly the same size. Bring to a simmer in lightly salted water with the butter. Cook over lowest heat until potatoes are just tender when pierced with a sharp knife, about 15-20 minutes. Drain, return to the pot and break apart slightly with a fork. Place potatoes in a mixing bowl with all other ingredients and toss to combine, adding salt and pepper to taste.
Cooled potato salad can be covered and stored in the fridge for up to 2 days. Bring back to room temperature before serving.
Serves 4-6

KERALA CURRY DRESSING
Place in a dry frypan 2 tbsp oil, 2 tsp mustard seeds, 1 tsp good-quality curry powder, 1 tsp turmeric, 1 tsp cumin seeds, ½ tsp cayenne pepper, 2 tbsp finely chopped fresh ginger and 3 cloves finely chopped garlic. Sizzle for 2 minutes over medium heat; do not burn. Remove from heat and mix in 1 cup home-made or good-quality commercial mayonnaise and 2 tbsp lemon or lime juice. Season to taste with salt and pepper.
Makes 1½ cups

AVOID GREEN POTATOES
Solanum tuberosum
Tradition has it in New Zealand that the first potatoes are planted at Labour Weekend in time for the Christmas dinner table. They can be planted right through to late summer with the final harvest just before the first frosts. Exposure to sunlight causes potatoes to turn green and produce a bitter-tasting chemical called solanine which is toxic in large quantities. Even fluorescent lighting at the supermarket can turn potatoes green. Store them in a dark place and cut off any green parts before cooking.
For more information on potatoes see page 77

'Sometimes in the weekends my kids will make fresh pasta. The alchemy of eggs, semolina and salt coming together to form tender ribbons of dough never fails to please, both in the making and the eating.'

Pasta with a twist

Lemon carbonara with spring greens

Prep 10 minutes
Cook 8-10 minutes

2 bunches asparagus, trimmed
100g snowpeas or sugar snaps
3 whole eggs plus 2 egg yolks
finely grated zest of 1 lemon
¼ cup lemon juice
½ tsp salt and grinds of pepper
1 cup (60g) finely grated fresh parmesan
400g dried or 600g fresh fettuccini
2 tbsp butter
8 rashers (180g) middle bacon, diced
2 cloves garlic, crushed
2 tbsp chopped parsley

The flavour of lemon in this simple one-dish dinner gives a bright freshness that is very appealing. For a more traditional carbonara, use cream instead of lemon juice.

Bring a large pot of well-salted water to the boil for the asparagus and the pasta. Boil asparagus for 1 minute, remove and cool under cold water. Drain and put in a bowl with raw snowpeas.

In a separate mixing bowl whisk together whole eggs, yolks, zest and lemon juice. Season and mix in parmesan. Place to one side. Cook pasta according to packet instructions; do not overcook.

While pasta cooks, heat butter in a frying pan and cook bacon over medium heat until crispy. Add garlic and vegetables and stir-fry until snowpeas are just softened and bright green, 2-3 minutes.

Drain cooked pasta and return to the pot off the heat. Toss through the raw egg and cheese mixture to coat. Pile into a serving dish with cooked bacon and vegetables and sprinkle over parsley. Toss to combine. Serve with extra parmesan at the table.
Serves 4

Variation: Substitute 400g sliced broccoli and 140g baby spinach leaves for the asparagus and snow peas used above. Follow the asparagus cooking method for the broccoli and add spinach in place of the snow peas.

BLANCHING TO SET COLOUR

Steeping vegetables very briefly in boiling water is known as blanching. You don't want to cook them, just set their colour and slightly alter their texture. As soon as the vegetables come out of the water they are cooled quickly in icy water. For snow peas and bean sprouts, blanching involves simply pouring boiling water over then draining and cooling. Thicker vegetables such as beans or carrots can be boiled for a minute then drained and cooled. If you plan to freeze vegetables such as green beans you need to blanch them first to prevent enzyme breakdown.

'More than half of the world's population now lives in cities, without access to the natural cycles of nature. As writer Barbara Kingsolver says, "food, like rain, is a process not a product". Value the process.'

Speedy pastas

Fettucini with prawns, asparagus & mascarpone
Prep 15 minutes
Cook 5-10 minutes

Cook 300g fresh or 200g dried fettucini according to packet instructions.
Heat 1 tbsp olive oil in a heavy pan. Add 200g raw prawns, 200g chopped fresh asparagus, 1 fat clove of garlic, crushed, and the finely grated zest of a lemon. Season with salt and pepper. Stir-fry over high heat until prawns change colour, 2-3 minutes.
Drain pasta, reserving ½ cup of the cooking liquid. Gently stir 80g mascarpone or softened cream cheese into the reserved cooking liquid until melted. Add the pasta and toss to coat. Mix in cooked prawn mixture, 2 tbsp lemon juice and 2 tbsp chopped parsley or chervil. Adjust seasoning to taste and serve.
Serves 2

Fusilli with peas, zucchini, bacon & parmesan
Prep 10 minutes
Cook 10-15 minutes

Boil 200g dried fusilli pasta according to packet instructions. Heat 2 tbsp extra virgin olive oil in a heavy frypan and cook 150g diced streaky bacon until crispy, stirring frequently. Add 2 cloves crushed garlic and sizzle for a few seconds then add 2 medium or 3 small zucchini, halved lengthways and angle-sliced 1cm, and the finely grated zest of 1 lemon.
Boil 1½ cups (about 200g) fresh or frozen peas until just tender. Using a potato masher, roughly mash peas several times so they start to break up; do not purée. Add cooked pasta to peas along with ¼ cup of the pasta water. Toss the pasta mixture with the bacon and zucchini and sprinkle with 60g freshly grated or shaved parmesan. Season with ½ tsp salt and grinds of black pepper and serve.
Serves 2; recipe easily doubled

The GMO debate is a complex issue for people to get their heads around. As Barbara Kingsolver says in her essay A Fist in the Eye of God, a sound-byte culture can't discuss science very well. What's the big deal? Well, I suggest you read Kingsolver's succinct and easily digested essay to understand the issues at play. The release of GMOs into the food chain is one of the biggest issues we face today. This essay can be found in Kingsolver's book Small Wonder. Read it online through the link www.organicconsumers.org/gefood/SmallWonders.cfm

*In New Zealand I sit on the Board of the Sustainability Council, which for the past five years has provided research and advocacy on the risks of GMOs to our food chain, environment and economy. It has identified ways to secure gains from improved seeds without using GM techniques so the nation can continue to position itself as a GM-free food supplier to the world's premium markets. The council is also undertaking research on climate change response options and better management of toxic chemicals.
For more information on the council visit www.sustainabilitynz.org*

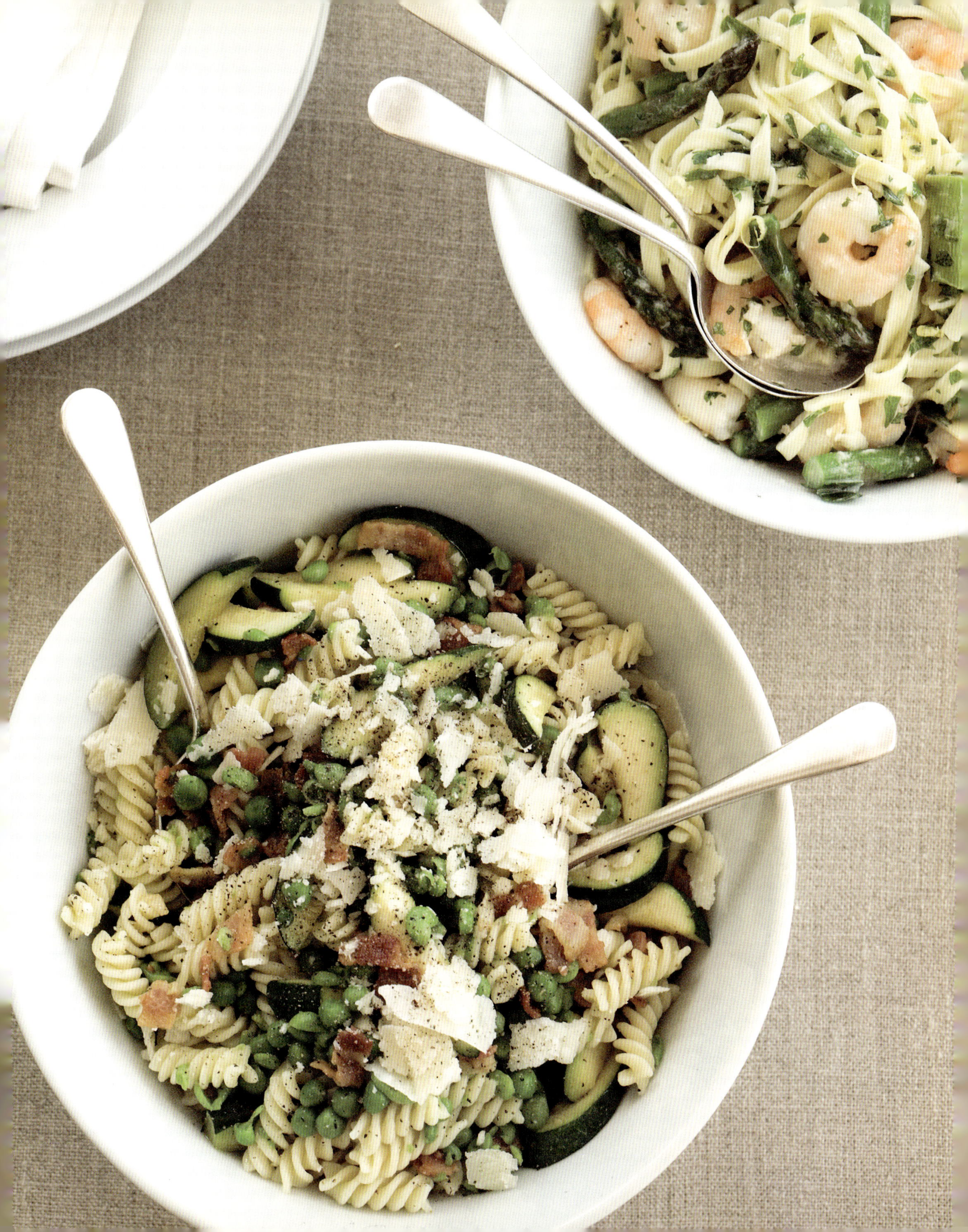

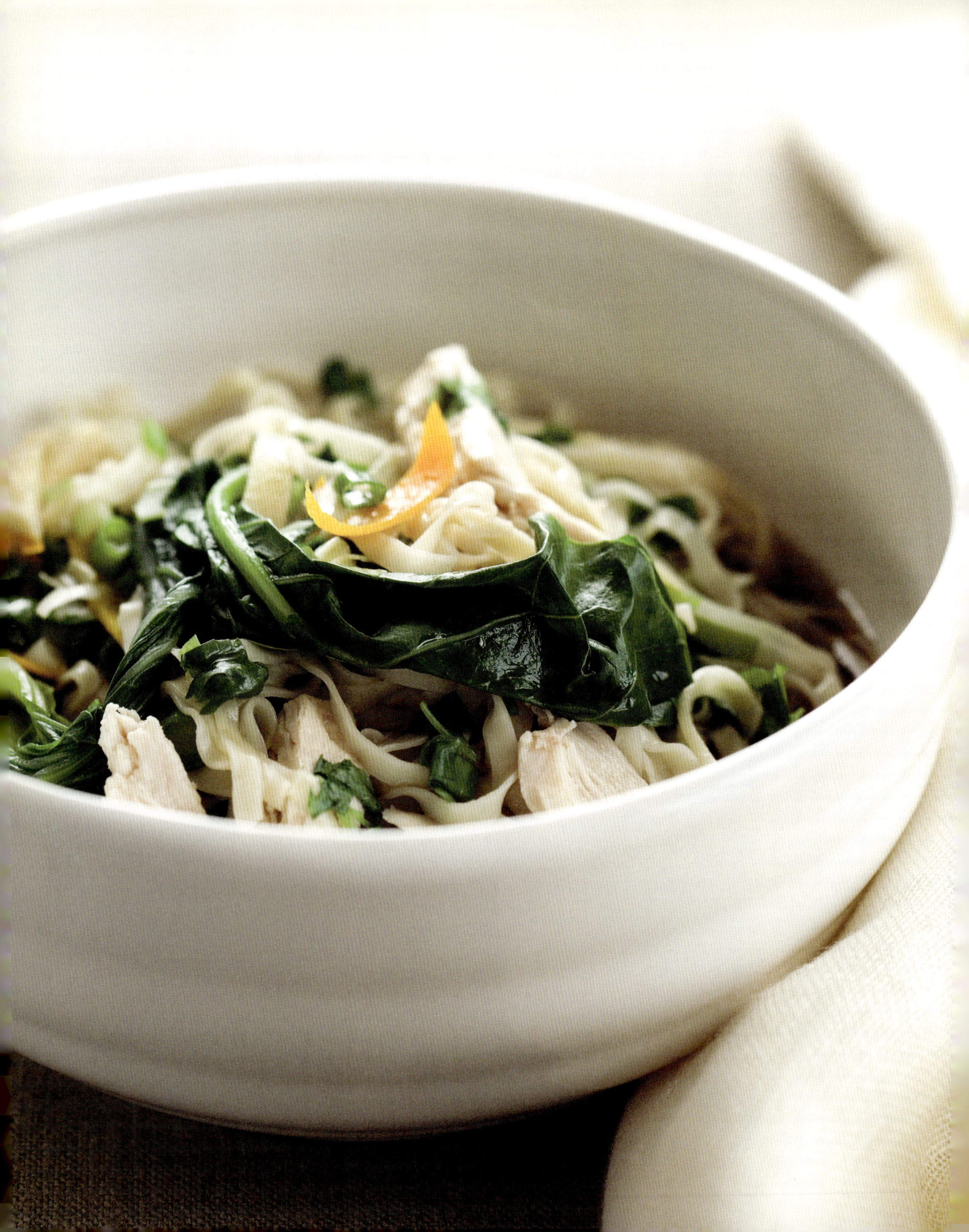

'Whether to slurp or eat your noodles quietly depends on your cultural bias. But no matter where you live, the act of sharing food around the table is a conduit to building friendships and families.'

Noodle bowls

Chinese chicken noodle bowl

Prep 10 minutes
Cook 25 minutes

2 heads baby bok choy, washed and quartered lengthways
3 cups good-quality chicken stock
2 boneless skinless chicken breasts
2 long thick strips of orange zest, cut with a peeler
1 tbsp grated fresh ginger
2 tbsp oyster sauce
4 "nests" dried Chinese egg noodles (250g)
1 spring onion, finely sliced
handful of fresh coriander or mint leaves
Garnish: 1 tsp sesame oil

Drop bok choy into a pot of boiling water to cook for 1 minute. Cool under cold water, drain and reserve. Place chicken stock in a pot with 2 cups water. Add chicken, orange rind, ginger and oyster sauce. Cover and bring to a simmer. Simmer gently for 10 minutes. Lift out chicken and when cool enough to handle, shred into bite-sized pieces.

Bring broth back to a boil, add noodles and boil for 1 minute less than their full cooking time before adding cooked chicken meat, bok choy, spring onions and coriander. Simmer another minute then divide between 2 serving bowls. Drizzle each with a little sesame oil.
Serves 2

CHINESE-STYLE COOKED GREENS

Here's a quick tip for flavoursome spring greens: place prepared greens, eg broccoli, bok choy, asparagus or choy sum, in a pot with ½ cup chicken stock and 1 tbsp extra virgin olive oil. Season lightly, cover and cook for 4-5 minutes until just tender and the liquid has all but evaporated.

PROTECT YOUR BODY WITH CRUCIFERS

The Cruciferae family carries lots of hot, spicy flavours. At the top end of the peppery scale we find horseradish, rocket, radishes, watercress and landcress. At the milder end of the taste spectrum are all the members of the Brassica genus – broccoli, bok choy, gai lan and all the other cabbages as well as collards and kale. Sweet pungent tastes predominate in brassicas such as swedes, turnips, cauliflower and brussels sprouts. The crucifer group of vegetables is highly nutritious and contains many beneficial phytochemicals that help protect the body from disease. You should try to eat at least one vegetable from this family every day.

Spicy beef & noodle bowl

Prep 5 minutes
Cook 7 minutes

2 cups good-quality beef stock
2 tsp Asian black bean sauce
½ -1 tsp Japanese 7 spices, eg togarashi, or ½ tsp chilli flakes
2 tbsp finely grated fresh ginger
220-250g cooked udon noodles
150g lean beef fillet (or other tender meat or chicken), sliced as thinly as possible into strips
100g fresh-water spinach or spinach, washed and coarse stems removed
Garnish: greens of 1 spring onion, thinly sliced, 100g mixed wild mushrooms or oyster mushrooms

Start with a spicy, brightly flavoured broth and add meat or chicken, noodles and veges to suit for a speedy meal in a bowl. Chicken stock and thinly sliced fresh chicken or pork also work well with these broth flavours and any type of vegetable or noodle can be used. If using long-life udon noodles, soak them in hot water to loosen and separate; drain before using.

Place stock in a medium-large pot with bean sauce, Japanese spices and ginger. Bring to a gentle boil and simmer 5 minutes. Add all other ingredients except garnishes and bring back to a simmer (for chicken, simmer 3-4 minutes to fully cook). Mix through garnishes and serve.
Note: If using denser Asian greens such as choy sum, drop them into a pot of boiling water for 1 minute before adding to soup.
Serves 2

'I remember my father getting us up to catch the tide for the whitebait run. We would light a fire on the beach and have a cook-up. Just a little egg to hold the whitebait, s & p, cooked to bliss in a buttery pan.'

Asian-style shellfish

Chilli lime & cockle noodle bowl

Prep   5 minutes
Cook   6-8 minutes

1 tbsp neutral oil, eg grapeseed
2 cloves garlic, crushed
½-1 tsp chilli flakes
2 stalks lemon grass, bruised
2 kaffir lime leaves
about 2.5kg fresh cockles or mussels
¼ cup sake
2 cups chicken or fish stock
2 tbsp lime juice
1 tbsp fish sauce
2 tsp brown sugar

To serve: ¼ cup chopped coriander, 1kg cooked udon noodles or 400g dried noodles

This light, tangy broth makes an excellent foil for any kind of shellfish. I prefer the texture of thick udon noodles but any type of noodle will do.

Heat oil in a large pot. Sizzle all the flavourings for a few seconds then add the shellfish and sake. Cover pot and cook over high heat, removing shellfish as they open. Remove kaffir leaves and lemon grass. Add all remaining ingredients except coriander and noodles to the liquid in the pot and bring to a boil. Add coriander.
Cook or heat noodles as per manufacturer's instructions. Divide hot noodles among bowls, top with cockles and pour over boiling broth.
Serves 4

SPRING PLANTINGS

The time it takes from planting a seed in spring to harvesting will depend on the weather (and how small you want your vegetables). Here is a rough guide to how long it takes from seed to harvest for some of my spring-planted vegetables. I usually work backwards from when I want to harvest – there are few things more frustrating than finding all your crops came on line while you were away on summer holidays.

basil: 6-8 weeks
beetroot: 8-10 weeks
broad beans: 13-14 weeks
spring carrots: 10 weeks
celery: 12 weeks
cucumbers: 14-18 weeks
french beans: 9-11 weeks
whole lettuces: 8-10 weeks
peas: 12-14 weeks
early potatoes: 9-10 weeks
radishes: 3-4 weeks
rocket and other salad greens: 3-4 weeks
spinach: 10 weeks
spring onions: 10 weeks
snowpeas: 8-10 weeks
tomatoes: 18-20 weeks
zucchini: 9-10 weeks

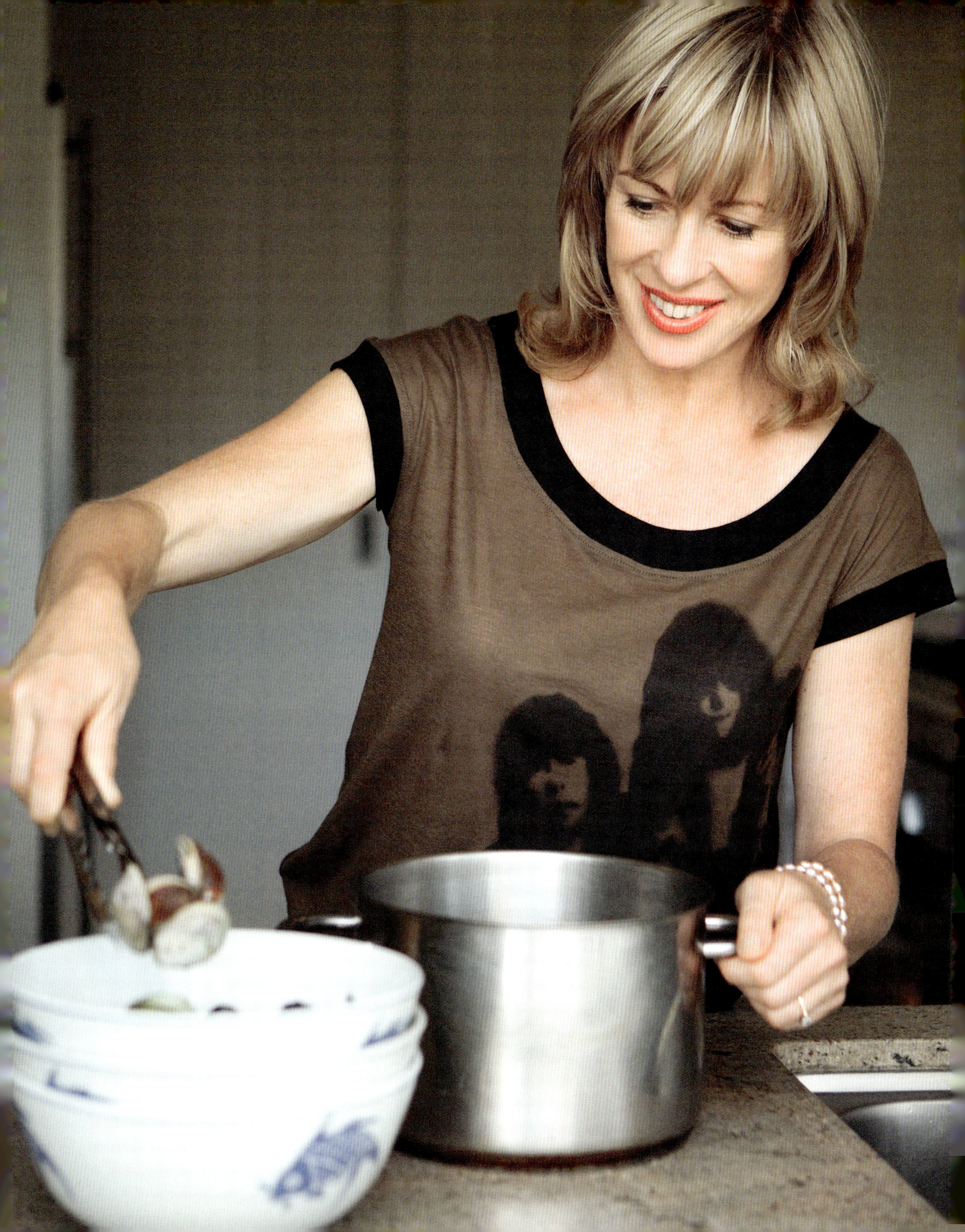

'In my teens I moved up the Whanganui River with two friends to live self-sufficiently on the old marae at Ranana. We had a vast organic vegetable garden, providing the freshest produce for everyone around.'

Spring stir-fries

Tofu & spring vegetable stir-fry

Prep   15 minutes
Cook   6-7 minutes

2 tbsp butter
3 tbsp soy sauce
2 tbsp finely chopped fresh ginger
2 fat cloves garlic, crushed
250g firm tofu, sliced 1cm thick and cut into 3cm batons
2 tbsp sesame seeds, toasted
1 large carrot, cut into batons
250g or 1 small head broccoli, cut into thin florets
150g asparagus or zucchini, sliced
1 bunch spinach (140g), washed and destemmed if large
½ cup roasted peanuts

Heat butter, soy sauce, ginger and garlic in a large wok or frypan. Add tofu and cook 2-3 minutes, turning to coat in sauce mixture. Remove from heat and sprinkle with sesame seeds.
While tofu cooks place carrot, broccoli and asparagus or zucchini in a pot with 2 tbsp water. Cover and cook for 3 minutes (or steam until crisp-tender).
Add vegetables and the liquids to tofu pan with spinach and stir-fry 1-2 minutes just to wilt spinach. Garnish with peanuts and serve.
The cooked sesame-tofu mixture without the vegetables also makes a great filling for stuffed baked pumpkin in the autumn.
Serves 2

Thai chicken & broccoli stir-fry

Prep   15 minutes
Cook   10 minutes

300g boneless chicken
1 tsp Thai green curry paste
2 cloves garlic, crushed
2 tsp finely chopped fresh ginger
finely grated zest of 1 lime
2 tbsp neutral oil
350g or 1 large head broccoli, cut into thin florets
200g or 1 head Shanghai bok choy, thinly sliced
165ml can coconut cream
4 tsp fish sauce
¼ cup coriander leaves, or in summer use basil

Stir-fries like this one lend themselves to endless interpretations. Use different meat or vegetables and change the flavours with ingredients such as kaffir lime leaves, lemon grass and curry powder in place of the green curry paste.
   Thinly slice chicken. Combine curry paste, garlic, ginger and zest and mix through chicken. Heat oil in a large frypan or wok and fry chicken over high heat to lightly brown. Add broccoli, bok choy, coconut cream and fish sauce. Cover and cook for about 5 minutes or until broccoli is just tender and chicken cooked through. Serve sprinkled with coriander or basil.
Serves 2

AVOIDING TRANS FATS

If you don't know the taste of rancid food, you should. If you have ever eaten an unpleasant-tasting peanut or sniffed a jar of stale oil, that's the whiff of rancidity. Rancid foods don't just taste horrid, they are also known carcinogens. And oils and fats turn rancid quite quickly, especially if they are stored in the light or kept in a hot place. To keep fats more stable and increase shelf life, manufacturers started to "hydrogenate" vegetable oils, a process that makes them more solid and stable for use in spreads such as margarine, cooking fats for deep-frying and shortening for baking.
However, in the process of partially hydrogenating vegetable oils, new types of fats are formed – trans fats. These trans fats increase the bad cholesterol (LDLs) and decrease the good cholesterol (HDLs). Trans fats can be found in some processed foods including french fries, potato chips, corn chips and many crackers. Unsaturated vegetable oils from plants, nuts and seeds such as olives, flax (linseed), macadamias, walnuts, peanuts, almonds, corn, safflower and sunflower (as long as they have not been subjected to the process of hydrogenation) are considered heart-healthy.

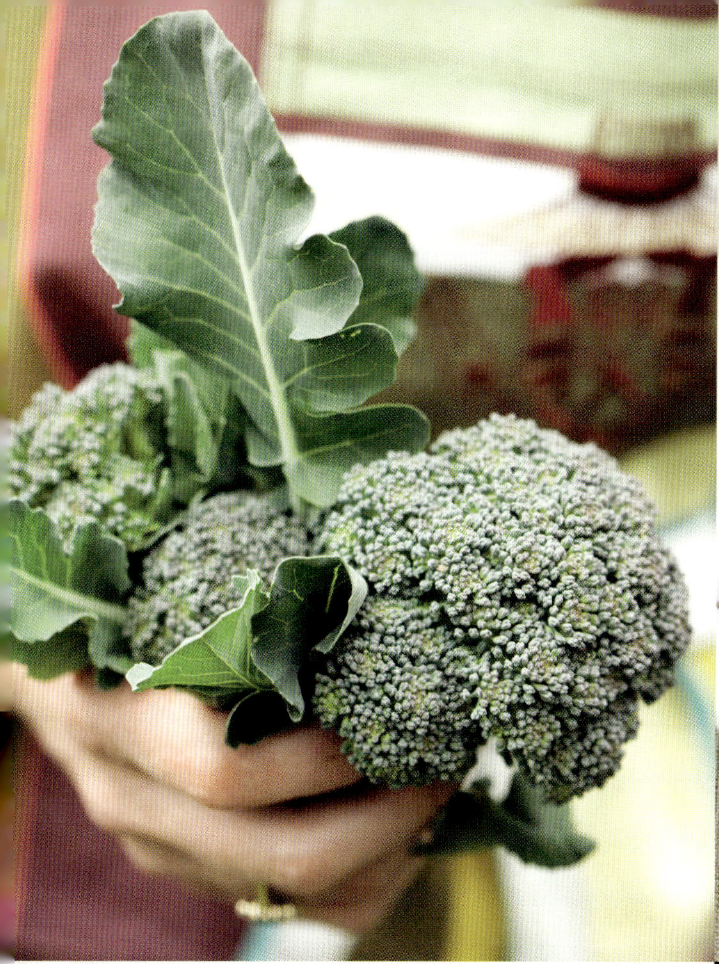
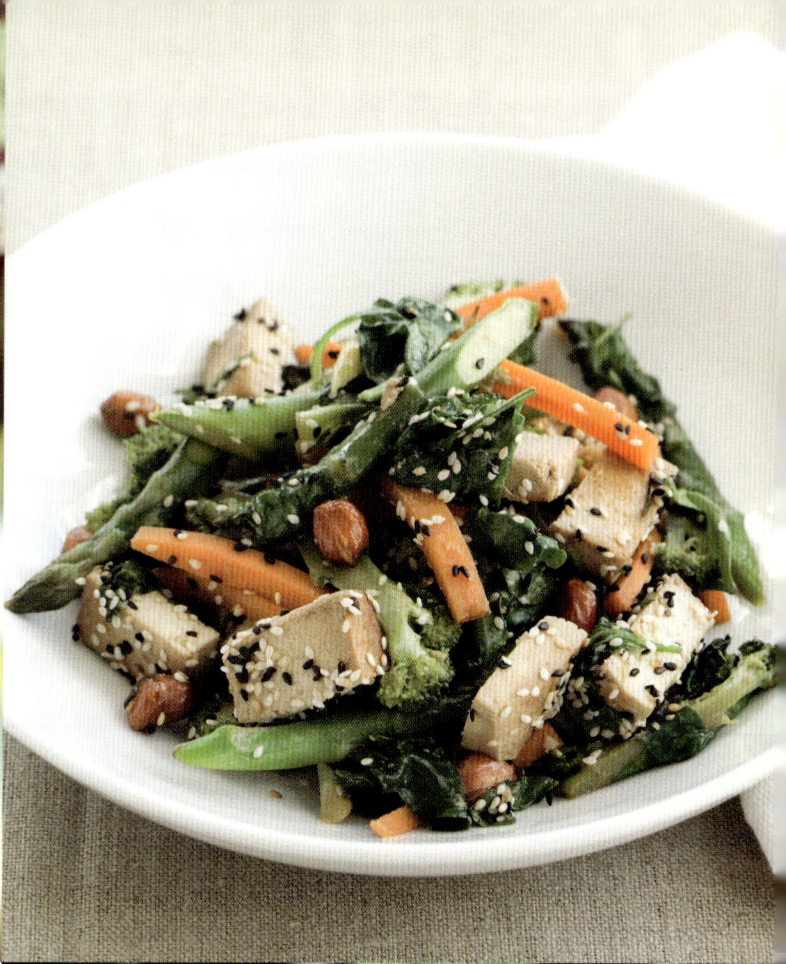
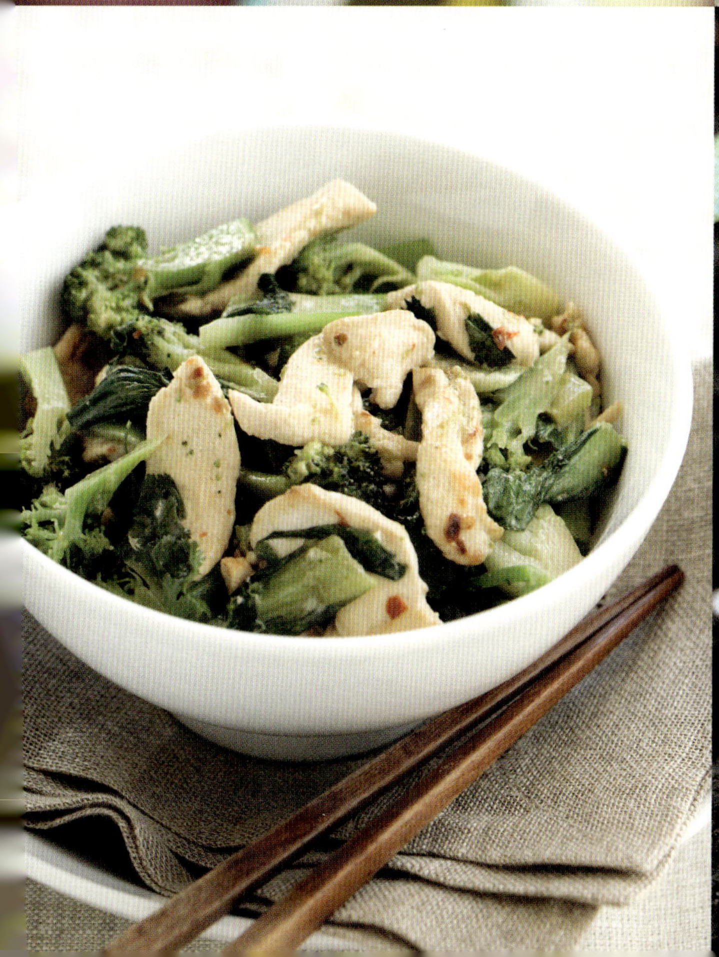
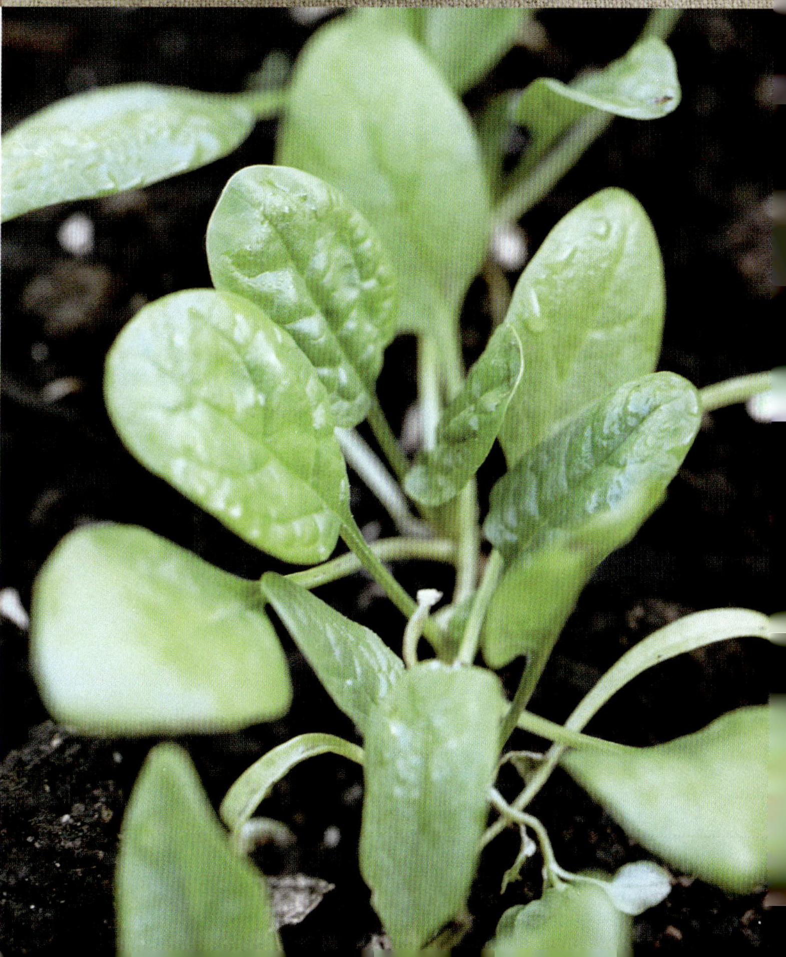

'You need to buy fish with your eyes and your nose. Really fresh fish smells of the sea, nothing fishy. Eyeball it for bright eyes and firm, glistening flesh.'

Fish in a flash

Roasted fish with lemon-caper crumb

Prep 20 minutes
Cook 10 minutes

Lemon-caper crumb:
2 canned anchovies (I use D'Amico or Ortiz)
1 tbsp capers
finely grated zest of 1 lemon
¼ cup olive oil
2 tbsp finely chopped flat-leaf parsley
20g grated parmesan
100g (2 thick slices) crustless artisan bread, eg sourdough, cut into chunks

18-24 spears asparagus
4 thick fillets blue nose or hapuku
salt and grinds of pepper
To serve: roasted cherry tomatoes or carrots

Place anchovies, capers, lemon zest, oil, parsley and parmesan in a food processor and blitz to a purée. Add bread and pulse mixture several times to form a coarse crumb. Don't let it get too fine. Put to one side until ready to cook.

Cook asparagus in boiling water for 1 minute. Cool under cold running water then drain.

Preheat oven to 220°C. Place fish and asparagus in a lined baking dish and season with salt and pepper. Sprinkle fish with a little of the crumb mix and spread out the rest in a separate shallow baking dish.

Bake fish, asparagus and crumbs until fish is just cooked (time will depend on thickness of fillets – about 10 minutes). Crumbs should be golden and crisp – if required, leave in the oven for an extra minute or two while fish rests. Serve fish sprinkled with extra crumbs. Accompany with asparagus and roasted cherry tomatoes.
Serves 6

HANDLING PEAS

Peas are best suited to cooler climates and most varieties will stop flowering once the temperature gets over 20°C. They need lots of water and because they fix their own nitrogen they don't need a very rich soil. It takes 2-3 weeks after flowering before the peas are ready. Flavour deteriorates very quickly if the peas are too ripe or left too long before cooking. Store in the fridge in an airtight container, but if possible pick them just before you plan to use them. Small fresh peas can be eaten raw, otherwise boil for 1-2 minutes.

HANDLING ASPARAGUS

Choose firm, heavy spears with tight heads and bases that look freshly cut. Place spears in a jar with the cut ends sitting in several centimetres of cold water. Stored thus in a cool place (even the fridge) they will keep fresh and in very good condition for a couple of weeks.

To remove tough ends, snap them at the base – they will break where they are tender.

Cook spears in boiling salted water for 3 minutes, stir-fry until green and crisp-tender or roast with a little olive oil and lemon zest.

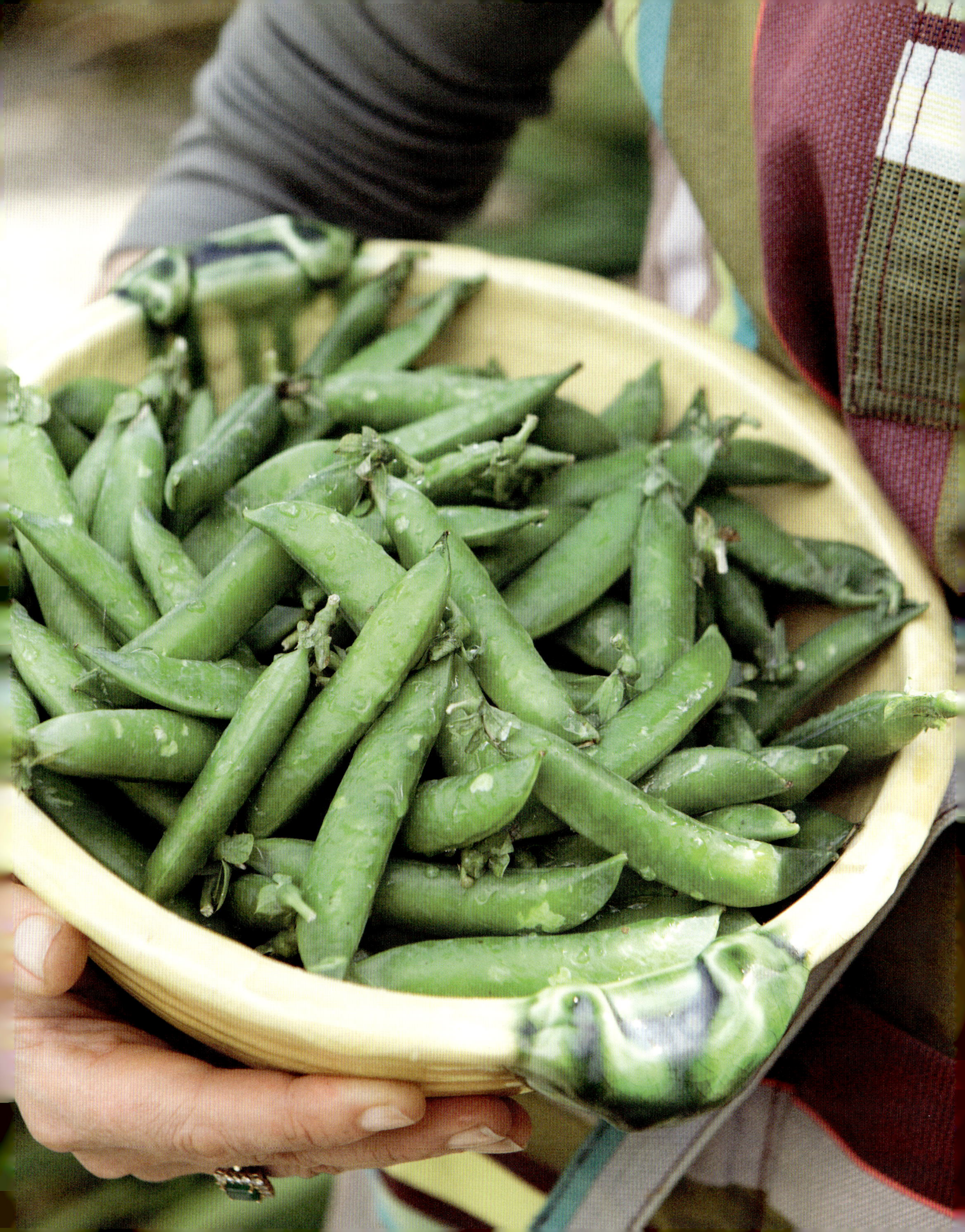

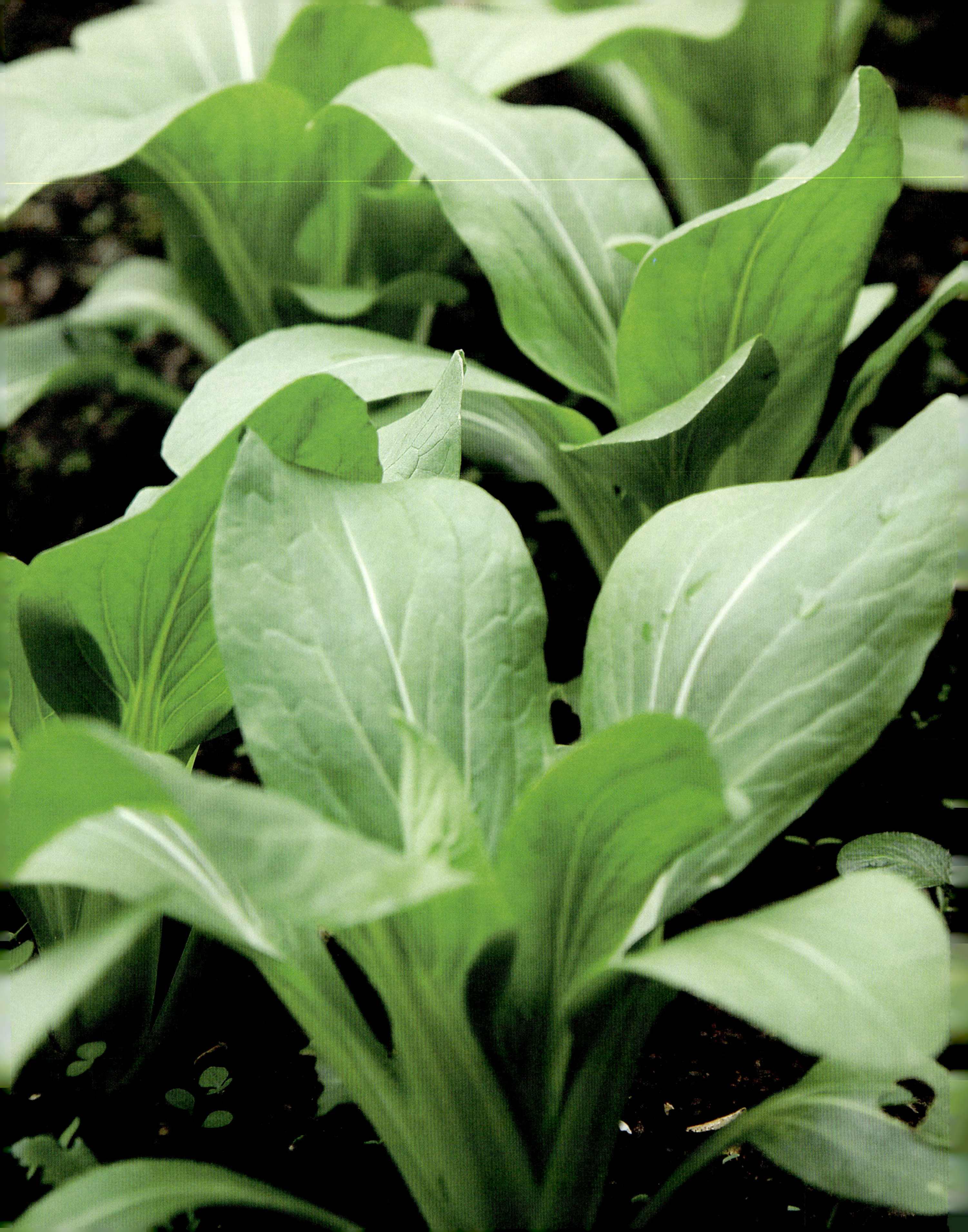

'Hanging a line over the side of a dinghy and pulling in an edible catch brings out the hunter-gatherer in all of us. All the work in preparing fresh fish for the table is more than made up for in the taste.'

Asian flavours for fish

Flash-roasted fish with Asian dressing

Prep 15 minutes
Cook 8-10 minutes

6 boneless and skinless fillets (about 185-220g each) of thick firm fish, eg sea bass, halibut or salmon
To serve: sushi rice and lightly cooked spinach or pea shoots
1 tbsp each white and black sesame seeds, toasted

Soy mirin dressing:
6 tbsp soy sauce
3 tbsp rice vinegar
2 tbsp mirin
2 tbsp neutral oil, eg grapeseed
2 tsp sesame oil
¼ cup (60g) young fresh ginger, peeled and cut into very fine julienne
2 spring onions, thinly sliced
freshly ground black pepper

Place fish in a large, shallow baking dish lined with baking paper. Place all dressing ingredients in a screw-top jar and shake together to combine. Spoon half the mixture over the fish, including most of the solids, and season with pepper (no salt will be needed). Cover and chill for at least 30 minutes or up to 3 hours.
Preheat oven to 230°C and bake fish until just cooked through, about 7-9 minutes (to test for doneness press flesh gently; it should bounce back). Serve fish on a bed of rice and lightly cooked greens. Spoon over remaining dressing and sprinkle with sesame seeds.
Serves 6

TOASTING SESAME SEEDS

Toss sesame seeds in a hot dry frypan over medium-high heat until they turn golden. Remove from heat and allow to cool before storing.

Sweet chilli & coriander-roasted fish

In place of the Asian dressing above, combine ½ cup Thai sweet chilli sauce, ½ cup chopped coriander, 2 tbsp finely minced fresh ginger and 2 tbsp lime juice. Spoon half over the fish and bake as above. Drizzle the rest of the sauce over at serving time.

'Growing up in a country where there were twenty times as many sheep as people has given me a real appreciation for the fine texture and sweet taste of lamb. It's still my favourite meat.'

Spring lamb

Lamb cutlets with bean & pecorino salad

Prep   20 minutes
Cook 5 minutes

Caper marinade and dressing:
2 tbsp salted capers, soaked and drained
2 lemons, juice and finely grated zest
2 cloves garlic, crushed
¼ cup extra virgin olive oil

12-16 lamb cutlets, trimmed
salt and grinds of pepper

Bean and pecorino salad:
500g peeled broad beans (2 cups) fresh or frozen, thawed
250-300g green beans
½ cup mint leaves, torn
50g pecorino, shaved with a potato peeler

Marinate the lamb and prepare the salad ahead of time, ready to assemble once the lamb is cooked. The broad bean and pecorino salad is terrific served with any kind of roasted or pan-fried lamb or beef.

    Chop capers finely and mix with lemon juice and zest, garlic and olive oil. Season with pepper.
Mix 2 tablespoons of this mixture through lamb and reserve rest for dressing the salad. Chill lamb if not cooking at once (it can be marinated in this mixture for up to 12 hours.)
Boil broad beans and green beans for 5 minutes, or if using frozen beans allow them to come just to a boil. Cool under cold water, drain and remove outer grey skins. Cover and, if not using at once, chill until serving time. Beans can be prepared to this point several hours ahead of serving.
Heat a heavy pan, season cutlets with a little salt and cook over high heat until browned and lightly rare, about 1½ minutes each side. Remove from heat and rest while dressing salad.
Toss beans with remaining dressing, pecorino and mint and place in a serving bowl or divide between serving plates along with lamb. Accompany with boiled new potatoes.
Serves 4

FLASH-ROASTING LAMB RACKS

Lamb racks are an expensive cut but require little effort to make them delicious and they cook quickly in a hot oven. At 220°C a whole lamb rack will take around 20-25 minutes to cook to medium-rare. Rest the meat for 5-10 minutes before slicing and serving. Various toppings and crusts can be used to add flavour and texture to the meat or it can be marinated. Use the marinade given at left for lamb cutlets or try the chermoula marinade, Greek lemon and herb marinade or spice trail marinade on page 101.

ROASTING A LEG OF LAMB

Preheat oven to 180°C. Place a 1.3-1.5kg carvery roast of lamb in a roasting dish and spread with toppings or crust of your choice or simply season well with salt and pepper. Place chunks of dense vegetables such as potatoes, onions, beets, pumpkin and kumara around meat to cook at the same time. Roast for 1-1¼ hours or until cooked to your liking (I think it is nicest served slightly rare). Remove meat from oven, cover to keep warm and rest for 10 minutes before carving.

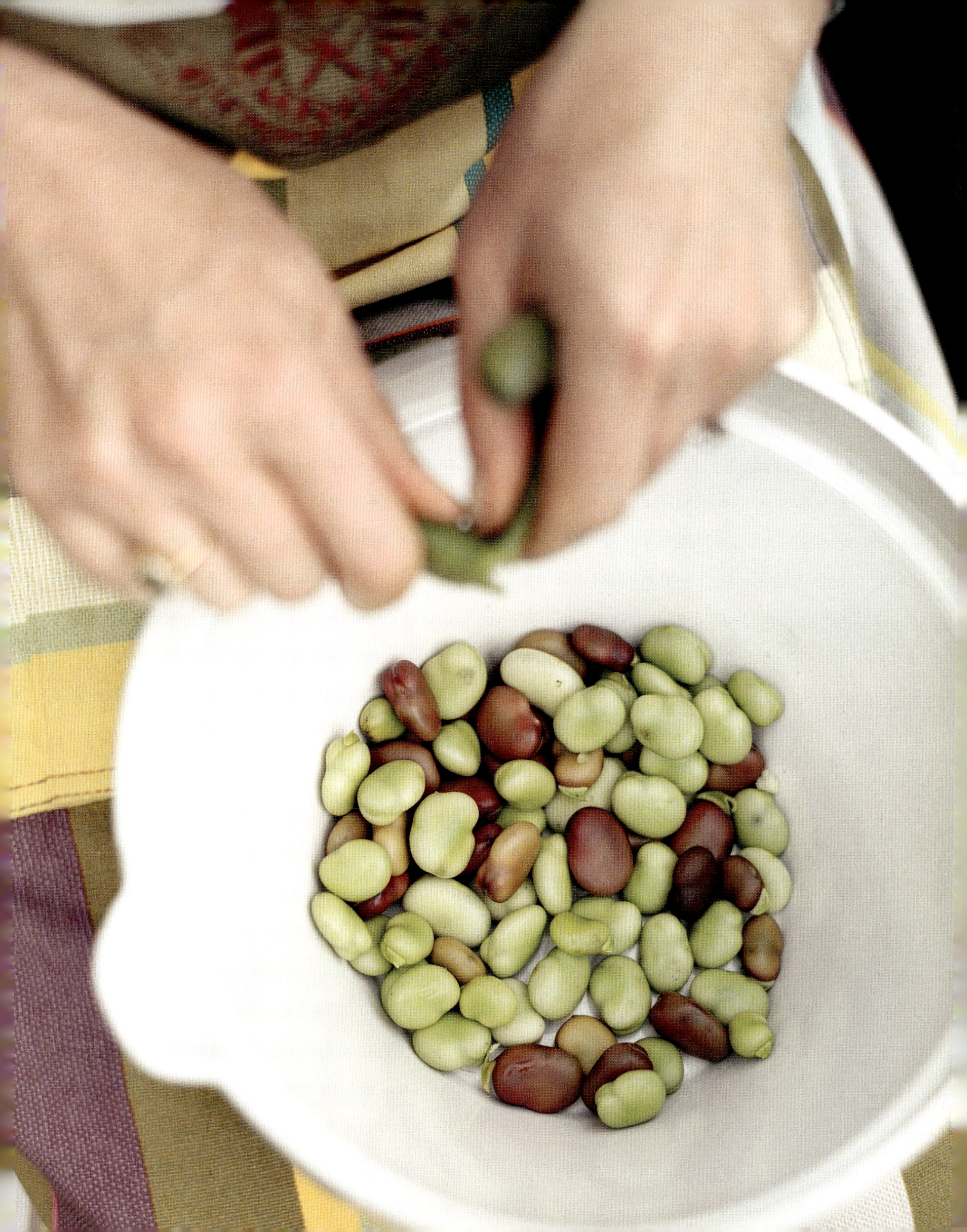

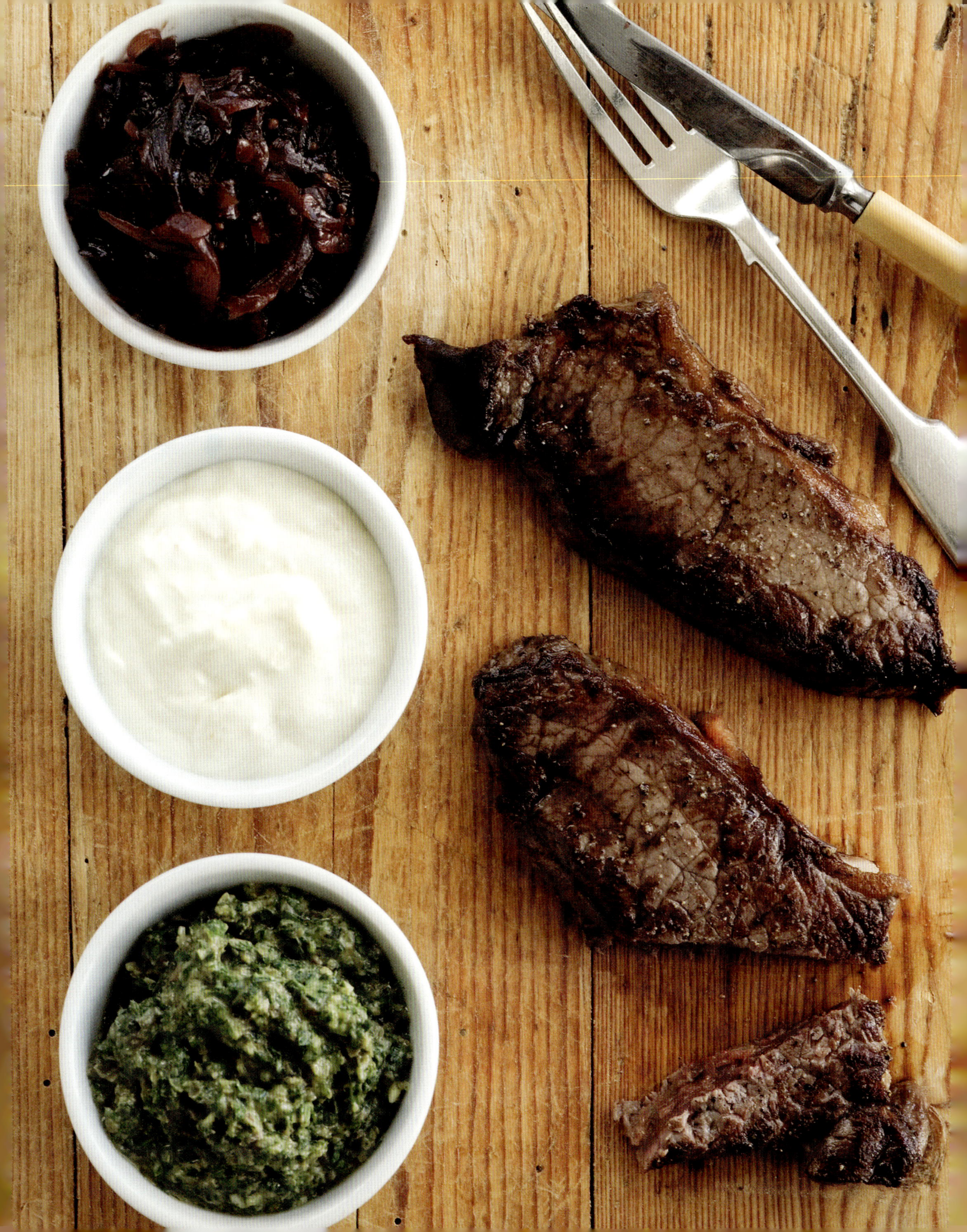

'It's easy to get stuck in a rut with cooking, dishing up the same old meals with the same ingredients. Serving a familiar dish with a new sauce or dressing is an easy way to bring new flavours to the table.'

Three sauces for steak

Balsamic red onion confit
Prep   15 minutes
Cook 1 hour 10 minutes

Peel, halve and thinly slice 3 red onions. Place in a large pan with 2 tbsp olive oil, ½ cup sugar, 1 cup red wine, ½ cup balsamic vinegar, 2 tsp mustard seeds and 3 tbsp dried currants and bring to a simmer.
Cover and simmer for 25 minutes then uncover and simmer until liquid is almost absorbed and reduced to a thick oniony syrup, about 45 minutes.
Confit will keep in the fridge in a covered container for several weeks and can be reheated as required.
Makes 2½ cups

Horseradish cream
Prep   5 minutes

Mix 50g peeled fresh horseradish, puréed in a blender, with 2 tbsp lemon juice, ½ tsp salt and 250g sour cream. Keeps in the fridge for weeks in a covered container.
Makes 1 cup

Salsa verde
Prep   5 minutes

In a food processor or blender, blend together until smooth 1 packed cup parsley leaves, 2 tbsp olive oil, ½ packed cup mint leaves, ¼ cup chopped chives, 2 tbsp capers, 3 cloves peeled garlic, 2 tsp Dijon mustard, ¼ onion, chopped, and 1 small can (50g) anchovies in oil. Store in the fridge for up to 5 days.
Serving ideas: Fabulous with grilled meats, chicken, green beans and asparagus. Mix a little through vinaigrette for a great dressing for chicken or meat salads.
Makes about 2 cups

STEAK AND GRAVY

Even though the smell is mouth-watering, you can do a lot more for a steak than serve it with fried onions. Store good-quality liquid stocks in the freezer for a sauce base that offers a natural depth of flavour. The brownings that accumulate at the bottom of the pan when you fry meat contain loads of flavour and with a little liquid will release their taste into a simple pan sauce.
To make a simple pan sauce for steak, add a spoonful of red currant or other fruit jelly, a splash of balsamic vinegar and a cup or two of vegetable cooking water or stock to the pan in which the meat has browned. Boil hard for a minute or two and season well. If you prefer a thickened gravy, mix 1-2 tsp cornflour with a little port or water then stir into sauce and simmer for a minute or two.
Stirring a small spoonful of miso into the sauce is a great way to enrich the flavour.

'Resourcefulness is the hallmark of farming cultures the world over. Finding the soft, sweet core of a thistle and turning it into a superb dish is a skill rooted in the land and the cycle of its harvests.'

Globe artichokes

Preserved artichokes in olive oil

Prep 20 minutes
Cook 25-30 minutes

fresh artichokes
olive oil to cover
1 tsp salt per potful
Optional additions: sliced lemons, cloves of garlic, fresh herbs

Leave tiny artichokes intact. For larger artichokes, halve them lengthways, remove hairy chokes with a spoon and trim off tough outer leaves.
Place artichokes in a pot so they fit snugly in a single layer. Add enough olive oil to cover and ½ teaspoon salt. Cover and cook over lowest heat for 25-30 minutes. The oil should never get so hot it sizzles.
Allow artichokes to cool in oil then pack into clean jars and cover with oil. They will keep for months in the fridge.
Cook's note: To vary the flavour, add a couple of cloves of garlic, a handful of herbs or some slices of lemon to the artichokes as they cook.

Sicilian artichokes, potatoes & olives

Prep 10 minutes
Cook 15 minutes

¼ cup extra virgin olive oil
2 cloves garlic, crushed
3 anchovies
8-10 cooked or preserved artichoke halves
300g potatoes, cut into chunks and boiled in lightly salted water until just tender
12 kalamata olives, pitted and chopped
¼ cup chopped fresh coriander

This makes a delicious accompaniment to grilled or barbecued red meats or chicken.
　　Heat oil in a large heavy-based pan and gently cook garlic and anchovies over low heat until anchovies soften to a pasty texture, about 5 minutes.
Add artichokes and potatoes, cover and cook over low heat for about 10 minutes, stirring occasionally.
Mix in olives and coriander. Cover and cook gently for another 3-5 minutes to heat through and infuse flavours.
Serves 4 as a side dish
Cook's note: To pit and chop olives, crush them with the side of a cook's knife, remove stones then chop.

FRESH ARTICHOKES
Cynara cardunculus L. var. scolymus
Preparing artichokes is a bit like preparing broad beans – there's not a lot left at the end but what is there is worth the effort. Have ready a bowl of water with the juice of a lemon squeezed into it – artichokes discolour quickly once sliced. Pull the outer layer of leaves off the base. Slice the top quarter off the head and use a small paring knife to remove all the dark green outer skin from around the base. Do the same to the stem so only the lighter-coloured, tender portion in the middle remains. Cut artichokes in half lengthways, remove the tough, prickly pink flower buds and use a spoon to scrape out the hairy choke. If the artichokes are very small you may not need to remove anything. Place the prepared artichokes in the lemon water as they are done. They are now ready for all manner of treatments. Boil them for 10-15 minutes before using in cooked dishes, or thinly slice and serve them raw, drizzled with olive oil or dressing. Preserve them as in the recipe at left.

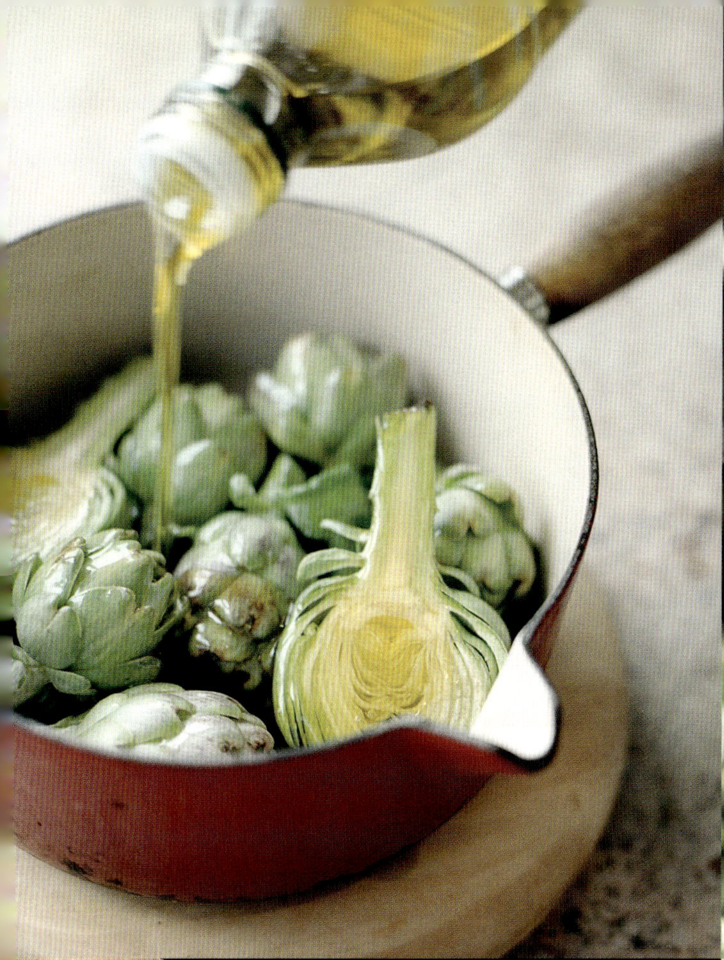
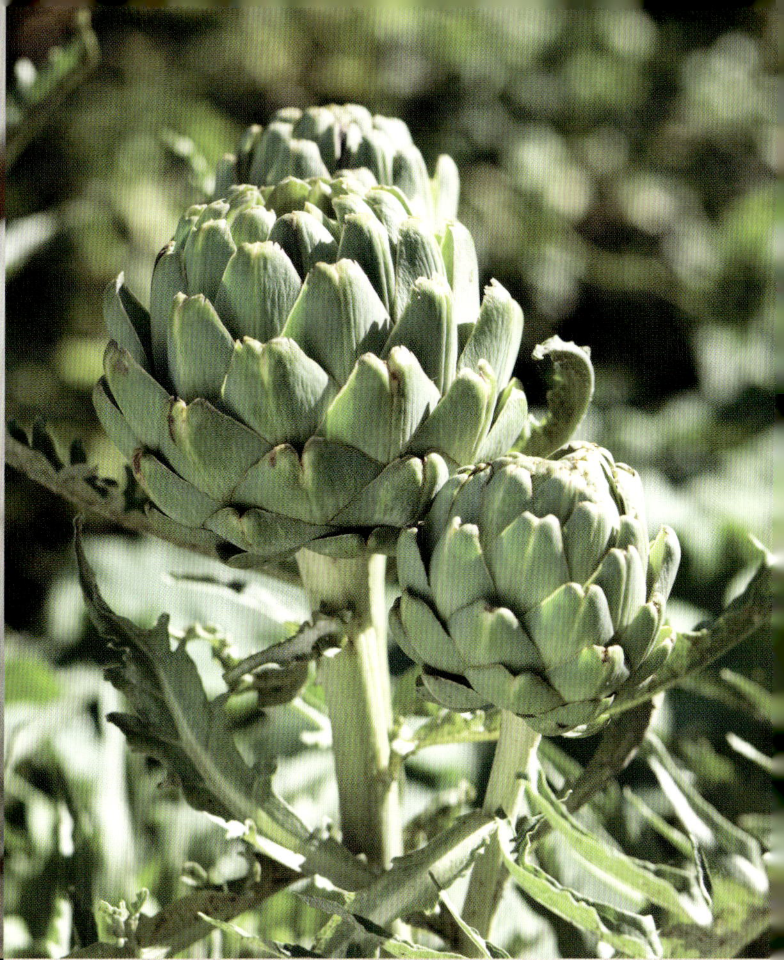
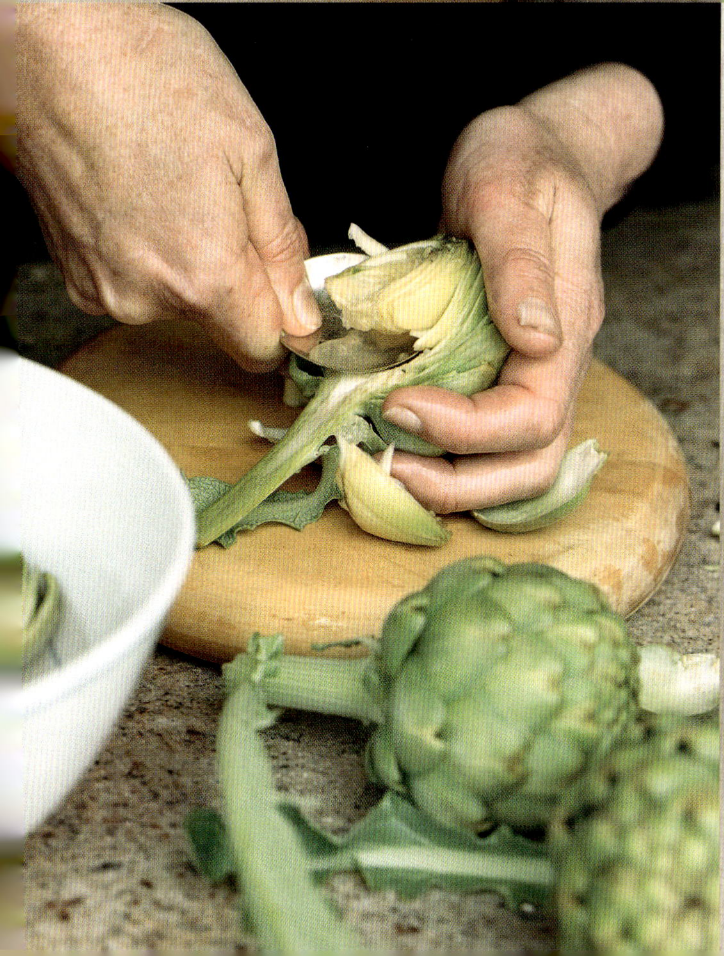
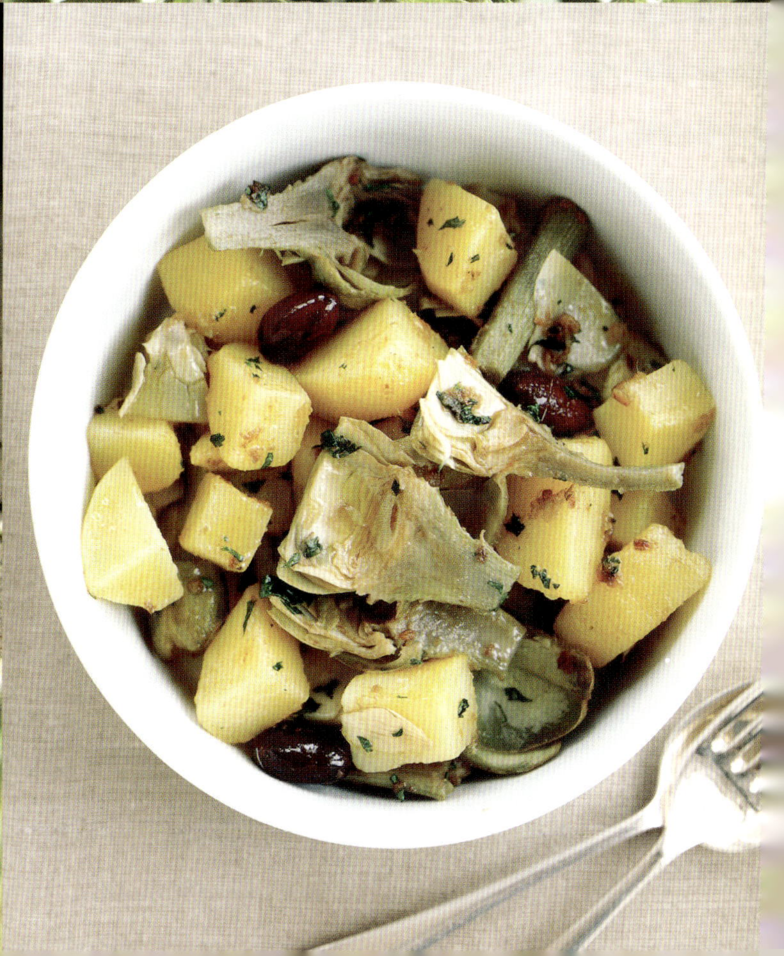

'For Christmas my husband Ted built me a cage to protect the raspberries from the birds. Being able to bring a big bowl of sweet fat berries to the table for dessert feels like such a luxury.'

Berry pleasures

Berry smoothie
Prep 5 minutes

In a blender place 1 cup frozen berries of any type, 1 small ripe banana, 1 cup plain yoghurt, 1-2 tbsp honey or maple syrup, 1 cup orange or apple juice and 2-3 ice cubes. Blend until smooth. Serve immediately.
Makes 2 large serves

Berry brûlée
Prep 10 minutes
Cook 30 minutes

Whisk 3 egg yolks with 3 tbsp caster sugar until creamy and smooth and sugar has dissolved. Stir in 1 tsp natural vanilla essence and 300ml cream. Divide 2 punnets (200g) boysenberries or blackberries between four 150ml ramekins or cups and pour over the cream mixture. Place the ramekins in a roasting pan and fill with hot water to about a third of the way up their sides. Bake at 160°C for 1 hour or until set. When set, remove from water and using a sieve, sprinkle tops evenly with brown sugar. Place under a hot grill and watch very carefully until brown-burnt. Chill until very cold before serving. They will keep in the fridge for up to 24 hours.
Serves 4

Strawberries in pinot noir
Prep 5 minutes +
1 hour standing

Place 3 tbsp caster sugar in a bowl with ⅔ cup pinot noir, several grinds of black pepper, a few drops of natural vanilla essence and 1 tsp lemon juice. Stir to dissolve sugar. Add 2 punnets (500g) hulled strawberries, stir gently and stand for an hour before serving, stirring now and then. Do not leave longer or they will get soggy. Garnish with fresh mint leaves.
Serves 4

*At the start of the summer holidays my friend Lizzie and I, aged 15, cajoled our parents into letting us go raspberry picking. We caught the ferry across Cook Straight and bussed over to Nelson, camping at my mother's cousins' farm out in the countryside near the berry farms.
A couple of bicycles were at our disposal and we set up camp in a lovely hollow near the river.
This was to be my first-ever real job. Out in the glorious sunshine picking my favourite berries and paid to boot – what could be better? My enthusiasm was short-lived. The work was backbreaking, clod-dull and the pay less than paltry.
And so we escaped, heading off over the hills on our bicycles with the smell of fresh-cut hay on the wind and skylarks rippling their summer tunes across the bluest skies. Cooking over a gas burner and washing in the river, we were free. No awful job to turn up to, no one to tell us what to do. And then it rained. Oh, did it rain. Our tent sat in the middle of a little lake, our possessions sunk and sodden.
Wet and exhausted, we made the slow trip back home – interminable hours on the bus, a rough ride on the ferry. Home to the welcome of warm beds and hot dinners. Home. How I appreciated it.*

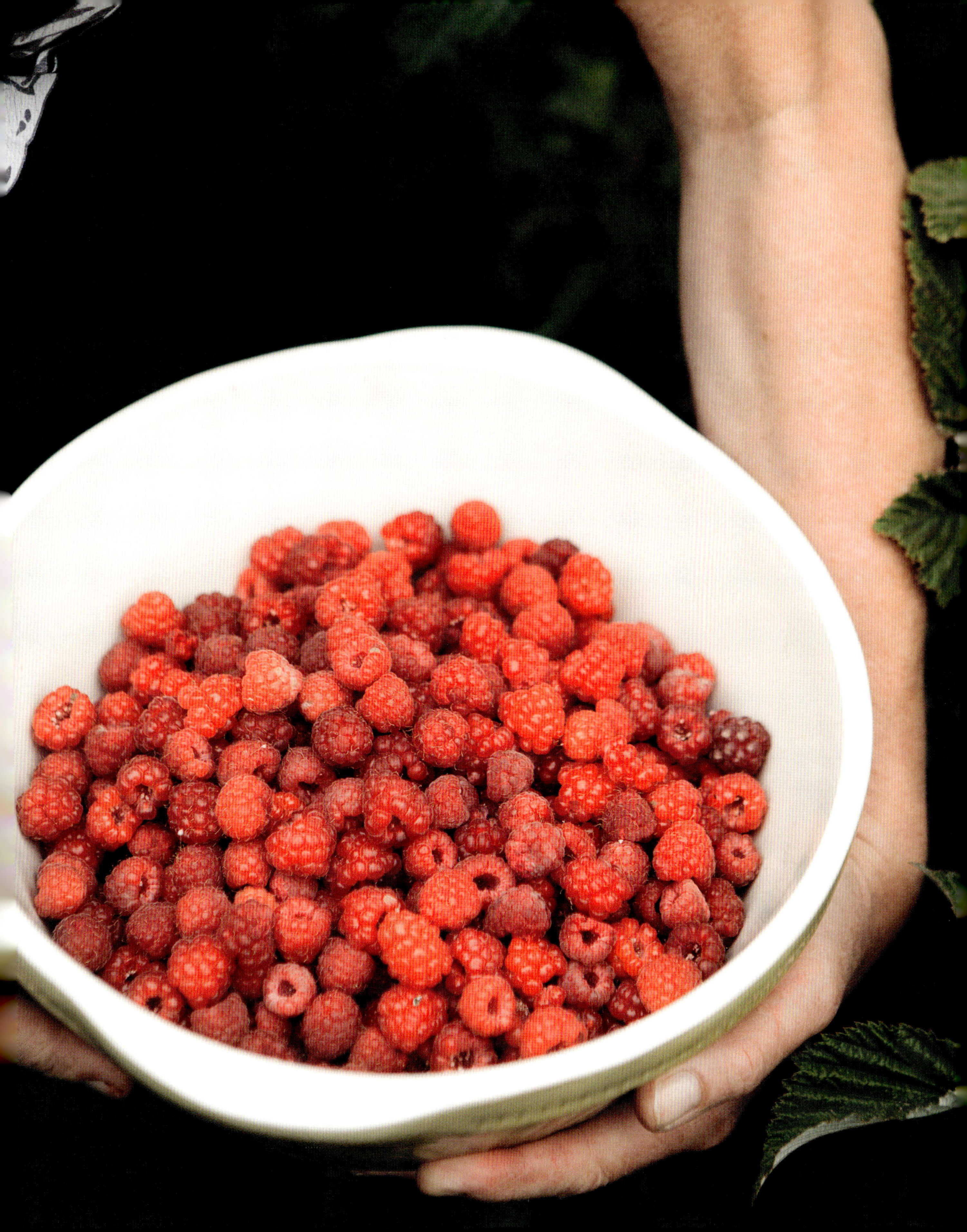

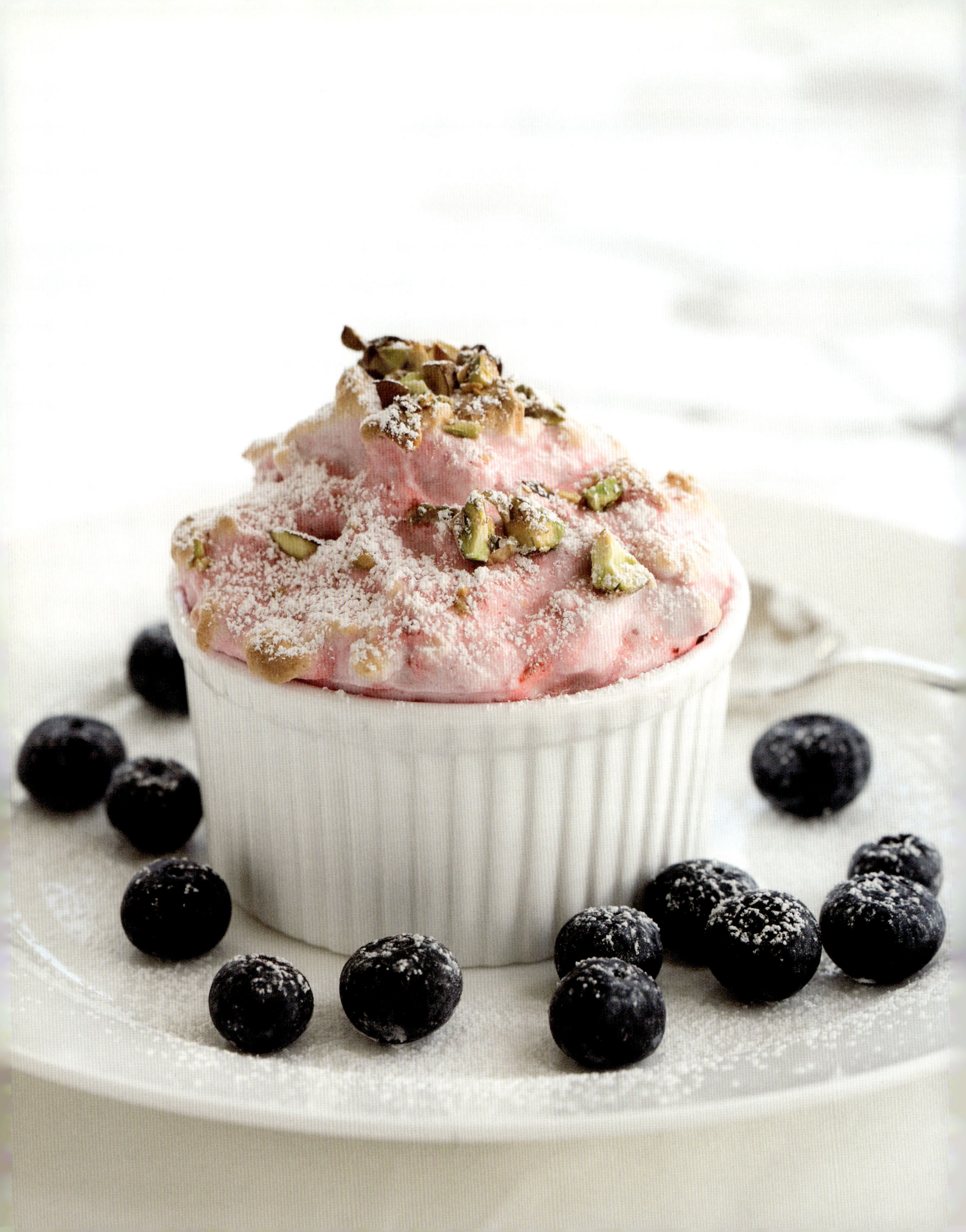

'I tend to avoid desserts that involve too much last-minute work. By pudding time, I want to relax. Make-ahead desserts that you can freeze or just put into the oven to finish deliver the goods.'

Make-ahead soufflé

Berry soufflés

Prep 15 minutes
Cook 5-6 minutes

Berry sauce
3 cups fresh or frozen raspberries or blackberries
½ cup sugar
¼ cup water
1 tsp natural vanilla essence
1 tsp lemon juice
1 tbsp cornflour mixed with 1 tbsp water

3 large egg whites, at room temperature
½ cup caster sugar
Optional: ¼ cup chopped pistachios

This simplified version of a soufflé (traditionally made with an eggy custard base) is foolproof and very light, using just sweetened whipped egg whites folded into a hot fruit purée. Even better, you don't need to be whisking when your guests arrive as the assembled soufflés will hold in the fridge for several hours, ready to bake when needed.

Combine berries, sugar, water, vanilla and lemon juice in a saucepan and bring to a simmer over medium heat. Add cornflour paste and stir until lightly thickened. Simmer for 2-3 minutes.
In a large, very clean mixing bowl beat egg whites and caster sugar until thick and glossy and sugar has fully dissolved (rub a little mixture between fingers to check). Bring berry mixture back to a boil. Gently fold ¾ cup of the boiling berry mixture into the meringue, swirling it into a marbled pattern. Divide remaining berry sauce between six ½-cup ramekins and top with meringue mixture. Sprinkle with nuts if using. If not cooking at once, place soufflés in the fridge for up to 4 hours. Preheat oven to 190°C. Bake soufflés until just beginning to brown, 5-6 minutes. Do not overcook or they will shrink. Remove from oven and serve.
Serves 6

Prune & orange soufflés

Prep 15 minutes
Cook 5-6 minutes

In place of berry sauce, prepare soufflés with a purée of prunes. Soak 150g pitted prunes with ½ cup white wine, ½ cup orange juice, the finely grated zest of 1 orange and 3 tbsp honey.
Cook until soft then purée until smooth. Heat purée to almost boiling and fold into meringue mixture as above.
Serves 6

In my early 20s my enthusiasm for cooking attached itself firmly to my thighs. Over a couple of years my weight increased by more than 20 kilos. It was not until I attended a nutrition course at the Culinary institute of America in upstate New York in 1985 that i figured out that what was making me fat was all the fat in my diet. Gram for gram, fat contains more than double the energy of either protein or carbohydrate. The guile of fat is its ability to carry flavours and give food mouth-feel. Take it away and it's easy to feel dissatisfied and hanging out for more.
The trick is to create dishes with little fat but loads of flavour. You need to find rich, strong flavours that aren't laden with fat – citrus juices, ginger, lemon grass, mint, spices and reduced berry flavours work on the sweet front, while for savoury dishes you can consider miso, reduced meat stocks, juices, ginger, fish sauce, tomato paste, mustard, dried mushrooms, capers and all herbs. High-fat foods like olives, anchovies and blue cheese provide depth of flavour in small quantities, so these are useful too.

'There's a sense of wonder in the transformation of egg white and sugar into a cloud-like meringue. Boil the egg and the white forms a rubbery solid. Part of the fascination of cooking lies in its endless possibilities.'

Melt-in-the-mouth

Stewed rhubarb

Prep 5 minutes
Cook 12-15 minutes

600g fresh rhubarb, chopped in small pieces
2 cups water
1 cup sugar

Place rhubarb in a pot with water and sugar. Bring to a simmer, stirring to dissolve sugar. Simmer for 12-15 minutes or until pulpy. Remove from heat. Cool and cover. Rhubarb will keep for 4-5 days in the fridge or can be frozen. Serve as a stewed fruit with cereal or yoghurt. To separate into syrup and pulp, cool stewed rhubarb and strain through a fine sieve, pressing firmly to extract all the juice. Use the juice as cordial with chilled soda or champagne. The purée makes a great pie filling or turn it into a fool by folding it through cream (see right).

RHUBARB CREAM
This is divine with meringues or pavlovas. Thoroughly drain chilled stewed rhubarb to give 1 cup of cooked pulp. Gently fold into 300ml chilled whipped cream. Leave some swirls of rhubarb showing through the cream.
Makes enough for 12 filled meringues or 1 pavlova.

Meringues

Prep 15 minutes
Cook 1 hour + cooling

5 large egg whites
pinch of salt
160g caster sugar
160g icing sugar
1 tsp natural vanilla essence

This recipe makes oodles of meringues but they keep for weeks in a sealed container and are incredibly useful to pull out for an emergency dessert.
Preheat oven to 180°C. In a very clean bowl and using an electric beater, beat egg whites with salt until stiff. Add caster sugar and beat on high speed for 10 minutes. Fold in icing sugar and vanilla.
Place tiny spoonfuls of mixture on lined baking trays or for larger meringues use about a tablespoon of mixture. Place in oven and immediately turn heat down to 120°C. Cook 1 hour. Turn off oven and leave meringues in oven to cool. Sandwich meringues with whipped cream up to an hour before serving.
Makes about 150 tiny or 60 medium meringues

TURKISH DRIED FRUIT COMPOTE
Dried fruits have a wonderfully intense flavour. Play around with the compote flavours by adding different spices and flavourings. Allspice berries are nice, as is fresh ginger, or a vanilla pod.
Place 3 cups water and 1½ cups sugar in a pot and bring to a simmer, stirring to dissolve sugar. Add 400g mixed dried fruits, eg pitted prunes, dried apricots, dried pears, apple slices or fig halves, the juice and zest of 1 lemon juice, 1 cinnamon quill and 5-6 cardamom pods and simmer over low heat for 20 minutes. Stand for at least 2 hours. Serve warm or chilled. Fruit will keep for several weeks in a covered container in the fridge.
Serves 6-8

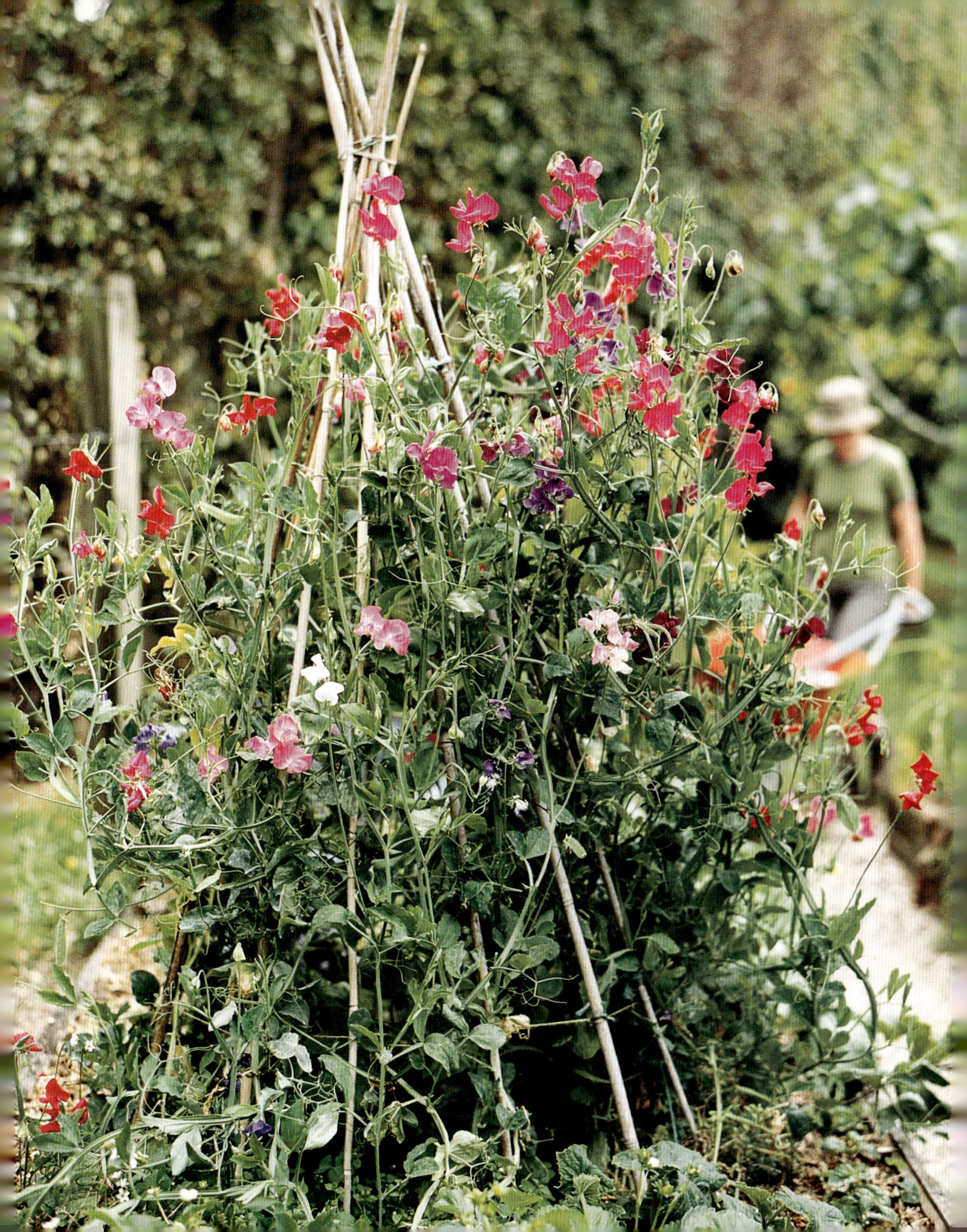

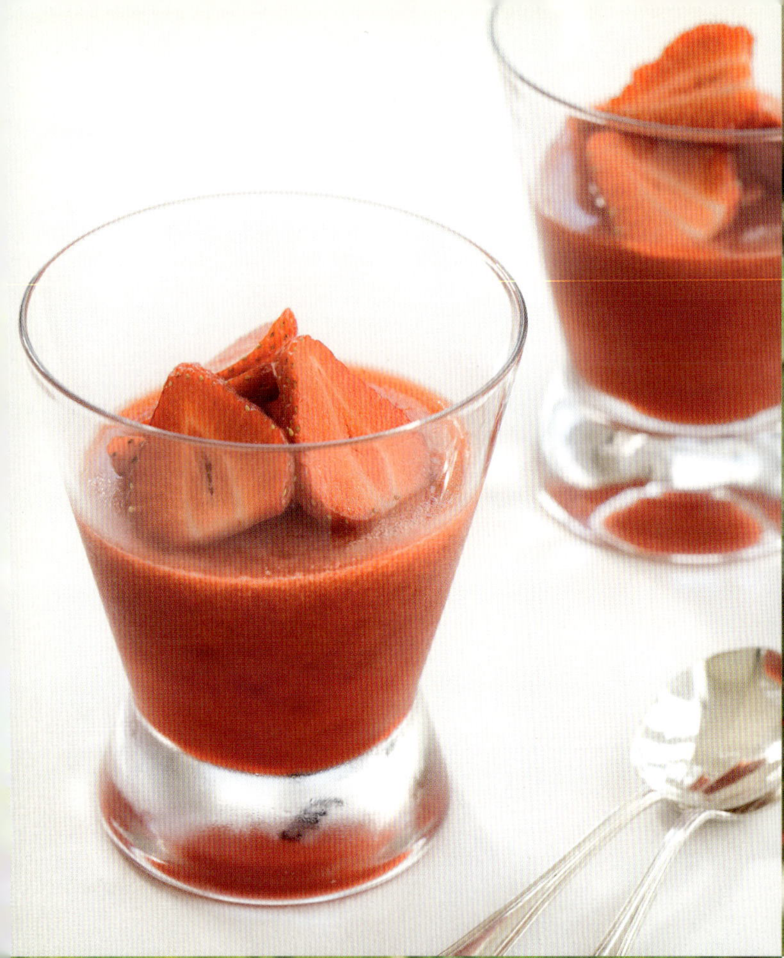
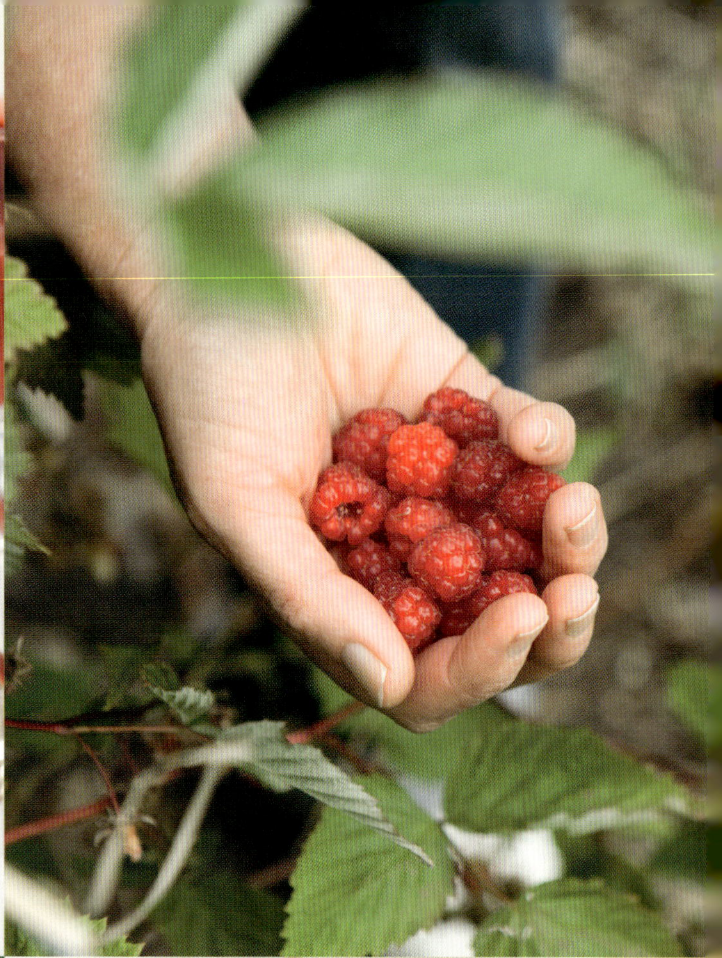
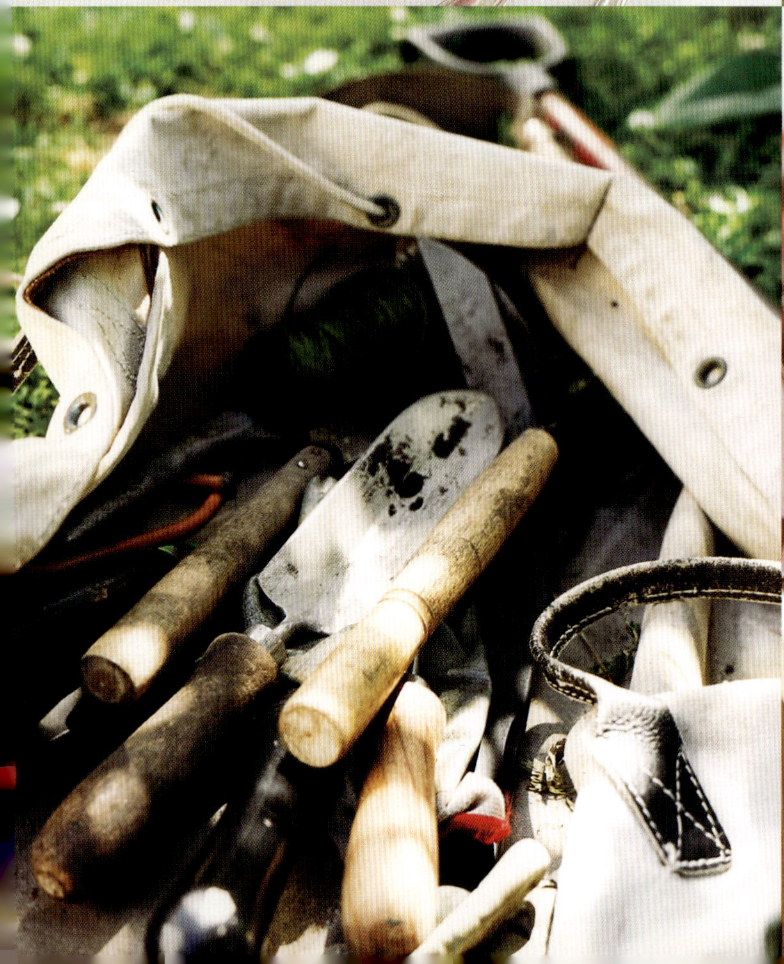
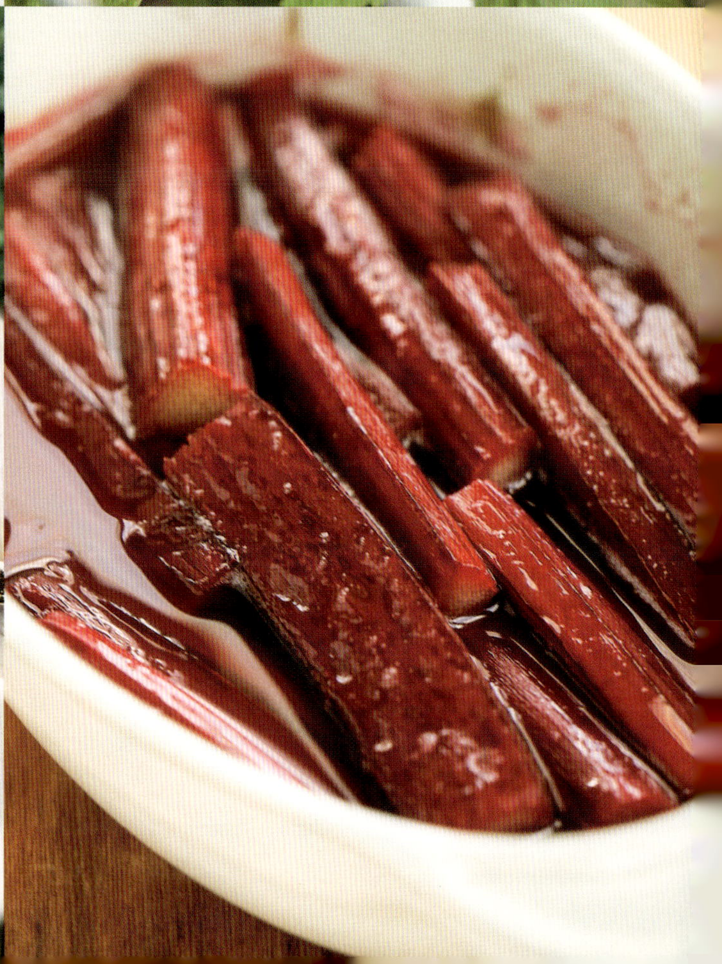

'It's a surprising fact that the same plant can be both edible and poisonous. Rhubarb, for instance, with its succulent stalks has leaves that are lethal enough to be used as a natural insecticide.'

Intensify fruit flavours

Scarlet strawberry jellies

Prep   15 minutes +
          3-12 hours chilling

500-600g fresh ripe strawberries
   (2 punnets), hulled
½ cup caster sugar
4 tsp gelatine
3 tbsp cold water
1 cup apple juice, heated to
   a boil
⅓ cup lime juice

Place three-quarters of the hulled strawberries in a blender or food processor with the sugar. Whizz to a purée. Sprinkle gelatine over cold water in a cup and leave to absorb for 2-3 minutes. Add the boiling apple juice and soaked gelatine mixture to puréed fruit and blitz for 30 seconds to dissolve sugar and gelatine. Pour into a 1 litre measuring jug, add the lime juice and if needed add extra apple juice to make 3 cups total volume.
Pour jelly mixture into 6 serving glasses and chill until set, about 3 hours or overnight. Slice remaining strawberries and use to garnish jellies.
Serves 6

Baked rhubarb

Prep   2 minutes
Cook   1 hour

400g fresh rhubarb
½ cup sugar
¼ cup water
Optional: juice of 1 orange

Preheat oven to 150°C. Trim rhubarb, peeling off tough outer strings. Cut stalks in half or thirds. Spread in a shallow baking dish. Sprinkle with sugar and add water and orange juice if using. Cover and bake for 1 hour.
Serves 4

Variation: For a rhubarb and berry compote, sprinkle over a punnet of raspberries or blueberries before adding sugar and water and baking. Cool and chill before serving.

FRUIT & VEGETABLE NUTRITION

In the nutrition stakes, not all fruit and vegetables are born equal. The nutritional powerhouses contain high levels of vitamins, minerals, antioxidants and phytochemicals. These fruits and vegetables provide the body not just with its requirements to fuction properly, but also offer protective nutrition against a number of diseases. Lettuce and cucumber are lightweights in the nutrients they offer compared to super-foods like broccoli and kiwifruit. Rhubarb is a rich source of calcium with a cup providing about 25% of your daily requirement, as well as some fibre and vitamnin C. Blueberries are rich in vitamin C and, like all berries, are a rich source of protective phtyochemicals that promote heart and vascular health.

HOME-MADE LEMONADE

Combine 400ml freshly squeezed lemon juice with 5 cups sugar, 2 tsp citric or tartaric acid and 1 litre boiling water. Stir to dissolve. Dilute to taste. Makes 2 litres of concentrate. Store in the fridge; it will keep for weeks.

'In the recall of a scent we are instantly transported back in time. Smell is our most potent sense and the most nostalgic; in it we find our warmest memories.'

Let them eat cake

Rhubarb & yoghurt crumble cake

Prep 15 minutes
Cook 50-60 minutes

140g butter, softened
1 cup sugar
2 eggs, at room temperature
1 tsp natural vanilla essence
¾ cup plain yoghurt
2 cups flour
3 tsp baking powder
½ tsp baking soda
3 stalks rhubarb, thinly sliced, or 190g berry fruits or other chopped fruits

Topping:
½ cup firmly packed brown sugar
½ cup slivered almonds or chopped walnuts
4 tbsp flour
1 tsp ground cinnamon
60g butter, melted

Preheat oven to 180°C. Grease a 25cm spring-form or loose-bottomed cake tin and line the base with baking paper. Beat butter and sugar together until creamy. Add eggs and vanilla and beat well. Beat in yoghurt then add sifted dry ingredients and stir gently to just combine (mixture will be a thick consistency). Spread into prepared tin and sprinkle over rhubarb.
Combine topping ingredients and sprinkle over cake. Bake until golden and a skewer inserted into the middle comes out clean, about 50-60 minutes. Stand 15 minutes before turning out. Allow to cool before cutting. Store in an airtight container.
Serves 8-10

Variations: In summer I like to make this cake with stone fruit. Use 6-8 stoned plums or apricots cut in wedges in place of rhubarb.
In autumn use feijoas or apples cut in chunks in place of rhubarb and flavour crumble topping with 1 tsp ginger in place of cinnamon.

THE CHEMISTRY OF BAKING

Baking is one area of cooking where you do need to be precise and measure carefully. Baking is essentially chemistry and as such ratios and proportions do matter. That said, even with careful and accurate measuring, recipes may turn out differently depending on the type of flour used or the humidity (or dryness) of the day. Take the time to read through the recipe carefully, check you have the ingredients and equipment at hand and stick to one set of measures – don't be tempted to mix and match your measurements between metric and cup. A recipe is usually more than just a single idea and generally offers scope for your own creativity, either in the flavourings or the type of fruit or nuts used. What you don't want to fiddle around with is the proportion of flour, sugar, fat and raising agent as this creates the formula that makes one type of cake or cookie different from the next.

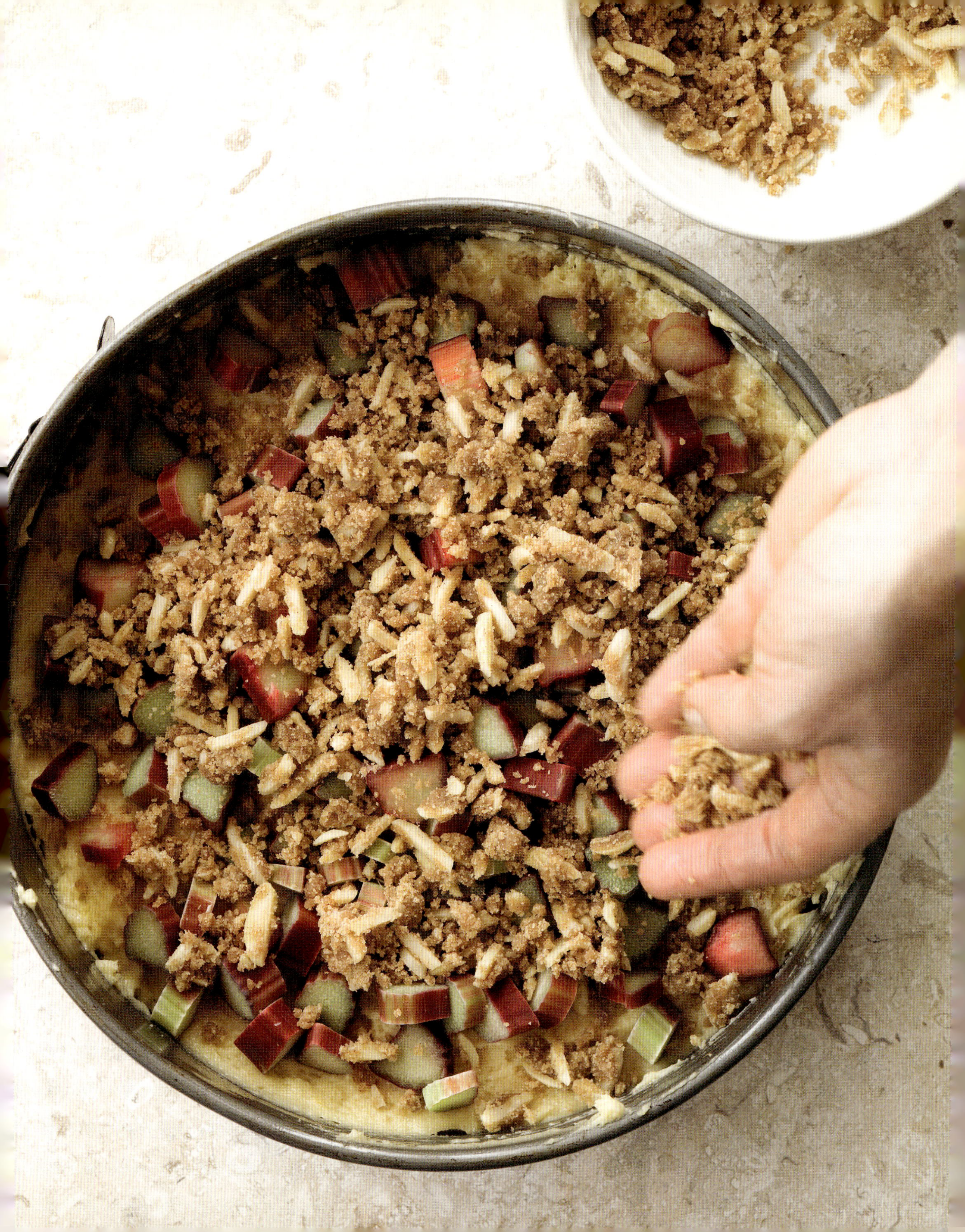

'Gooseberries, along with currants, are such old-fashioned fruit. Their fleeting season makes them hard to find in the shops. Up on the hills behind Wanaka these fruits grow wild, ripe for the picking.'

Fruit and cream

Gooseberry fool

Prep 5 minutes + at least 90 minutes to chill
Cook 8 minutes

300g fresh or frozen gooseberries
½ cup water
¾ cup sugar
500ml cream
1-2 tbsp icing sugar to taste
Optional: 2 tbsp chopped pistachios or walnuts

Combine gooseberries, water and sugar in a saucepan. Cover and cook over low heat, stirring occasionally, until fruit is tender and breaks up easily, about 8 minutes. Transfer to a food processor or blender and purée. Taste and add more sugar if needed. Cover and chill until cold – at least 1 hour – or store for up to 3 days.

In a deep bowl, whip cream to soft peaks, adding icing sugar to taste. Fold in half the chilled fruit purée, swirling gently to combine without fully mixing. Layer cream and remaining fruit in 4 serving glasses, swirling gently with a fork between layers to slightly combine. If not served at once, fool will keep covered and chilled for up to 6 hours. Just before serving garnish with nuts if using.

Serves 4

Rhubarb & strawberry fool

In place of gooseberry purée use 1 cup stewed rhubarb (page 60) mixed with 1 punnet strawberries, hulled and finely chopped.

WHIPPING CREAM

Fresh whipping cream needs a fat content of at least 32% to achieve a thick consistency. It also needs to be chilled before whipping.

THICKENED CREAM

In the spring fresh cream can contain up to 60% fat which gives it a very thick, spoonable consistency. To emulate this year round, manufacturers add gelatine to whipping cream, producing thickened cream.

CLOTTED CREAM

Clotted cream needs a fat content of at least 55%. Cream is heated to 82°C and cooled for about 4½ hours. The crust is then skimmed off. It has its own special, almost caramel flavour and colour and is very thick.

CRÈME FRAÎCHE

Crème fraîche is produced from unpasteurised, fermented fresh cow's cream. A substitute is to add 1 tbsp plain full-fat yoghurt to 150ml whipping cream. Heat slightly over a bowl of hot water to activate the enzymes. Take out of water bath, cover and place in a warm spot. It will take about 12-36 hours. Chill before using – it will thicken further.

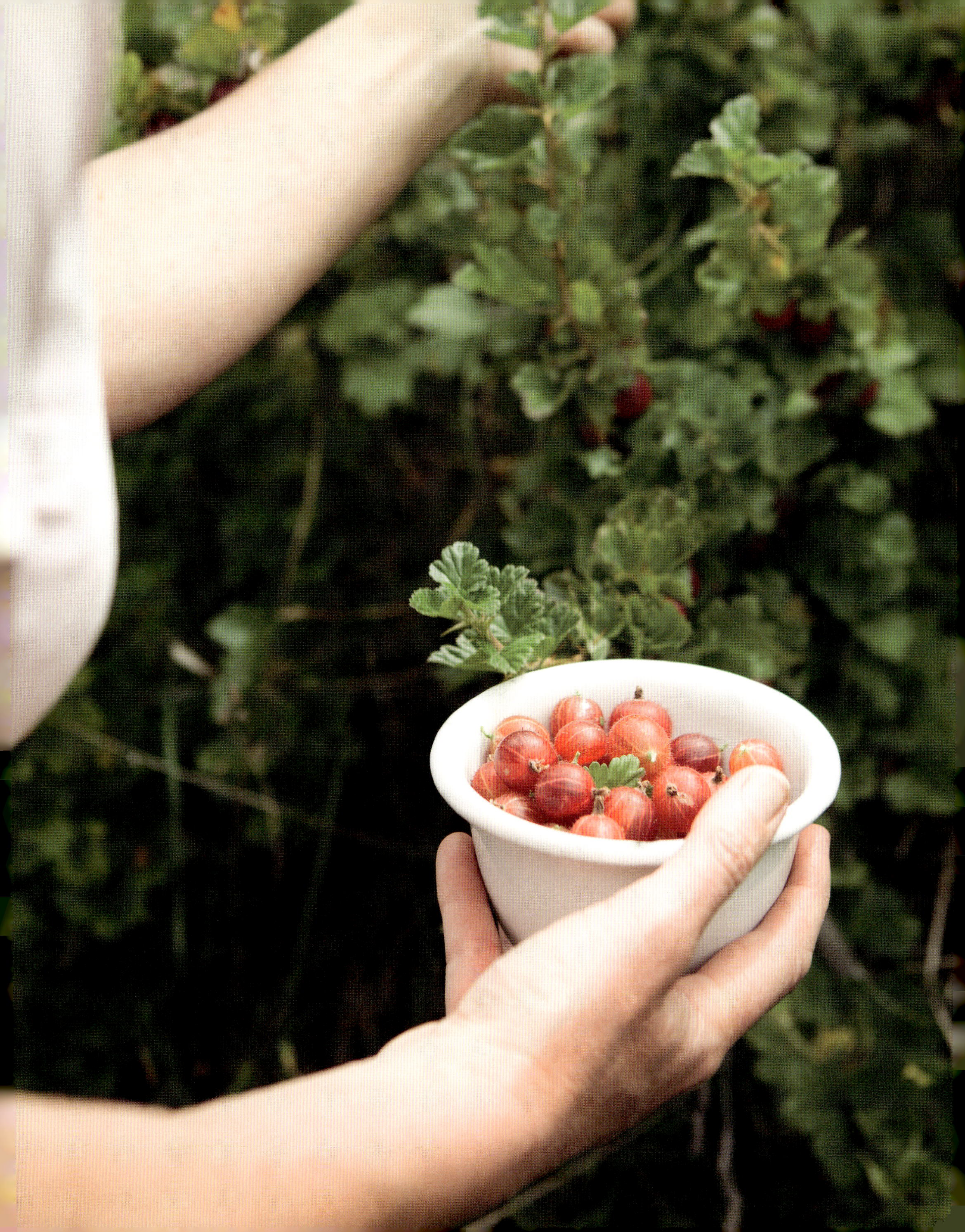

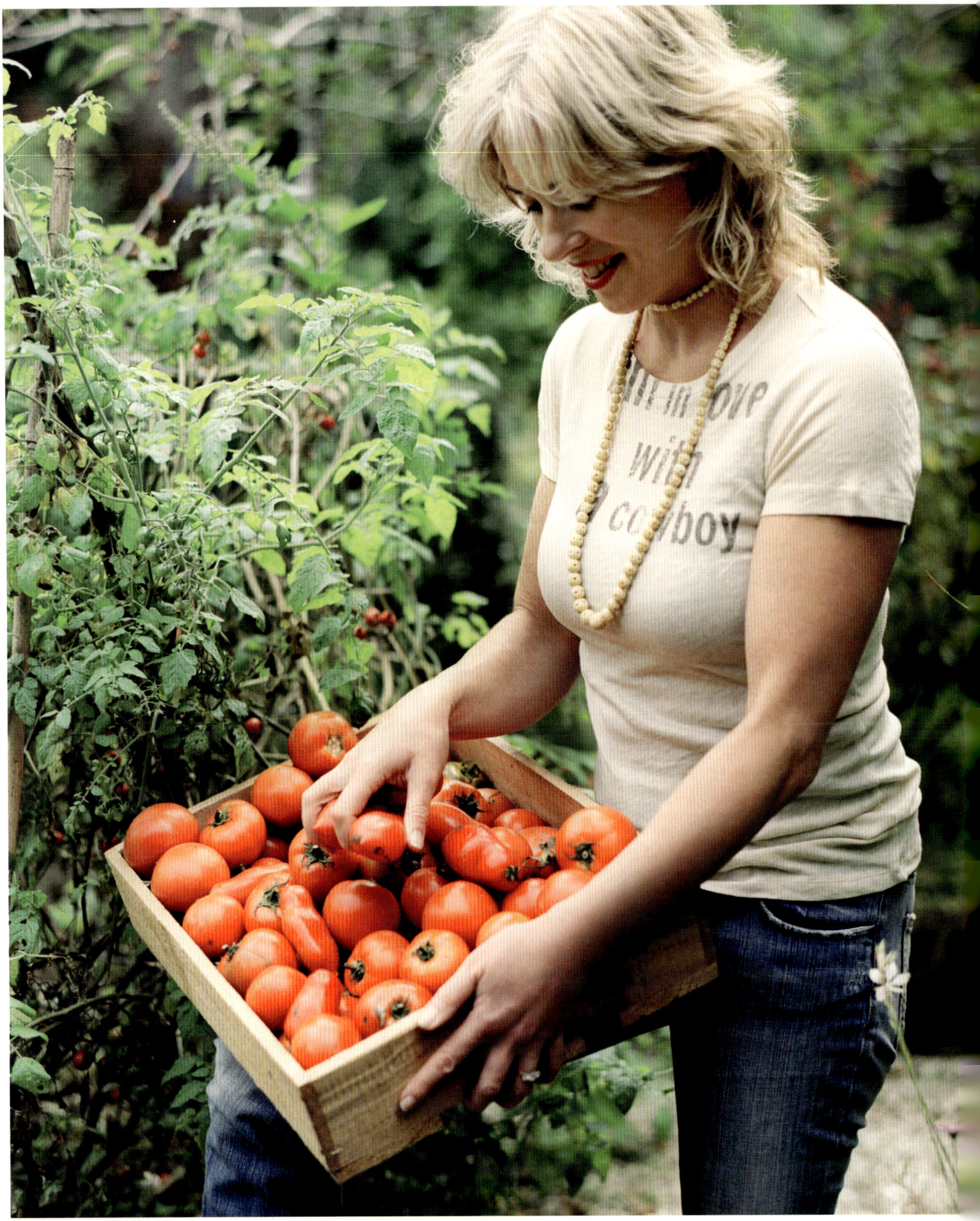

Summer

Through the peak of summer's heat our bodies seek respite in foods with clean, fresh tastes. True to form, the season's harvests echo our own natural rhythms, delivering a progression of offerings to satisfy our appetites. Those quintessential tastes that we associate with summer – from tomatoes, corn, green beans and zucchini through to all the berries and stone fruits – find successful partners with a range of flavours from around the globe. Simplicity reigns in salads and grills – deliciously easy meals that keep us out of the kitchen, free to enjoy summer's many pleasures.

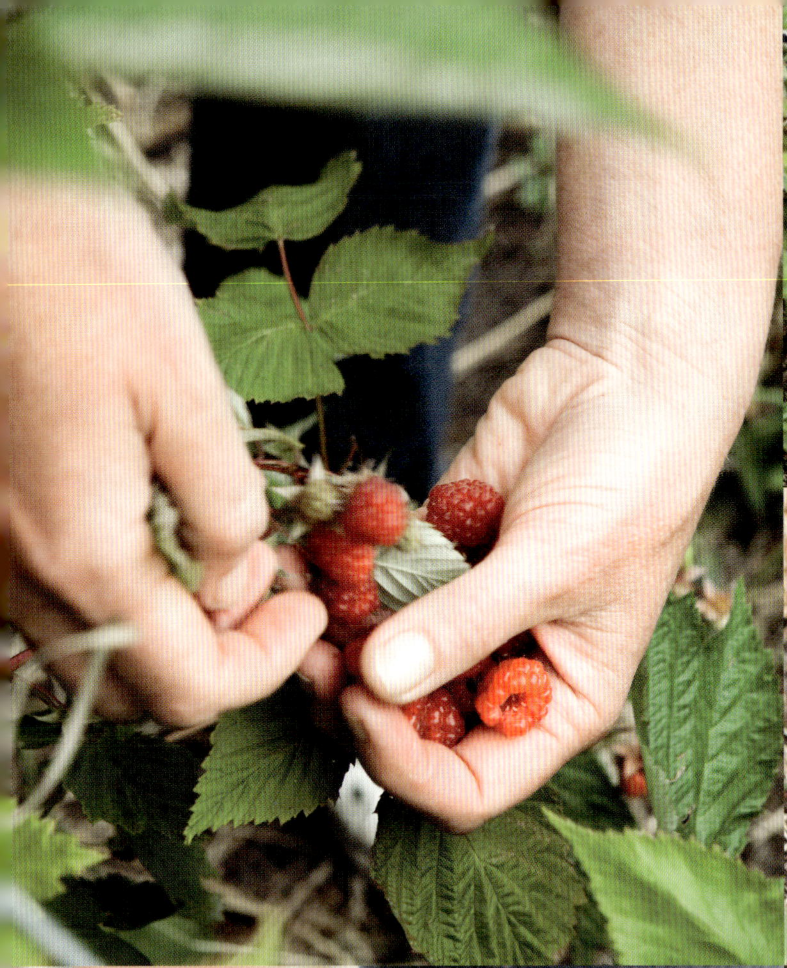
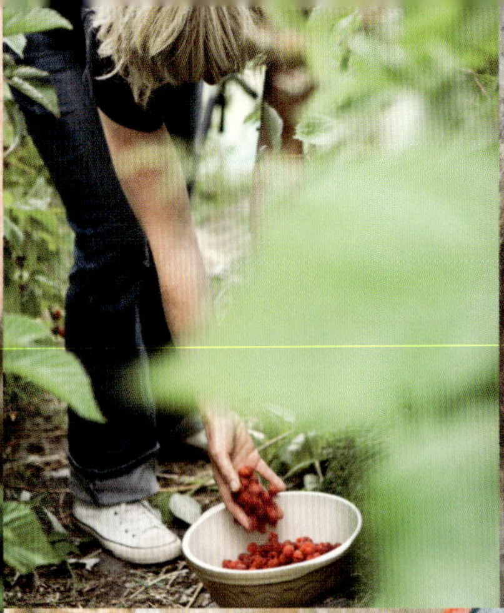
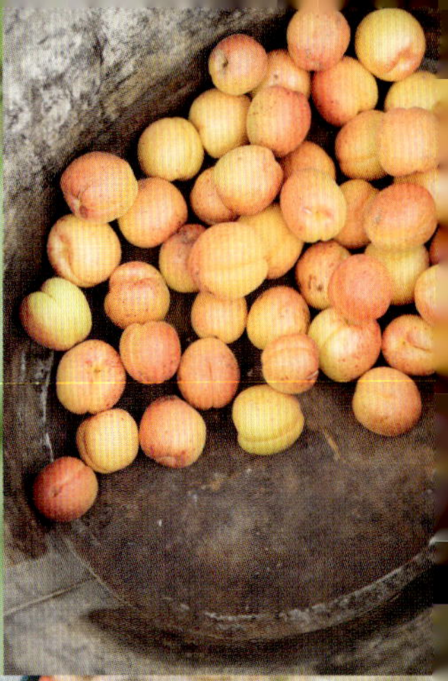
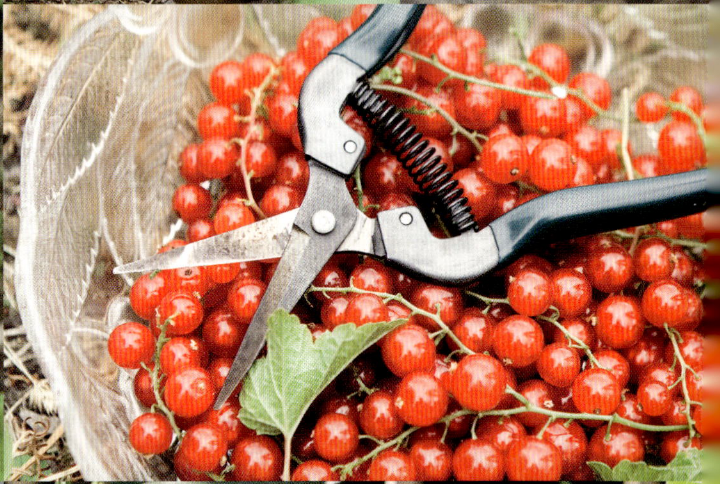
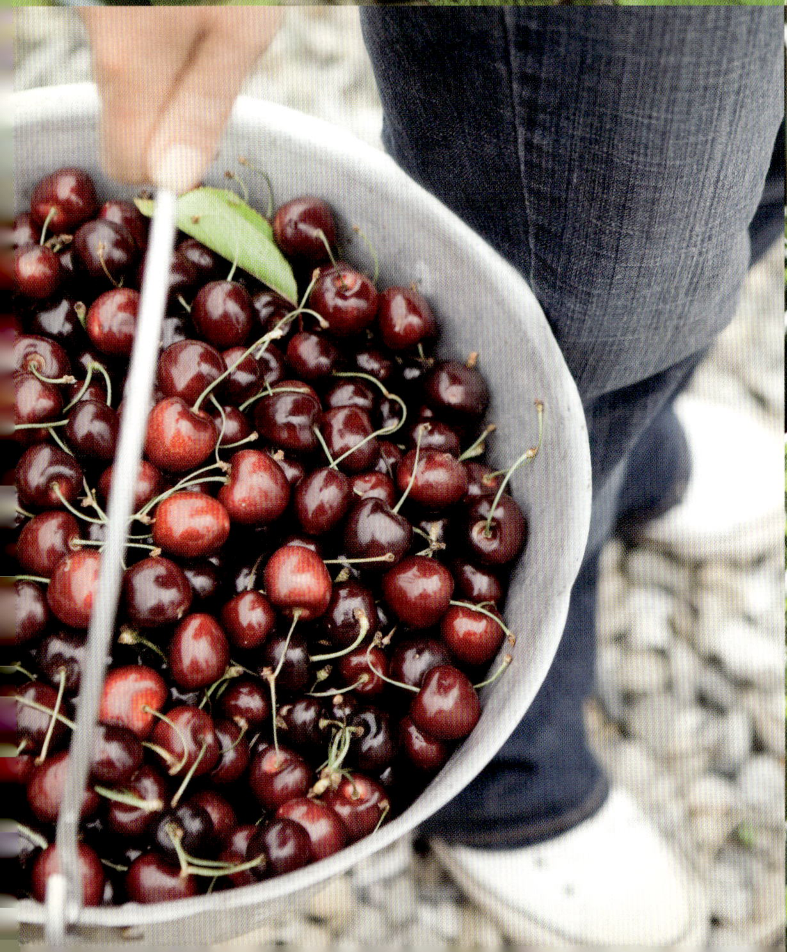
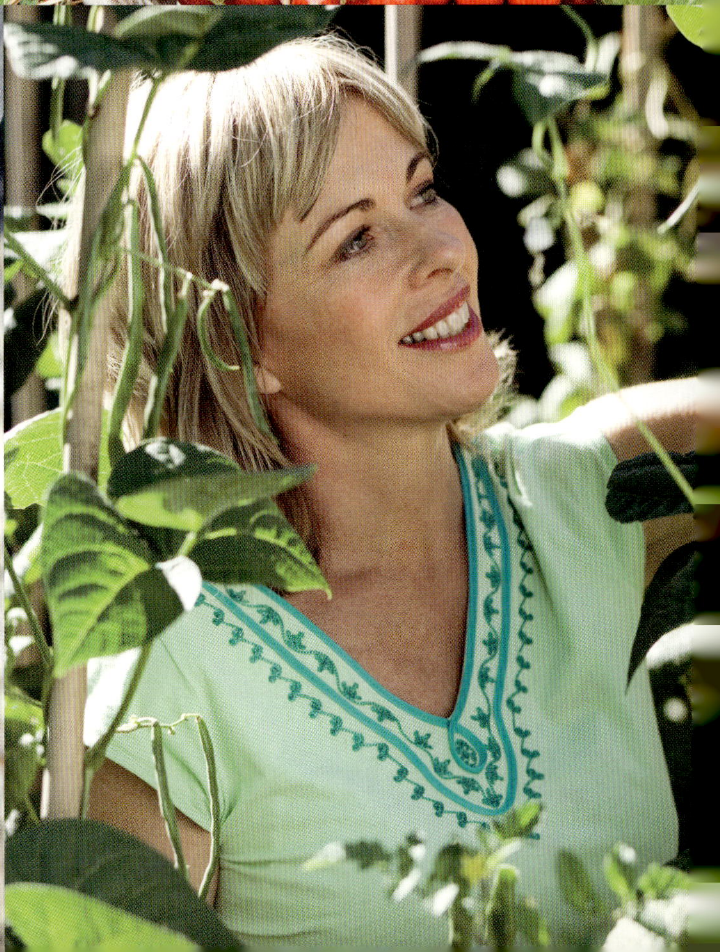

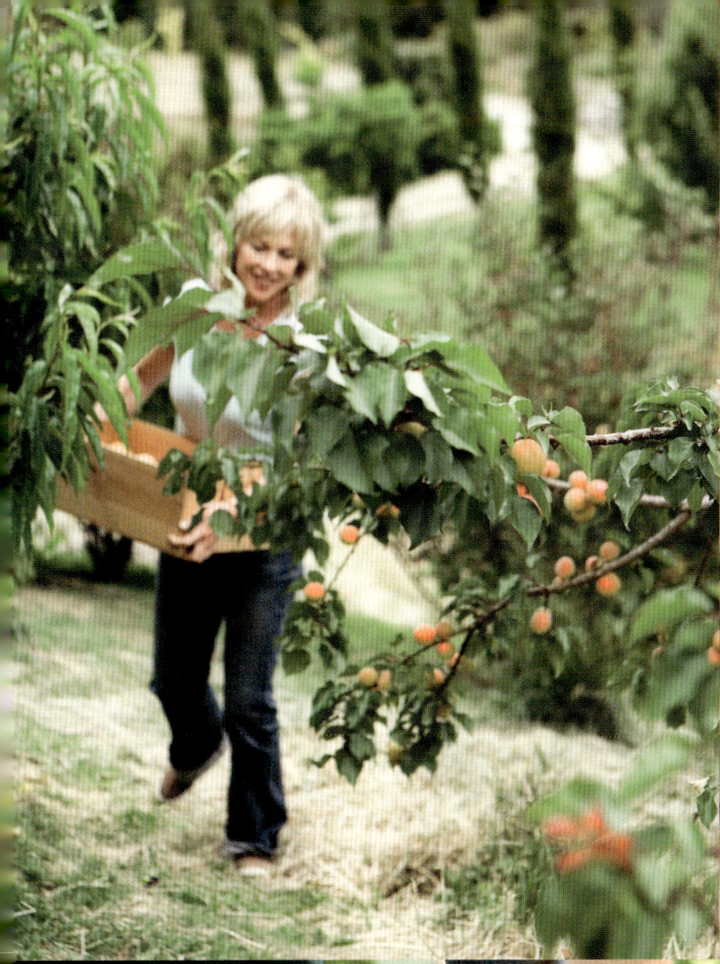
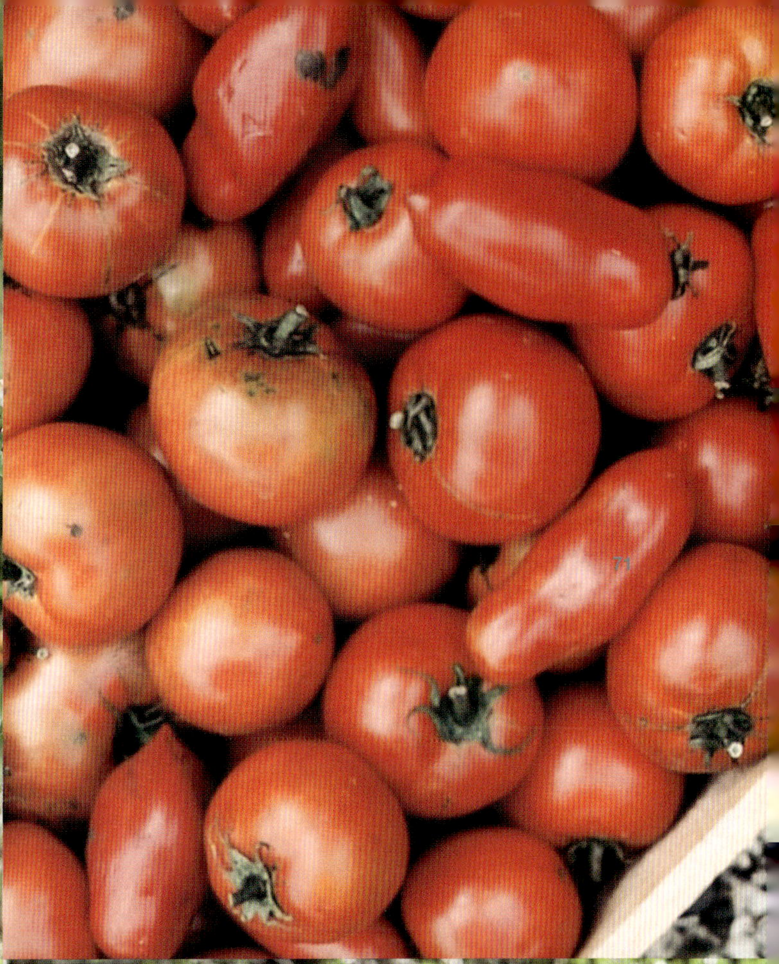
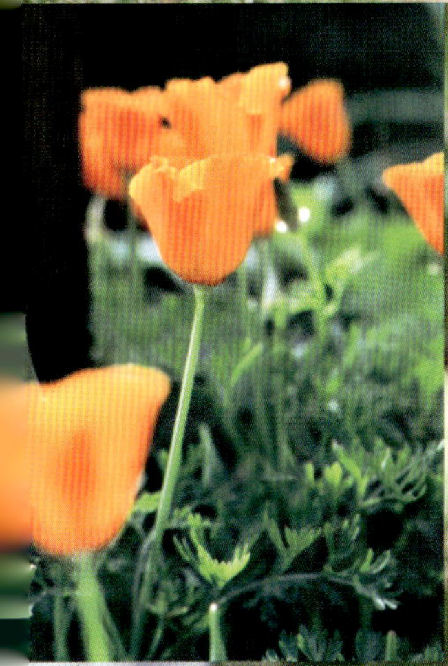
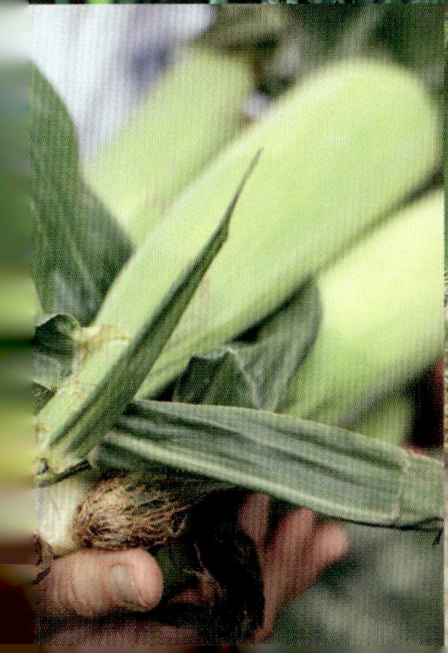
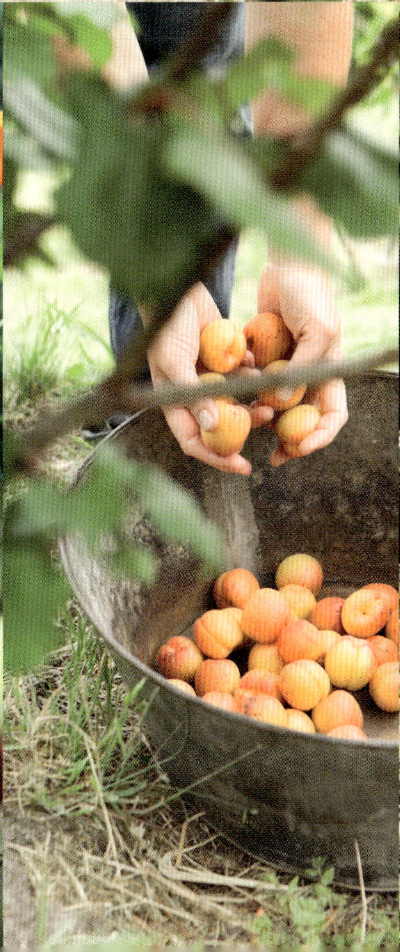
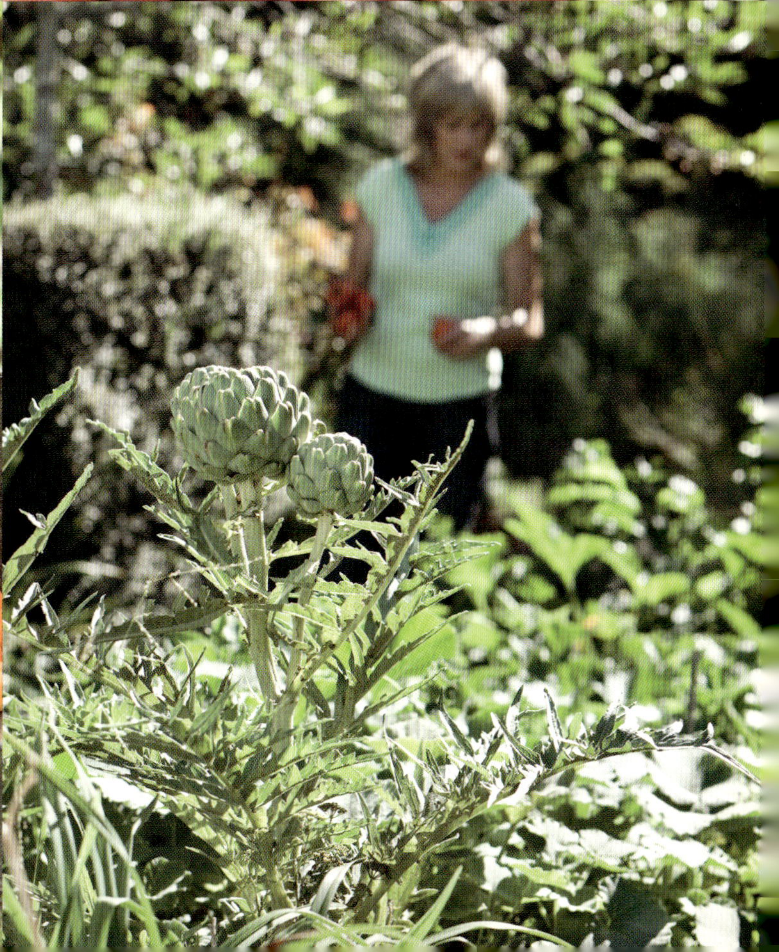

'Toss and serve is a simple mantra for summer dining. The season's meals are a riff on whatever fresh food is at hand. Good dressings and marinades bring it all together in great-tasting salads and grills.'

The summer palate

Fresh in summer
avocados
beans
beetroot
berries
broccoli
cabbage
cape gooseberries
celery
corn
cucumbers
fennel
lettuces
mangos
pineapple
potatoes
radishes
rhubarb
shallots
spring and red onions
stone fruit
the first apples and pears
tomatillos
tomatoes
zucchini

Flavours
basil
chillies
chives
coriander
dill
garlic
lemon grass
marjoram
mint
sage
tarragon
thyme

Returning to our city garden after the summer holidays I am greeted by a wilderness of lush Amazonian growth. Zucchini have turned triffid-like into giant watery marrows, vines of self-seeded pumpkins rampage over the garden beds and the runner beans climb ever skyward on their bamboo stakes. Spring's leftover fennel, leeks and Italian parsley have seeded, as have the coriander, chervil, watercress and rocket. These can be planted again once the longest day has passed. Abundance is the hallmark of summer and we are spoilt for choice. Taking the season's harvests, we can combine them with different herbs and spices to make tasty dressings, sauces and marinades. Thus, with the same base produce, it's easy to create an array of enticing summer dishes.

Rosemary, garlic and lemon are a natural triumvirate that provides Mediterranean tones. Substitute the rosemary for basil, oregano or tarragon or mix the herbs together for flavours that deliver the taste of a Mediterranean summer. If Asian flavours take your fancy, create zesty combinations with lemon grass, chillies, ginger and mint or coriander. Moroccan flavours such as lemon, cumin, chilli, paprika, garlic and coriander bring the spicy Casbah to your table.

Chilli comes to the fore as the summer heats up. You would imagine that eating chillies would make you feel even hotter but in fact capsaicin, the heat-causing compound that is manufactured in the ribs of the chilli, has a cooling effect on the body.

1. Kaffir lime leaf
   Citrus hystrix
2. Cayenne chilli
   Capsicum annuum
3. Scotch bonnet chilli
   Capsicum chinense
4. Jalapeno chilli
   Capsicum annuum
5. Lemon grass
   Cymbopogon
6. Thai bird's eye chilli
   Capsicum annuum
7. Tahitian or Persian lime
   Citrus latifolia
8. Mint
   Mentha

THE ULTIMATE CHILLI SAUCE
Purée together until smooth 3 cloves garlic, peeled, ¼ cup finely chopped fresh ginger, the juice and finely grated zest of 2 limes, 2 stalks chopped lemon grass and ½ cup fresh coriander. Place in a pot with 1½ cups Thai sweet chilli sauce, 2 tbsp fish sauce, 2 tbsp light soy sauce and 1 tbsp rice vinegar. Simmer for 5-8 minutes. Leave to cool. Sauce will keep in the fridge for several months.
Makes 2 cups

HOT STUFF
The Scoville scale is used to rate the hotness of chillies. The hottest Naga Jolokia, at up to 1,000,000 heat units, rate at half that for pepper spray. Capsicums rate at zero.

1.

2.

3.

4.

5.

6.

7.

8.

'As my husband Ted says, we try not to eat barcodes. It's easy to become reliant on packaged, processed foods, especially when life is busy. You feel healthier with fresh, locally grown food on the plate.'

Summer salsas

Fresh nectarine or mango salsa
Prep   10 minutes

In a mixing bowl combine 4 nectarines, very finely diced (or 2 peeled diced mangos), ⅓ cup lime juice, 1-2 small red chillies, finely minced, 1 spring onion, finely diced, ¼ cup chopped mint or coriander and 1 tbsp Thai sweet chilli sauce. Season with salt and pepper. Chill until ready to serve, up to 2 hours. Serving ideas: great with any grill. *Makes 2 cups, 6-8 serves*

Avocado salsa
Prep   15 minutes

In a mixing bowl combine 2 large just-ripe avocados, chopped and roughly mashed, 2 tomatillos, finely diced (optional), 2 tbsp chopped coriander, ¼ cup lime juice, ½ green chilli, finely chopped, ¼ tsp salt and grinds of black pepper. Stir until evenly combined. Serve within 2 hours to prevent discolouring. (If tomatillos are used, they will hold the colour for up to 24 hours.) *Makes 1½ cups*

Mexican fresh tomato salsa
Prep   20 minutes

In Mexico and southern American states this refreshing, addictive salsa is called pico de gallo. As well as being the standard accompaniment to corn chips, it makes an excellent partner for grilled fish or chicken. It's also very good without the chilli.

Combine 2 large tomatoes (300g), finely diced, with 1 small red onion, finely diced, 2 cloves garlic, finely chopped, 1-2 small chillies, finely minced (optional), 4 tbsp chopped coriander, 2 tbsp lime juice, 1 tbsp olive oil, ½-1 tsp salt, several grinds of pepper and a pinch of sugar. Stand for at least 30 minutes before serving to draw out the flavours. Keeps in the fridge up to 24 hours. *Makes 2 cups*

SALTED CAPERS
Capparis spinosa
The best capers in the world come from the island of Pantelleria, off the coast of Sicily. These tiny, tight buds are preserved in salt. To use salted capers, cover them with hot water, stand for 10 minutes then drain and rinse thoroughly.

TOMATILLOS
Physalis ixocarpa
Also known as the Mexican husk tomato, and from the same family as the cape gooseberry. Once established, tomatillos will self-seed in the garden to provide annual harvests throughout summer. Widely used in Mexican cooking, especially in traditional guacamole recipes, where they add a distinctive flavour and also prevent the avocado from browning. Like the smaller cape gooseberry, the plant has a sprawling habit and the fruit forms inside a papery calyx. It has a distinctive yet delicate, tangy melon flavour. Use in sauces, salads and chilled gazpacho-style soups. No real substitute in terms of flavour, but green tomatoes can be used.

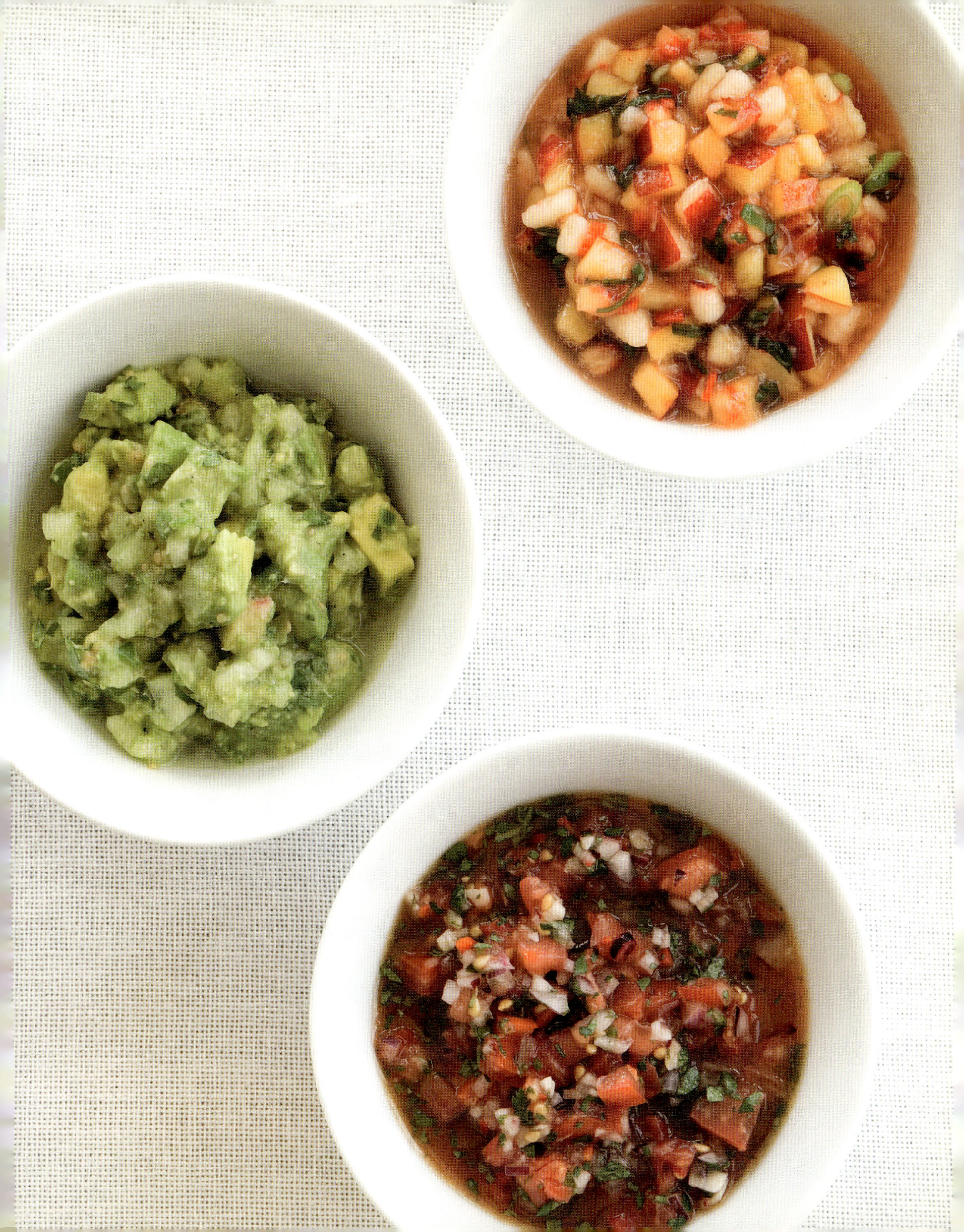

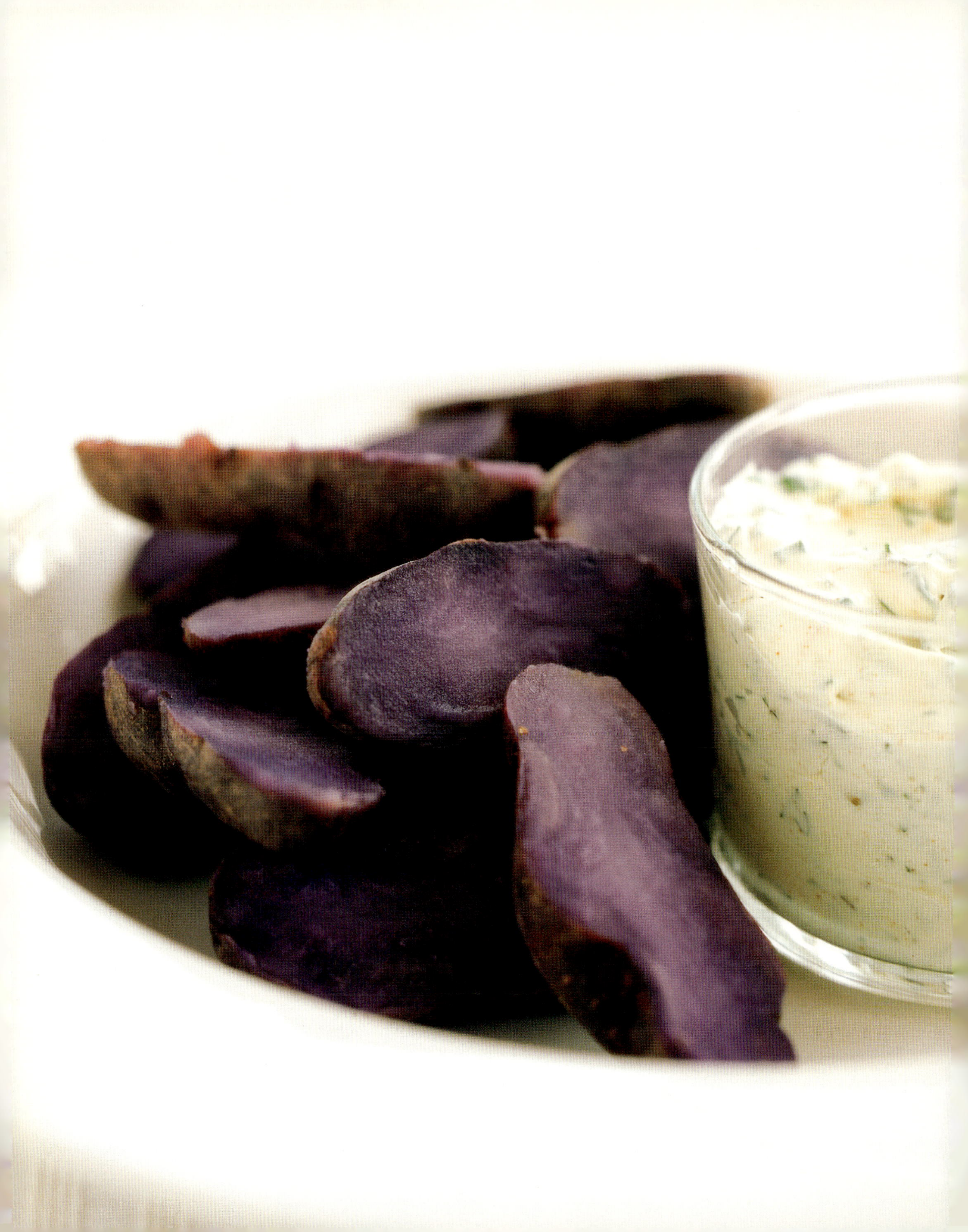

'Home cooking should never try to emulate restaurant food. There are no hard-and-fast rules at home; everyone makes a recipe differently, improvising where needed. That's what gives it your own touch.'

Potatoes with sauce

Baby potatoes with three sauces
Prep 5 minutes
Cook 20 minutes

Simmer a pot of new potatoes or Maori potatoes in lightly salted water until just tender. Drain and, when cool enough to handle, halve. Serve warm or at room temperature with horseradish and wasabi cream, mint and caper sauce or south-of-the-border sour cream.

Horseradish & wasabi cream
Prep time 5 minutes

Mix 1 cup light sour cream with 2 tbsp horseradish sauce, 2 tsp wasabi paste, 1 tsp lemon juice, 1 tbsp finely chopped chives and a little salt and pepper. Will keep chilled for several days.
Makes 1 cup

Mint & caper sauce
Prep time 10 minutes

Place 1 tightly packed cup mint leaves in a sieve and pour over boiling water to wilt. Cool under running cold water; drain thoroughly. Blend in a food processor with 1 tbsp capers, ½ tsp salt (omit if using salted capers), the finely grated zest of 1 lime and ½ cup neutral oil. Purée to form a semi-smooth sauce. Will keep chilled for several days.
Makes 1 cup

South-of-the-border sour cream
Prep time 5 minutes

Place 250g sour cream (lite or regular) in a mixing bowl and beat lightly until creamy. Mix in 1 tsp Cajun spice mix, ½ tsp garlic salt and 1 tbsp each chopped coriander and mint. Add a little chopped chilli if you like the kick. Will keep chilled for several days.
Makes 1 cup
Pictured left with purple Urenika potatoes.

GROWING POTATOES

Buy seed potato tubers in the late winter and set them out in a box or egg tray with the end where the tiny buds can be seen – the 'rose' end – upwards. Store in a cool, frost-free, light place (if it's too dark they will grow lanky and weak). Once they have produced short, deep-green shoots, and provided there is no risk of frost, plant them out in trenches about 10cm deep and 15cm apart. This sprouting process, known as chitting, encourages the tubers to produce sturdy sprouts. As the potatoes start to grow, mound the soil up around the stems. When they flower they are ready to harvest. Do not eat any part of the plant that grows above the ground as it is poisonous.

NEW POTATOES AND OLD POTATOES

Early-season potato varieties, along with any other immature potato, tend to be low in starch. This means they have a waxy texture and do not break up during cooking. They are ideal for boiling, in salads and any dish in which you want them to retain their shape. Main-crop varieties have more starch and therefore less structural integrity and break up more easily. These are good to mash, roast and chip.

'Taste as you cook, adjusting the flavours to your preference to be more or less sweet, sour, salty, spicy or bitter. That way you create some ownership in the food you prepare and get to eat it the way you like it.'

Salad rolls

Chicken & mint salad rolls

Prep 30 minutes

100g rice vermicelli noodles
1 iceberg lettuce, very finely shredded
1 large carrot, peeled and coarsely grated
½ tsp sugar
1 cup torn mint leaves (60-70 leaves)
3 tbsp chopped coriander leaves
2 cooked chicken breasts (200-250g), very finely shredded
30 small or 20 large rounds rice paper

The kids often whip up rice-paper salad rolls like these for a summer snack. They are wonderfully light and refreshing to eat. Adding lots of mint is the key to their zingy taste. They can also be made with pork or shrimps.

Place noodles in a bowl, pour over boiling water and soak for 10 minutes. Drain and cut in several places with kitchen scissors.

Place lettuce and carrots in a mixing bowl with sugar and chopped herbs. Mix through noodles and chicken.

Dunk sheets of rice paper into warm water to fully immerse then transfer to a bench covered with a clean, damp cloth. Wait for a minute for the paper to soften and become flexible. (If you try to roll them before this they will split.)

Place a small handful of the chicken mixture on the centre of each wrapper. Roll up tightly, tucking in the sides as you go. Transfer rolls to a plate, seam side down, and cover with a damp paper towel or plastic wrap. Chill if not serving at once; they will hold their shape for 24 hours. Serve with peanut chilli dipping sauce.

Serves 8-10

Vegetarian salad rolls

Omit the chicken and substitute 1 cup bean sprouts and 2 lebanese cucumbers, seeded and cut into thick matchsticks.

Prawn salad rolls

Use 200g cooked prawn meat, chopped, in place of chicken.

PEANUT CHILLI DIPPING SAUCE

Mix 2 tsp peanut butter with 2 tbsp boiling water to soften. Stir in ½ cup Thai sweet chilli sauce, 2 tsp fish sauce, 2 tbsp lime juice and 2 tbsp chopped roasted peanuts. *Makes 1 cup*

NUOC CHAM (VIETNAMESE DIPPING SAUCE)

Combine ¼ cup fresh lime juice, 2 tbsp sugar, 2 tbsp Asian fish sauce (nam pla), 2 garlic cloves, crushed, and 1 small red chilli, finely minced with seeds (or 1 tsp dried chilli flakes). Sauce will keep in the fridge for weeks. Mix in half a finely shredded small carrot or some finely chopped ginger just before serving if you like. *Makes ½ cup*

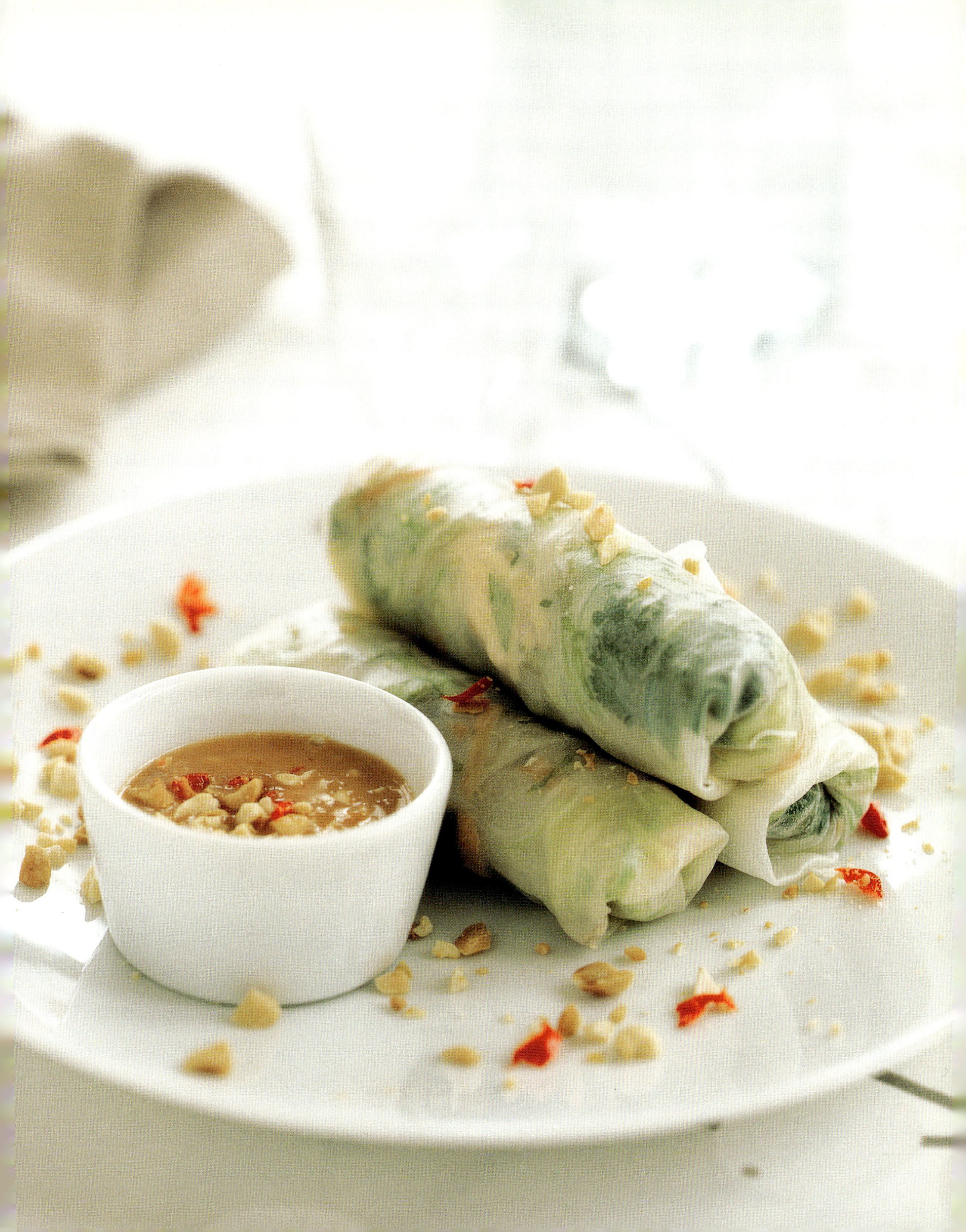

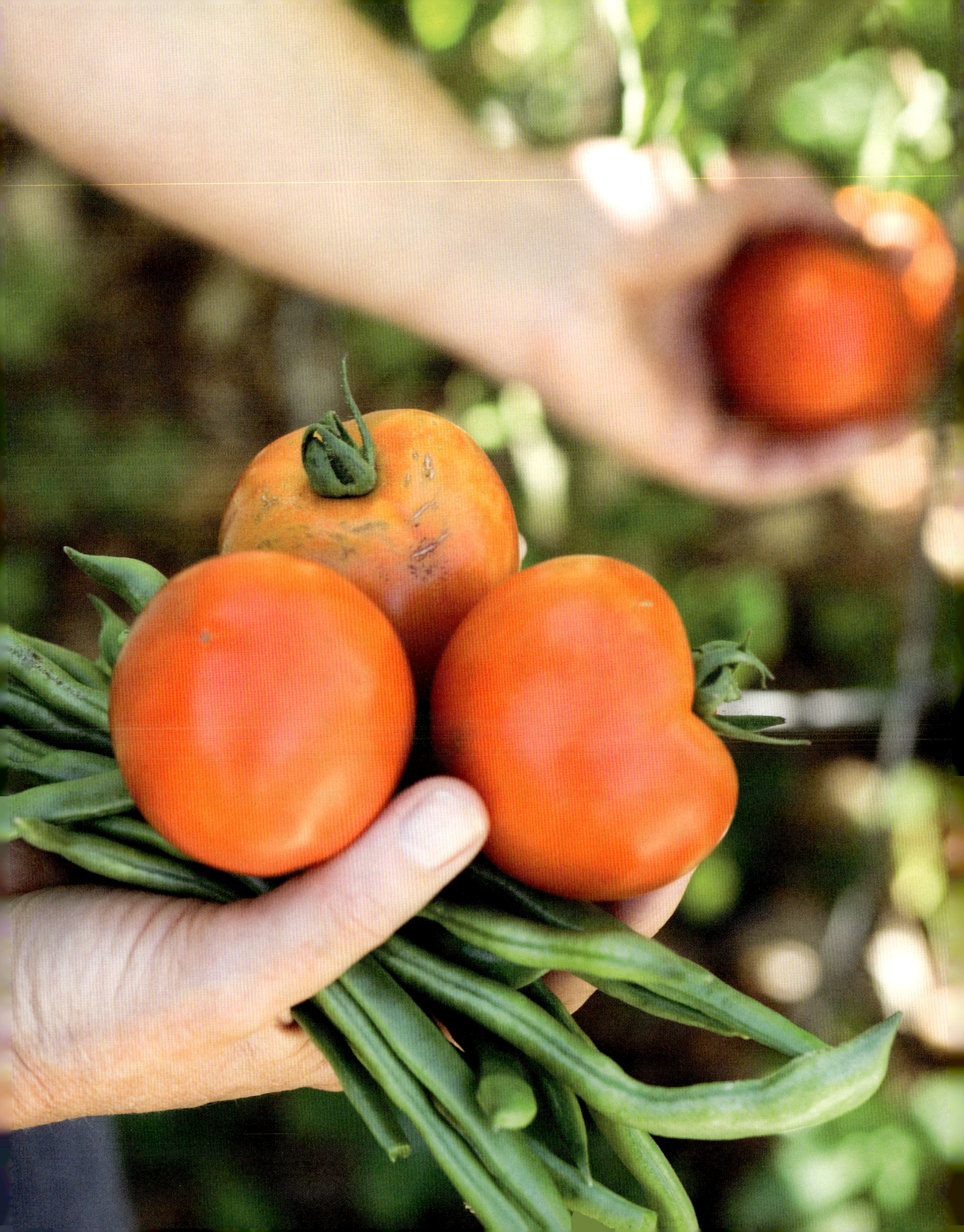

'Most of us hanker for authentic food experiences when we travel. Friends on the ground take you to the heart of a food culture – here the inspiration comes from Paris, the epicentre of culinary elegance.'

Fill with goat's cheese

Chèvre-filled summer vegetables

Prep   20 minutes

250g creamy goat's cheese or chèvre (Puhoi goat's cheese is ideal)
finely grated zest of ½ lemon
2 tsp chopped fresh marjoram or mint leaves
pinch each salt and pepper

Vegetables:
2 lebanese cucumbers, cut in 3cm lengths, centres scooped out with a melon baller
16 cherry tomatoes or 6-8 small vine-ripened tomatoes, tops cut off and seeds scooped out
2 stalks celery, cut into 3cm lengths or 1 head witloof, leaves separated
Garnish: 2 tbsp chives, very finely chopped

At the Lanvin boutique in Paris I enjoyed an elegant lunch plate of blanched zucchinis, cucumbers and cherry tomatoes stuffed with a creamy goat's curd mixture. In France, celery is not used in this manner but I've included it in this recipe as it is delicious. Celeriac and witloof are also good.

Use a wooden spoon to beat cheese until smooth and creamy. Mix in zest, herbs and salt and pepper to taste.

Place cucumber in a bowl, cover with boiling water and stand for 1 minute, then drain and cool. (Do this also for zucchini, if using.) Spoon mixture into prepared vegetables to fill. Sprinkle with chives.

Prepared vegetables can be filled and chilled several hours in advance. Take them from the fridge 10-15 minutes before serving to allow them to come to room temperature.

Serves 4 as a light meal (makes about 24)

MARINATING SOFT CHEESES

Soft cheeses such as feta and chèvre are excellent when marinated in flavoured oil. I like to use fresh rosemary, garlic and lemon zest mixed into olive oil or, for a lighter flavour, a neutral oil such as grapeseed or sunflower. Cut the cheese into cubes or chunks and add enough oil to fully cover the cheese, then cover and refrigerate. It will keep for several weeks.

'When I was 21 I landed a job cooking in a little Italian restaurant. I had no formal training, only the gift from my mother of Elizabeth David's Italian Food, *which proved a worthy guide. I still refer to it.'*

Zucchini pleasures

Zucchini & basil bruschetta

Prep 5 minutes
Cook 5 minutes

3 zucchini (400g), coarsely grated
3 tbsp olive oil
2 large cloves garlic, crushed
finely grated zest of 1 lemon
¼ tsp chilli flakes
½ tsp salt and grinds of pepper
50g feta, finely crumbled
10-12 basil leaves, finely torn
To serve: about 16 grilled bruschetta bases or crostini

Grate zucchini on to a clean tea towel, then pull up the sides and twist and squeeze tightly to remove as much liquid as possible.
Heat oil in a large frypan over medium heat. Add zucchini, garlic and lemon zest and stir-fry for about 5 minutes until zucchini has softened without browning. Remove from heat and season with salt and pepper. Cool for 5 minutes.
Mix in feta and basil. Spoon on to bruschetta bases and serve.
Makes about 16 (or 24 if made with smaller bruschetta); serves 5-6 as a snack

Warm zucchini & prawn salad

Prep 15 minutes
Cook 2-3 minutes

1 fennel bulb (about 130g), halved and very thinly sliced
1 tsp salt
80-100g raw prawn tails
3 tbsp extra virgin olive oil
finely grated zest of 1 lemon
4 zucchini, cut very thinly using a Benriner slicer, vegetable peeler or mandolin
50g feta, crumbled
3 tbsp lemon juice
2 tbsp pine nuts, toasted
1 tbsp chopped mint
freshly ground black pepper

Place fennel in a non-reactive container and sprinkle with salt. Leave to stand for 15 minutes then rinse under cold water until it no longer tastes overly salty. Place in a bowl. Boil prawns until pink, 2-3 minutes. Drain and add to bowl with olive oil and lemon zest.
Pour boiling water over sliced zucchini and leave for 1 minute. Drain thoroughly and add to bowl. Toss to combine. Cover and chill if not serving at once; salad will hold for a couple of hours. At serving time, toss through feta, lemon juice, pine nuts and mint and season with pepper.
Serves 4

ZUCCHINI FLOWERS
Curcubita pepo
Once a zucchini plant is up and running you need to harvest the crop every few days. In the flash of an eye those tender, fingerling babies turn into fat, insipid marrows. Both male and female flowers are good to eat. In Italy they are often stuffed and either fried or steamed. To stuff zucchini flowers, carefully prise open the petals and fill the cavity inside – a combination of ricotta, garlic and parmesan is nice, as is a seasoned minced chicken or seafood mixture. The flowers are also delicious battered and fried.

CRISPY FRIED ZUCCHINI FLOWERS
I make a version of Elizabeth David's frying batter from her book *Italian Food*. Stir 3 tbsp olive oil into a cup of flour with a pinch of salt. Add 150ml tepid water and stir until smooth and creamy, adding more water if needed. Add some lemon zest or torn basil or parsley leaves as desired. Stand for at least 2 hours. Just before using, gently fold in 1 stiffly beaten egg white. Dunk flowers into batter to lightly coat and shallow-fry in a small pan in about 1cm oil, turning as they brown. Drain on paper towels and serve hot.

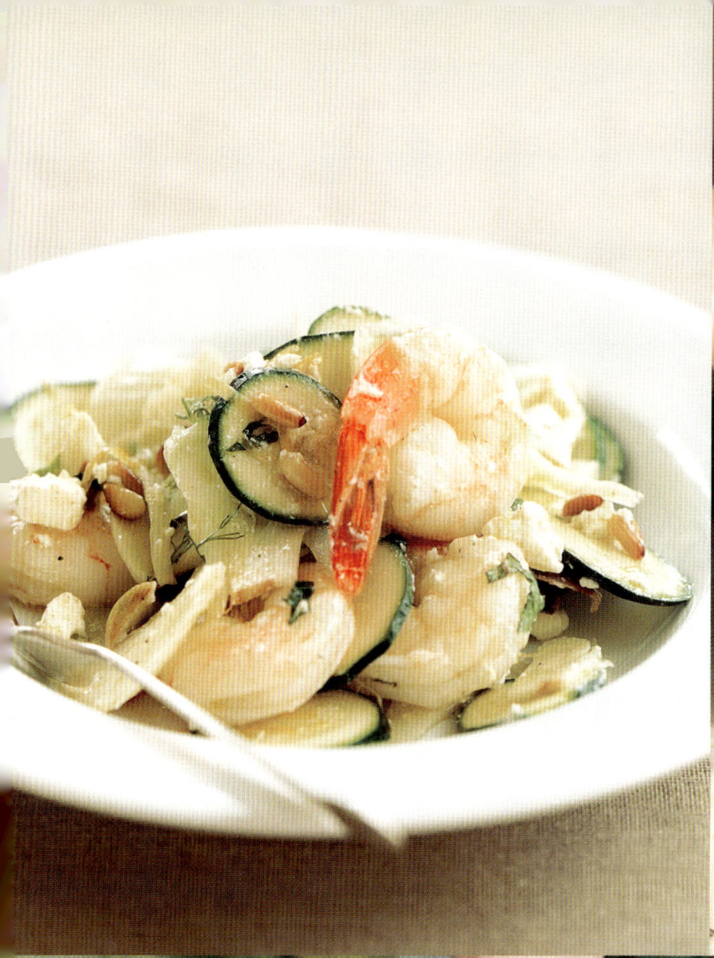
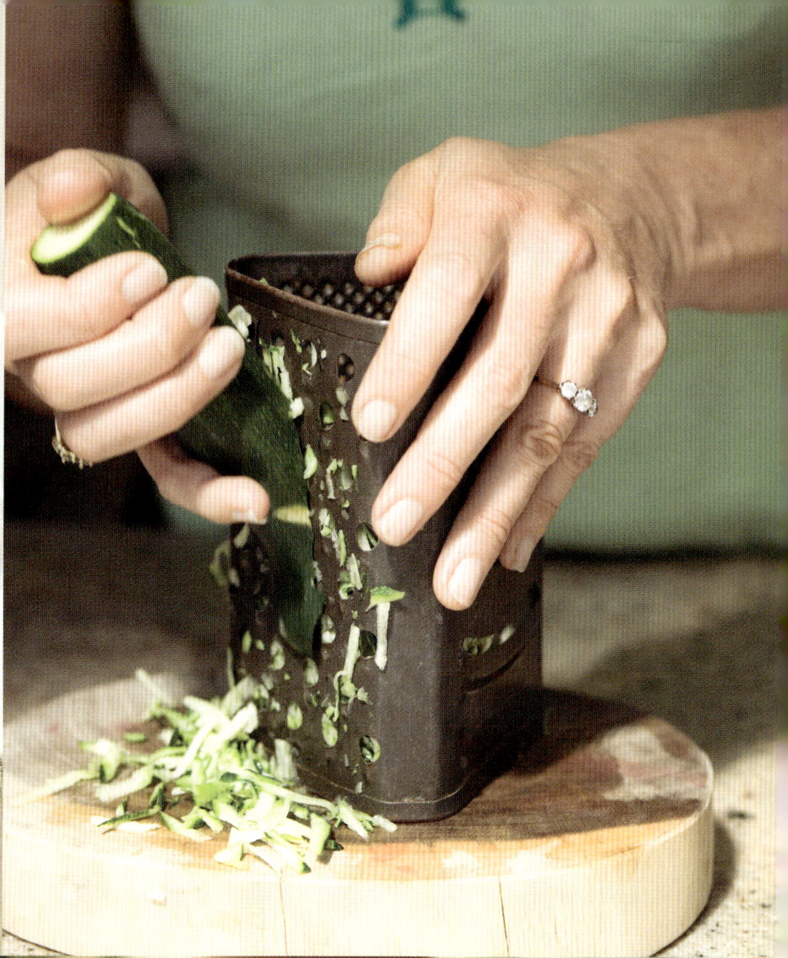
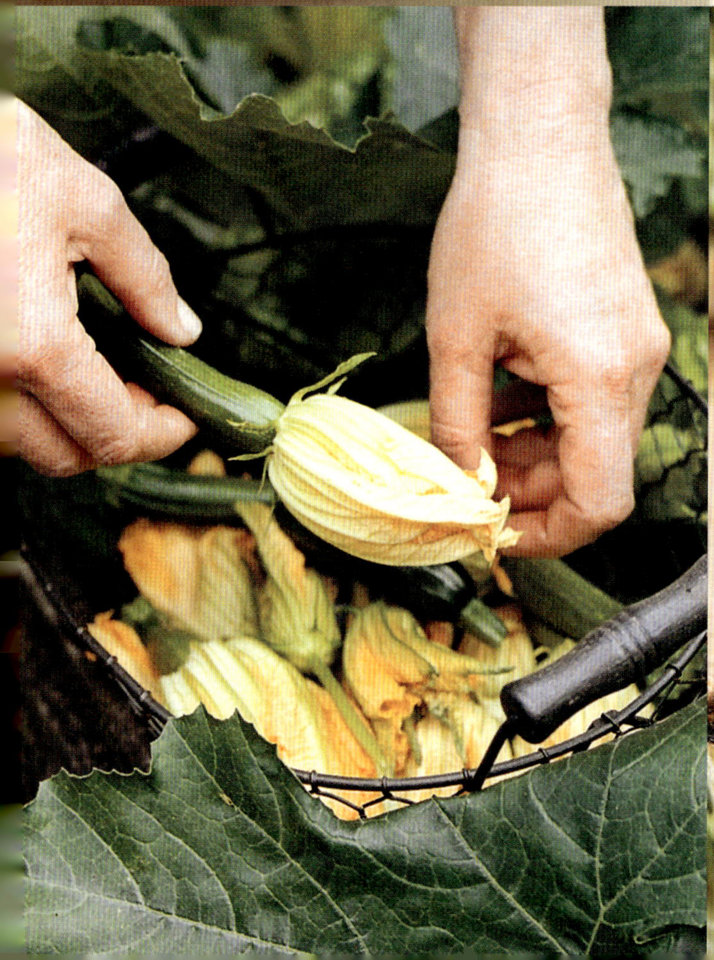
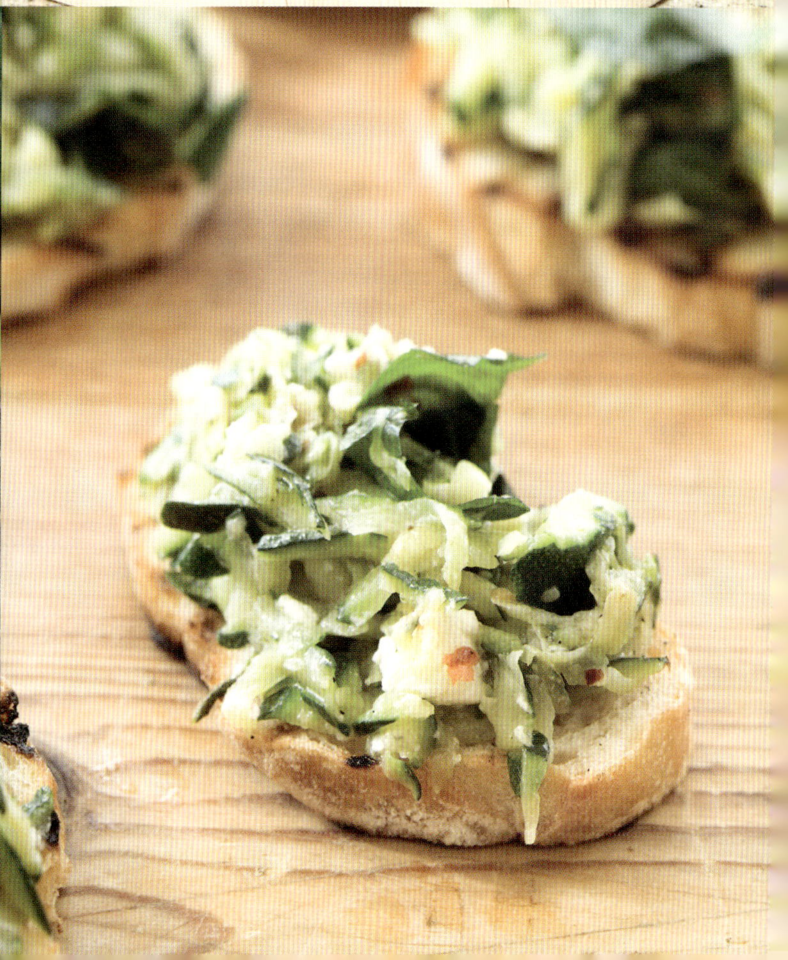

'The difference between a good salad and a lousy one lies largely in the dressing. I like to make my own; the result tastes so much better than anything store-bought and is much cheaper.'

Easy dressings

Mustard red wine vinaigrette
Prep 2 minutes

A classic french dressing, useful for any green salad.

Shake together in a jar 4 tbsp extra virgin olive oil, 2 tbsp best-quality red wine vinegar, 1 tsp Dijon mustard and ½ tsp each salt and sugar. Store in the fridge; dressing will keep for weeks. Good to make in bulk.
Makes ⅓ cup

Chilli lime dressing
Prep 2 minutes

Great over any salad where you want an Asian twist.

In a small jar shake together ¼ cup freshly squeezed lime juice, 2 tbsp fish sauce, 1 tbsp sugar, 1 tbsp neutral oil, 1 tsp oyster sauce, 1-2 small hot red chillies, seeded and very finely diced, the finely grated zest of 1 lime and 1 kaffir lime leaf, finely shredded (optional). Cover jar and chill if not using at once. Dressing will keep in the fridge for 2 weeks. Good to make in bulk.
Makes ⅓ cup

Honey mustard dressing
Prep 10 minutes

This is my everyday dressing used for green salads and any tomato or avocado-based salad.

Shake together in a jar ¼ cup neutral oil, ¼ cup olive oil, 2 tbsp white wine vinegar, 2 tbsp lemon juice, 2 tsp honey, 2 tsp wholegrain mustard, 1 tsp Dijon mustard, ½ clove crushed garlic, ½ tsp salt and lots of freshly ground pepper. Store in the fridge. Good to make in bulk.
Makes 1 small cup

Spiced oil dressing
Prep 2 minutes
Cook 1 minute

A wonderful dressing for roasted vegetables and potatoes.

Heat 2 tbsp neutral oil with 2 fat cloves garlic, crushed, 2 tsp finely grated fresh ginger, 1 tsp curry powder, 1 tsp coriander seeds, coarsely crushed, 1 tsp salt and grinds of pepper. Sizzle about 1 minute then remove from heat.
Makes 3 tablespoons

HANDLING SOFT GREENS
Wash and spin-dry salad greens or place them in a clean towel and shake out moisture. Place dry, clean greens in a plastic bag and seal. They will keep for at least a week in the fridge.

CHOOSING OLIVE OIL
Buy a bottle of really good-quality estate-grown olive oil to drizzle over salad leaves and dunk crusty bread into. Around November each year, at the beginning of the European bottling season, I import two dozen cans of oil from my favourite Italian organic producer, Mario Tortella of Le Magnolie in Aprutino Pescarese, Abruzzo. I try to eke it out (usually unsuccessfully) to last through the year.

HOW TO DRESS A GREEN SALAD
All leafy salads need to be dressed just prior to serving or they will wilt and go soggy. Place salad ingredients in the biggest bowl you can lay your hands on and drizzle over just enough dressing to lightly coat – ¼-⅓ cup is usually enough for a bowl of greens for 4-6 people. Use clean hands or salad servers to toss the dressing gently through the salad, coating evenly. There shouldn't be any swimming in the bottom of the bowl. Serve at once.

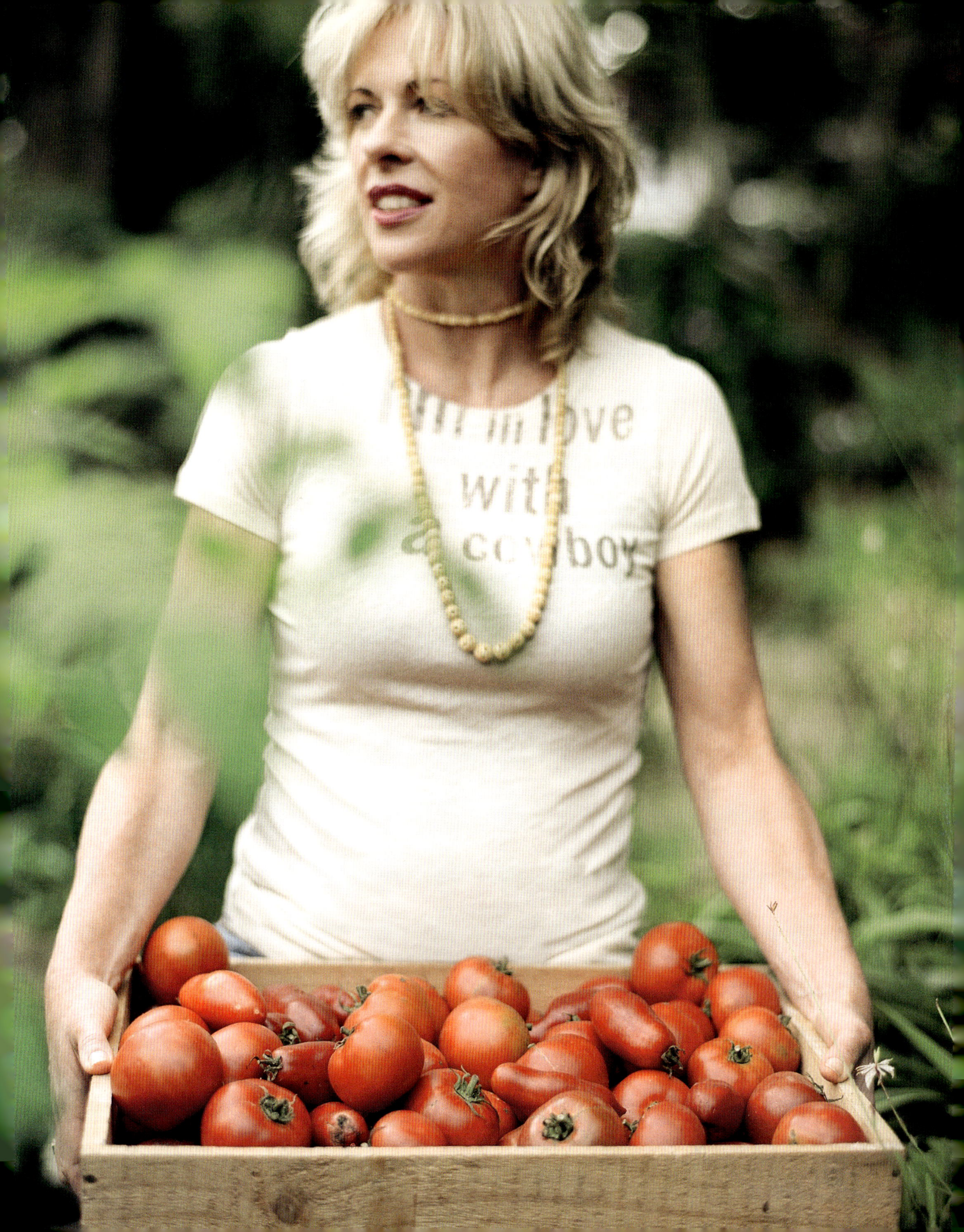
love
with

'Fresh corn served with nothing more than salt, butter and pepper, and sweet tomatoes tossed with the best olive oil, are tastes that epitomise the simplicity of summer dining. Nature does all the work for you.'

Summer corn

Chilli bean & corn salad

Prep 20 minutes
Cook 1 minute

400g can black beans or butter beans, drained and rinsed
2 tbsp extra virgin olive oil
2 cloves garlic, crushed
1 tsp dried oregano
1 small red onion, very finely diced
2 tomatoes, finely diced
1 red or yellow capsicum, finely diced
1 cup cooked corn kernels
⅓ cup lime or lemon juice
½ cup chopped coriander leaves
Optional: 1-2 tsp hot pepper sauce or Tabasco
½ tsp salt and grinds of black pepper
1-2 avocados, diced

This useful salad makes a great base for a simple summer meal as well as being an excellent side dish for grilled meats and chicken. Turn it into a meal-in-one with a can of tuna, some sliced lightly fried chorizo or slices of rare beef.

Drain beans and place in a pot with oil, garlic and oregano. Cover and sizzle over medium heat for 1 minute to infuse flavours. Mix in all other ingredients except avocados. Chill for at least 2 hours to allow flavours to blend. Add avocados just before serving. Serve with grilled chicken or meat.
Serves 4-6

SWEETCORN
Zea mays var. rugosa
Corn needs to be eaten when freshly picked as the longer it's kept, the more the natural sugars turn to starch. As the corn ripens the tassels intensify in colour and generally once they are black the corn is too ripe and will not be as sweet. Choose cobs that feel plump with glossy tassels that are deep brown rather than black.

COOKING CORN
For maximum flavour, cook and eat corn as soon as possible after it has been harvested. Pick cobs while the kernels are still pale and plump, before the sugars have converted to starch.
To boil fresh corn cobs, remove the husks and tassels and drop cobs into a large pot of salted boiling water to cook for 3 minutes. Drain and serve with butter, salt and pepper.
To freeze, throw whole cobs in their husks into the freezer.

Summer cob salad

Prep 10 minutes
Cook 3 minutes

2 cooked corn cobs or 2½ cups cooked corn kernels
4-5 tomatoes, cored and cut in wedges
2 just-ripe avocados, diced
handful of basil leaves
¼ cup Tuscan herb oil (page 96) or 2 tbsp basil pesto mixed with 2 tbsp olive oil and a pinch of chilli flakes (optional)

Makes a great side dish for grilled meats or chicken.

Cut kernels off cobs and place in a mixing bowl with tomatoes, avocados and basil. Add Tuscan herb oil and toss to combine.
Serves 4 as a side salad

CUTTING CORN FROM THE COB
Hold cobs of cooked corn upright on a chopping board and use a sharp, heavy knife in a downward motion to remove kernels from the cob. Cooked corn can be frozen in a sealed vacuum bag.

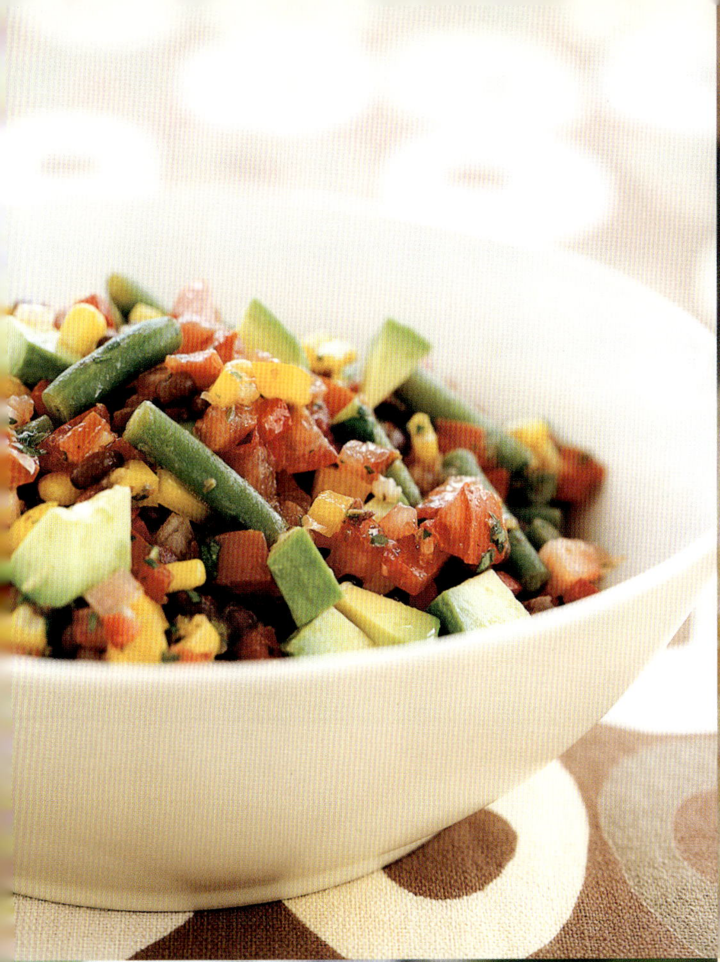
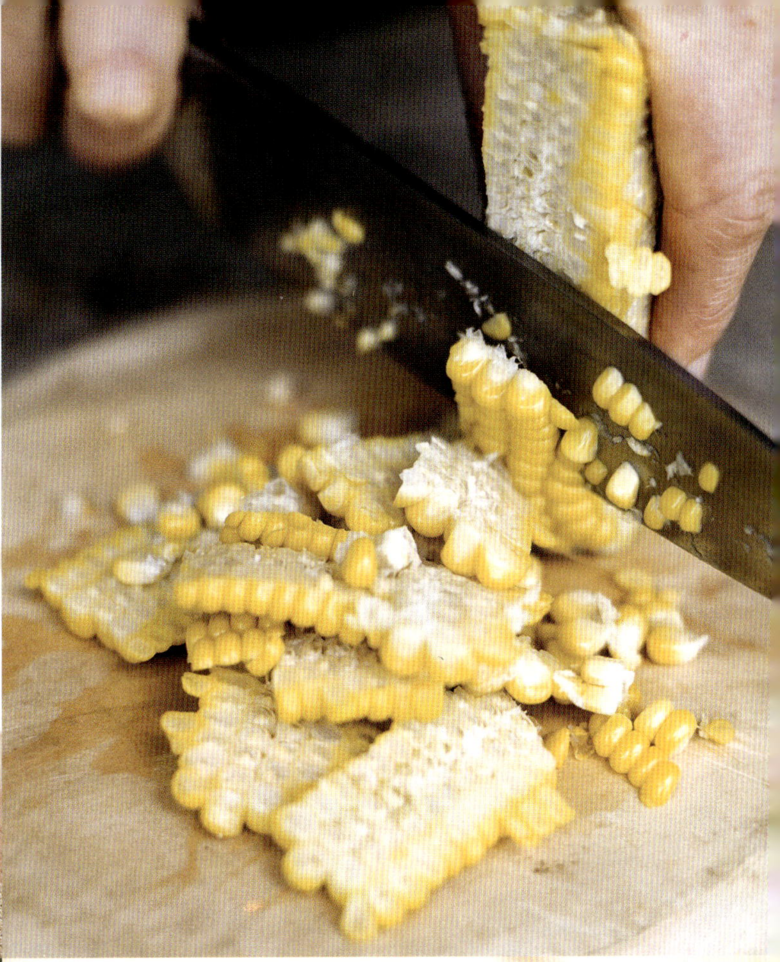
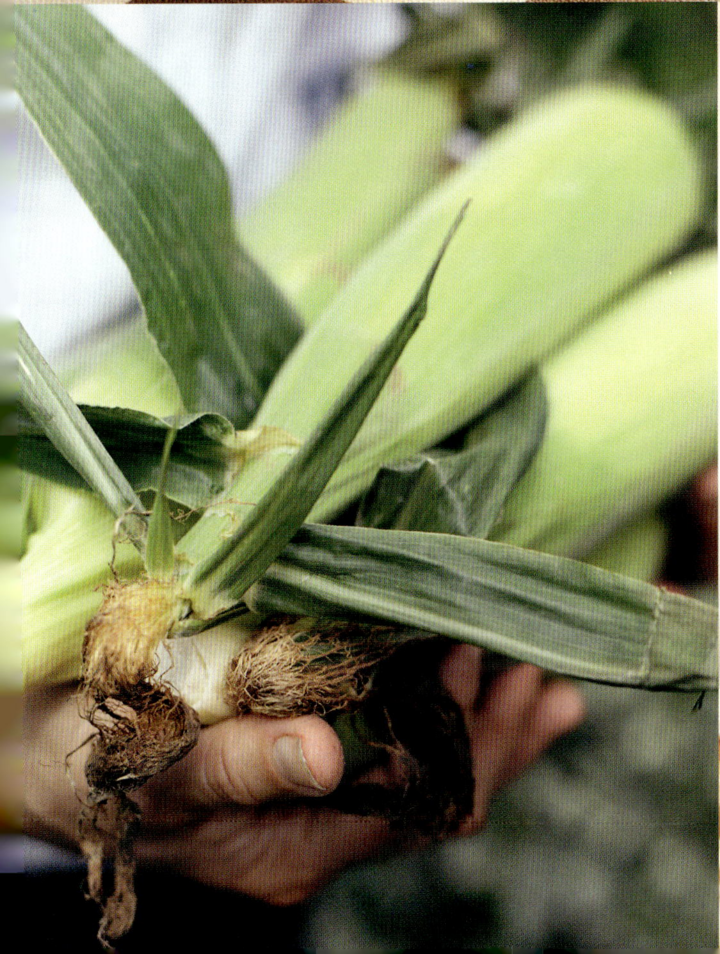
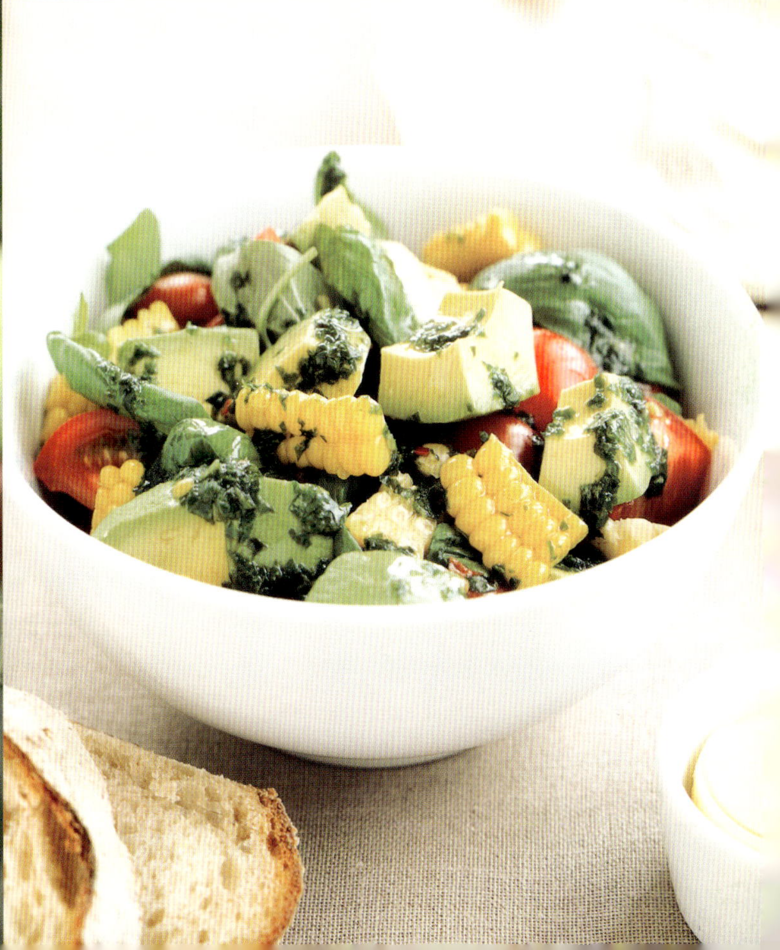

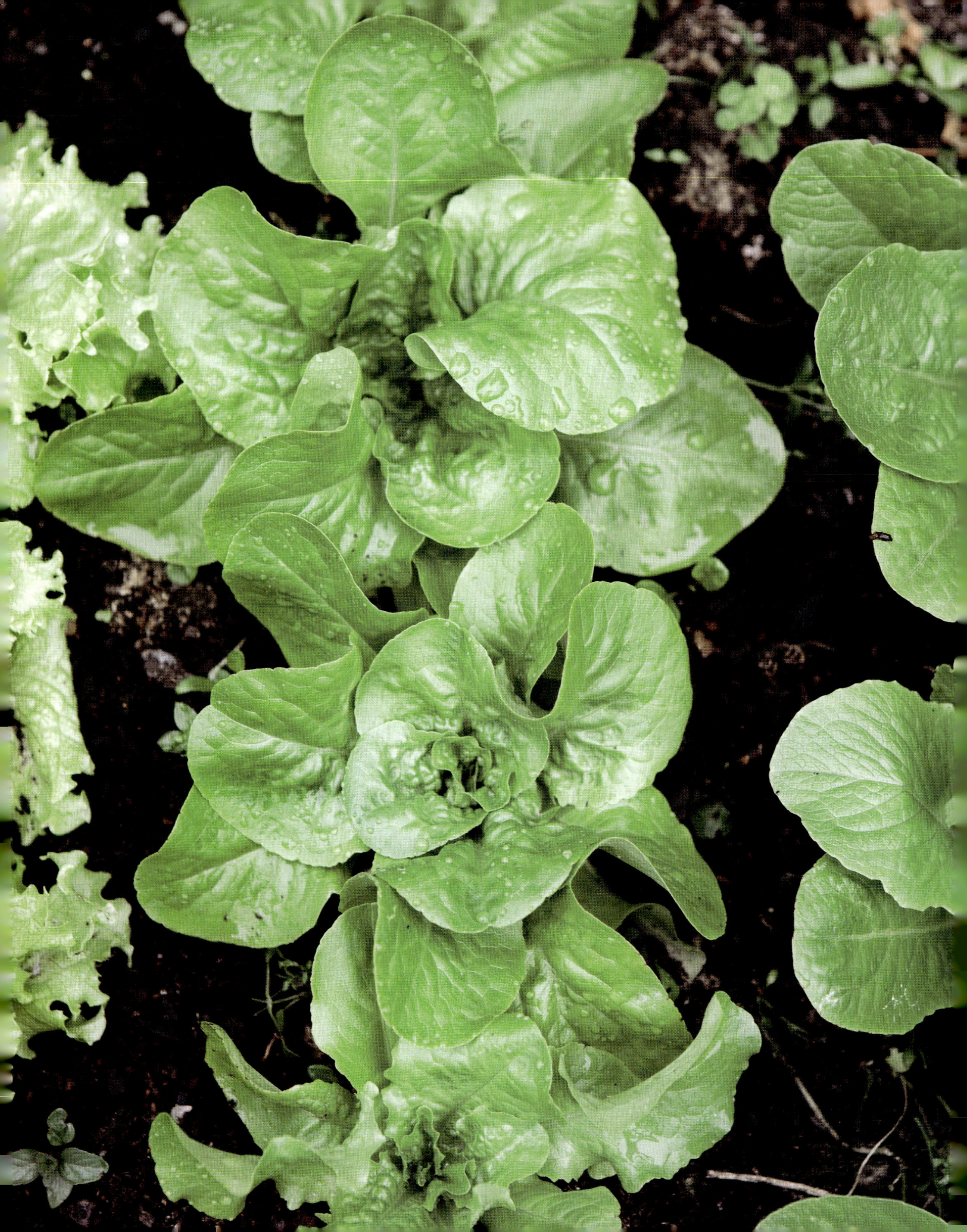

'Show me a person who likes doing dishes. Anyway, food eaten with your fingers always tastes better.'

A salad in hand

Spicy ginger pork salad cups

Prep   5 minutes
Cook   8-10 minutes

375g pork mince
1 tbsp Thai sweet chilli sauce
1 tbsp fish sauce
1 tbsp neutral oil, eg grapeseed
1 tsp sesame oil
1 red capsicum, finely diced
3 tsp minced fresh ginger
1 clove garlic, crushed
2 tbsp oyster sauce
375g can water chestnuts, rinsed, drained and diced
2 spring onions, whites and greens, sliced very thinly
2 tbsp chopped coriander
To serve: 20-24 crunchy green lettuce leaves, washed and trimmed

Combine mince with chilli sauce, fish sauce, oils, capsicum, ginger and garlic. Heat a wok or large frypan and stir-fry mixture over high heat until cooked through, all liquid has evaporated and it starts to brown, about 8-10 minutes.
Remove from heat and mix in oyster sauce, water chestnuts, spring onions and coriander. Serve warm or at room temperature.
To serve, place pork in a serving bowl. Arrange lettuce leaves in a stack on a platter with pork. Allow guests to make their own rolls by placing a little of the mixture on a lettuce leaf and rolling up.
Serves 6 as an appetiser

GINGER
Zingiber officinale
Fresh or young ginger has a thin skin like a new potato, is very mild and juicy and perishes quickly. Use it as a vegetable or for pickling. As ginger matures, its skin thickens and it becomes denser and more fibrous with a stronger fllavour. Peel ginger before grating, mincing or chopping. Store ginger rhizomes in the fridge, or freeze and cut off as required. You can also preserve it in sherry or vinegar.

Spicy ginger chicken salad cups

Substitute 375g lean chicken mince for the pork.

Duck finger rolls

Prep   10 minutes

1 roasted duck, skin, bones and fat removed, flesh finely sliced (or 3 cups cooked chicken or turkey meat, finely sliced)
2 tbsp oyster sauce
2 spring onions, finely shredded
leaves of 1 large iceberg lettuce, cut into 6-8cm ovals
Optional (and good to extend): 227g can water chestnuts, drained and diced

Pick up a roasted duck or chicken and assemble these crisp, fresh rolls. They make a great casual starter.
Mix duck with oyster sauce and spring onions and place in a serving bowl. Accompany with lettuce ovals. Place a teaspoon of duck mixture on a lettuce wrapper, fold in sides and pop into your mouth.
Serves 4-6

'This year tomatoes with names like Box Car Willie, Aunt Ruby's German Green and Brandywine Pink grace my summer garden. Once you have eaten a ripe, sweet, home-grown tomato there's no going back.'

Ideas with summer tomatoes

Summer tomato salad
Prep 5 minutes

Place 1kg sweetest summer tomatoes, sliced as preferred, in a large mixing bowl. Scatter over 250g crumbled feta (or use sliced fresh mozzarella or crumbled ricotta) and 20-30 fresh basil leaves. Sprinkle over 1 tbsp fresh marjoram or oregano leaves, the finely grated zest of 1 lemon and salt and pepper to taste.
Drizzle over ¼ cup of the best-quality extra virgin olive oil you can lay your hands on and gently toss together.
Serves 4-6, pictured right

Chilled Mexican tomato soup
Prep 20 minutes

Make the Mexican fresh tomato salsa on page 74, with or without the chilli as preferred. Add 1 cup chilled tomato juice, 1 cup finely diced cucumber, 1 tsp ground cumin and 1-2 diced tomatillos (optional). Season to taste.
Makes 1 litre, serves 4

Slow-roasted tomatoes
Prep 10 minutes
Cook 1½ hours

Core, halve and thickly slice 1kg tomatoes. Arrange on a lined baking tray. Sprinkle with 2 tsp sugar, 1 tsp flaky salt and grinds of pepper. Drizzle over 2 tsp red wine vinegar and 2 tablespoons extra virgin olive oil. Bake at 150°C for 1½ hours or until starting to shrivel and caramelise. Cool, cover and chill. Tomatoes will keep in the fridge 4-5 days.
Serves 4 as a side dish

Roasted tomato salad with tamari-almond & basil pesto
Prep 10 minutes

Divide 1 recipe of slow-roasted tomatoes between 4 serving plates. Top each plate with a small handful of washed and dried salad greens or micro greens. Dice 1 just-ripe avocado and scatter over the top. Drizzle each salad with a tablespoon of tamari-almond & basil pesto (page 18).
Serves 4

ROASTED TOMATOES ON THE MENU
Slow-roasted tomatoes have many uses:
Purée as a sauce for pasta.
Use as a base for salads.
Mix into couscous.
Use as a base for baked chicken, fish or lamb dishes.
Serve for breakfast on grilled bread with crispy bacon and a spoonful of basil pesto.
Serve with corn fritters, sour cream and sliced avocado for an easy brunch.

My father Fred grew the best tomatoes. His secret ingredient was potash, derived from the frequent applications of seaweed and wood ash he piled on his vegetable garden. While nitrogen makes things grow lush and leafy, potash promotes flowering and fruiting and in the case of tomatoes gives them a particularly dense, rich flavour. Several times a year, and after a big storm had blown through, we would pile into the Plymouth and head for the sea-grass flats at Pauatahanui, north of Wellington. The next few hours would be spent gathering huge sacks of fine brown sea grass thrown up by the storm. The trip home was a slow one, with an overloaded boot of stinky seaweed, but the taste of those tomatoes is something I have yet to better.

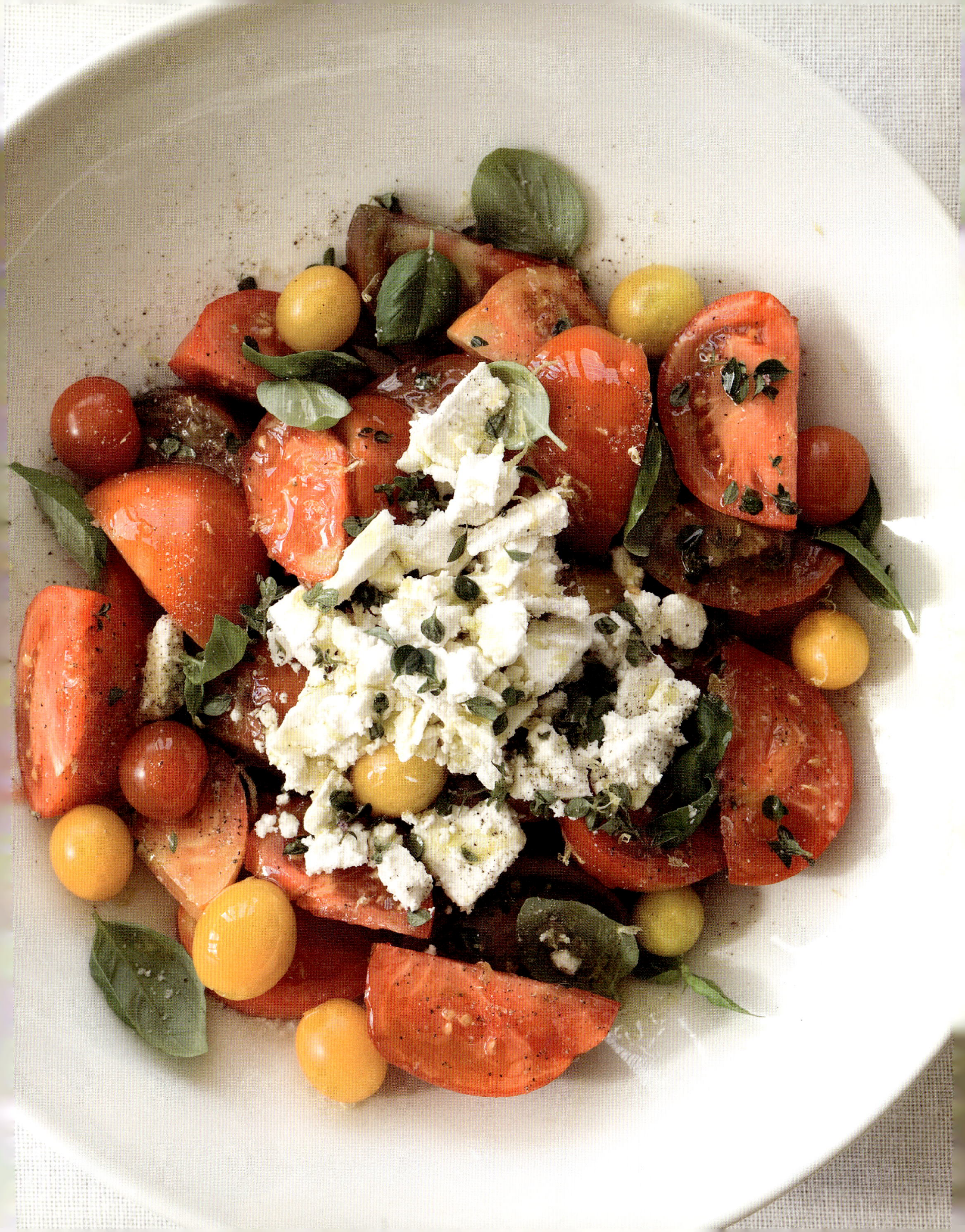

'As kids we would head out to D'Urville Island on my grandfather Put's launch for days on end to fish for cod and hapuku. As fast as we landed our catches he would be down in the galley cooking them.'

Gourmet seafood

Moroccan seafood salad

Prep 10 minutes

1 recipe creamy Moroccan dressing (see right)
2 cooked crayfish tails, flesh chilled and sliced in chunks, or 400g cooked prawn tails
800g baby potatoes
1 spring onion, finely sliced
2 tbsp lemon juice
salt and grinds of pepper
To serve: 150g mache or salad leaves

Prepare dressing and seafood and boil potatoes until just tender; cool and halve. Combine prepared creamy Moroccan dressing with all other ingredients. Serve on a bed of salad greens.
Serves 4

Variation: Use cooked mussels in place of crayfish. Steam open 3 dozen mussels. Cool and remove from shells. Mix with all other ingredients.

Grilled prawn & mango salad

Prep 15 minutes + marinating
Cook 3 minutes

500g raw prawn tails
2 fat cloves garlic, crushed
1 lemon, finely grated zest and juice
salt and grinds of pepper
2 tbsp olive oil
To serve: 4 small handfuls (140g) baby salad leaves
1 fresh mango, peeled and cut in chunks
1 red capsicum, thinly sliced
roast capsium and coriander sauce (page 130)

Mix prawns with garlic and zest and season with salt and pepper. Cover and marinate in the fridge for at least 10 minutes or up to 2 hours.
Heat oil in a heavy pan or on a barbecue hotplate and cook prawns over medium-high heat until pink and lightly caramelised, about 1½ minutes each side. Remove from heat and drizzle with lemon juice.
Place salad greens on a platter and top with mangos and capsicum. Pile on the prawns with their juices. Serve with roast capsicum and coriander sauce.
Serves 4

Variation: In place of the mango and capsicum use 200g cherry tomatoes and 1 large just-ripe avocado, diced. Accompany with creamy Moroccan dressing (see right).

CREAMY MOROCCAN DRESSING
In a small mixing bowl combine ½ cup mayonnaise, ½ packed cup chopped coriander leaves, 2 cloves garlic, crushed, 1 tbsp lemon juice, ½ tsp smoked paprika or plain paprika, 1 tsp ground cumin and ¼ tsp cayenne pepper. *Makes ¾ cup*

GREEN BEANS
(Phaseolus vulgaris)
Like zucchini, beans grow very quickly. Check the plants daily, as beans quickly get tough and stringy if left too long. Cut off the stalk ends and check for any strings, running a potato peeler down each side if required. My favourite way to cook green beans with lemon is to drop them into a pot of boiling water for 2 minutes then cool them under cold water and drain. When I'm ready to serve I heat 2 tbsp extra virgin olive oil with the finely grated zest of 1 lemon, add the beans and a little salt and pepper and stir-fry for 2-3 minutes until just tender. Green beans go well with crispy bacon and almonds — you could add either to the dish above. They're also great in potato salads and with the spiced oil dressing on page 84.

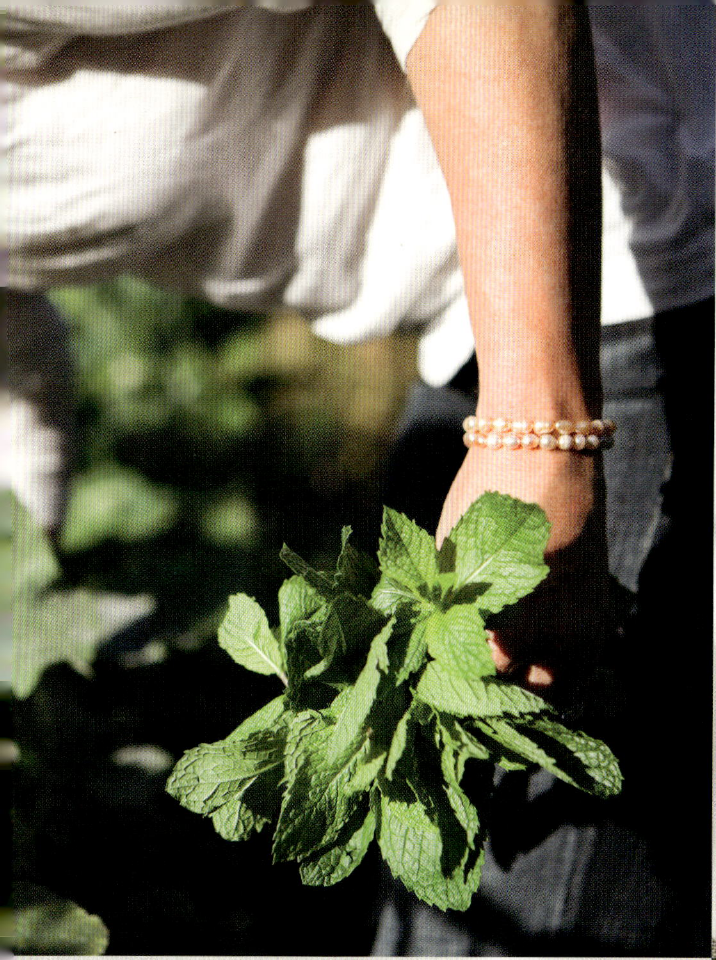
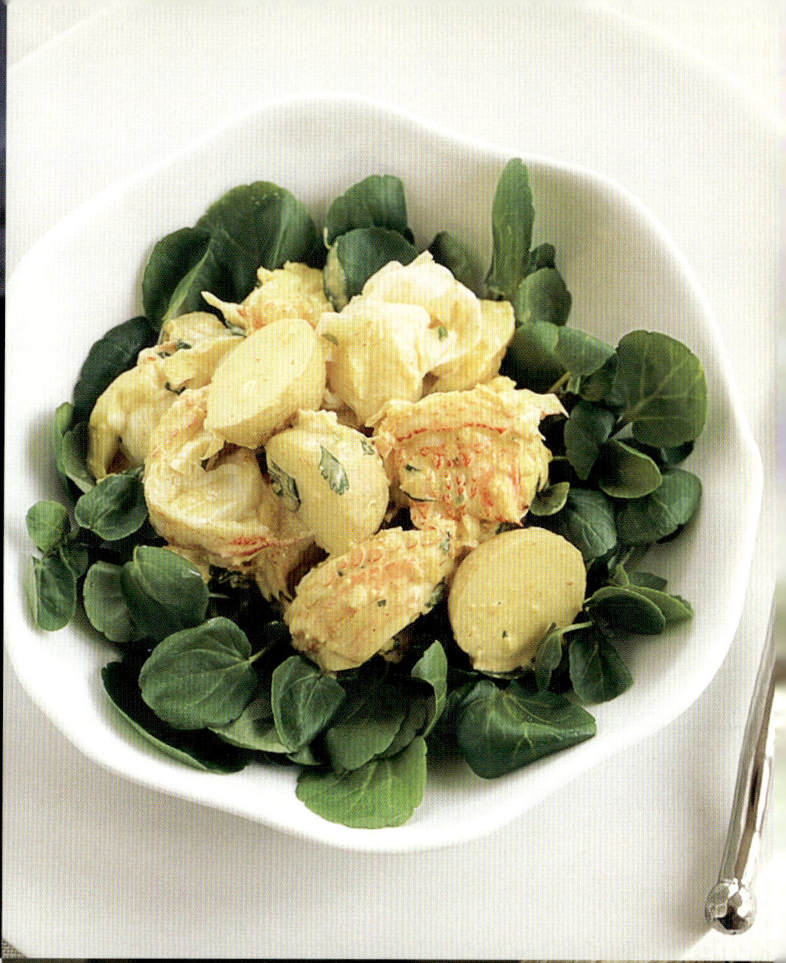
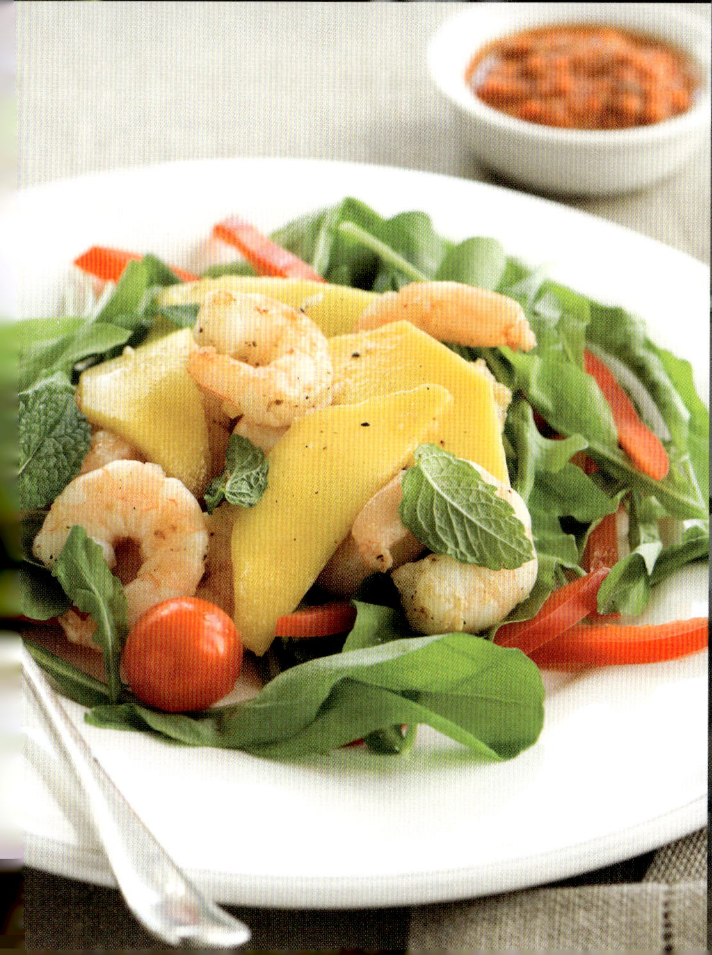
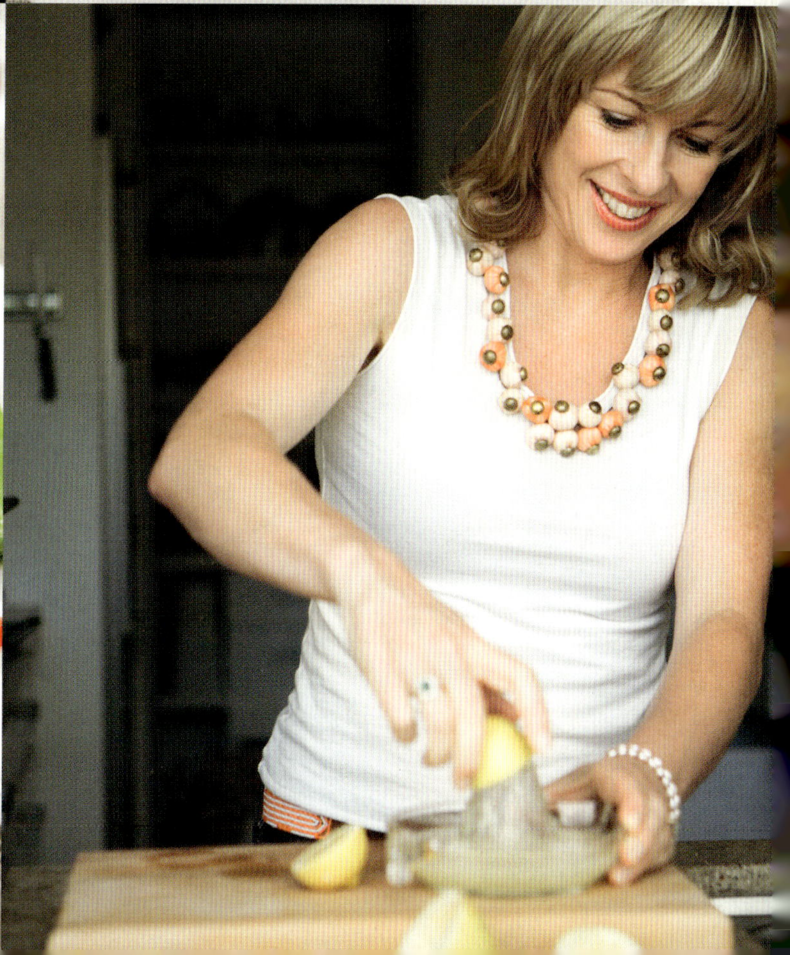

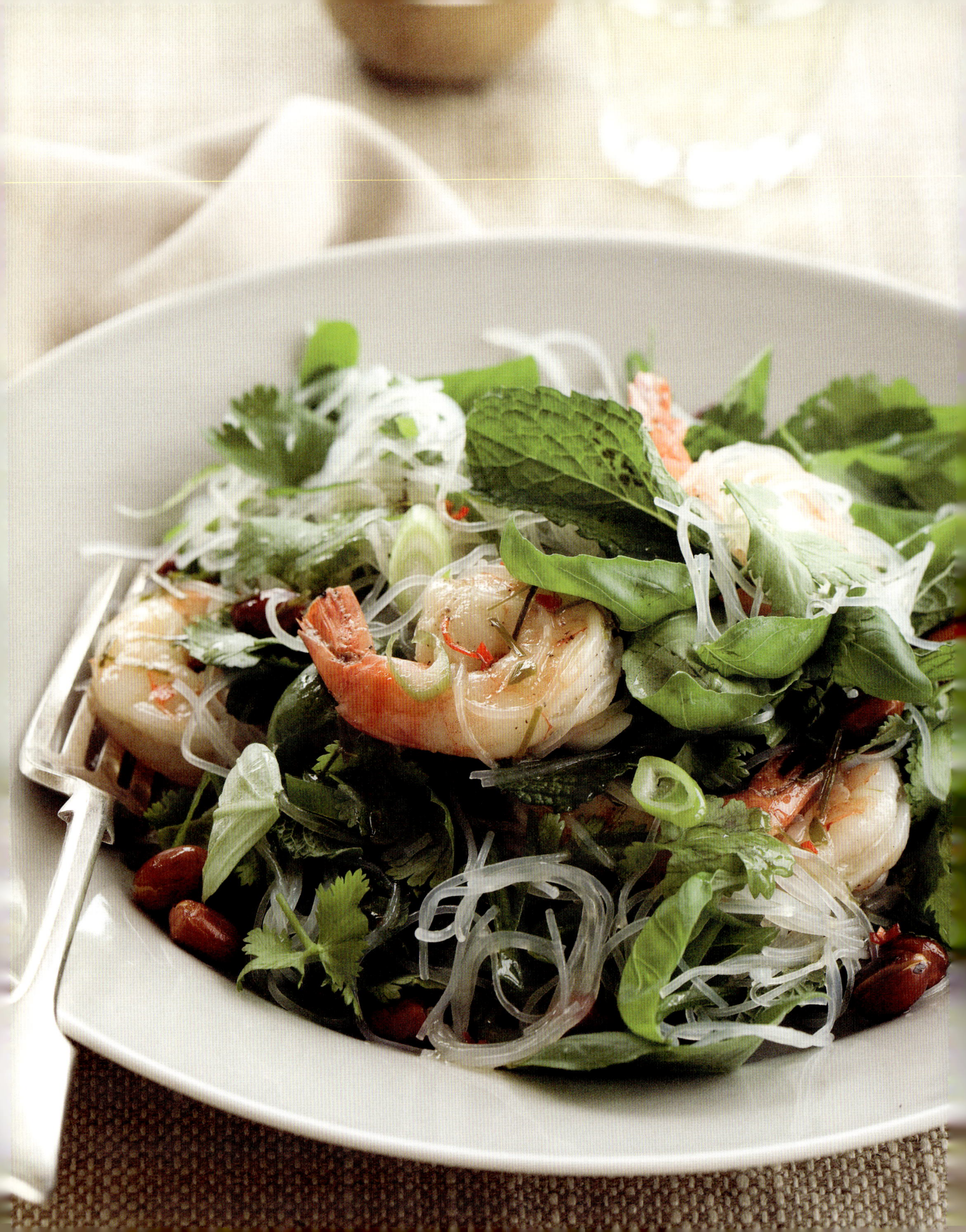

'No other herb elicits as much controversy as coriander – you either love it or hate it. Coriander is the most widely used herb in the world, but if it's not to your taste, use fresh mint for a zing of flavour.'

Asian summer salad

Spicy prawn & glass noodle salad

Prep 20 minutes
Cook 4-5 minutes

1 recipe Chilli lime dressing (see page 84)

500g raw prawns, shelled

Glass noodle salad:
60g (1 small packet) glass noodles (bean thread noodles)
2 spring onions, whites and greens, sliced very finely on the diagonal
3 packed cups mixed fresh Asian herbs, eg 1½ packed cups torn mint and ¾ cup each coriander and torn basil leaves
Garnish: ½ cup chopped roasted peanuts

Place dressing ingredients in a jar and shake thoroughly until sugar has dissolved. Mix half dressing through prawns in a bowl or clean plastic bag and reserve remainder. Cover prawns and chill for at least 30 minutes or up to 2 hours.

Preheat a heavy pan or grill plate until very hot, add a little oil and cook drained prawns 2-3 minutes each side or until cooked through.

Place prawns in a bowl, pour over reserved dressing and mix through. Leave to stand while preparing the rest of the salad components.

Place glass noodles in a separate mixing bowl and pour over boiling water to cover. Stand until transparent, about 2 minutes, then rinse under cold water, drain thoroughly, dry with paper towels and cut into shorter threads.

Combine noodles, spring onions and herbs with cooked prawns and dressing, tossing to combine. Mound salad in centre of serving plates and scatter over chopped peanuts. Serve immediately.

Serves 6 as a starter or 4 as a summer meal

GLASS NOODLES

Glass noodles, also known as bean thread noodles or mung bean vermicelli, are made from ground mung beans. These fine, translucent noodles are tough and hard when dried but on soaking transform to a slippery, silky mass. For easy handling, I usually buy a packet containing smaller packets, as trying to cut into a large amount is really messy. You can fast-soak them by pouring boiling water over and leaving for 2 minutes, or soak in warm water for 7-8 minutes until they become clear and slippery. Good to add to richly flavoured soups and stir-fries as they will take on the flavour of the cooking liquid.

ASIAN SLAW

Place 2 cups finely shredded Chinese cabbage (or regular cabbage) in a large mixing bowl. Work cabbage between your fingers to soften and moisten. Mix in 1 cup bean sprouts, 2 tbsp chopped coriander, 1 tbsp chopped garlic chives or plain chives, ¼ cup roasted chopped peanuts and 2 tbsp sesame seeds. In a small bowl combine 1 tsp sesame oil, 1 tsp soy sauce and 2 tsp rice vinegar. Mix through salad to dress.
Serves 4

'Cooking terms like "poach" can be off-putting. There's a sense that this is something the pros do and therefore could be tricky. To poach you cook in liquid at a low heat so it does not boil. Sounds simple? It is.'

The art of poaching

Tender poached chicken breasts

Prep   5 minutes
Cook   8-10 minutes +
       1½ hours cooling

Provençal chicken flavours: add a handful of fresh thyme leaves, 2 bay leaves, ½ lemon, thinly sliced, 1 tsp salt and several peppercorns to the poaching water.

Asian chicken flavours: add 2cm fresh ginger, thinly sliced, the zest of ½ lime, 3 whole star anise, 1 spring onion, 1 tsp sesame oil, 1 tsp salt and several peppercorns to the poaching water.

I always used to think poaching food made it pale and uninteresting. Now I have discovered that there is no better way to deliver a moist, tender result. Adding seasonings to the cooking liquid ensures good flavour. I generally allow 1 single chicken breast (about 100-120g) per serve, or less if it is going into a mixed salad with other ingredients.

Place chicken breasts in a pot that fits them snugly in a single layer. Cover with cold water, fully submerging the chicken by a finger joint, about 3cm. Add flavours as you prefer – see side panel.

Cover and bring to the boil. As soon as mixture boils, remove pot from heat and leave to cool without removing the lid (about 1½ hours). Chicken can be left in a cool place for 2-3 hours. If storing for longer, chill in the poaching liquid; it will keep for 2-3 days.

Serves 6-8

Mediterranean chicken salad

Prep   15 minutes

3 poached chicken breasts
2 tbsp lemon juice
½ tsp salt and grinds of pepper
300g cherry tomatoes, halved
2 red capsicums, thinly sliced
½ cup kalamata olives
130g rocket leaves
Optional: 1 red chilli, minced
½ cup Tuscan herb oil (see right)
2 just-ripe avocados, sliced

Shred chicken breasts and place in a bowl with lemon juice. Season with salt and pepper. Add all other ingredients except Tuscan herb oil and avocados. When ready to serve, add herb oil and avocados and toss to combine.

This salad is also delicious made with grilled prawns or baby octopus in place of chicken.

Serves 4

THE BEST CHICKEN SANDWICHES

Finely shred 2 poached chicken breasts, discarding the skin. Mix with 6 tbsp best-quality mayonnaise, 1 stalk finely chopped celery, 2 tbsp toasted pine nuts, 1 tbsp finely chopped tarragon, parsley or rocket, 2 tsp lemon juice, ½ tsp salt and lots of freshly ground pepper. Spread mixture over 4 slices of lightly buttered, very fresh bread. Top with watercress, rocket or lettuce leaves and cover with 4 more slices of bread. Cut off crusts, slice and serve. If not serving at once, cover with a damp paper towel then plastic wrap and chill. Prepared sandwiches will keep for up to 6 hours before serving.
Serves 4

TUSCAN HERB OIL

This is great to use with any summer vegetables or with roasted vegetables, chicken or seafood.
In a food processor blend together until smooth 3 large handfuls basil leaves, stems removed, 2 peeled cloves garlic, the finely grated zest of 1 lemon, 1 tsp salt and 1½ cups extra virgin olive oil. Transfer to a storage jar, cover and chill. The flavoured oil will keep in the fridge for 5-6 days and can also be frozen.

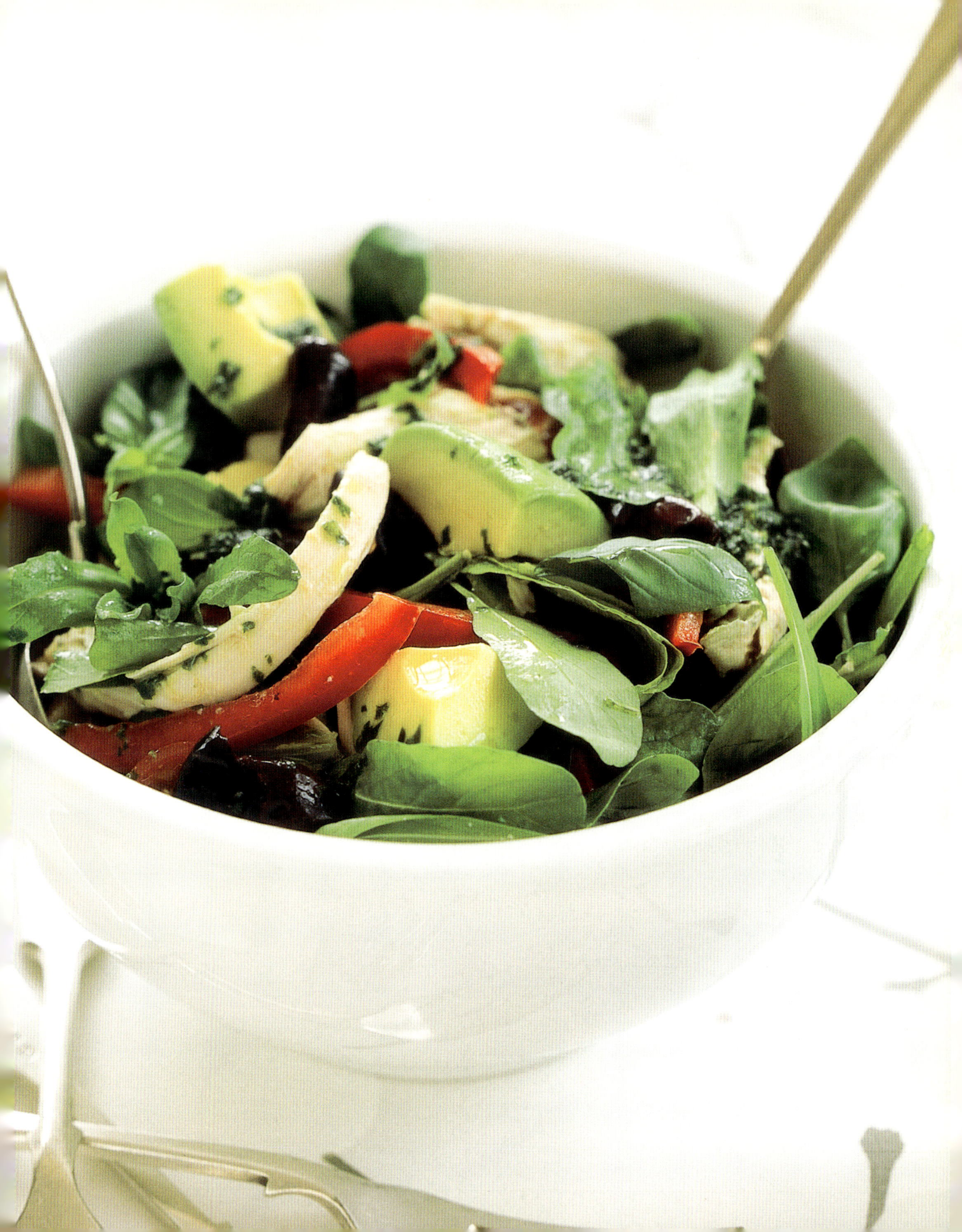

'Expand your repertoire with an assembly approach. Mix and match fresh ingredients with different flavours and dressings. Use Indian spices instead of Moroccan or chermoula dressing instead of curry.'

Chicken salads

Lemon chicken & fennel salad

Prep 15 minutes + standing

1 large or 2 small fennel bulbs
1 tsp salt
Champagne vinegar dressing:
2 tbsp champagne vinegar or white wine vinegar
1 tsp Dijon mustard
3 tbsp extra virgin olive oil
finely grated zest of 1 lemon
2 tbsp lemon juice
ground black pepper

2 cooked chicken breasts
140g watercress tips
1 just-ripe avocado, finely diced
Optional garnish: 2 tbsp almond slivers, toasted

Cut fennel heads in half lengthways and trim off tough bases. Slice fennel as finely as possible (use a mandolin or potato peeler). Place in a non-reactive bowl and mix through salt. Stand 15-20 minutes to allow fennel to soften then rinse very well until it no longer tastes overly salty. Drain.
Combine vinegar, mustard, oil, lemon zest and juice and season with pepper. Toss this dressing through sliced fennel.
Divide watercress between 4 serving plates. Thinly slice chicken and arrange on top. Place a mound of fennel on top, drizzle with dressing and scatter over chopped avocado and optional almonds.
Serves 4

ⓥ Moroccan chicken & chickpea salad

Prep 15 minutes
Cook 2-3 minutes

2 x 300g cans chickpeas, rinsed and drained
3 tbsp olive oil
1 tsp sweet smoked paprika
2 tsp ground cumin
finely grated zest of 1 lemon
½ tsp salt and grinds of pepper
3 tbsp lemon juice
4 cooked chicken breasts, shredded into bite-sized pieces
8 tomatoes, quartered
2-3 roasted red capsicums, thinly sliced
140g baby spinach leaves
¼ cup Greek yoghurt
Garnish: 4 tsp dukkah

Place chickpeas in a pot with oil, spices, lemon zest and seasoning and stir over heat for 2-3 minutes until mixture sizzles and smells aromatic. Remove from heat and allow to cool 5-10 minutes.
Mix in lemon juice and place in a large mixing bowl with chicken, tomatoes, capsicums and spinach. Gently toss to combine then divide between 4 serving plates. Dollop on yoghurt and scatter over dukkah.
Serves 4

VERSATILE FENNEL
Foeniculum vulgarum
Sown from mid to late summer, the sweet tender bulbs of Florence fennel take a good three months from planting to reach maturity. Their crisp texture and light anise flavour make an excellent match for a wide variety of foods.
For a great **fennel and walnut slaw**, halve bulbs and slice lengthways as thinly as possible. Sprinkle with a little salt to soften for 10-15 minutes then rinse well and mix with chopped walnuts, mint, thinly sliced spring onions, currants soaked in orange juice and a little olive oil.
Finely sliced and gently **sautéed fennel** makes an excellent addition to any kind of seafood stew or soup. Add a splash of Pernod, stock, canned tomatoes and saffron.
A loin of **pork with fennel and apples** makes a great weekend dish. Cook the pork slowly on a bed of sliced fennel and apples with a little apple juice or stock.

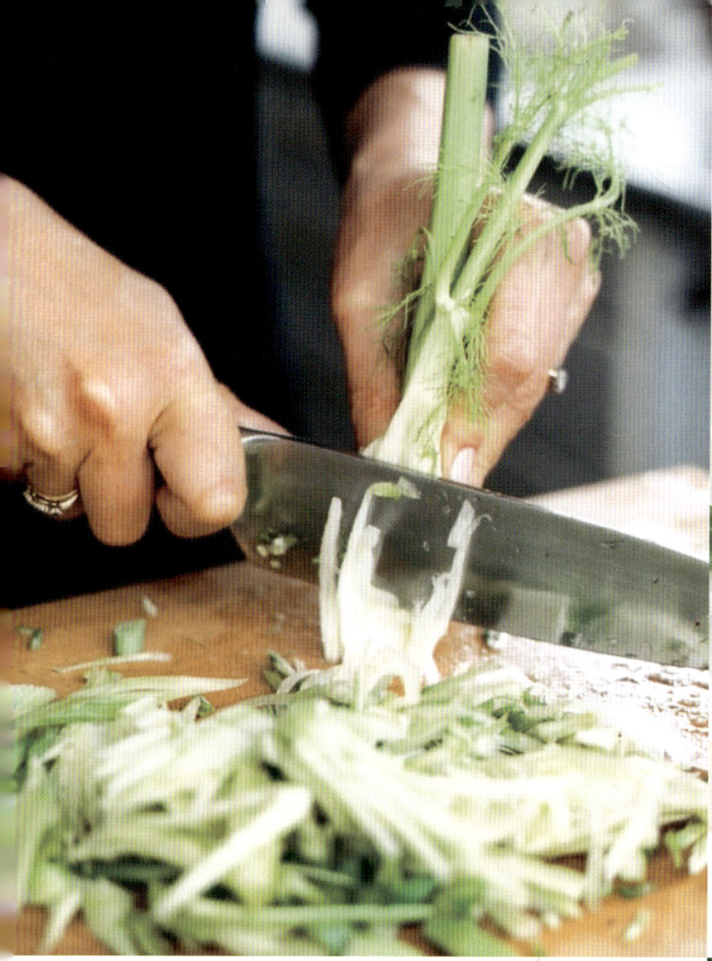
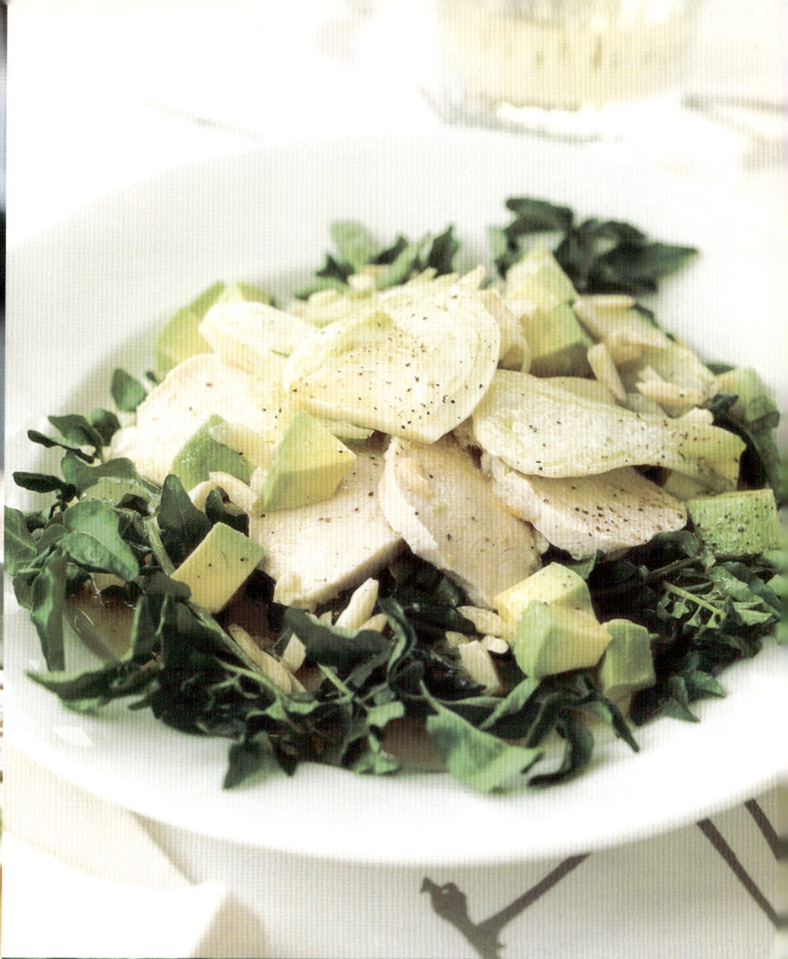
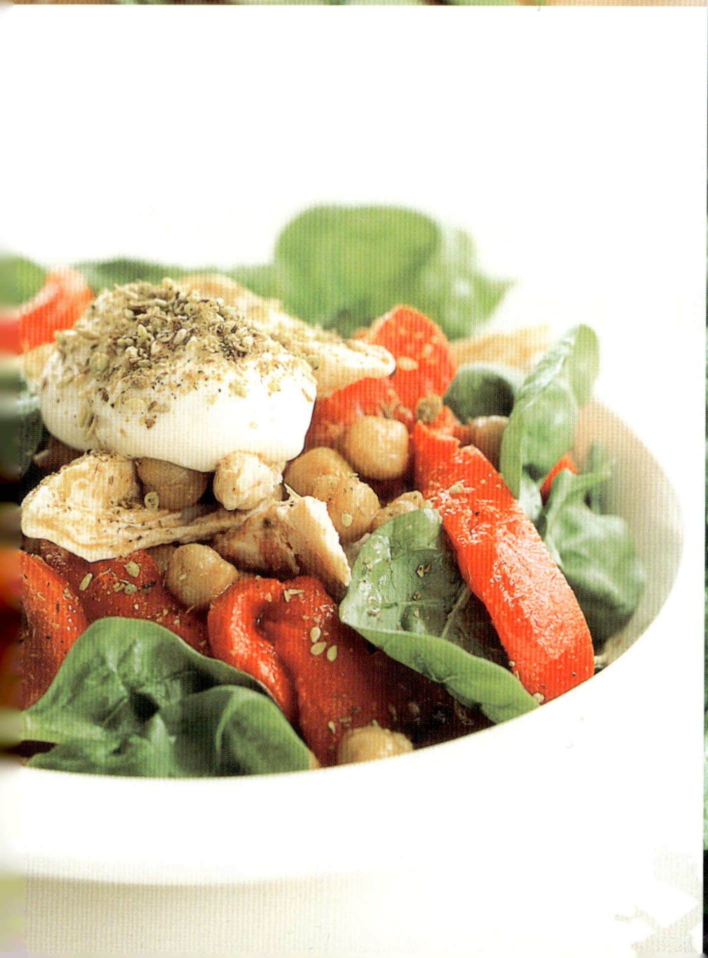
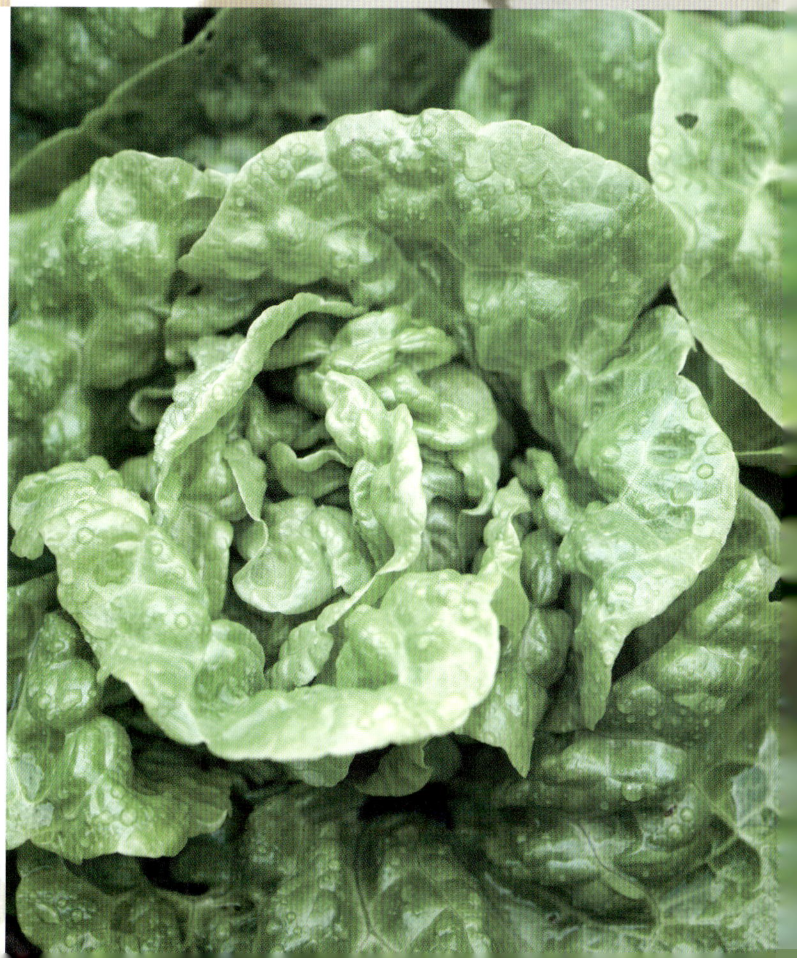

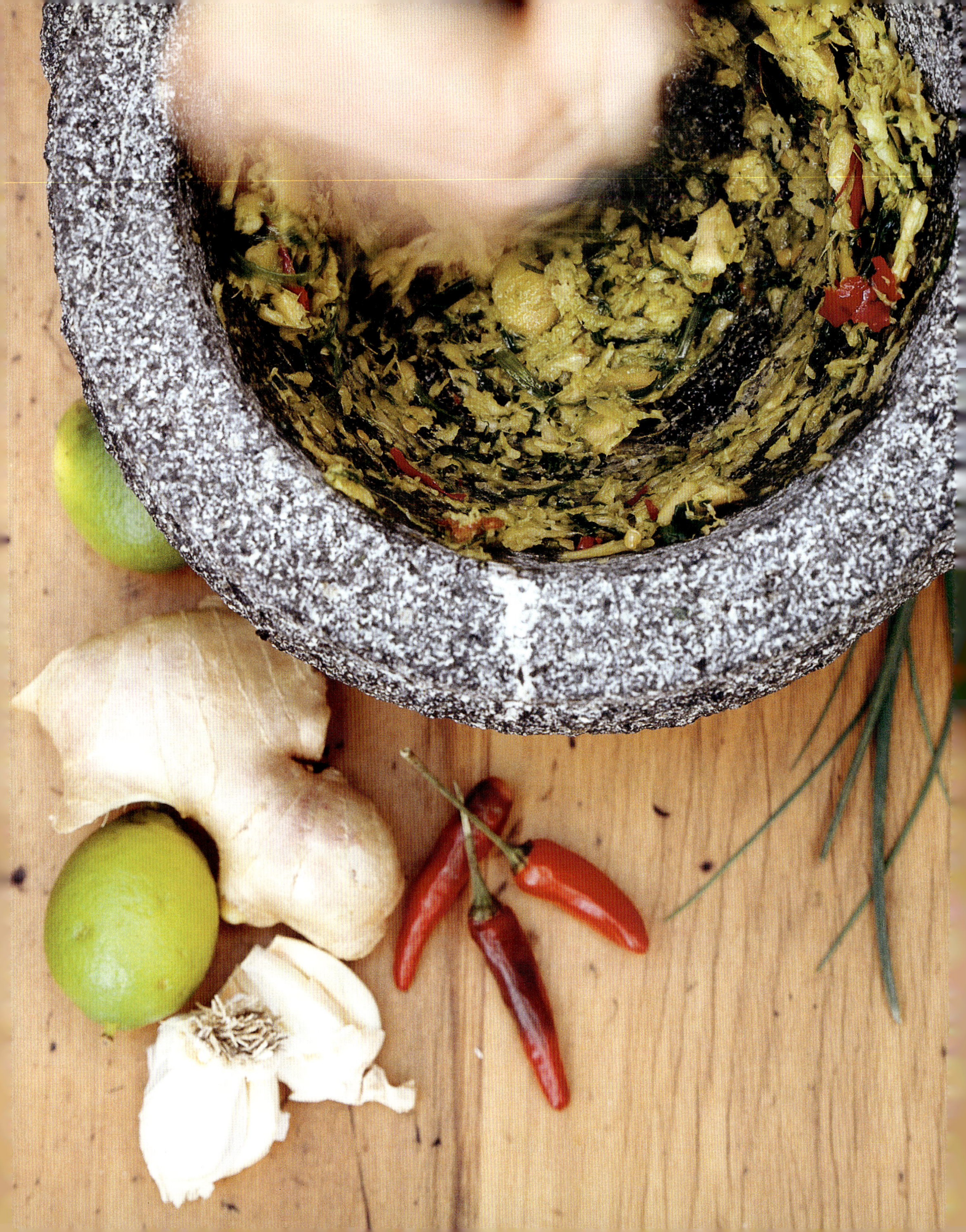

'It's not enough to just char your steak on a naked flame. You need a marinade to tenderise and add flavour. Every culture has its own distinctive barbecue tastes. Go easy on the oil to avoid flare-ups.'

Marinades for summer grills

Chermoula paste
Prep   10 minutes

This Moroccan spice paste can be used in marinades, spicy butters for cooking seafood (prawns and scallops are delicious), mayonnaise and as a rub.

Toast 2 tsp ground cumin, 1 tsp ground turmeric, ¼ tsp cayenne pepper and 1 tsp paprika in a dry frypan for 30 seconds to release aromas. Combine with 2 cloves garlic, crushed, 1 tsp brown sugar, ½ tsp salt, the finely grated zest and juice of 1 juicy lemon, 1 whole coriander plant, roots and tough stems removed (1 cup packed leaves), finely chopped, and 1 spring onion, finely sliced.
Makes enough for a whole chicken or a leg of lamb or 1kg seafood

CHERMOULA BUTTER
Mix paste with 100g melted butter.

CHERMOULA MARINADE
Mix paste with ¼ cup olive oil.

USING SPICE PASTES, RUBS AND BLENDS
Any kind of spice rub or paste such as Cajun spice mix, curry mix or Moroccan spice mix can be combined with butter for a tasty coating for potatoes, grilled fish or chicken, mixed into mayonnaise for a dressing or combined with oil for a wet marinade.

Greek lemon & herb marinade
Prep   10 minutes

This is my favourite marinade for lamb and chicken.

Combine ½ cup lemon juice with 2 tbsp olive oil, 1 tbsp chopped oregano or thyme leaves (or 1 tsp dried), 1 tsp chopped rosemary leaves, 2 cloves garlic, crushed, 1 tsp salt and several grinds of black pepper.
Makes enough for 1 chicken or 1 butterflied leg of lamb

Spice trail marinade
Prep   2 minutes
Cook   1-2 minutes

Great with chicken and fish.

Heat 2 tbsp oil in a frypan. Add 2 tsp coriander seeds, coarsely crushed, 2 tsp cumin seeds, coarsely crushed, 2 tsp sesame seeds and the finely grated zest of 1 lemon and sizzle for a minute or two. Mix in 2 tsp garam masala and ½ tsp each salt and pepper.
Makes enough for 300-400g chicken or seafood

'There is a real sense of freedom in cooking outdoors. Simply by virtue of being outside, our gastronomic expectations are lessened and everyone loosens up and has a good time.'

On to the grill plate

Grilled chicken with israeli couscous salad

Prep   15 minutes + marinating
Cook 10-12 minutes

12 chicken tenderloins or 8 boneless skinless chicken thighs
Spice trail marinade (pg 101)
Spiced oil dressing (pg 84)

1½ cups israeli couscous
2 stalks celery, thinly sliced
2 spring onions, thinly sliced
¼ cup dried cranberries, very finely chopped

The toothsome texture of israeli couscous is very appealing and goes well with all kinds of dressings. Here's my current favourite, lightly spiced with Indian flavours. Unlike regular couscous, Israeli couscous requires boiling. You can also make this salad with regular couscous. Use the same quantity and follow the manufacturer's guide to cooking.

Mix chicken with marinade. Cover and marinate for 30 minutes or up to 4 hours in the fridge.
Heat a large pot of salted water (1 tbsp salt per 8 cups water) and boil couscous for 8 minutes. Drain well and combine with spiced oil dressing. Toss through celery, spring onions and cranberries.
Grill chicken over medium heat, turning frequently, until cooked through, about 10 minutes for tenderloins and 12 minutes for thighs. Remove from heat and allow to stand for 5 minutes before serving with couscous.
If preferred, slice cooked chicken into large pieces and toss through salad.
Serves 4

When you are new to cooking it's easy to think that making a dish more complex or adding more ingredients will make it better. But actually the opposite applies. Simplicity rules. Find the freshest, best-quality ingredients and make them shine ... like a little salad of lettuce, hard-boiled eggs, freshly cooked sweet prawns and a good red-wine vinaigrette. You might be tempted to add more, but don't. I was lucky enough to enjoy such a dish in the home of Madame Bernard in Paris. This wonderful woman, now in her mid-80s, prepared from her tiny kitchen a marvellously simple yet stunning lunch for six people. The prawn and egg salad was the starter. It was followed by pan-fried fresh fish with seasonal vegetables and finished with a plate of cheeses and fresh figs from her garden. Such welcoming hospitality and simple good tastes are richly memorable.

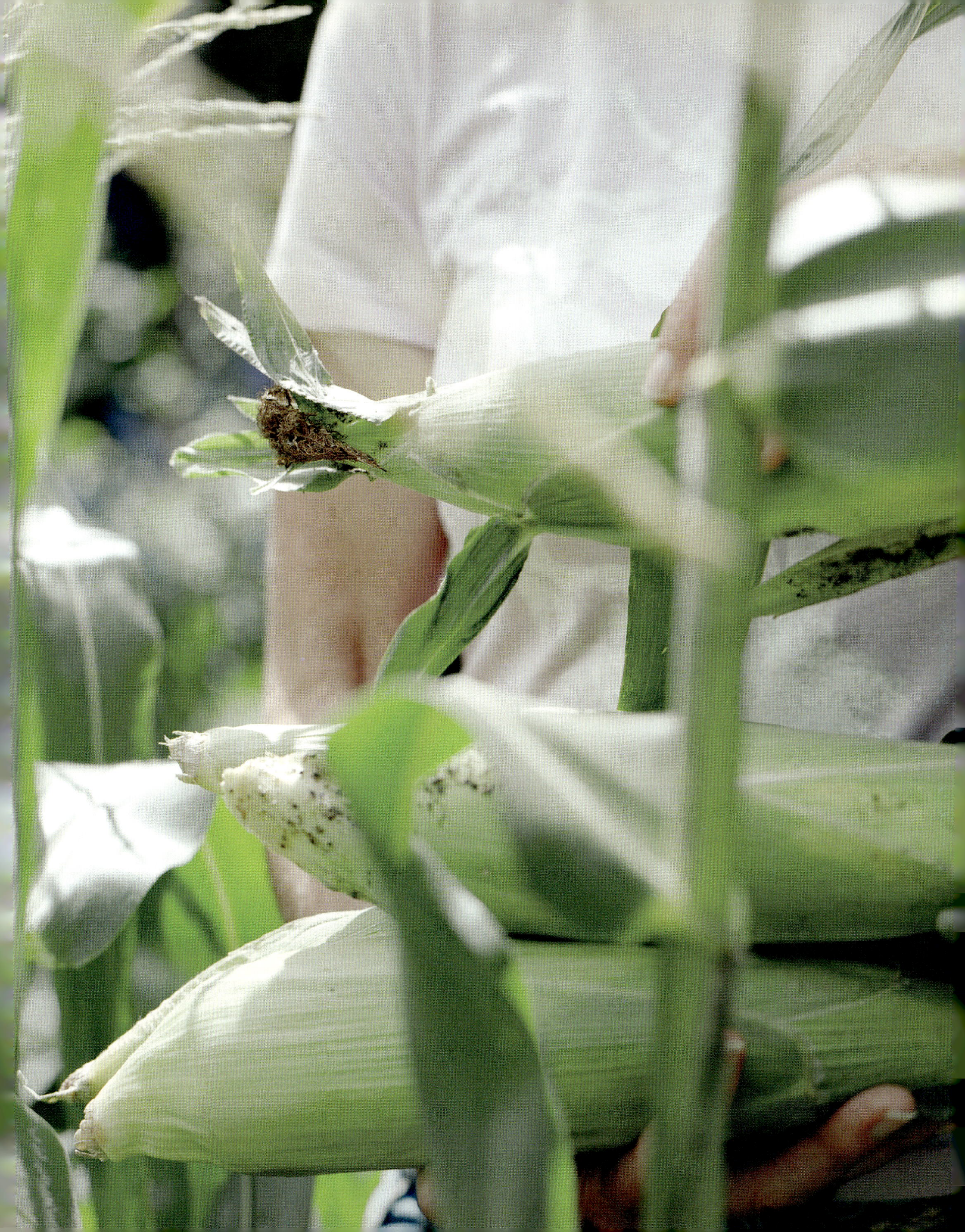

'What memories can be found in the uniformity of takeout and ready meals? In nourishing the food memories of our children we provide them with the fabric of culture and an appetite for tradition.'

Quick grills

Grilled lime & coriander chicken

Prep 5 minutes +
 30 minutes marinating
Cook 5 minutes

6 boneless, skinless chicken
 breasts, angle-cut into
 5-6 slices
Lime & coriander marinade:
finely grated zest of 2 limes
¼ cup lime juice
2 tsp brown sugar
1 tbsp minced fresh ginger
½ cup finely chopped coriander
1 tbsp wholegrain mustard
salt and ground black pepper

Mix chicken with all other ingredients except salt. Chill for at least half an hour.
Slide chicken on to skewers, one slice per skewer, and season with salt. Chill until ready to cook.
Heat a barbecue hotplate or heavy pan and cook skewers over medium-high heat until fully cooked, about 2 minutes each side.
Serves 6; makes 30-36 skewers, pictured with Chilli bean & corn salad, page 86.

BALSAMIC VINEGAR

In his lovely book *Cooking By Hand* Paul Bertolli shares a letter written to his new-born son telling him about the special gift they have received in honour of his birth: six beautiful casks built for storing balsamic vinegar. Why all this fuss over vinegar, he asks. There is insufficient room here to share his memorable soliloquy. Suffice to say that balsamic is a legacy, a taste from another time in which you are reminded of people optimistic enough to imagine an heir who will continue a tradition.

Grilled steak on rocket salad with balsamic glaze

Prep 10 minutes +
 30 minutes marinating
Cook 4-6 minutes

1 tbsp balsamic vinegar
⅓ cup extra virgin olive oil
6 steaks, 2-3cm thick
salt and grinds of pepper
2 cloves garlic, thinly sliced
1 tbsp rosemary leaves
¼ cup balsamic glaze
 (page 143)

Rocket salad:
120-150g rocket leaves
6-8 tomatoes, cut in wedges
2 avocados, cut in wedges
100g snow peas, blanched

Rub balsamic vinegar and 1 tablespoon of the oil over steaks. Season with salt and plenty of pepper and stand for at least 30 minutes or up to 4 hours in the fridge. Bring to room temperature before cooking. Heat a hotplate or heavy pan and cook steaks over high heat to rare or medium-rare (2-3 minutes each side). While the steaks cook, heat remaining oil with garlic and rosemary until garlic just starts to sizzle; do not allow it to brown.
Transfer cooked steaks to a chopping board and rest for 3-4 minutes before slicing thinly on an angle across the grain. Arrange rocket, tomatoes, avocados and snow peas on a large serving platter or divide between 6 individual plates. Top with steak, pour over the flavoured oil and drizzle with balsamic glaze.
Serves 6

BALSAMIC GLAZE OR CREMA

The rare and expensive taste of a carefully barrel-aged balsamic vinegar produced by Italian artisans is a heady experience. For everyday pleasure make a simple balsamic glaze. You'll find the recipe on page 147. This mixture produces something akin to commercial balsamic crema, which can be purchased from specialist Italian food stores. Whether home-made or store-bought, it is very useful and keeps for months.

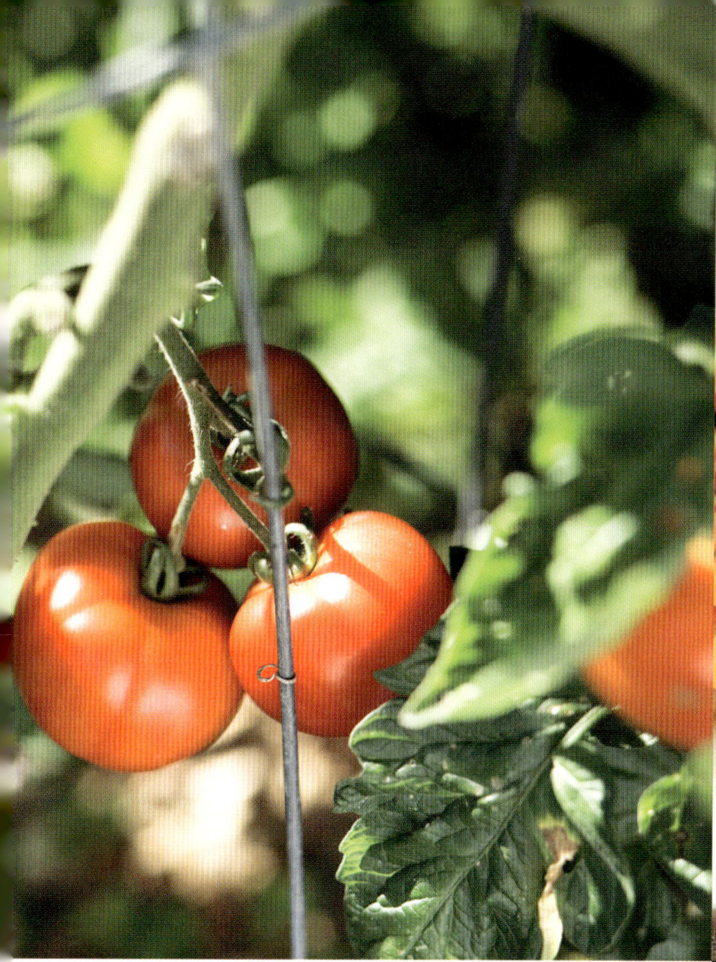
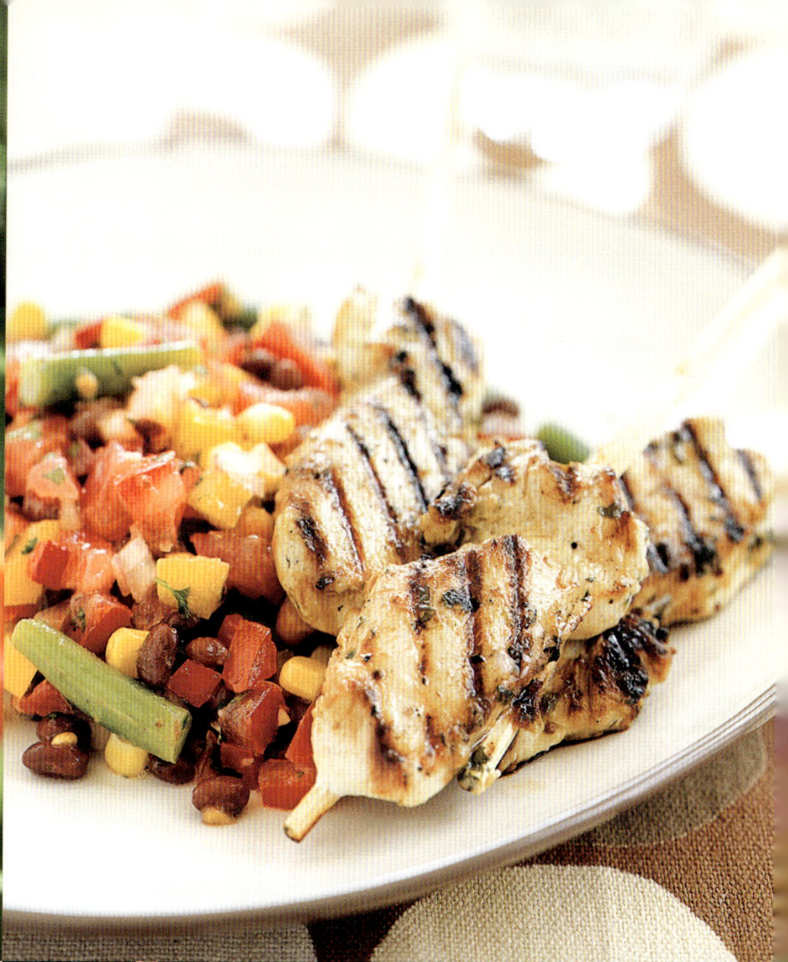
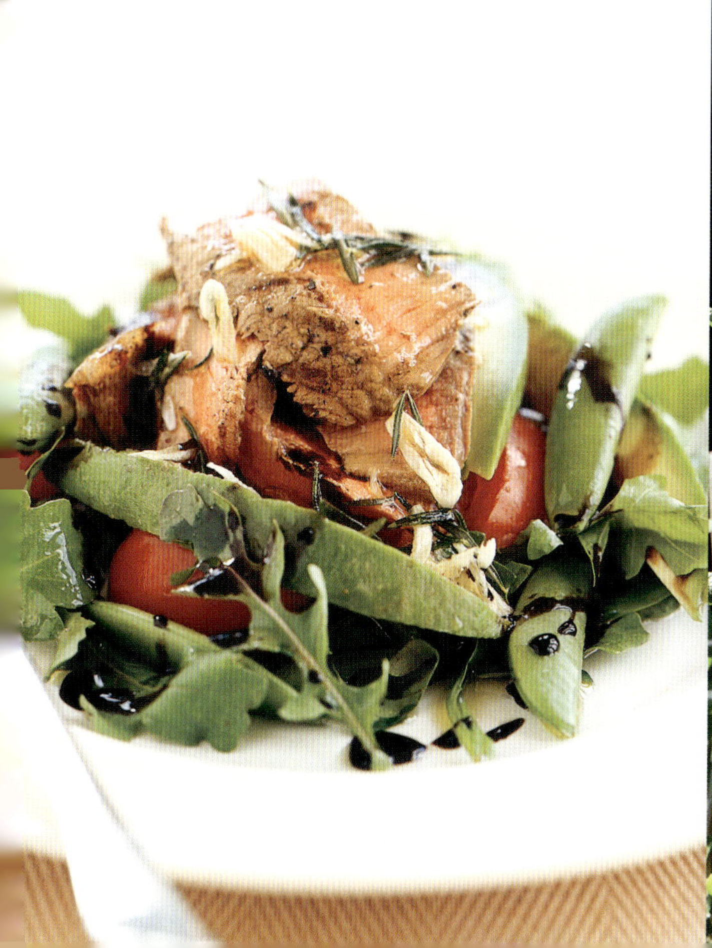
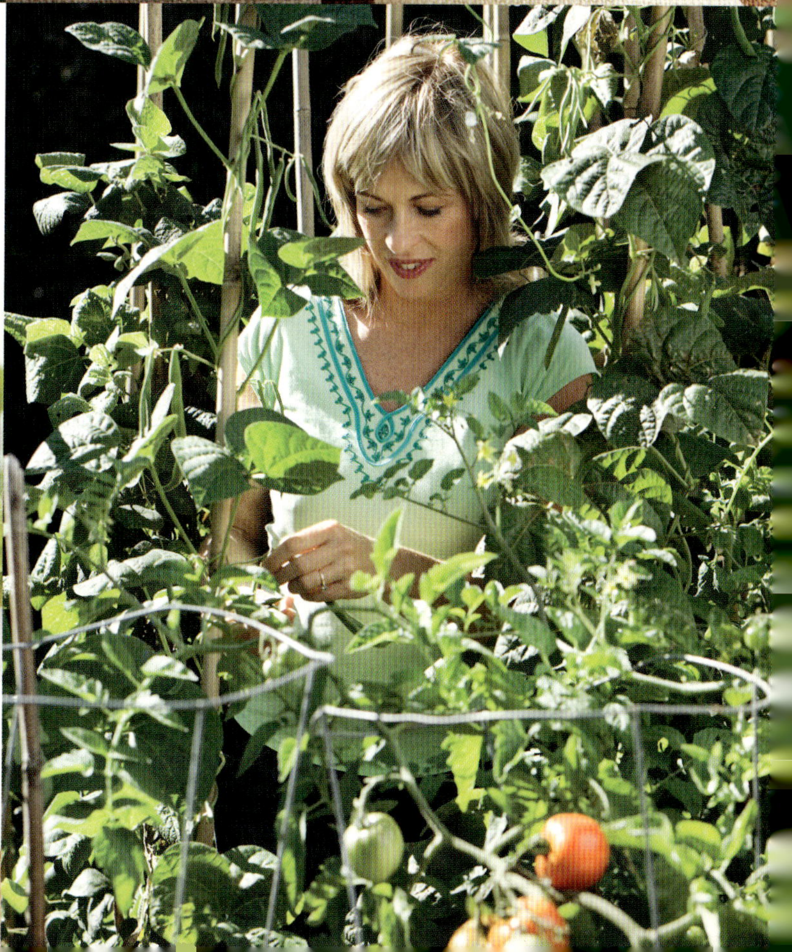

'My first taste of chargrilled lamb from a roadside stall in Greece is one I won't forget. I can never replicate that particular food moment, but there's a lot of pleasure to be had in the recall of its flavours.'

Take a leg of lamb

Grilled butterflied leg of lamb

Prep 10 minutes + marinating
Cook 40-50 minutes

1 whole leg of lamb, boned and butterflied open
1 recipe greek lemon and herb marinade (page 101) or other marinade of your choice
salt and grinds of pepper
fresh rosemary to garnish

Ask your butcher to bone and butterfly the leg of lamb for this dish. Butterflying the meat ensures quick and even cooking.

Trim meat of excess fat and place in a clean plastic bag with marinade. Seal and refrigerate for at least 2 hours or up to 48 hours, turning occasionally. Preheat barbecue grill over medium-high heat. Remove meat from marinade and season with salt and pepper. Cook until lightly browned, about 5 minutes each side. Weight the meat with a brick wrapped in tinfoil or place a tray on top of meat and weigh down with a couple of heavy stones. Lower the heat and cook a further 20 minutes each side or until done to your liking. Remove from heat, cover and stand for 10 minutes before carving in thin slices across the grain. Sprinkle with fresh rosemary and serve with grilled vegetables (see below) and your favourite sauce, eg salsa verde (page 53) or roast capsicum and coriander sauce (page 130).
Serves 6-8

TIPS TO BETTER GRILLS

Avoid an open flame and have a water bottle at hand to douse any flare-ups.
Use untreated wood or charcoal and avoid kerosene or fire-starters.
Use well-trimmed low-fat meat cuts and limit use of fat or sugar in marinades to reduce flare-ups and charring.
Use indirect heat to cook larger cuts. On a covered gas barbecue, turn all elements on full and when ready to cook place food in middle, turn off middle elements but leave outer elements on full to create an 'oven' effect of indirect heat.

Grilled vegetables

Prep 10 minutes
Cook 10-20 minutes

3-4 small red onions, skins on, cut in half (or in quarters if using larger onions)
3-4 red capsicums, halved and cored
200g kumara, cut 2cm thick or baby kumara halved lengthways

Grill onions, turning frequently until fork-tender, about 35 minutes.
Brush capsicum halves with oil and grill 8-10 minutes each side.
Make a hatchet pattern on cut surfaces of kumara and brush with oil. Grill, turning frequently until fork-tender, about 15 minutes.
Serves 6-8

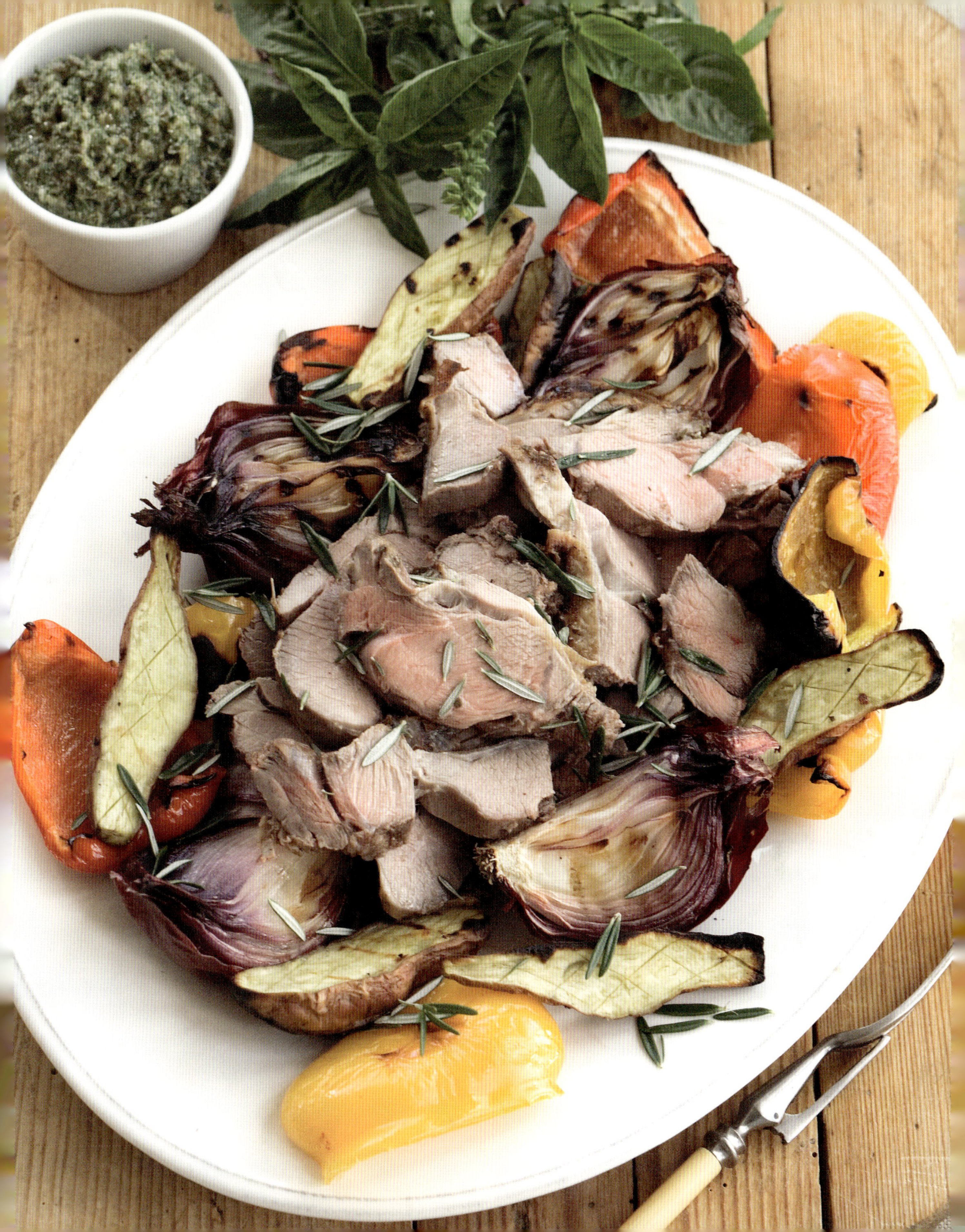

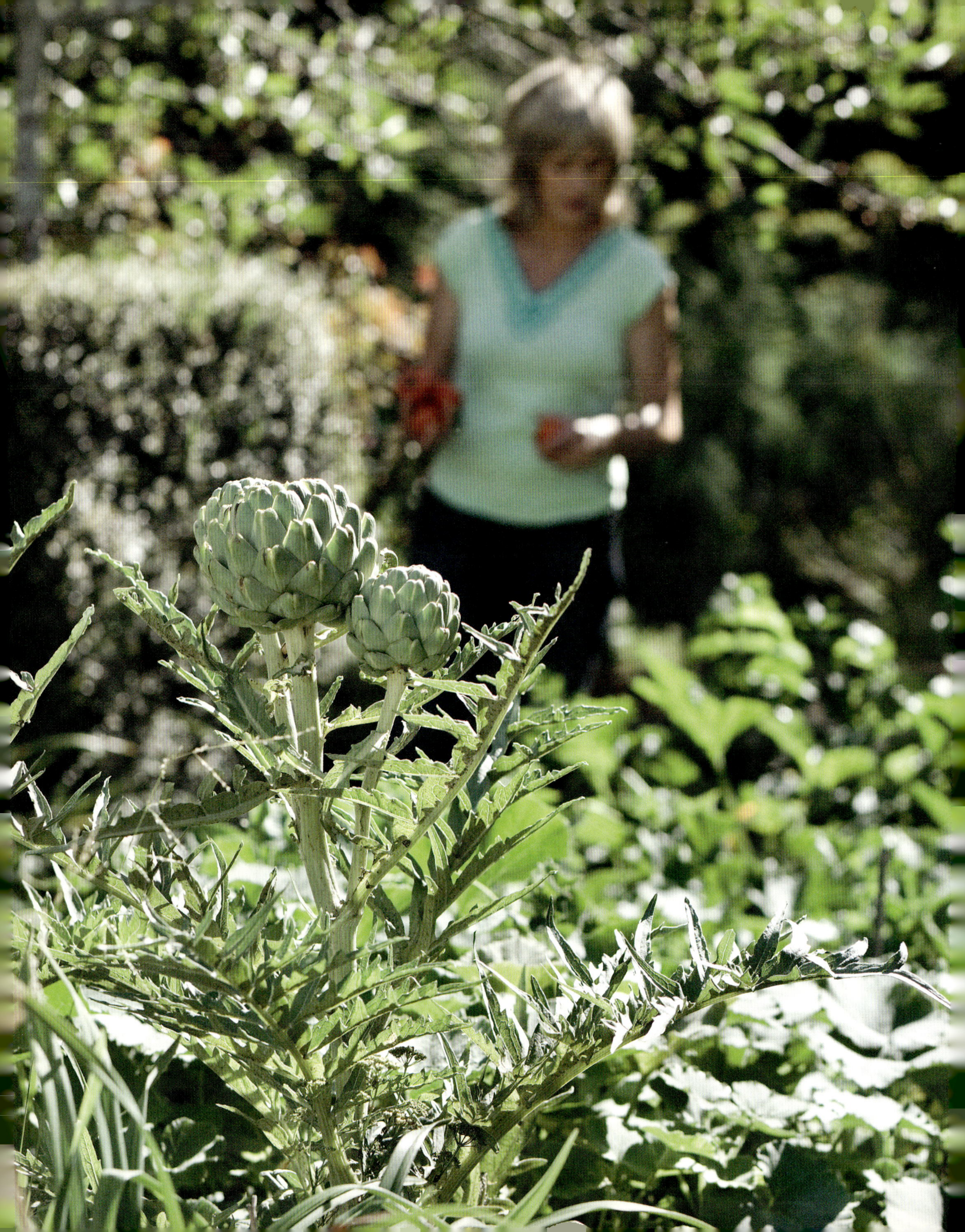

'As a teenager I learnt to make my own cray pots on an old metal jig in my boyfriend's garage. Lobster thermidor was the hit of that era. These days my cooking has become much lighter and simpler.'

Flavours that zing

Chermoula grilled crayfish

Prep 15 minutes
Cook 5-7 minutes

½ recipe chermoula paste (page 101)
50g butter, melted
2 whole raw crayfish, halved lengthways and digestive tracts removed

Crayfish is the ultimate luxury treat. Prepare the chermoula paste on page 101 and use half for the crayfish and half for the potato salad in this celebratory dish.

Combine chermoula paste with melted butter. Spread mixture over cut surfaces of crayfish. Chill until ready to cook.
Heat a barbecue hotplate or grill pan. Place crayfish cut side down on hotplate, cover with a lid and cook for about 5-6 minutes until shells turn bright red. Alternatively, roast crayfish in the oven at 220°C, butter side up in a baking tray, until red and the flesh in the deepest part of the tail is white and juicy, 6-7 minutes. Serve with the following potato salad.
Serves 4

MAKING FLAVOURED BUTTERS

In the recipe at left I have prepared a sensational flavoured butter by mixing the chermoula base with melted butter. This method can be used with other flavourings – lemon zest and juice and chopped herbs are a good combination. Commercial spice rubs and marinades can also be mixed through butter. Doing this will carry through the flavours of the marinade and give food a richer mouth-feel.

Moroccan potato salad

Prep 10 minutes
Cook 15 minutes

½ recipe chermoula paste (page 101)
600g (6 medium) new potatoes, boiled until just tender
¾ cup good-quality mayonnaise
1 spring onion, finely sliced
about 2 tbsp lemon juice
salt and grinds of pepper

Mix chermoula paste with cooked potatoes, mayonnaise and spring onions. Check seasonings and adjust to taste. Chill if not serving at once and bring to room temperature to serve.
Serves 4

'Industrial foods win us over on the promise of time-saving convenience but often they're full of fat and sugar. Staples like couscous offer stir-and-serve ease without the compromise.'

Grains on the side

Couscous with beets & almonds
Prep 15 minutes
Cook 15 minutes

Roast or boil 2 beetroot until tender (see page 136 for roasting instructions). Cool, peel and dice into 1cm cubes. Mix through 2 tbsp olive oil and season with salt and pepper. In a separate bowl mix 2 cups couscous, the finely grated zest of 1 lemon, 1 tsp salt and 2 cups boiling water. Stand about 10 minutes then break up with a fork. Mix in 2 finely diced spring onions, 2 sliced stalks celery or ¾ cup thinly sliced, peeled kohlrabi, 100g crumbled feta, ½ packed cup mint and/or coriander leaves and ¼ cup lemon juice. Transfer to a serving bowl and top with ½ cup toasted, slivered almonds, ¼ cup chopped pistachios and the beets or, if preferred, toss everything together.
Serves 4-6, pictured right

Summer orzo salad
Prep 15 minutes
Cook 12-15 minutes

Cook 400g orzo according to packet instructions. Drain and place in a large mixing bowl with 400g cherry tomatoes, halved, ½ cup toasted pine nuts, 50g freshly grated parmesan, ¼ cup chopped parsley, 2 tbsp chopped capers and 1 red capsicum, diced (optional). Mix through ½ cup Tuscan herb oil (page 96) and season to taste. Instead of Tuscan herb oil this salad can be also be dressed with Riviera dressing (page 26).
Serves 4-6

Spicy chickpea salad
Prep 15 minutes
Cook 5 minutes

Heat 2 tbsp olive oil in a frypan over medium heat. Add 2 fat cloves garlic, crushed, and 2 tsp each cumin seeds, fennel seeds and curry powder. Sizzle for 1-2 minutes. Add 3 cups cooked chickpeas or two 400g cans, drained, and stir over heat for a minute or two. Cool then add 2 tbsp lemon juice and season with salt and pepper to taste. Mix in 2 stalks celery, thinly sliced, 1 spring onion, thinly sliced, and ½ cup roasted cashews, chopped.
Serves 4-6

KOHLRABI
Brassica oleracea var. gongyloides
The Yugoslav woman who sells her husband's produce at my local farmers' market introduced me to this fabulous vegetable, which tastes like a crunchy cross between cabbage and Chinese turnip. With its terrific crispness it makes a great salad simply grated and tossed with a little honey-mustard dressing, or Asian-style with a dash of sesame oil and soy sauce, a little lime juice and toasted sesame seeds.
In winter kohlrabi is traditionally cooked long and slow, but in summer it is best enjoyed raw. You need to peel off the thick outer skin until you reach the lighter, tender core, then chop or grate as desired. Choose smaller, heavy bases over larger ones, which may be coarser and tougher. Stored in the crisper in the fridge, they will keep for several weeks.
Raw kohlrabi can be substituted for celery and vice versa in salads.

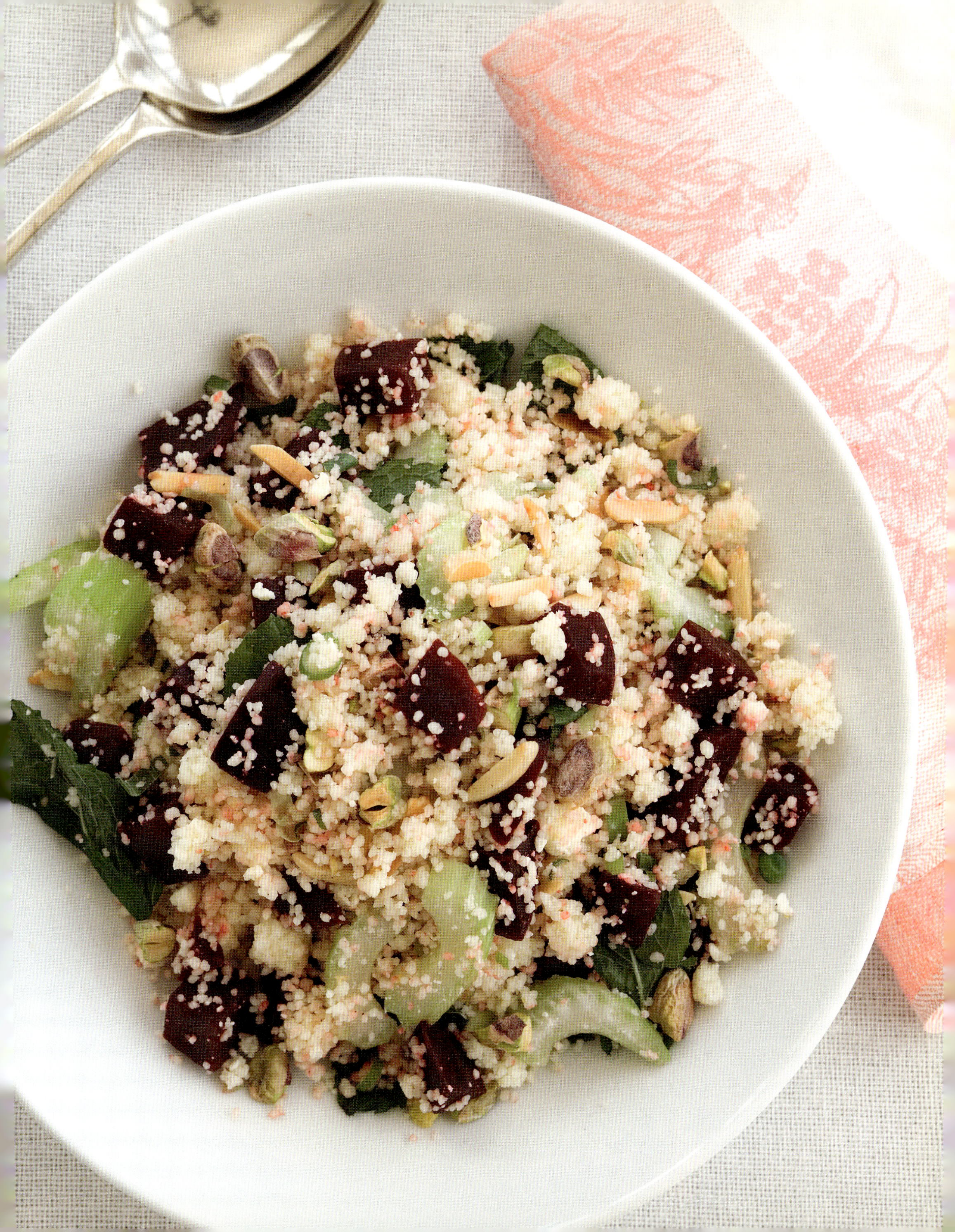

'The ambrosial taste of a fragrant, perfectly ripe peach from the tree, with juices that run down your chin and flood your senses, is a food experience you will not find from varieties grown for shelf life'

Two tones of sweetness

Nectarine compote & semi-dried nectarines

Prep 15 minutes
Cook 45 minutes + 1¼ hours for semi-dried nectarines

12 ripe sweet-smelling nectarines
½ cup sugar
1½ cups water
1 vanilla pod, split and scraped
½ lime, juice and finely grated zest

Finely dice the flesh from 6 of the nectarines and place in a saucepan with sugar, water, vanilla pod and scrapings, lime juice and zest. Bring to a simmer, stirring to dissolve sugar. Cover and simmer gently for 45 minutes.

Place a strainer over a bowl and pour fruit and syrup into it. Leave fruit to drain for 15 minutes.

To prepare the semi-dried nectarines, take the cooked, strained nectarine chunks and spread them out in a single layer on a lined baking tray. Slow-bake at 150°C until pieces are shrivelled and chewy, 1¼ hours.

To make the compote, bring the strained nectarine syrup to a boil. Dice remaining fresh nectarines and place in a heatproof bowl. Pour over the boiling syrup and leave to stand for at least 30 minutes or up to 24 hours. Chill if not using within 4 hours.

Serve nectarine compote with Greek yoghurt, garnished with slow-roasted nectarine pieces, or serve with vanilla panna cotta (page 114).

The slow-roasted nectarine dice will keep in the fridge in a covered container for several weeks.

Serves 6

Mas Masumoto is a third-generation Japanese-American farmer, writer and farm activist who grows organic peaches in Del Ray, California. His lyrical writings include Four Seasons in Five Senses, Things Worth Savoring, Epitaph for a Peach, Four Seasons on my Family Farm *and* Letters to the Valley, *a harvest of memories. I have been lucky enough to hear him speak and describe the epiphany of the perfect peach experience – that transforming moment of taste, an overwhelming culinary experience. A bite from an old-fashioned peach, fragile and fragrant, ripened by the sun, a peach that won't last more than three or four days when picked, is a taste you will never forget. In a world that values production and volume above all, such a taste is increasingly hard to find.*

For more information visit www.masumoto.com

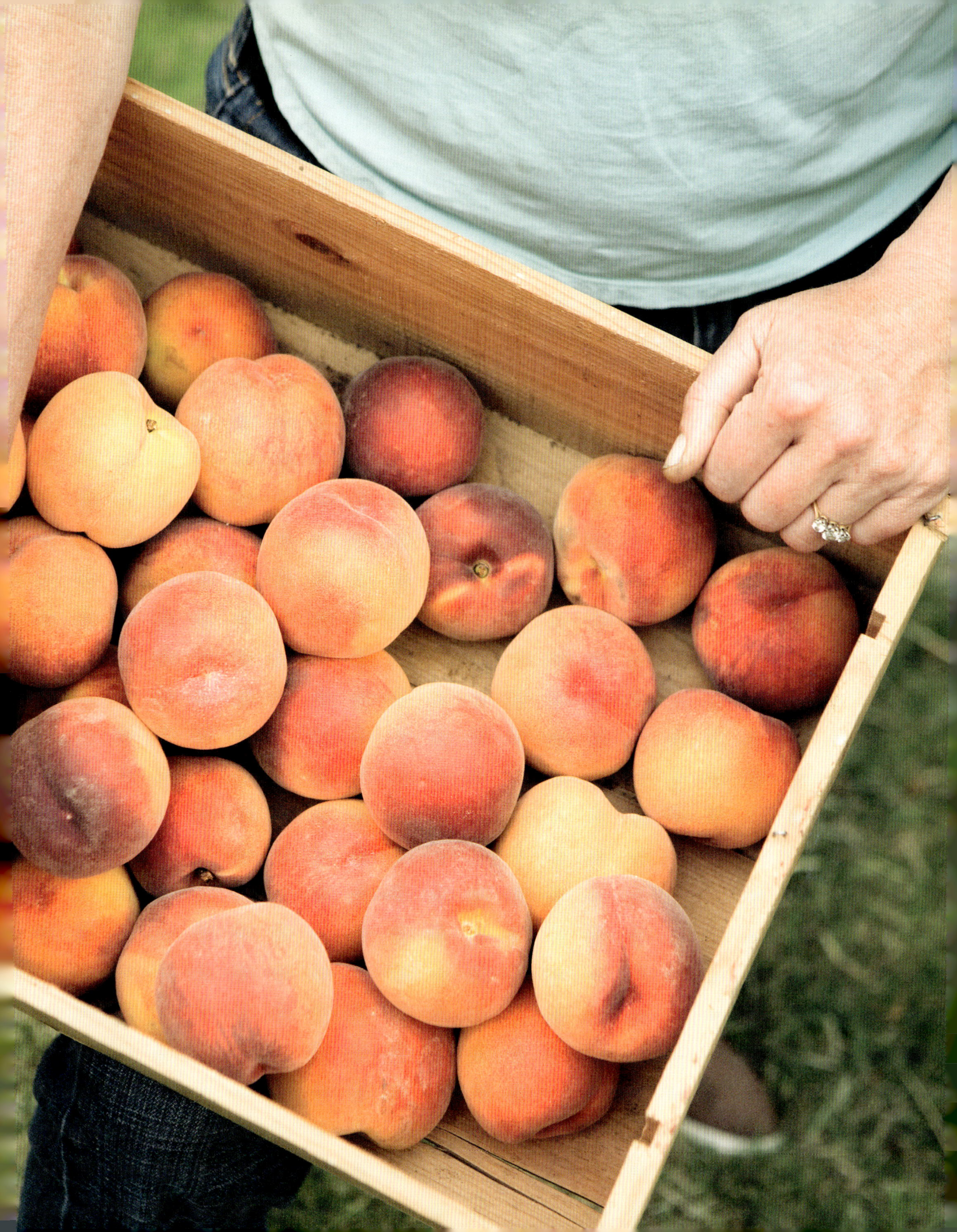

'In our Central Otago garden I have planted all those fruits that need a cold winter and love a hot summer. It's such a pleasure to be able to walk outside and pick ripe fruit, sweet and warm from the sun.'

Vanilla fragrance

Vanilla-lime panna cotta

Prep 15 minutes
Cook 6-8 minutes + at least 4 hours to set

¼ cup cold water
3 tsp gelatine
1 cup boiling water
½ cup sugar
15 fresh mint leaves
finely grated zest of 1 lime
2 tbsp lime juice
2 cups cream
1 tsp natural vanilla essence
To serve: nectarine compote and semi-dried nectarines (page 112) or fresh blueberries

Combine cold water and gelatine in a small saucepan. Add boiling water, sugar, mint, lime zest and juice. Bring just to the boil, stirring to dissolve sugar and gelatine. Remove from heat and stand for 10 minutes to allow flavours to infuse.

Strain liquid into a bowl, discarding solids. Whisk in cream and vanilla. Divide between 6 serving glasses or cup moulds. Cover with plastic wrap and chill until set, about 4 hours or overnight. Panna cotta can be kept in the fridge for up to 2 days.

Serve panna cotta topped with nectarine compote and syrup and garnished with semi-dried nectarine chunks or with fresh blueberries.

Serves 6

Slow-roasted late-season peaches

Prep 5 minutes
Cook 1 hour in individual dishes, 2 hours in a large roasting dish

1 cup sugar
1 cup riesling or other sweet wine
1 cup water
1 vanilla pod, split lengthwise or 1tsp natural vanilla essence
2 cinnamon quills, broken up
8-10 shavings fresh ginger, cut with a potato peeler
6 fresh peaches, washed
½ cup raspberries

Preheat oven to 150°C. Place sugar, wine, water and flavourings in a deep-sided roasting dish large enough to hold peaches in a single layer. Alternatively, divide ingredients between 6 cocottes (mini casserole dishes). Stir to partially dissolve sugar. Add peaches and sprinkle raspberries around. Cover and bake for 2 hours, turning after an hour. (If cooking in cocottes, cook for 1 hour and turn peaches after 30 minutes.)

Serve warm or allow to cool and chill. Peaches will keep in their syrup for a week in the fridge, or can be preserved while very hot in sterilised jars with pop-top or preserving lids.

Serves 6

STORING STONE FRUIT

Peaches, apricots, plums and cherries are often sent to market in an under-ripe state so they won't become bruised and damaged. This means they have much less flavour than fruit that is picked fresh and ripe straight from the tree. The best way to ripen early-picked stone fruit for maximum flavour is in a paper bag at room temperature. Like tomatoes, stone fruit should not be kept in the fridge as this flattens the taste.
Gauge ripeness (and flavour) by smell – the more aromatic the fruit, the better the taste will be.

PICKLING CHERRIES AND CRAB APPLES

Serve these simple pickles with cold meats and terrines or mix into stuffings and pie fillings. In a large saucepan heat together 1 cup water, 1 cup white vinegar, ½ cup sugar, 3-4 thin slices fresh ginger, 1 tbsp whole black peppercorns and 3 whole star anise. Bring to the boil. Add 500g fresh cherries or crab apples, stems on, and bring back to the boil. Boil for 3 minutes then remove from heat, spoon into sterilised jars and seal with screw-top seal lids. Once opened, store in the fridge.
Makes 2 medium jars

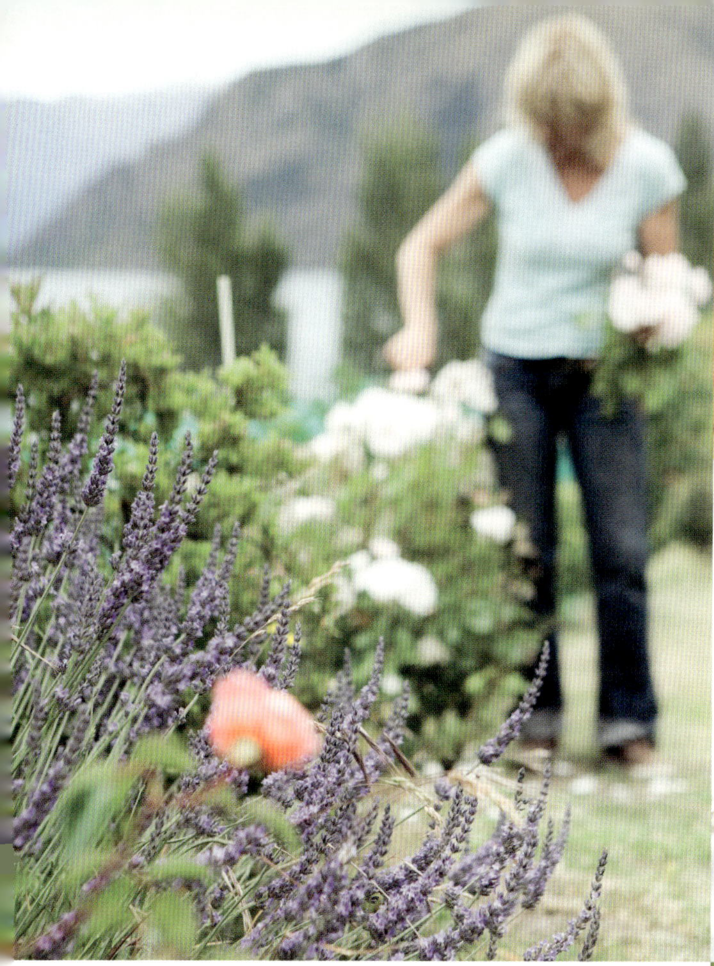

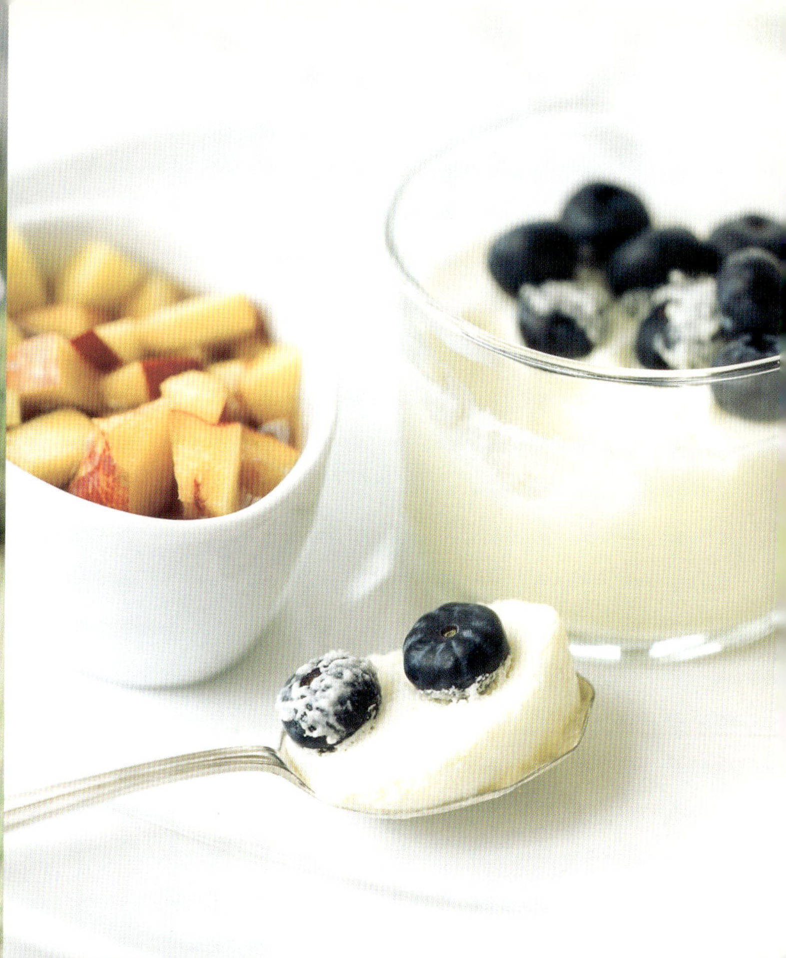

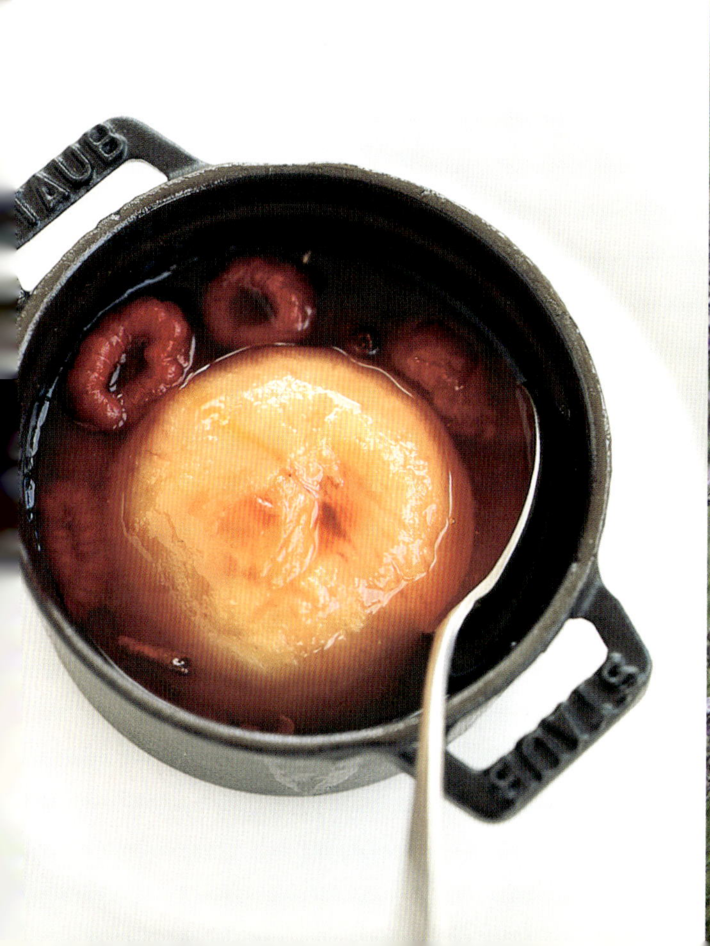

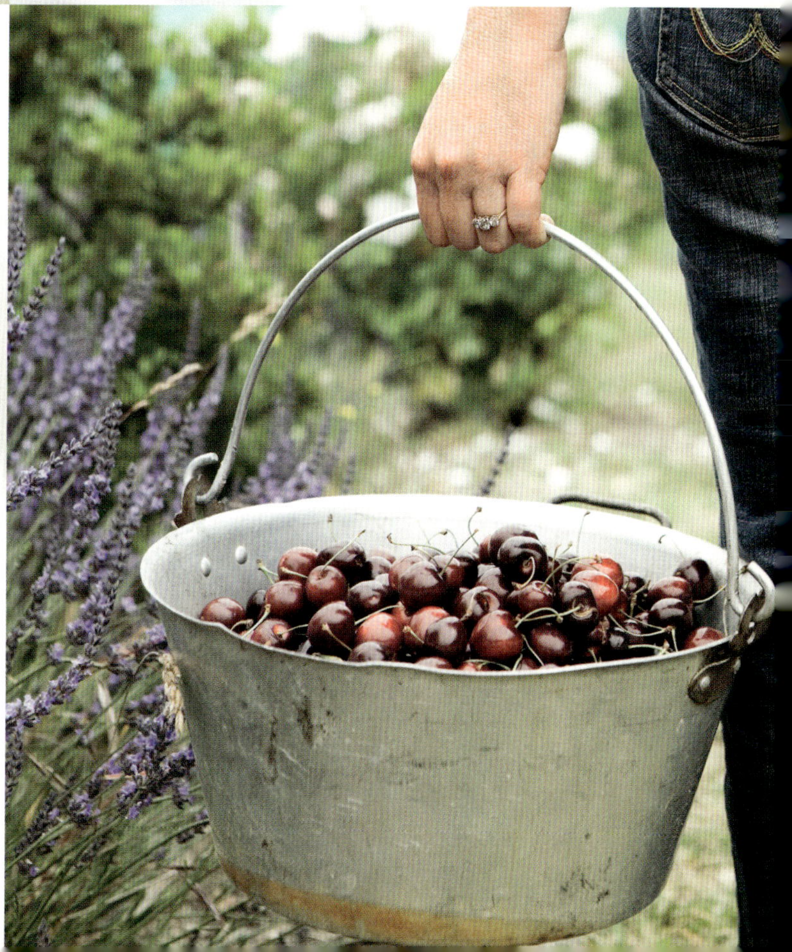

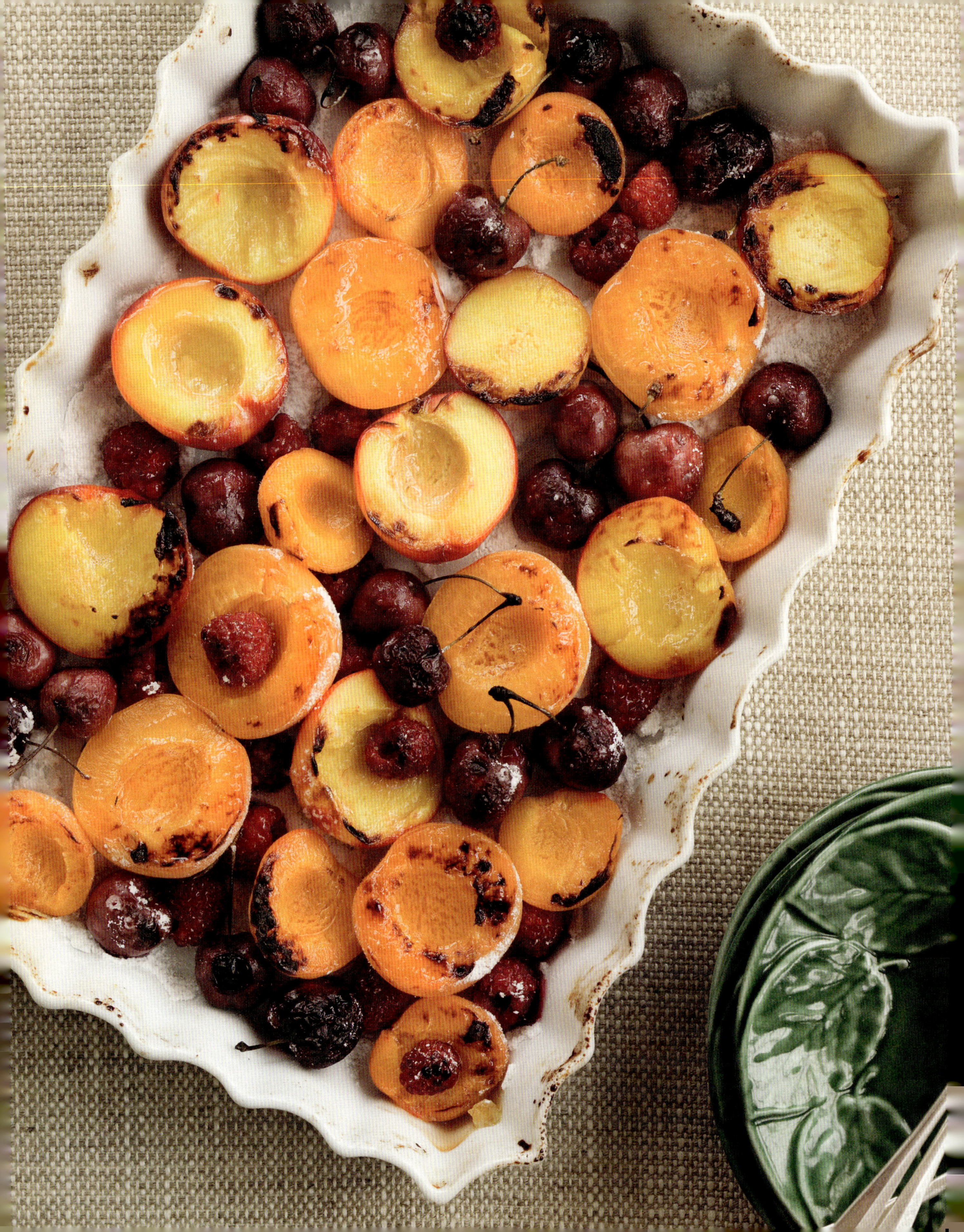

'Browning food under a grill or in a pan produces sweet, caramel flavours that add depth and richness. Sprinkling the food with sugar before grilling, or adding some sugar to the pan, increases the effect.'

Flambé & grill

Flambéed fruit

Prep 5 minutes
Cook 2-3 minutes

2 tbsp butter
½ cup sugar
400g cherries or other stone fruit, pitted
¼ cup fruit juice or water
1 tsp natural vanilla essence
6-8 whole cloves or cardamom pods
¼ cup rum

Pan-frying cherries or other stone fruits with butter, sugar and some aromatic flavours and then flaming them makes a simple, spectacular dessert.

In a heavy pan heat butter and sugar until bubbling. Add cherries, fruit juice or water, vanilla and cloves or cardamom pods. Cook over high heat for 2-3 minutes or until juices are thick and syrupy and mixture is just starting to caramelise.

Add rum and set alight with a match. Serve hot with clove-spiced mascarpone cream (see right).
Serves 4

CLOVE-SPICED MASCARPONE CREAM

Whisk together 100g mascarpone, 2 tbsp icing sugar and ½ tsp ground cloves until creamy and fluffy.
Recipe doubles easily.
Makes ½ cup, enough for 2-3 serves.

CARAMEL SAUCE

A useful make-ahead sauce, this keeps for about a week in the fridge. Place 1 cup cream, 1 cup brown sugar, ¼ cup golden syrup and 1 tsp natural vanilla essence in a pan and stir over heat until sugar has dissolved. Boil 5 minutes or until slightly reduced and a rich brown colour.

Grilled summer stone fruit

Prep 10 minutes
Cook 8-10 minutes

1kg mixed summer stone fruits, eg plums, apricots, nectarines, peaches, cherries
½ cup icing sugar
Optional: 2-3 tbsp kirsch or other liqueur

Halve stone fruits and remove stones (leave cherries whole). Place cut side up in a roasting dish. Sift icing sugar evenly over fruit.
Place under a hot grill about 10cm from the heat source. Grill until bubbling and starting to caramelise, 8-10 minutes. Drizzle over liqueur if using.
Serves 6

'My interest in cooking began at my mother's elbow while she baked, waiting for the moment when I could lick the beater. It starts with a taste, then before you know it you are in there chopping and mixing.'

Light as air

Chocolate raspberry pavlovas

Prep 15 minutes
Cook 45 minutes

6 egg whites (at least a week old), at room temperature
pinch of salt
1¼ cups caster sugar
2 tsp cornflour
1 tsp white vinegar
130g good-quality dark chocolate, melted and cooled
Optional: 6-8 tbsp raspberries, fresh or frozen

Topping:
300ml cream, chilled
1 tbsp icing sugar
1 tsp natural vanilla essence
1 cup fresh raspberries

Ensure there's not a skerrick of fat on the beater or mixing bowl when making meringue otherwise the egg whites will not beat up properly. Cooked meringue, without the topping and raspberry filling, will keep fresh in an airtight container for up to a week.

Preheat oven to 160°C and line a baking tray with baking paper. Place egg whites in the bowl of an electric mixer. Add salt and beat to soft peaks. Slowly add sugar with the beater running. Beat 10 minutes or until mixture is glossy and very thick. Whisk in cornflour and vinegar then fold in melted chocolate, swirling through the mixture very lightly so it is marbled.

Using three-quarters of the mixture in total, dollop 8 spoonfuls on to a tray. Make a hollow in the centre of each and if using raspberries, place 1 tbsp fresh or frozen berries in each hollow. Use remaining quarter of meringue mixture to form a cover over the raspberries. Bake 3 minutes then reduce oven temperature to 120°C and cook 1 hour or until pavlova shells are crisp to the touch. Turn off oven and leave to cool in oven. Store in an airtight container if not using the same day.

To serve: Whip chilled cream to soft peaks with icing sugar and vanilla. Dollop cream on to pavlovas and garnish with berries.
Serves 8

Variation: For plain pavlovas, leave out raspberries and chocolate, mix and cook as above.

MERINGUE KNOW-HOW

You need to pick a dry day to make any kind of meringue because if there's even a hint of humidity in the air the mixture will collapse. If the yolks break when you are separating the eggs do not use them as the tiniest amount of yolk in the whites will stop them from beating to a peak. If the eggs are very fresh the mixture may bleed a clear liquid as it cooks; I find it best to use egg whites that are at least a week old.
Don't add the sugar all at once as it can collapse the mixture. Once you have prepared the meringue it can be flavoured in many ways. Ground almonds or hazelnuts, coffee or cocoa are popular additions, as is coconut.
Whatever flavour you choose, stir it gently into the meringue right at the end. Don't beat it in as any oils in the flavouring will deflate the delicate structure of the meringue.

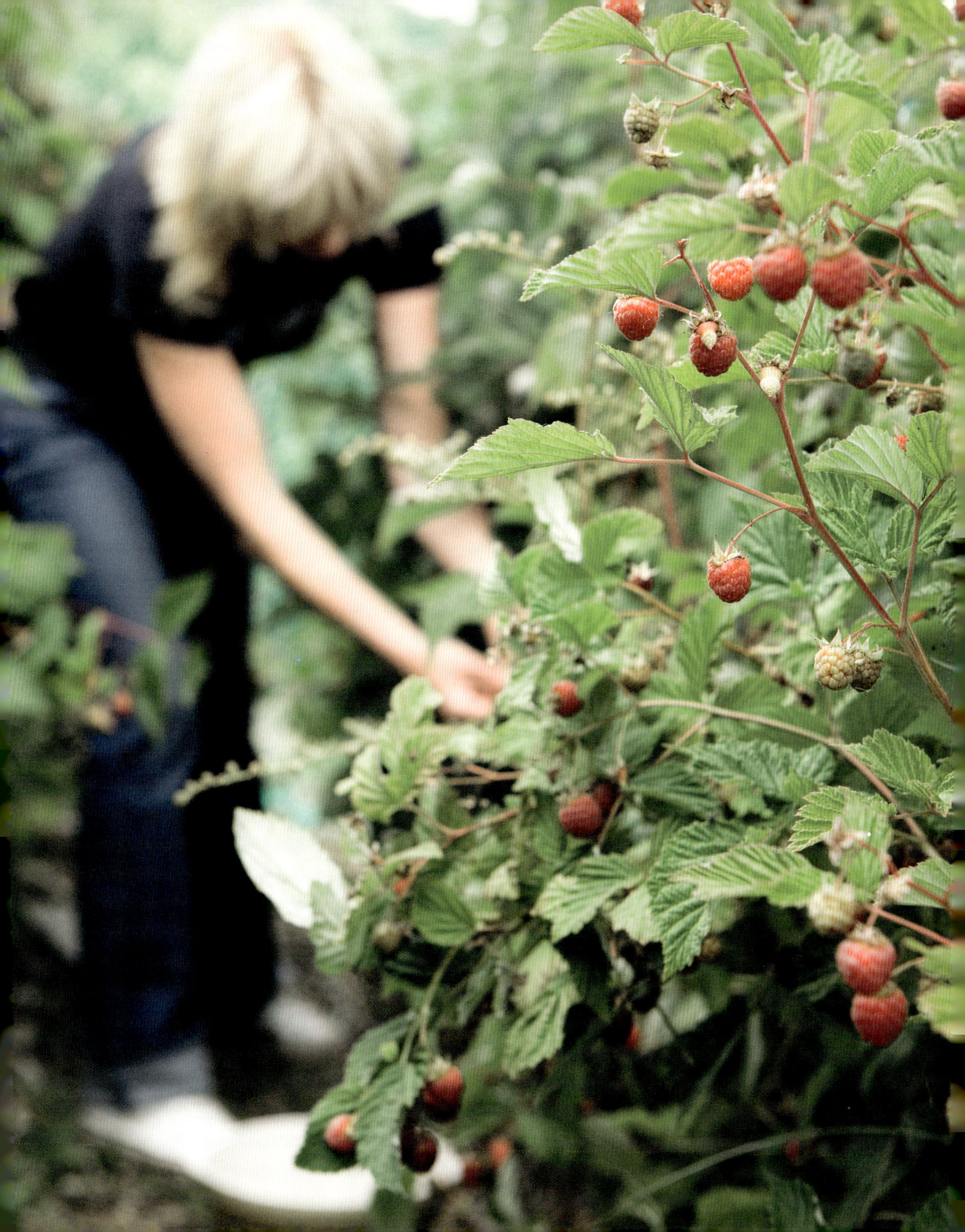

'Store-bought butter pastry is one convenience food I find useful. Check the ingredients and avoid anything with trans fatty acids (ie no margarines). The more solid a margarine the more trans fatty acids.'

Sweet baked aromas

Summer harvest fruit tart

Prep 10 minutes
Cook 45 minutes

1 sheet ready-rolled sweet buttercrust pastry or 250g rolled thinly (5mm)
⅓ cup jam, preferably same flavour as the fruit used
400-500g apricots or plums, each cut into 4-6 wedges
1 tbsp icing sugar, plus extra to dust board

Preheat oven to 180°C. Dust a board with a little icing sugar and roll out pastry sheet to increase its size by an additional 5cm top and bottom. Line a 22-25cm shallow tart tin with the pastry, covering the base and sides. Spread with jam. Top with fruit and sprinkle with icing sugar (a sieve makes this easy). Bake 12-15 minutes then reduce heat to 160°C and cook a further 30-35 minutes until fruit is starting to caramelise and pastry is cooked through. If fruit appears dry, brush with a little warmed jam. Serve warm or at room temperature. Tart is best eaten the day it is made.
Serves 6

Plum friands

Prep 15 minutes
Cook 15-20 minutes

1 cup icing sugar
½ cup flour
½ tsp baking powder
¾ cup (70g) ground almonds
6 egg whites
1 tsp natural vanilla essence
1 drop almond essence
100g butter, melted
6 plums, halved

Friands contain lots of egg whites, ground almonds and butter, which make them moist, tender and very rich. They will keep for several days or can be frozen. Use other seasonal fruit as available.

Preheat oven to 170°C. Sift icing sugar, flour and baking powder into a mixing bowl. Add ground almonds. Stir in 2 of the 6 egg whites with vanilla and almond essences to moisten the mixture evenly.
Beat remaining 4 egg whites to soft peaks. Use a large, flat spoon to mix in one quarter of the whipped egg whites, then gently fold in the remaining whites. Gently mix in melted butter until evenly incorporated.
Spoon heaped tablespoons of mixture into 12 greased friand moulds or muffin pans to half fill. Top each one with a plum half. Bake for 15-20 minutes or until lightly golden and set to the touch and an inserted skewer comes out clean. Cool before removing from moulds.
Makes 12

The aromatic wafts of stone fruit stewing on the stove take me back to my mother Anne's kitchen and her annual rituals of bottling. For weeks on end our kitchen was filled with cases of fruit and the sweet summer smells of cooking apricots, peaches, plums and pears.
Mother would rise early to head down to the auction markets to examine the lines she would bid for. Back home with her loot, she would transform our tiny kitchen into a little factory, dispatching case after case of perfect summer produce into glorious jars of preserves. They had none of the quick "stew it and throw it into jars with an overflow of syrup" look of my meagre efforts. Hers had the hallmarks of every good home science graduate: neatly packed in perfect overlapping layers and water-bathed to tender perfection. Through winter and spring, her larder of preserves formed the mainstay of our childhood breakfasts.

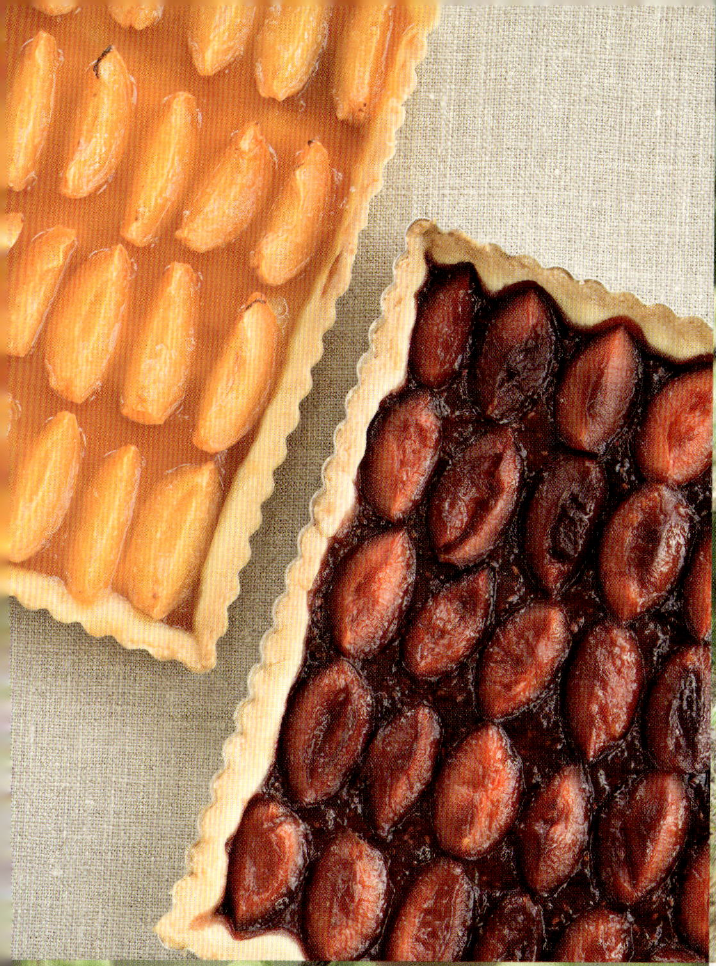
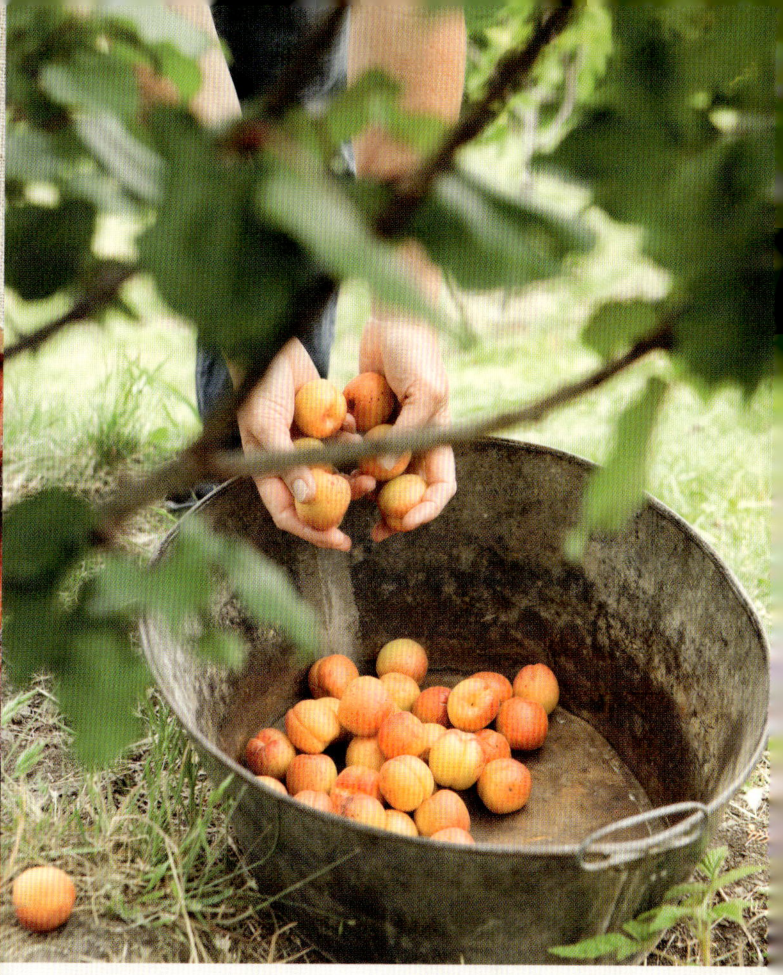
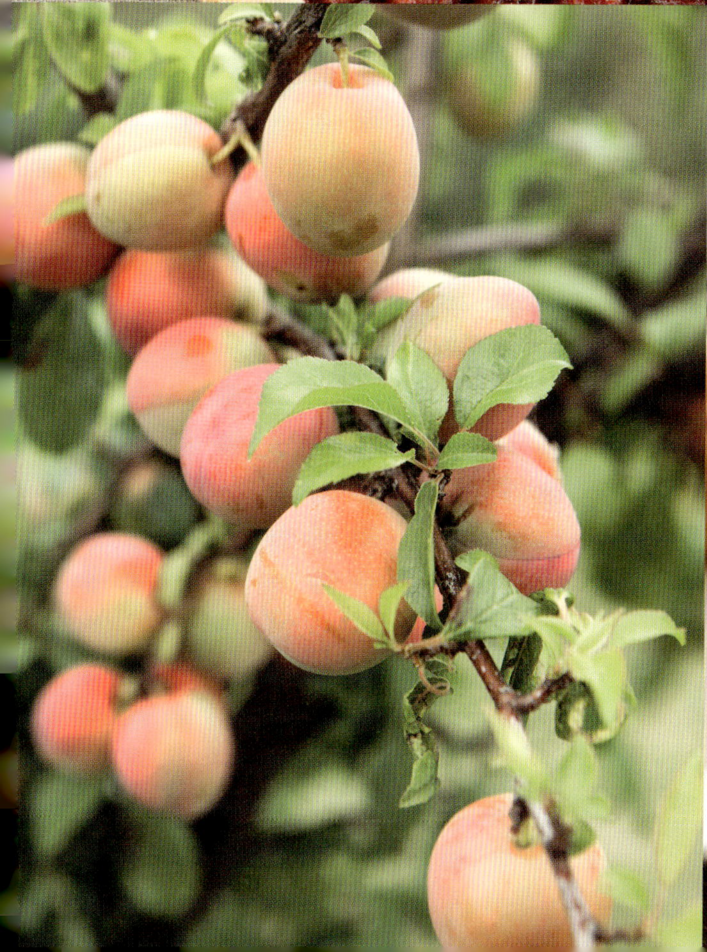
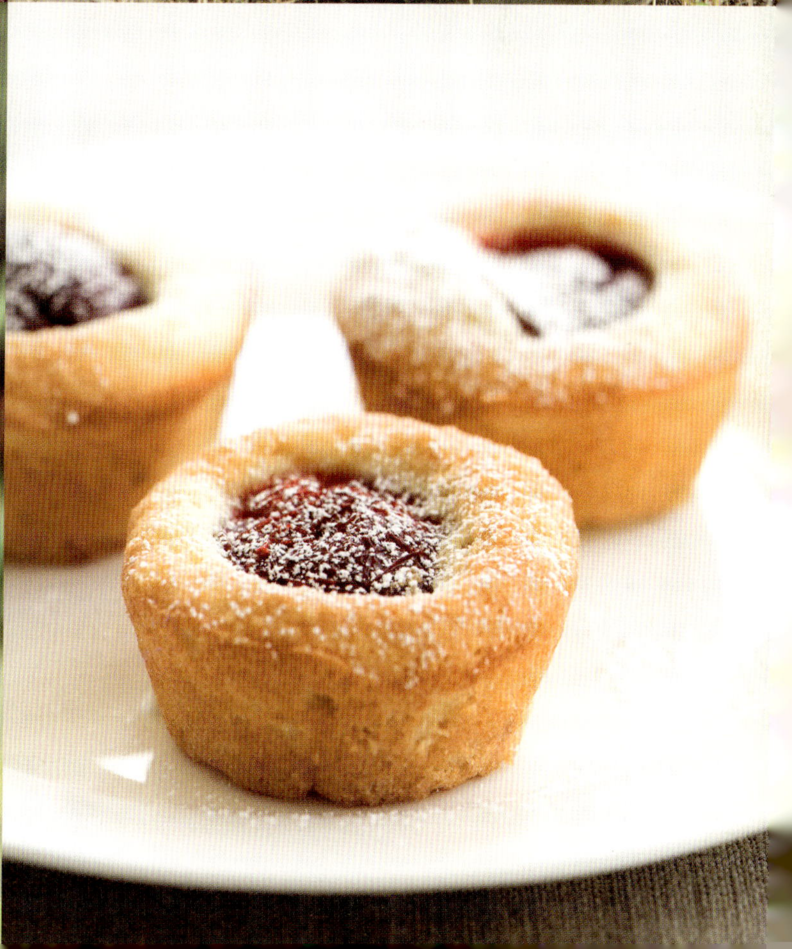

'Phytochemicals found in vegetables, fruits, herbs and whole grains are biologically active molecules that help boost immunity and promote good health. Eating fresh foods increases your body's ability to protect itself.'

Essence of flavour

Five-berry confit

Prep 5 minutes + standing time
Cook 2 hours

200g each fresh or frozen strawberries, raspberries, blueberries, red currants and blackberries or boysenberries (or a mixture to a total of 1kg)
1¼ cups sugar
1 tsp natural vanilla essence
Optional: brandy or kirsch

Place berries in a baking dish and sprinkle with sugar and vanilla. Stand for at least an hour or up to 4 hours. Preheat oven to 120°C. Cover dish tightly and bake berries for 2 hours. Remove and allow to cool (or serve hot with winter puddings). Chill if folding through cream. Confit will keep in the fridge for up to a week and can be served cold or reheated as needed. To preserve confit for a longer period, bottle in sterilised jars with pop-top lids while still very hot or freeze.
Makes 3 cups

Brandied berry confit

Add ½ cup brandy with sugar.

Summer berry coulis

Prep 5 minutes
Cook 5 minutes

500g fresh or frozen raspberries or mixed berries
½ cup caster sugar
¼ cup water
1 tsp natural vanilla essence
Optional: 2 tbsp cassis or kirsch

Place berries in a large saucepan. Add sugar, water and vanilla and bring to simmering point over medium heat. Remove from heat and add cassis or kirsch if using. Quickly pulse a few times in a food processor to loosely blend. If desired, strain through a sieve to remove seeds. Pour hot coulis into a jug or, to preserve, pour into sterilised jars and seal with pop-top lids. Leave to cool at room temperature.
Store in the fridge. Berry coulis will keep 3-4 weeks.
Makes 3 cups

FRUITS FROM THE ROSE FAMILY
Many temperate-climate dessert fruits come from the family *Rosaceae*. Each genus in this family is differentiated by the way the seeds or pits form in the fruit. Within the genus *Prunus* are the stone fruit – peaches, nectarines, plums, apricots and cherries. From the genus *Rubus* are blackberries, raspberries and other berry canes. *Fragaria* includes strawberries and *Malus* encompasses apples. The *Cydonia* genus provides us with quinces and the genus of those flowers we so enjoy as cut blooms – no surprises here – *Rosa*.

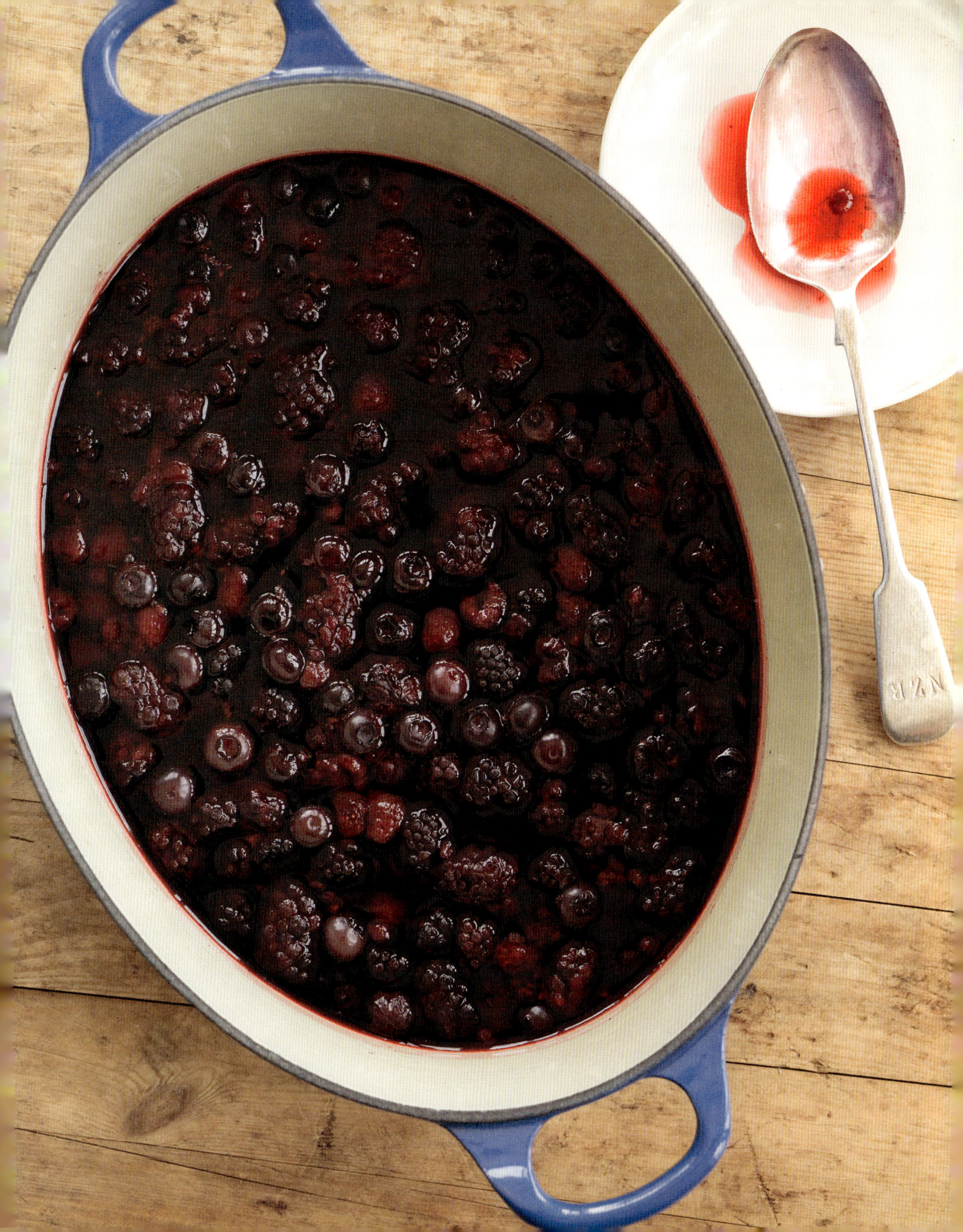

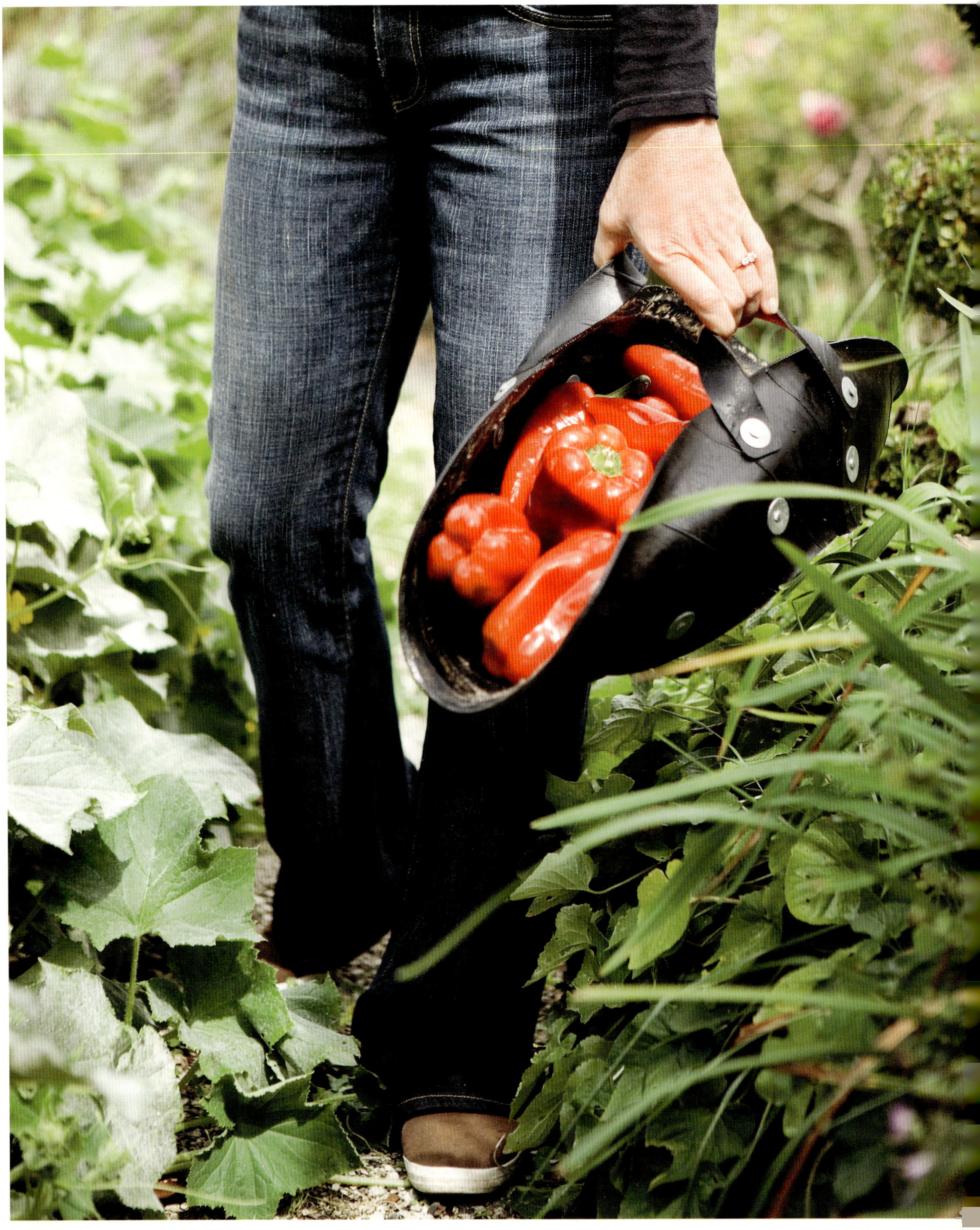

Autumn

Before you know it, summer is over. The mornings arrive crisp and heavy-dewed, there's a bite in the air, the light of day starts to dwindle noticeably earlier and the evenings draw in. Sensing the shift, our palates seek something more substantial and satisfying than the light, fresh tastes enjoyed over summer. Like squirrels, we gather our harvests and set about preserving the season's flavours in preparation for the cold months ahead.

As we light the first fires, there's a sense of celebration as another cycle of nature turns.

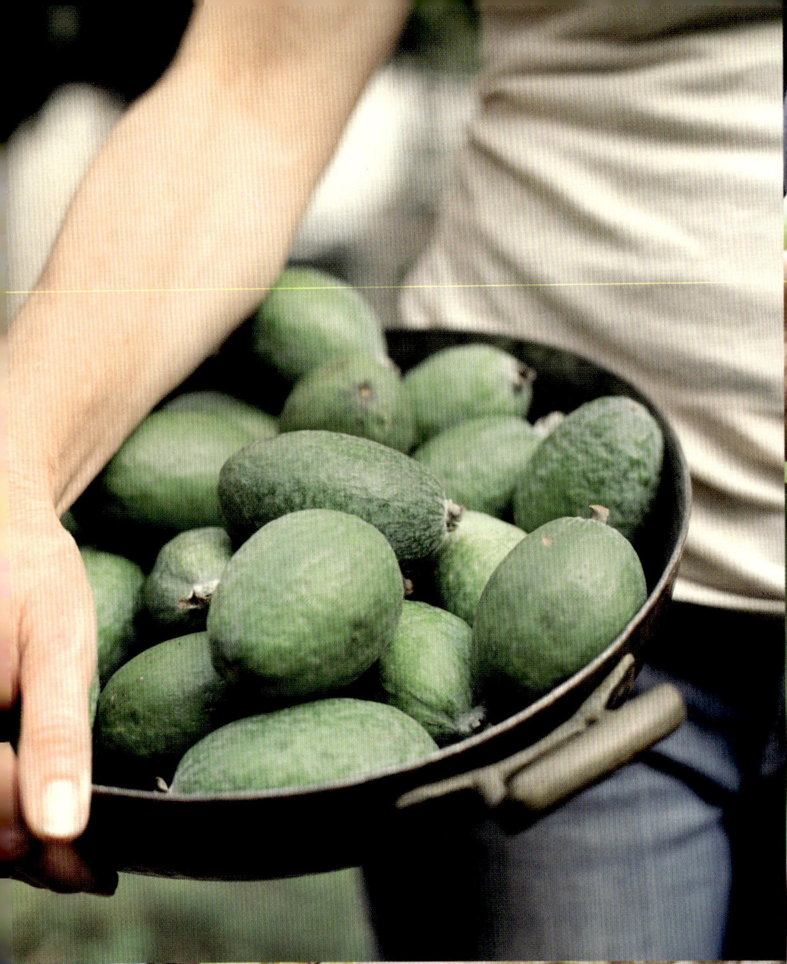
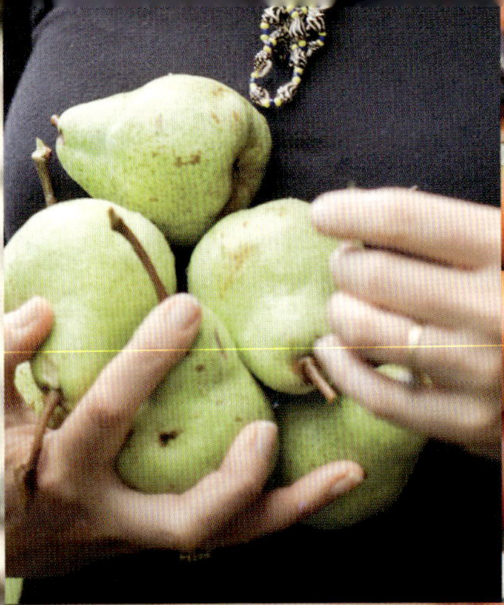
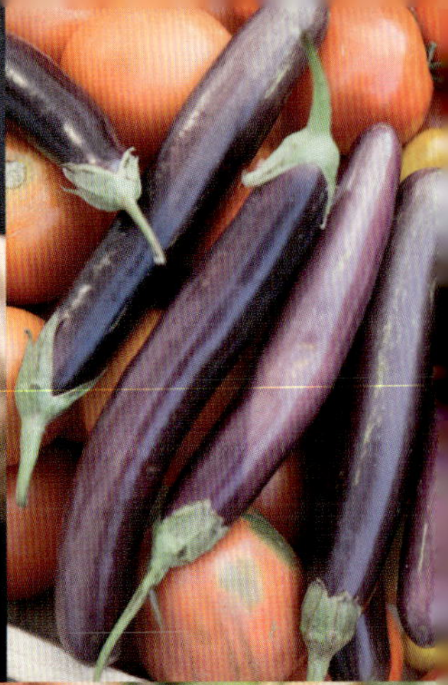
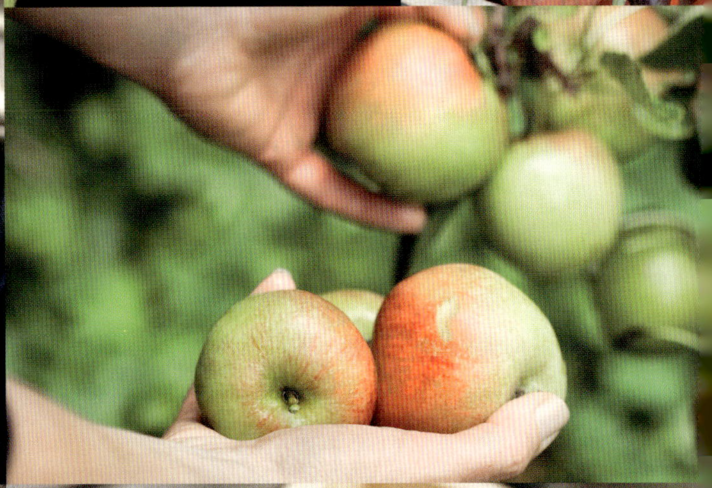
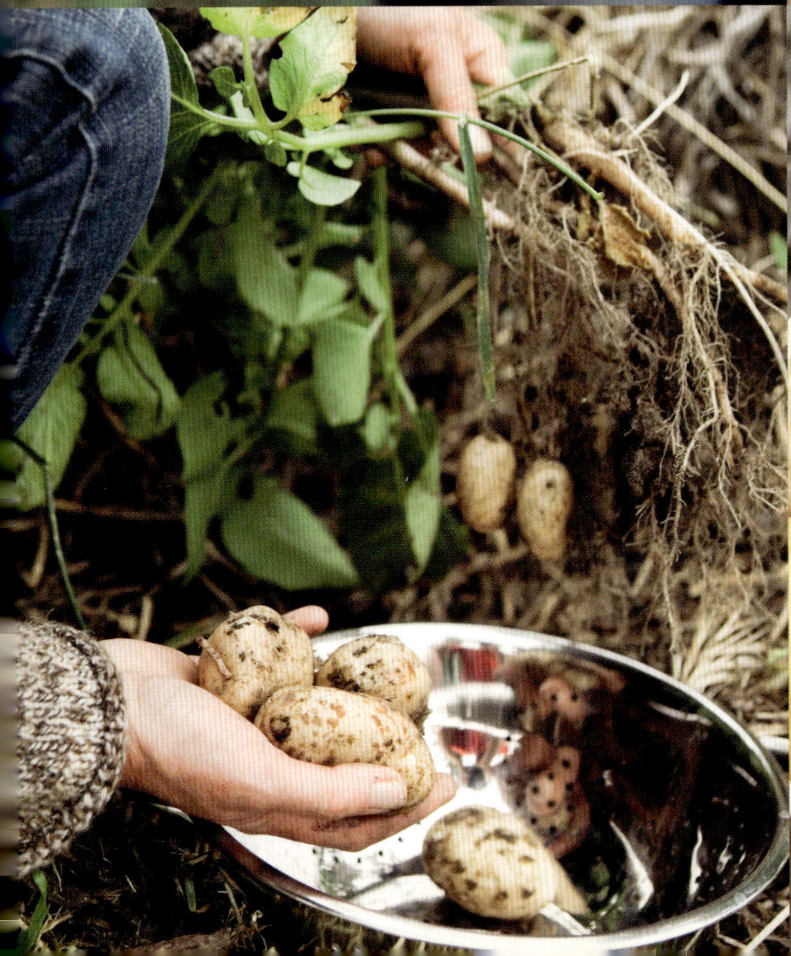
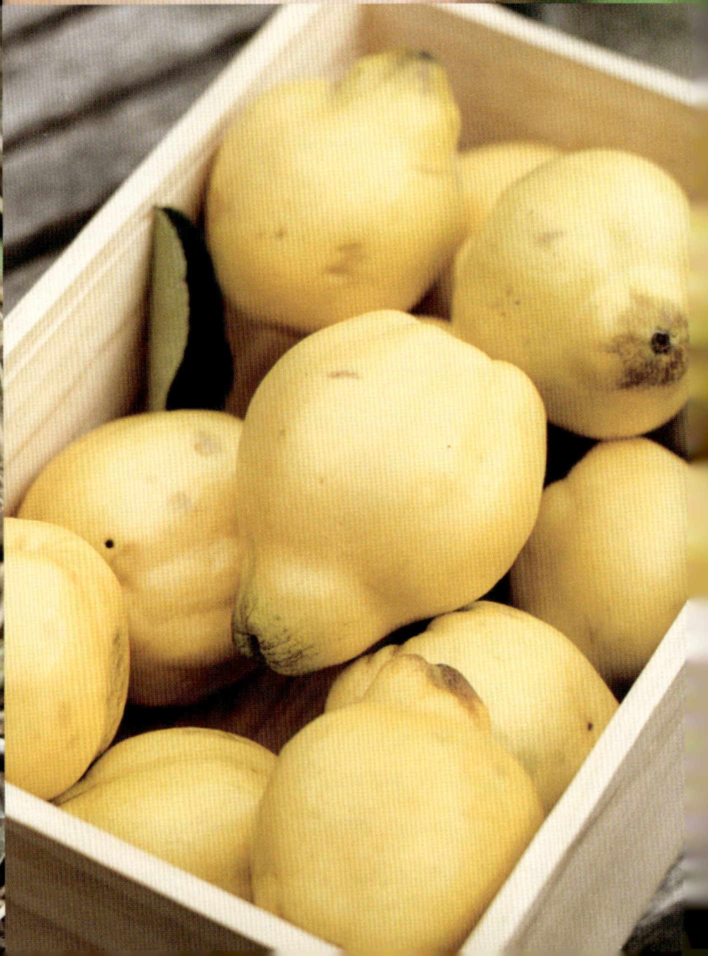

127

'Cooks aren't there just to make dinner. We like to socialise, drink and have a good time, too. None of this stuck-in-some-dark-room-alone slaving. Bring people into your kitchen and let them help.'

The autumn palate

Autumn harvests

- beans
- beetroot
- brassicas
- capsicums
- carrots
- corn
- cress
- cucumbers
- eggplant
- feijoas
- figs
- globe artichokes
- Jerusalem artichokes
- kumara
- melons
- mushrooms
- onions
- passionfruit
- persimmons
- pip fruit
- potatoes
- pumpkins
- quinces
- radishes
- raspberries
- rhubarb
- salad greens
- spinach
- stone fruit
- tomatillos
- tomatoes
- zucchini

As all the annual summer crops race to procreate and set seed for the next season, the year's growing rhythm reaches a crescendo of sun-drenched harvests. It's a race against time for tomatoes, peppers, eggplants and other members of the Solanacae family. Along with the Curcubits – cucumbers, zucchini, pumpkins and marrow – they are destined to collapse at the first whack of frost. As the days start to shorten and the mornings dawn crisp and dewy, I find myself craving richer, deeper flavours. Roasting comes to the fore as my preferred way to cook through the autumn. It's a simple means of intensifying flavours and requires very little effort on the part of the cook. Trays of summer produce emerge as meltingly tender, dense, sweetly caramelised tastes, from slow-roasted tomatoes, caramelised onions and beets, tender eggplants, honey-sweet pumpkin and kumara, through to sticky pears and juicy figs. From here it's simple to springboard off into a vast array of salads, pasta dishes, sauces and soups.

In the cooler evenings we light the first fires, gather in the crops to store away for the winter. It's a time to stock up, put up and celebrate the harvest.

1. Rosemary
   Rosmarinus officinalis
2. Fennel
   Foeniculum vulgare
3. Sage
   Salvia officinalis
4. Parsley
   Petroselinum crispum
5. Thyme
   Thymus
6. Oregano
   Origanum vulgar

OLIVE PASTE

I make this useful blend in bulk and keep it in the fridge. It's great spread on pizza bases, tossed into pastas or spread over fish or chicken before roasting. Blend until smooth 50g pitted olives, 2 anchovies, 2 tsp capers, 1 clove garlic, 1 tbsp chopped flat-leaf parsley, 2 tbsp chopped basil, ⅓ cup olive oil and lemon juice to taste. Store paste covered in the fridge – it keeps for several weeks.

Flavours

- basil
- coriander
- dill
- fennel
- garlic
- lemon grass
- marjoram
- mint
- rosemary
- sage
- shallots
- thyme

1.

2.

3.

4.

5.

6.

'Umami is defined as "savoury deliciousness". This fifth taste, only recently discovered, occurs naturally in fish sauce, beef bouillon, bonito flakes, tomatoes, mushrooms, miso, soy sauce, seaweed and green tea.'

Harvest sauces

Roast capsicum & coriander sauce
Prep 25 minutes
Cook 20 minutes

Roast 4 large red capsicums and 3 chillies on an oven tray at 220°C until skins start to blister and char, about 20 minutes. Place in a plastic bag or sealed container and leave to cool (the steam produced makes them much easier to peel). Peel off skins and discard seeds and pith. Purée chilli and capsicum flesh with 2 cloves garlic, 1 bunch (1 packed cup) coriander, ⅓ cup extra virgin olive oil and ½ tsp each salt and pepper. Sauce will keep in the fridge for 4-5 days or can be frozen in ice-block containers for a dense, rich taste to enjoy throughout the year. Terrific with seafood, chicken, beef or lamb, or mixed through vegetables or couscous.
Makes about 3 cups

Roast tomato sauce
Prep 15 minutes
Cook 1½ hours

Preheat oven to 160°C. Purée together ¼ cup tomato paste, 2 tbsp sugar, 2 tbsp olive oil, 2 cloves garlic, 1 tsp chopped rosemary leaves, ½ tsp smoked paprika, ½ tsp chilli flakes, 1 tsp salt and grinds of black pepper. Mix this evenly though 1.3-1.5kg tomatoes cut into wedges, 2 red capsicums cut into thin strips and 1 large onion cut into thin wedges.
Spread vegetables in a single layer in a very large roasting dish lined with baking paper. Bake for 1½ hours or until starting to caramelise and shrivel.
Serve chunky or purée if you want a smooth, deep red sauce. Store in the fridge for up to a week or freeze.
Use as a sauce for pasta, a base for soup with stock and vegetables, in casseroles and pan sauces.
Makes about 8 cups, pictured right

THE LILY FAMILY
Alliums
This gives us the edible bulbs of onions, garlic, shallots and leeks. Asparagus also falls into this family, although in a different genus (*Asparagus offiicinalis*).
The Alliums all share a certain pungency, with garlic and onions being the most potent and leeks and shallots being the sweetest. Chives and spring onions fall somewhere in between. Given their strong raw tastes, it seems surprising that with long, slow cooking they sweeten to soft, rich flavours. If you slow-cook a whole head of garlic it emerges as a full-flavoured buttery purée (see page 192). Roasted garlic is great to use for aioli and in risottos or stirred into meat sauces for added depth. Leeks and shallots cooked gently in butter render into rich, tender sweetness for soups, sauces, pies and toppings. There's a recipe on page 167 for a red wine sauce for beef using shallots, which break down to thicken the sauce. Brown onions, the biggest and most biting of the *Alliums*, become almost jam-like in their sweetness when cooked long and slow, and give a nutty depth when fried until crisp. See page 53 for a recipe for balsamic red onion confit.

'By stocking my pantry with different ethnic seasonings, I can take the same fresh ingredients and create a new dimension to the dishes I serve simply by changing the flavourings.'

Quick-cook scallops

Stir-fried scallops with capsicums & spinach

Prep   5 minutes
Cook   2-3 minutes

16 large fresh scallops
1 tsp ground cumin
1 tsp ground coriander
finely grated zest of 1 lemon
½ tsp sugar
½ tsp salt and grinds of pepper
1 tbsp olive oil
1 roasted red capsicum, peeled and cut into large dice
50g spinach leaves, washed
1 tbsp lemon juice

Mix scallops with cumin, coriander, lemon zest, sugar, salt and pepper.
Heat oil in a large frypan and when very hot add the scallops, half at a time, frying for 30-40 seconds each side. Remove to a plate as they are cooked.
Add capsicum and wet spinach to pan and cook for a few seconds until spinach is just wilted. Mix through scallops with lemon juice and serve.
Serves 2, pictured below

Spicy scallops in the half shell

Prep   10 minutes
Cook   6 minutes

1 cup roast capsicum and coriander sauce (pg 130)
16 freshest scallops
4 tsp butter

Divide sauce between 4 scallop shells or small ramekins and place 4 scallops in each one. Dot with butter. Preheat oven to 250°C and cook scallops until juices start to bubble, about 6 minutes.
Serves 4

Variation: Prepare scallops using other sauces of your preference, eg roast tomato sauce (page 130).

HANDLING FRESH SCALLOPS AND OTHER SHELLFISH
Freshness is the most important factor when it comes to seafood, along with accessing it from a safe, clean water source. (These species are filter feeders so are particularly vulnerable to any kind of pollution.)
The fastest way to ruin a tender, sweet scallop – or any other shellfish – is to overcook it. If you give it a minute or two too long, that tender succulence will be rendered bullet-proof tough.
Start with a very hot heat source, be it pan, grill or oven. Do not overcrowd shellfish in the cooking container as if they start to sweat and lose liquid they will toughen.
Test for doneness by touch. Press with your finger – they should still feel squidgy. If they bounce back like a rubber ball you have overdone it.

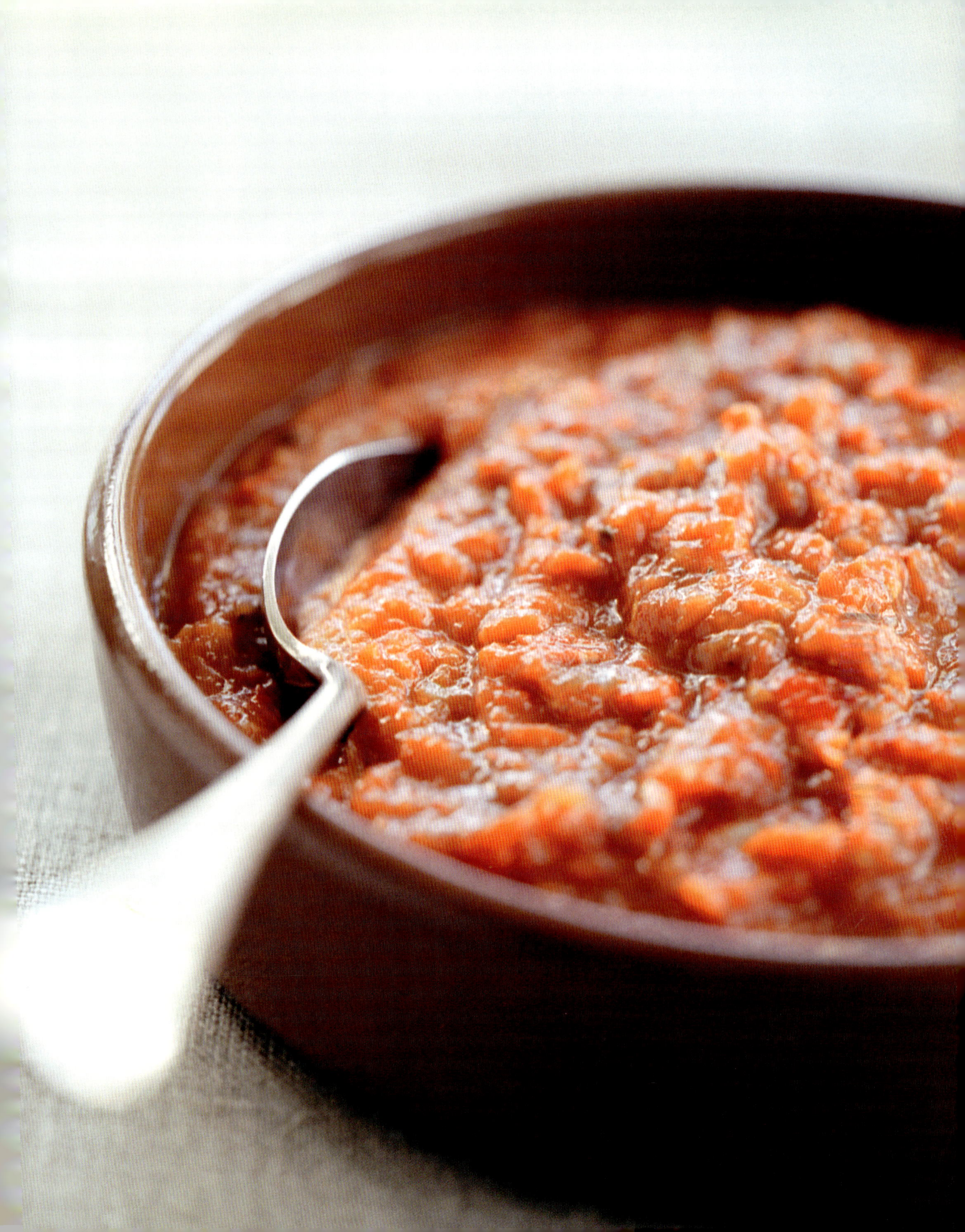

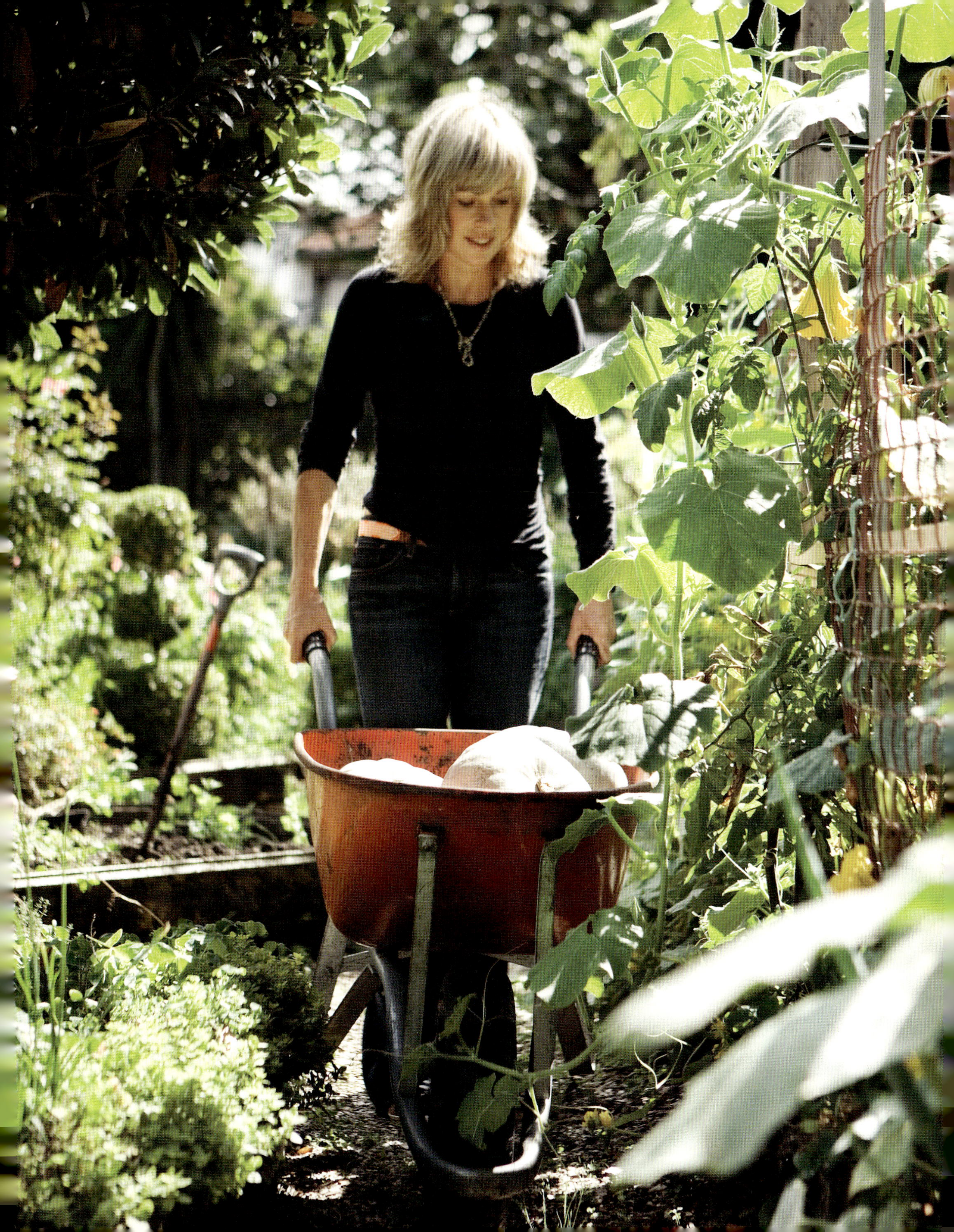

'In the Western world we each use an average of 300 plastic bags a year. Every single person. Plastic bags can take up to 500 years to break down in a landfill. Get yourself a big, durable bag to use when you shop.'

Kumara snacks

Cumin grilled kumara slices

Prep 10 minutes
Cook 8-10 minutes

700g kumara or other sweet potatoes, preferably organic
2 tbsp oil
salt and grinds of pepper
2 tsp cumin seeds
1 tsp curry powder
1 tsp brown sugar

Scrub kumara under running water and cut into 1.5cm-thick slices. Toss with oil to coat. Season with salt and pepper. Mix cumin seeds, curry powder and sugar together and sprinkle evenly over slices.
Grill slices over medium heat until tender and golden, about 4 minutes each side, or roast on an oven tray at 220°C for about 15 minutes. Serve with roast capsicum and coriander sauce (page 130).
Serves 4-6

Spicy kumara & prawn fritters

Prep 10 minutes
Cook 15 minutes

¼ cup self-raising flour
¼ cup rice flour (or use all self-raising)
½ tsp baking soda
½ tsp curry powder
½ tsp salt and grinds of pepper
1 egg white
⅔ cup coconut cream
1 packed cup grated raw kumara (90g)
150g raw prawn meat, chopped
2 tbsp chopped coriander
1 spring onion, finely sliced
2 tbsp Thai sweet chilli sauce
1 tsp fish sauce

2-3 tbsp neutral oil (eg grapeseed) for frying

We usually start our evenings kitchen-side with a tasty snack or nibble before heading to the table. Little fritters like these prepare the tastebuds for dinner. With any batter mixture it's a good idea to cook just one fritter, taste and adjust the seasonings as needed before cooking the rest.
   Place flours, baking soda, curry powder, salt and pepper, egg white and coconut cream in a mixing bowl and beat to a smooth batter. Mix in all other ingredients. Chill until ready to cook.
Heat a little oil on a barbecue hotplate or in a heavy pan (use enough to just cover the base of the pan). Cook spoonfuls of the mixture over medium heat, about 3 minutes each side or until cooked through and springy to the touch. Add more oil to the pan as needed between batches, ensuring it heats fully before cooking the next fritter. Cooked fritters can be reheated in a hot oven. Accompany with sweet chilli sauce.
Makes about 20 medium or 30 small fritters

FRITTER COOKING TIPS
Cooking fritters can be time consuming, especially if you make a big batch for a party (any fritter recipe can easily be doubled). To speed things up I brown the fritters quickly on each side in a frypan then finish cooking them in the oven. Spread the fritters out on a baking tray and bake for 5-6 minutes at 200°C or until springy to the touch.

KUMARA AND OTHER SWEET POTATOES
Ipomoea batatas
The tubers of this warm-weather perennial are harvested during autumn and will store over winter. Throw out any that are mouldy as the mould is very toxic. Like potatoes, the tubers start to sprout late in winter. The strong, thin sprouts are broken off where they attach to the sweet potato and then rooted in water for planting out in early spring once all danger of frost has passed. Traditionally the seedlings are placed in a shallow ditch with the root facing south and the tip facing north. The plants sprawl out over the bed and their spade-shaped leaves can be eaten like spinach. Boil or roast the tubers.

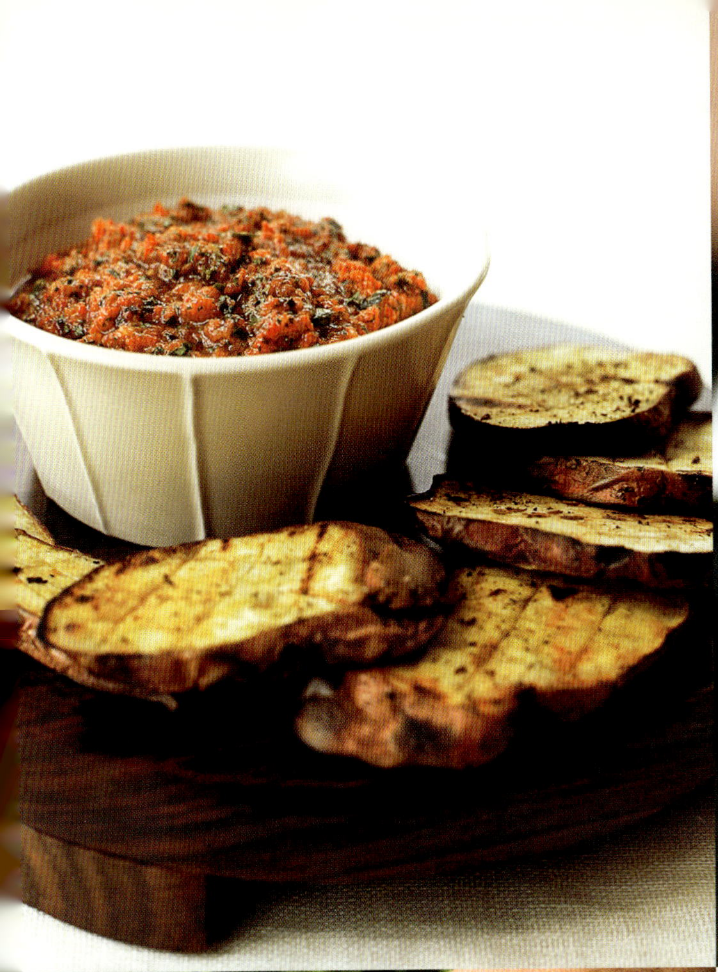
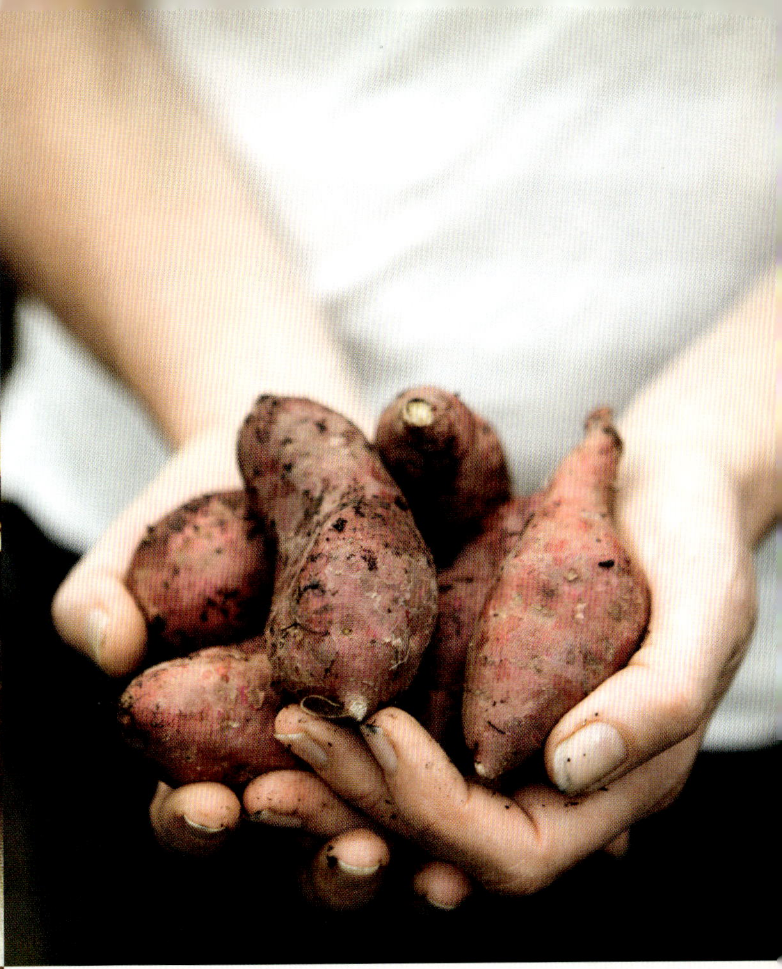
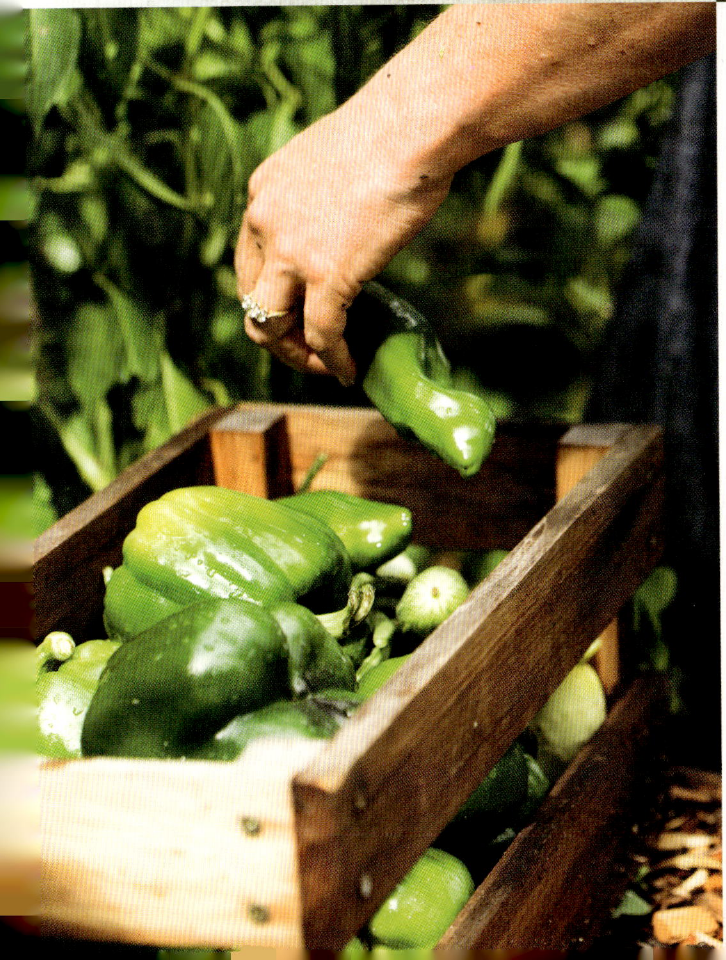
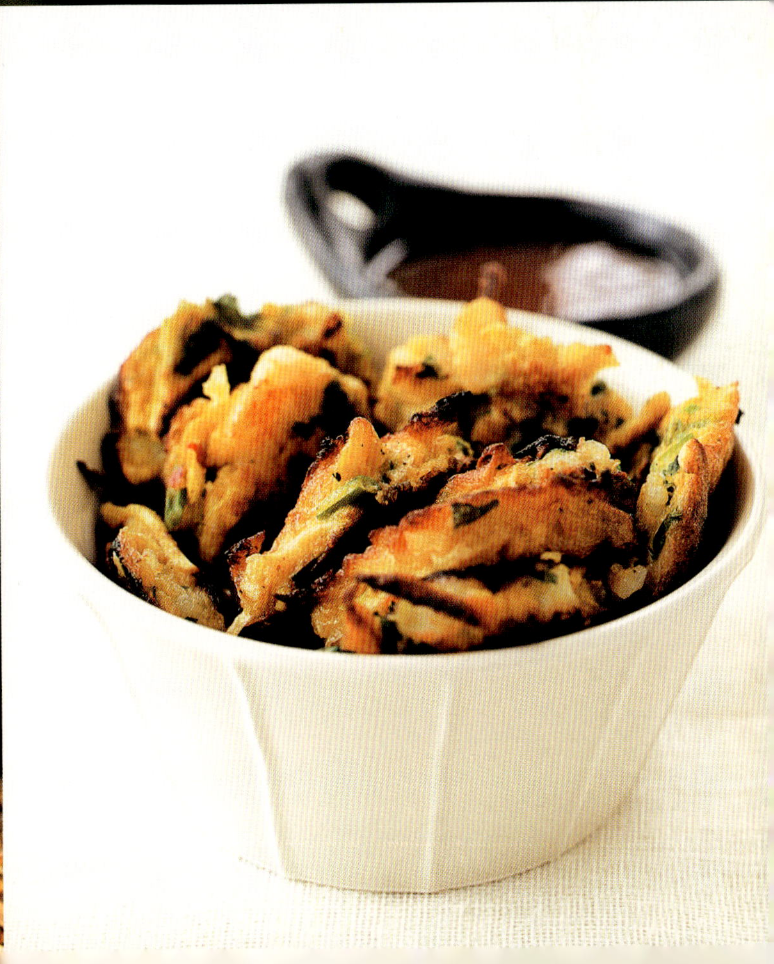

'From the ages of about five through to 14, kids are often vegetable-phobic. I found the easiest way to get veges into mine was in disguise – grating carrots and pumpkin into meatballs and pasta sauce or cakes.'

Sweeten flavours by roasting

Sweet & sour beets and onions
Prep 10 minutes
Cook 60 minutes

Preheat oven to 180°C. Peel 2 beetroot and 2 red onions and slice into 1cm wedges. Place in a large roasting dish lined with baking paper. Drizzle over 3 tablespoons each extra virgin olive oil, red wine vinegar and maple syrup or honey and ¼ cup water. Season with 1 teaspoon salt and a generous grinding of pepper. Toss to coat and spread out in a single layer. Roast until all liquids have evaporated and vegetables are tender and just starting to caramelise, about 60 minutes. Cool in pan.
Serves 4 as a side dish

Roasted eggplant slices
Prep 10 minutes
Cook 25 minutes

Preheat oven to 220°C. Slice eggplant into 2cm-thick rounds and brush both sides with olive oil. Place slices on a baking tray lined with baking paper. If desired, cover top surface with a flavoursome spread, eg sun-dried tomato pesto or harissa. Bake eggplant until tender and lightly golden, about 25 minutes. Allow to cool on the tray. Slices will keep at room temperature for several hours or can be covered and chilled for 4-5 days.
Serves 4 as a side dish

Roasted red capsicums
Prep 10 minutes
Cook 20 minutes

When capsicums are in peak supply, roast them in bulk and store in the fridge or freezer. I usually allow half to one capsicum per serve for pasta dishes or salads.

Preheat oven to 220°C. Wash red capsicums and place on an oven tray. Roast until blistered and starting to char, about 20 minutes. Cool in a sealed container or plastic bag then peel off skins and remove seeds and pith. Reserve juices as they have lots of flavour. Store in the fridge (they will keep about a week) or freeze.

ROASTED BEETROOT
The sweetness of roasted beetroot is delicious with roast meats. Scrub baby beets or peel if large and cut in wedges. Rub with a little oil and season with salt and pepper. Drizzle over a spoonful of maple syrup or honey and roast at 200°C until tender, about 30-40 minutes.

ROASTED STARCHY VEGETABLES
Peel a mixture of dense, starchy vegetables such as potatoes, parsnips, yams, pumpkin and kumara, allowing about 200g per person. Place in a large roasting dish. Mix through 2-3 tbsp olive oil and season with a little salt and sprigs of rosemary. Spread out in dish to a single layer. Roast at 200°C until crisp and golden, about 50 minutes.

HANDLING ROASTED VEGETABLES
Roasted vegetables will hold at room temperature for several hours or can be covered and chilled for up to 3 days. Bring to room temperature before serving. For a great salad to serve with roast chicken or grilled meats, toss a couple of handfuls of rocket through the cooled roasted vegetables in the dish and add some roasted almonds and a little crumbled feta.

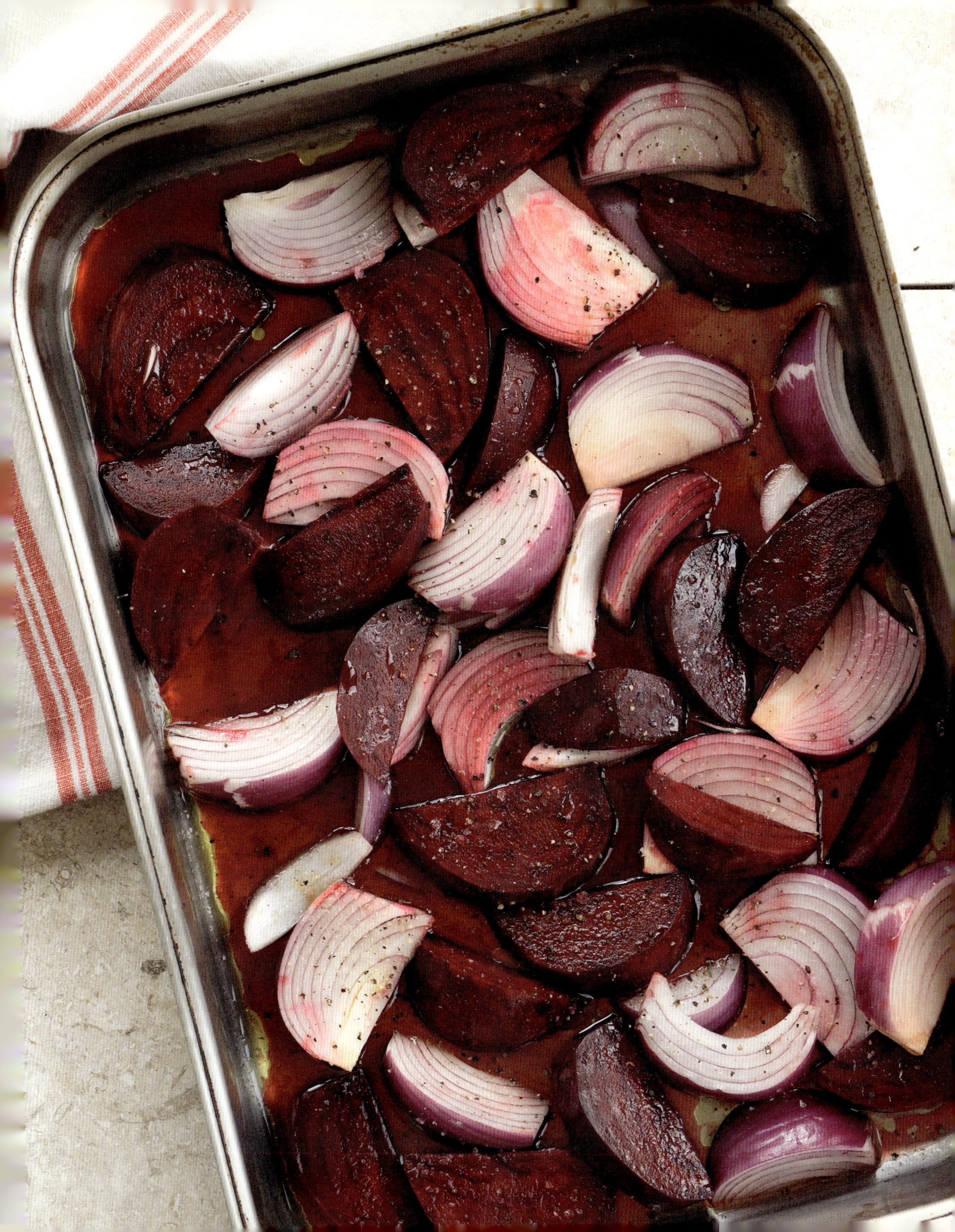

'The trilogy of the '70s alternative cooking scene – lentils, bean sprouts and brown rice – got bad rap for being bland. Using Indian and Moroccan spices gives them the attention they deserve.'

Lentil power

Spicy lentils

Prep 15 minutes
Cook 20-30 minutes

2 tbsp olive oil
1 large onion, finely diced
2 cloves garlic, crushed
1 tsp ground cumin
½ tsp ground turmeric
¼ tsp smoked paprika
5 cups water
1 cup puy lentils
1 tsp salt and grinds of pepper
1 tbsp rice vinegar or white wine vinegar

Serve these tasty lentils hot with roast chicken, pork or duck, or at room temperature as the base for a range of salads.

Heat oil in a medium pot and gently cook onion until clear, 6 minutes. Add garlic and spices, stir and allow to sizzle for a minute. Add water and lentils and cook uncovered on a low simmer until lentils are just tender and water has fully evaporated, about 20-30 minutes. If mixture dries out before lentils are tender, add more water. Season with salt and pepper and gently stir in vinegar. Allow to cool to room temperature, about 20-30 minutes, before serving.

Lentils will keep for several days in the fridge or can be frozen.
Serves 4 (makes 2¼ cups cooked lentils)

Vegan lentil salad

Prep 10 minutes

Cooked lentils combined with roasted beets and onions and garnished with hummus make a great vegan salad.

Divide 4 handfuls of mixed salad leaves between 4 serving plates. Spoon over half a recipe of spicy lentils and top with 1 recipe sweet and sour beets and onions. Garnish with a dollop of hummus, drizzle with a little extra virgin olive oil and if desired scatter each salad with a spoonful of dukkah (page 151).
Serves 4, pictured top right

Lentil & feta salad

Prep 10 minutes

Prepare lentil salad above without hummus or dukkah and divide between 4 plates. Crumble over 100g feta and top with 2 tbsp chopped tamari-roasted almonds (see right) and 4 tbsp coriander pesto.
Serves 4

HOME-COOKED CONVENIENCE

Lentils, dried beans and chickpeas rank up there as "power foods". They are very good sources of cholesterol-lowering fibre and contain magnesium and folate. They're also considered especially useful for keeping prostates healthy. Lentils can be cooked without prior soaking, which makes them very handy in our time-hungry lives. When cooking beans, chickpeas or rice, for that matter, make more than you'll need and freeze the extra for easy use another time. Drain cooked beans, etc, really well and freeze on a tray. When fully frozen, free-flow into airtight bags.

TAMARI-ROASTED ALMONDS

I buy tamari-roasted almonds at my local wholefoods shop but you can also make them very easily. This method also works well with sunflower seeds. Place 2 cups or 300g raw whole almonds on a baking tray. Pour over 1 tbsp tamari or Japanese soy sauce and 2 tbsp neutral oil and mix through evenly. Spread almonds evenly in dish and roast at 180°C until fragrant and crisp, about 15 minutes. Cool before storing in a sealed jar; they will keep for several weeks.
Makes 2 cups

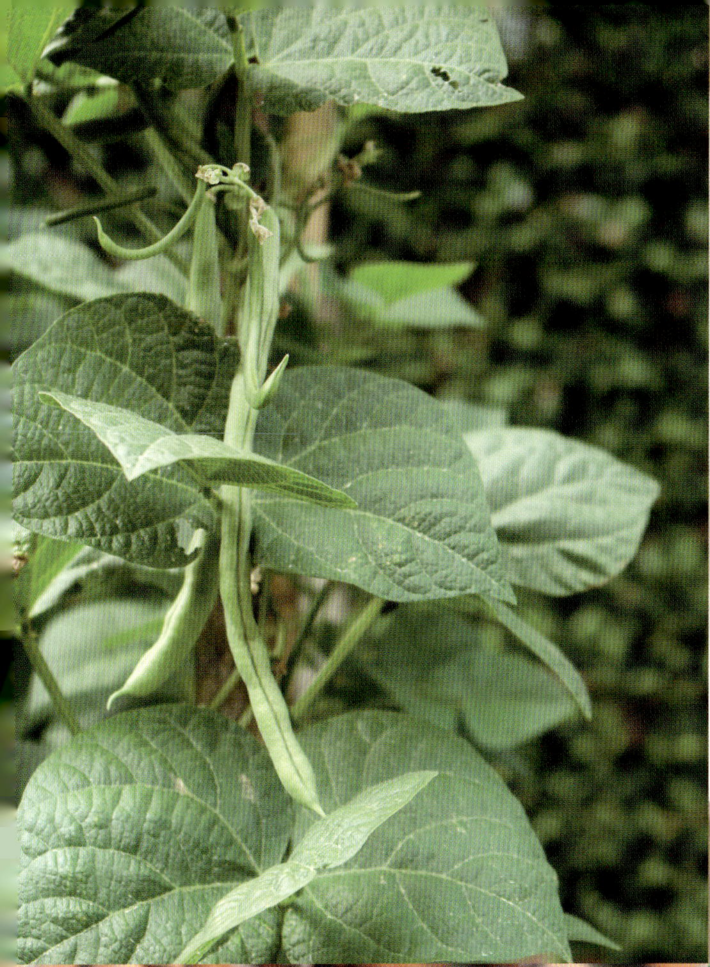
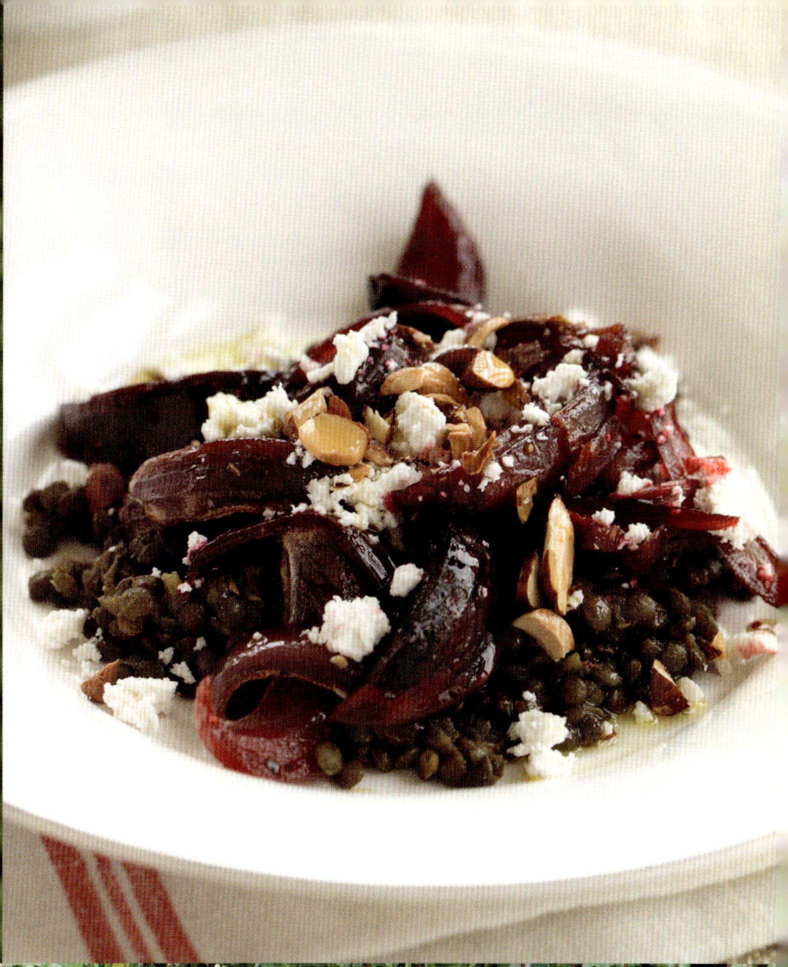
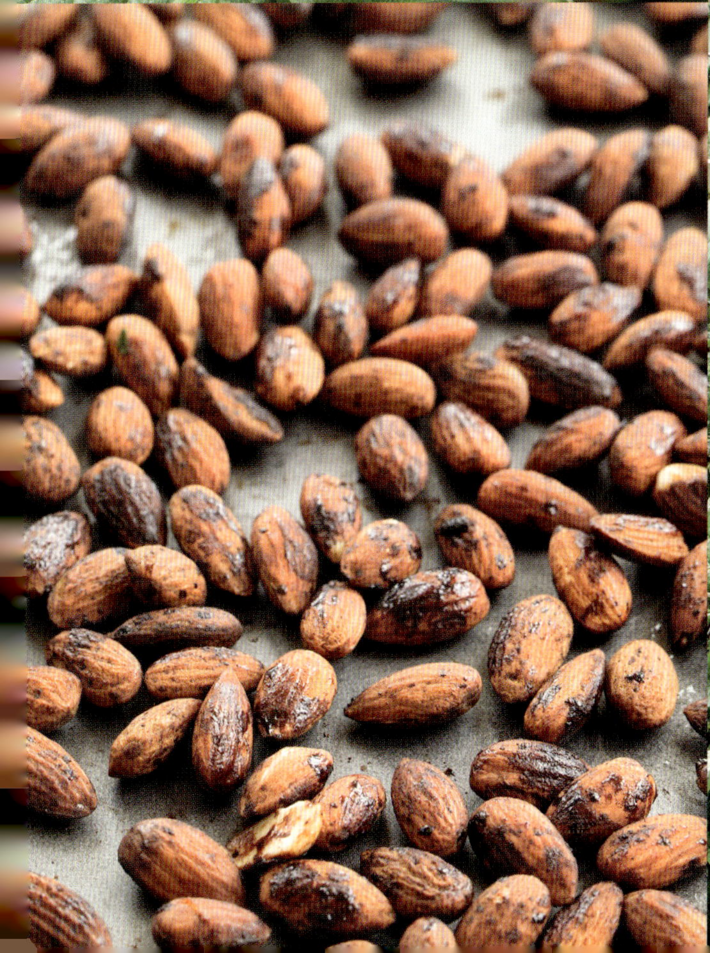
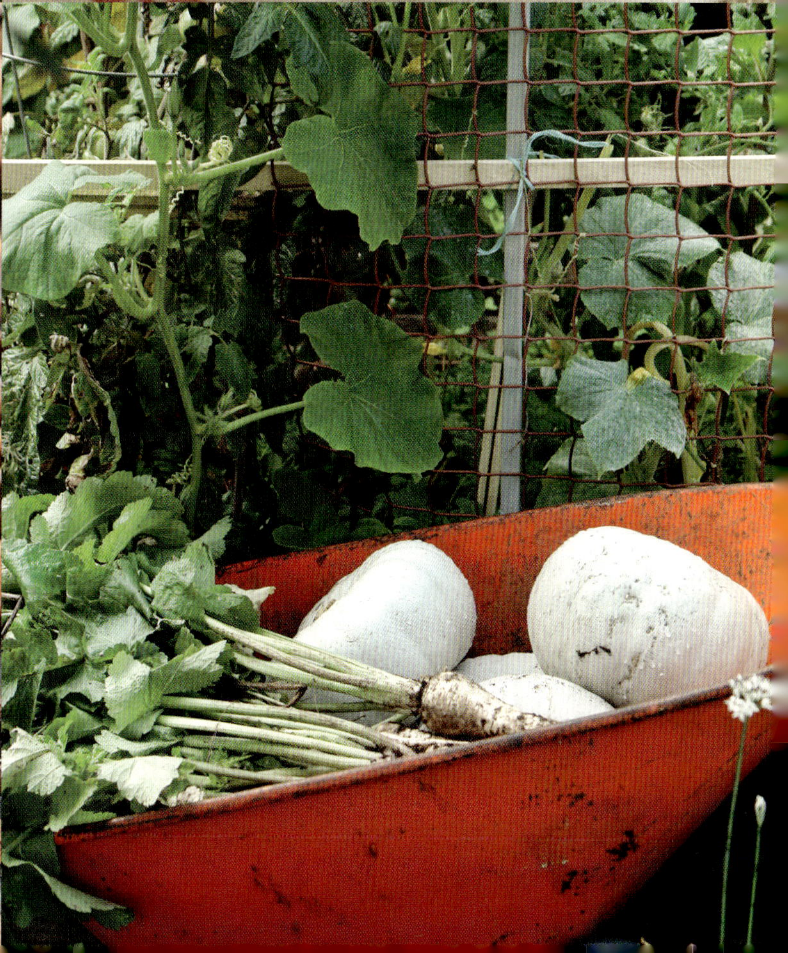

'Make a fruity vinegar with the last flush of berries. Just throw a handful of raspberries into a bottle of white wine vinegar and leave for a few weeks. It turns a pretty pink and has a soft, fruity taste.'

Savoury roasted pears

Roasted pear & walnut salad

Prep 15 minutes
Cook 25 minutes

2 just-ripe pears
1 tbsp extra virgin olive oil
1 tsp rice vinegar
1 tsp sugar
salt and grinds of pepper
½ cup fresh walnut pieces
6 handfuls (160g) baby spinach leaves
2 avocados, cut into chunks
1 recipe raspberry balsamic dressing (page 26)
50g parmesan, shaved with a potato peeler

Partner this delicious autumnal salad with a roast chicken or grilled meats or bulk it out with smoked chicken or soft goat's cheese.

Preheat oven to 200°C. Halve and core pears and slice each half into 6-8 wedges. Place oil, vinegar, sugar, salt and pepper in a bowl. Add pears and toss to coat. Spread out in a single layer in a baking dish lined with baking paper.
Roast for 20 minutes then add walnuts and cook another 10 minutes until pears are lightly caramelised and nuts lightly toasted. Cool.
Place pears and walnuts in a large mixing bowl with spinach, avocados and dressing and gently toss to combine. Pile on to a serving platter and garnish with parmesan.
Serves 4

Variations: For a main course autumn salad, great for a simple light lunch or supper, add the sliced flesh of 2 chicken breasts to the salad above.
If you like blue cheese, prepare the roasted pear salad as above using watercress in place of spinach. In place of parmesan, crumble over 120-150g creamy blue cheese and garnish with a few muscatels or dried cranberries.

SOME SALAD GREENS
Selecting salad greens from different plant families melds sweet, spicy, peppery and bitter tastes for enjoyment.

MIZUNA
Small, green, cut leaf with mustardy flavour, popular in Japan. Self sows easily.

ROCKET, ARUGULA
I grow both the bushy, tooth-edged, yellow-flowered wild rocket and the milder and larger-leafed white-flowered annual. Grows well over autumn, winter and spring.

RADICCHIO
Sometimes known as Italian chicory. Deep red leaves and quite a bitter taste that mellows when grilled or roasted. Adds colour, texture and a little bite to salads. Also available as a pale green open-leaf curly endive, which is pretty in salads.

CORN SALAD, LAMB'S LETTUCE, MÂCHE
Small, sweet, succulent leaves that can be grown through autumn, winter and early spring.

MINER'S LETTUCE, WINTER PURSLANE
Mild, slightly sweet spade-shaped leaves with succulent texture. Tolerates frosts.

For information on preparing a tossed salad see page 26.

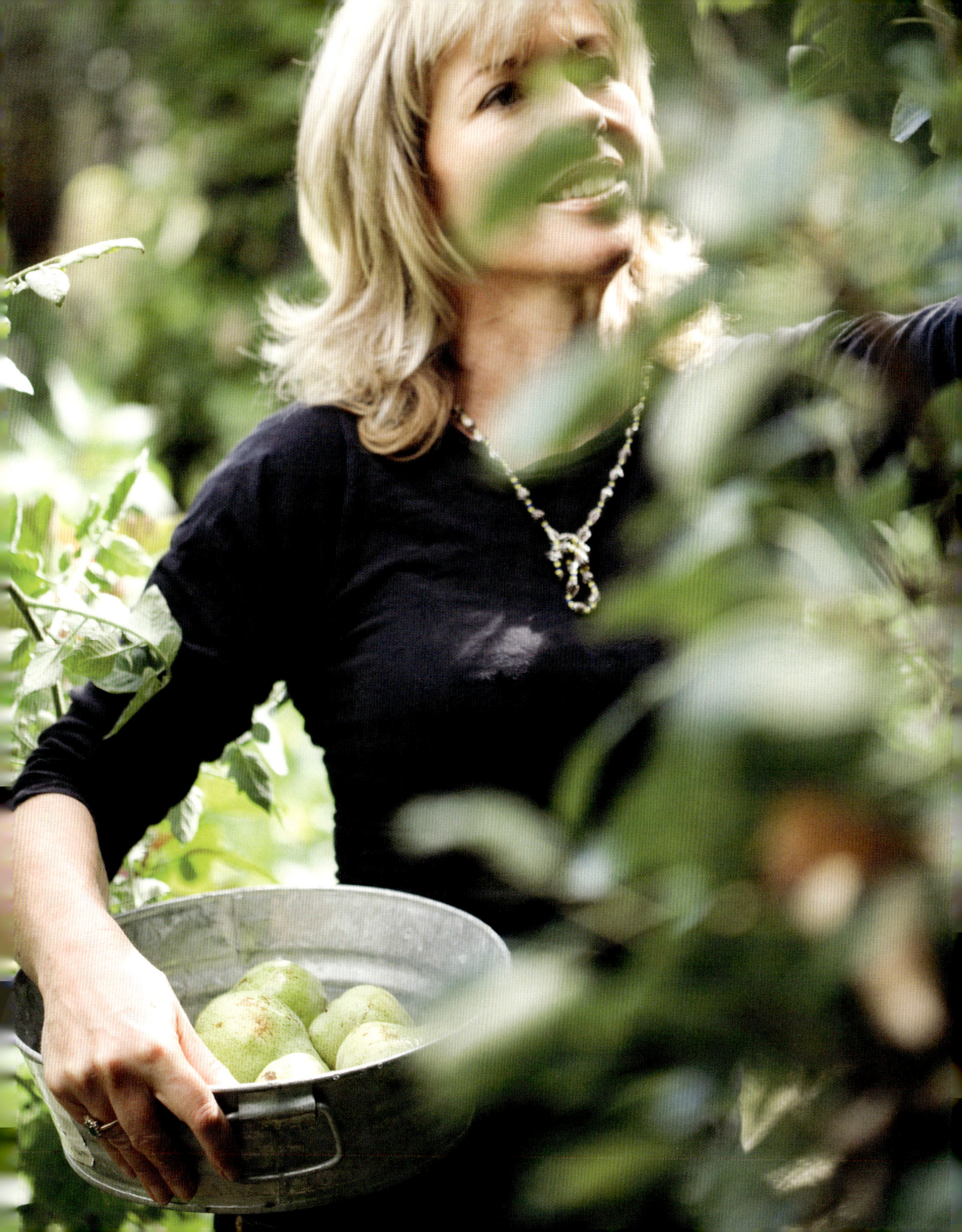

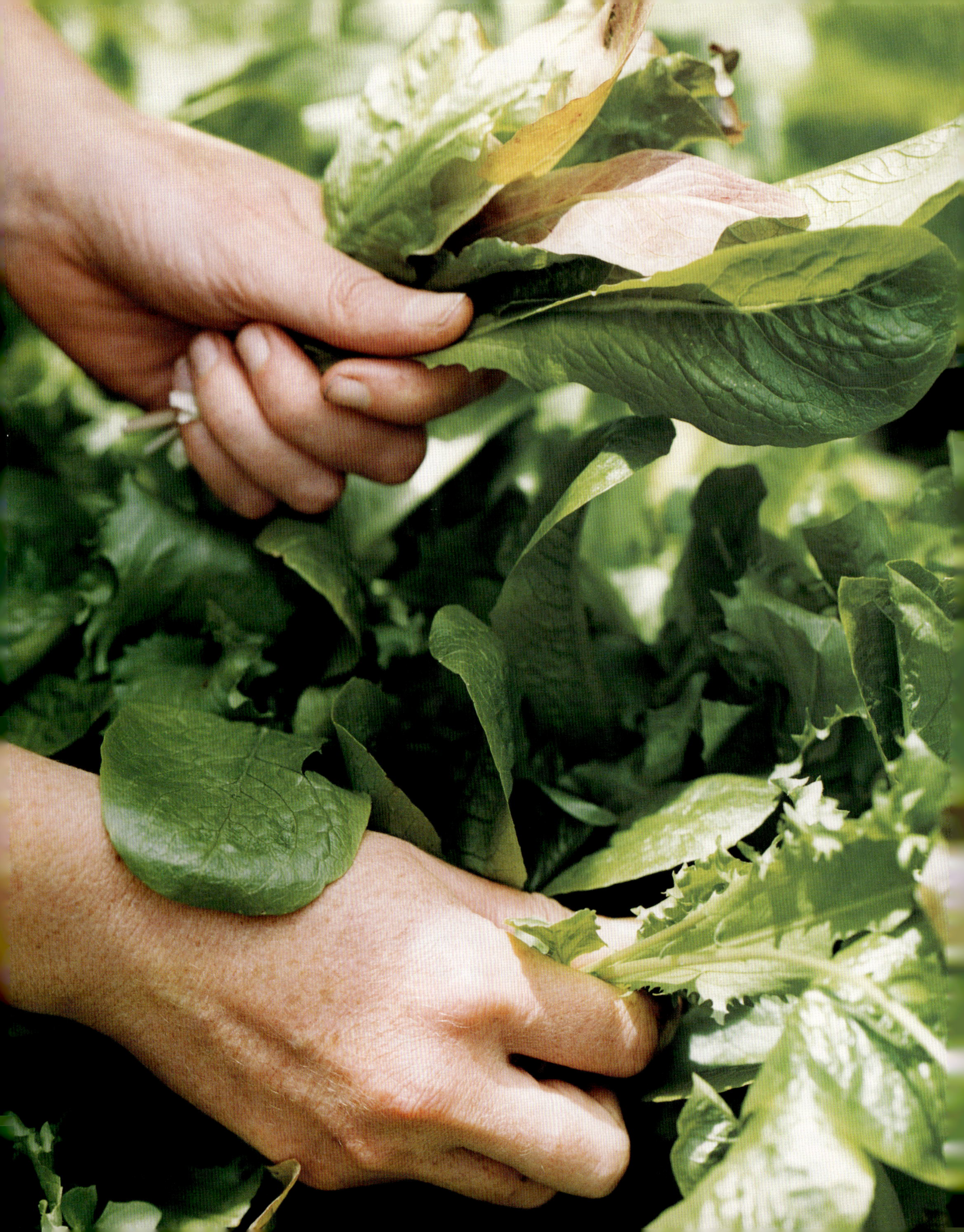

'Setting out stuffed socks in a just-picked cornfield before dusk might sound like an odd thing to do but it's a great way to attract squab when you're shooting. A brace of squab is such a treat, as is wild duck.'

Warm duck salad

Balsamic-glazed duck salad

Prep 15 minutes
Cook 2 hours

12 dried or fresh figs
½ cup freshly squeezed orange juice
6 large duck legs
salt and grinds of pepper
3 red onions, each cut into 8-10 wedges
1 tbsp extra virgin olive oil
1 tbsp honey
1 recipe balsamic glaze (recipe follows) or commercial balsamic crema
½ cup chicken stock

To serve: 150g watercress or rocket, 2 oranges, peeled and segmented

Preheat oven to 220°C. Place figs and orange juice in a pot and simmer for 2 minutes.
Prick duck legs all over with a sharp fork and season with salt and pepper. Place in a large, shallow roasting dish and roast until most of the fat has been rendered out and the skin is golden, about 45 minutes. Transfer legs to a platter and discard fat from the dish.
Reduce oven temperature to 190°C. Arrange figs and onion wedges in the roasting dish. Drizzle over the fig cooking liquid, olive oil, honey and 1 tablespoon of the balsamic glaze. Season with salt and pepper.
Arrange duck legs on the onions and figs, pour chicken stock around and bake until duck is very tender, 1-1¼ hours. Remove from oven and stand for 20-30 minutes before serving.
Divide watercress and oranges between 4 serving plates. Place duck legs, onions and figs on top.
Pour the pan juices over and drizzle with a little balsamic glaze.
Serves 4

*Sitting in a mai mai on the opening day of the shooting season in the first weekend of May, waiting for the mallards to fly in, is a tradition of rural Kiwi life. It's always fiendishly cold, and in the pre-dawn haze when the frost is deciding whether or not to settle, you really do wonder why you are there. Beginners' luck often plays a part in the fishing and hunting stakes and my first double-barrel landed two plump birds.
By the end of the day, with a bag in hand, I was hooked. However, like my first attempt at fly-fishing (when I caught more trout than I knew what to do with), I've never managed to replicate the score card.*

Balsamic glaze

Prep 5 minutes
Cook 10-15 minutes

1 cup balsamic vinegar
½ cup apple juice

Combine balsamic vinegar and apple juice in a small saucepan and bring to the boil. Simmer until thickened and reduced to ⅓ cup, about 10-15 minutes. Pour into a bottle and cool to room temperature. Glaze will keep for weeks. Reheat gently to bring to a spoonable consistency.
Makes ⅓ cup
For more information on balsamic vinegar and balsamic glaze or crema see page 104.

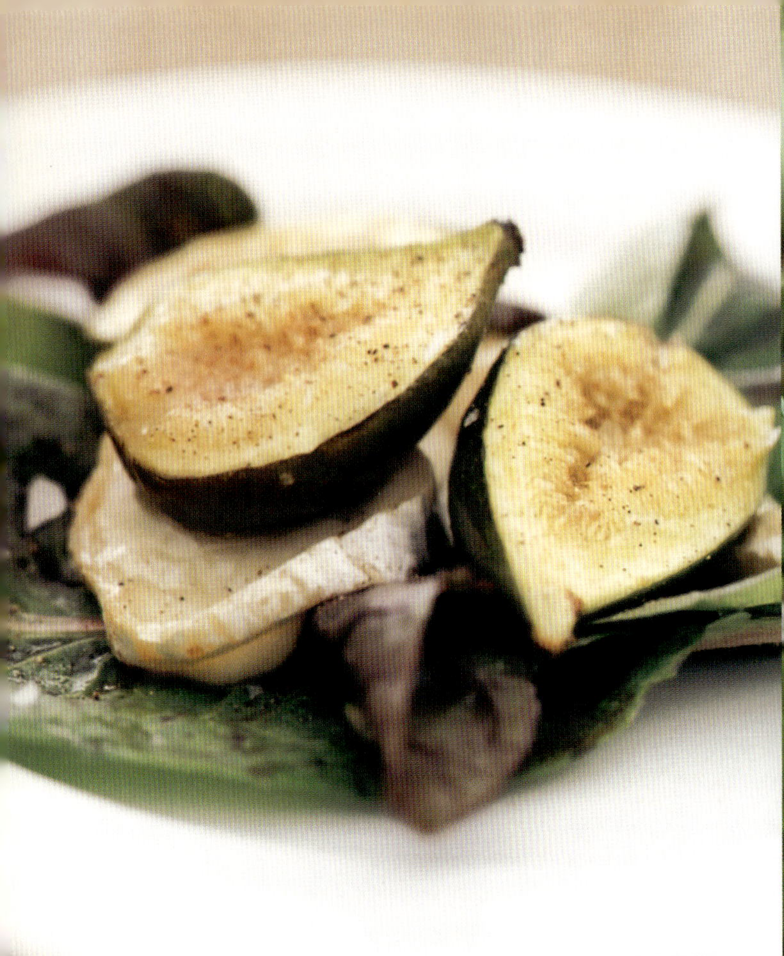
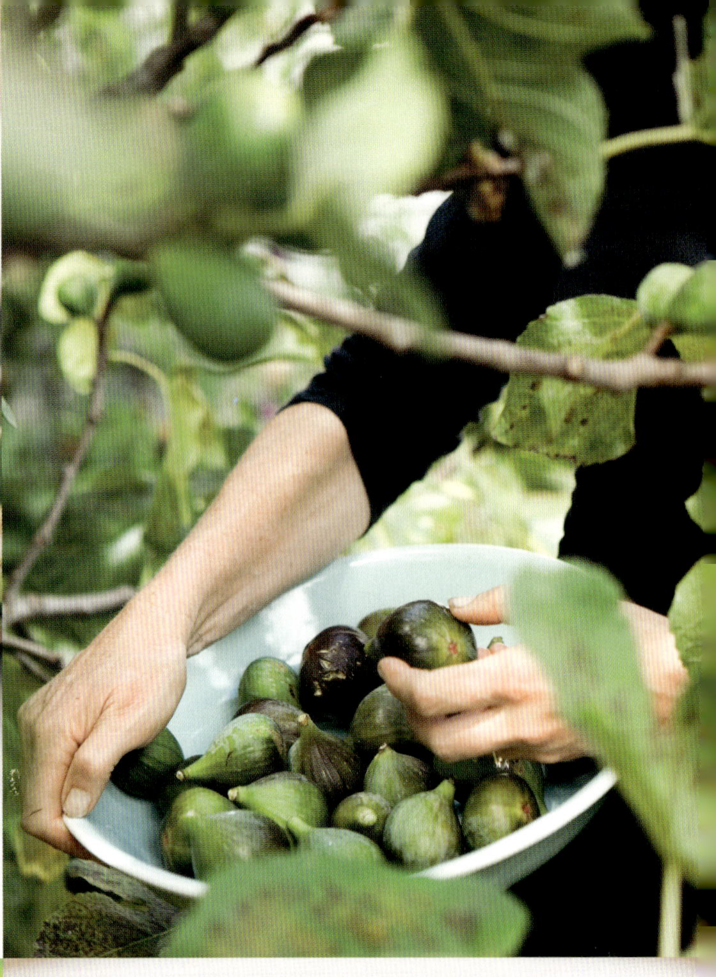
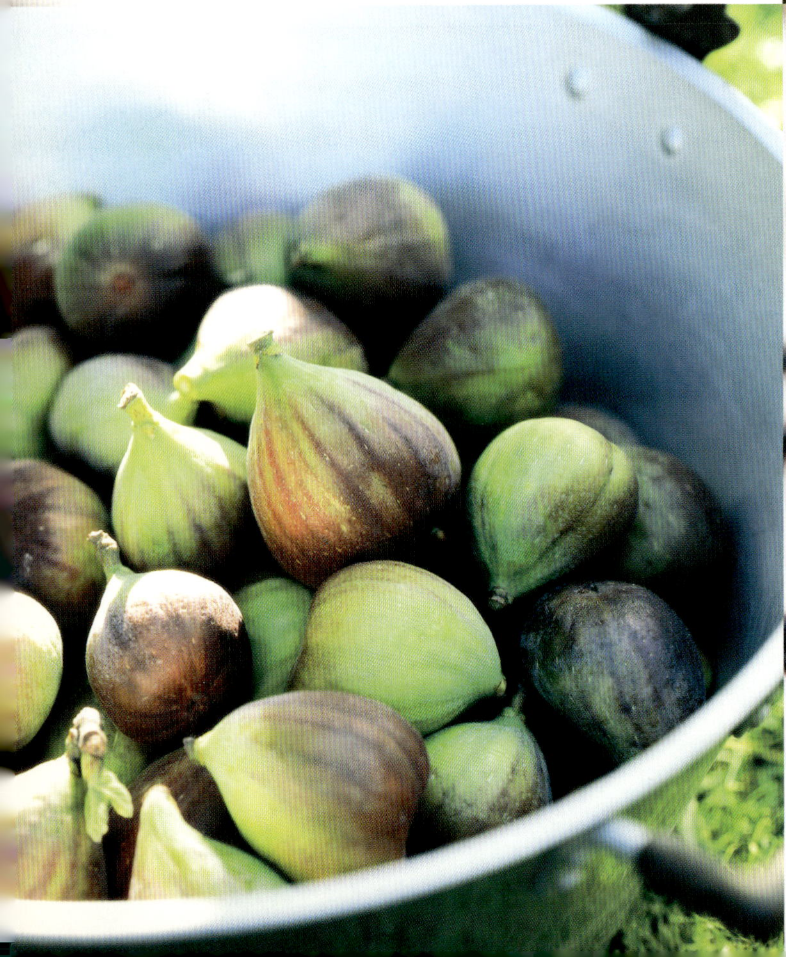
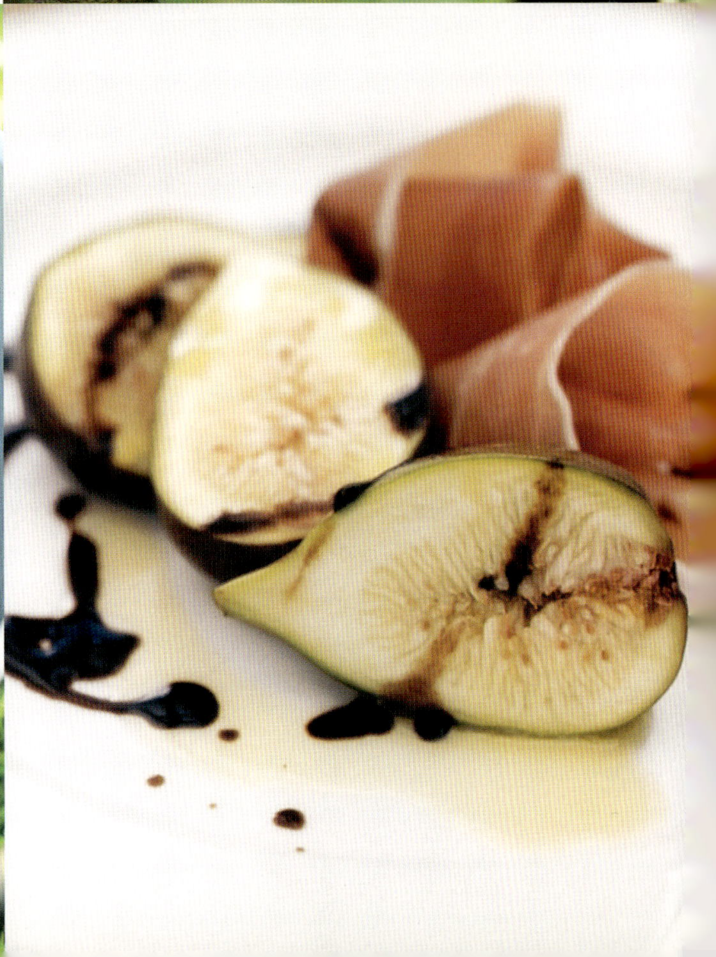

'My enduring memory of Ibiza is a summer spent high in its wild hills eating figs – blissfully fat, scarlet-centred figs – and daily pilgrimages to the lone fig tree near our little cottage with rug and book.'

Fig harvests

Grilled goat's cheese & fig salad

Prep   10 minutes
Cook 6-8 minutes

6 figs, halved
liquid honey or maple syrup
240g St Maure or other soft goat's cheese or camembert log
4 handfuls salad leaves
4 tbsp honey mustard dressing (page 84)

Place figs on a baking tray and brush with a little honey or maple syrup. Cut cheese log into thin slices (about 12). Arrange slices on baking tray with figs, allowing a little space between them.
Grill about 12-15cm from heat source until cheese is bubbling and figs are starting to caramelise, about 6-8 minutes.
Toss salad leaves with dressing and divide between 4 plates. Top with grilled cheese and figs.
Serves 4

Fresh figs and prosciutto

Prep   5 minutes

8 fresh sweet figs
8 slices prosciutto, halved
Optional: 4 tbsp balsamic glaze (page 143)

Make a simple starter salad with fresh figs and prosciutto.
Halve figs and place them on a small plate with very thin slices of prosciutto or parma ham. Drizzle with a little balsamic glaze and serve.
Serves 4

Figs with port glaze

Prep   10 minutes

12 ripe juicy figs
1 recipe port glaze (page 173), warmed
Optional garnish: 1 cup fresh raspberries

Divide figs between 4 plates and cut a cross in the top of each one so it opens out like a flower. Drizzle with warm port glaze. Garnish with fresh raspberries if desired.
Serves 4

When you first start gardening you don't always give thought to specifics. You think, "I want a fig tree", not "I want a late-season Adriatic fig with deep scarlet, juicy centres" or "a sweet, early-season black fig with a succulent, creamy-pink heart". You go to the garden shop and buy a fig tree with a label that says "reliable producer". And so I have a brown turkey fig, bland and dull, but okay to bottle. And now the tree is so big and so prolific that duty and greed mean it will never be removed.
The tree sits right outside my office window and as I write a million birds are gloatingly devouring the figs, blatantly ignoring my window bashing and yelling. I leap into the garden to shoo them away. They flop off lazily, returning almost the moment I am back at my desk. And so the battle continues until the tree is all but bare.
With the figs I do manage to harvest I always set some aside to bottle. Pulled from the store cupboard in the depths of winter, these figs deliver a succulent, sun-filled taste and make a handy dessert served with mascarpone or Greek yoghurt. I have included a recipe for preserved figs on page 174.

'If you are picking wild watercress, be sure it's not from a source near sheep or cattle as it could be infected with liver fluke. This parasite is carried by snails living in the water the farm fields drain into.'

Seasonal vege soups

You don't really need a recipe to make a good soup. Depending on the weather (the colder it is the heartier the brew should be) and your flavour preferences, you can improvise to your heart's content. A simple mix of finely diced onion cooked gently in butter and good-quality chicken stock forms the base of many wonderful vegetable soups. As a thickener you can use potato, kumara or pumpkin cooked until pulpy. For leek and roasted garlic soup, gently cook 1-2 large sliced leeks with onion, add 4-5 cups chicken stock, 2 diced potatoes, a pinch of nutmeg and the cloves from a head of roasted garlic. Season and simmer until tender before mashing or puréeing. For a spicy Thai-style pumpkin soup, cook onion and add 2 cloves crushed garlic, 1-2 tsp green curry paste, 2-3 cups diced pumpkin, 3-4 cups chicken stock and a little coconut cream. Simmer until tender and finish with chopped coriander. For a creamy winter cress soup, add several big handfuls of fresh cress to cooked onion along with stock and a diced potato. Cook until tender, purée and season with salt, pepper and nutmeg.

FLAVOURING SOUPS & VEGETABLES

Mixing spices or herbs, be they a curry paste or a herby pesto, through a tray of vegetables with a little oil before roasting is a great way to add different flavour profiles to vegetable dishes. To make great soups, add stock to the flavoured roasted vegetables and simmer until soft then purée and season to taste.
For a Moroccan-style pumpkin or kumara soup, roast chunks of pumpkin or kumara with ground cumin, coriander, garlic, a little orange zest and chilli. Simmer with stock and thicken with freshly roasted and ground almonds. For a more French style, flavour with garlic, bacon and thyme.

COOL BEFORE CHILLING

Always fully cool soups or big pots of stew before chilling. If you put large volumes of hot liquid in the fridge before they have evenly cooled the inside will stay warm, providing an ideal environment for undesirable bacteria to grow.

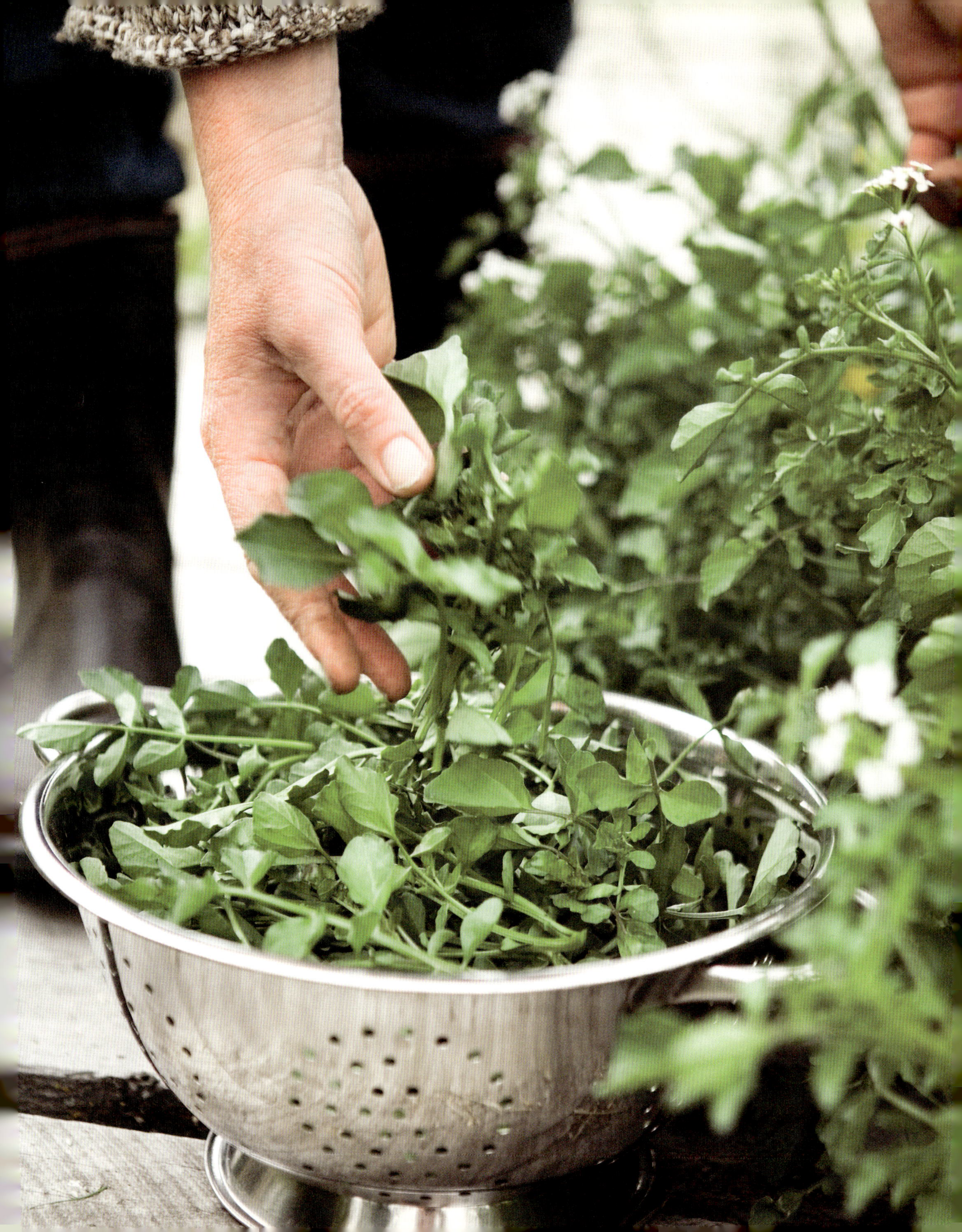

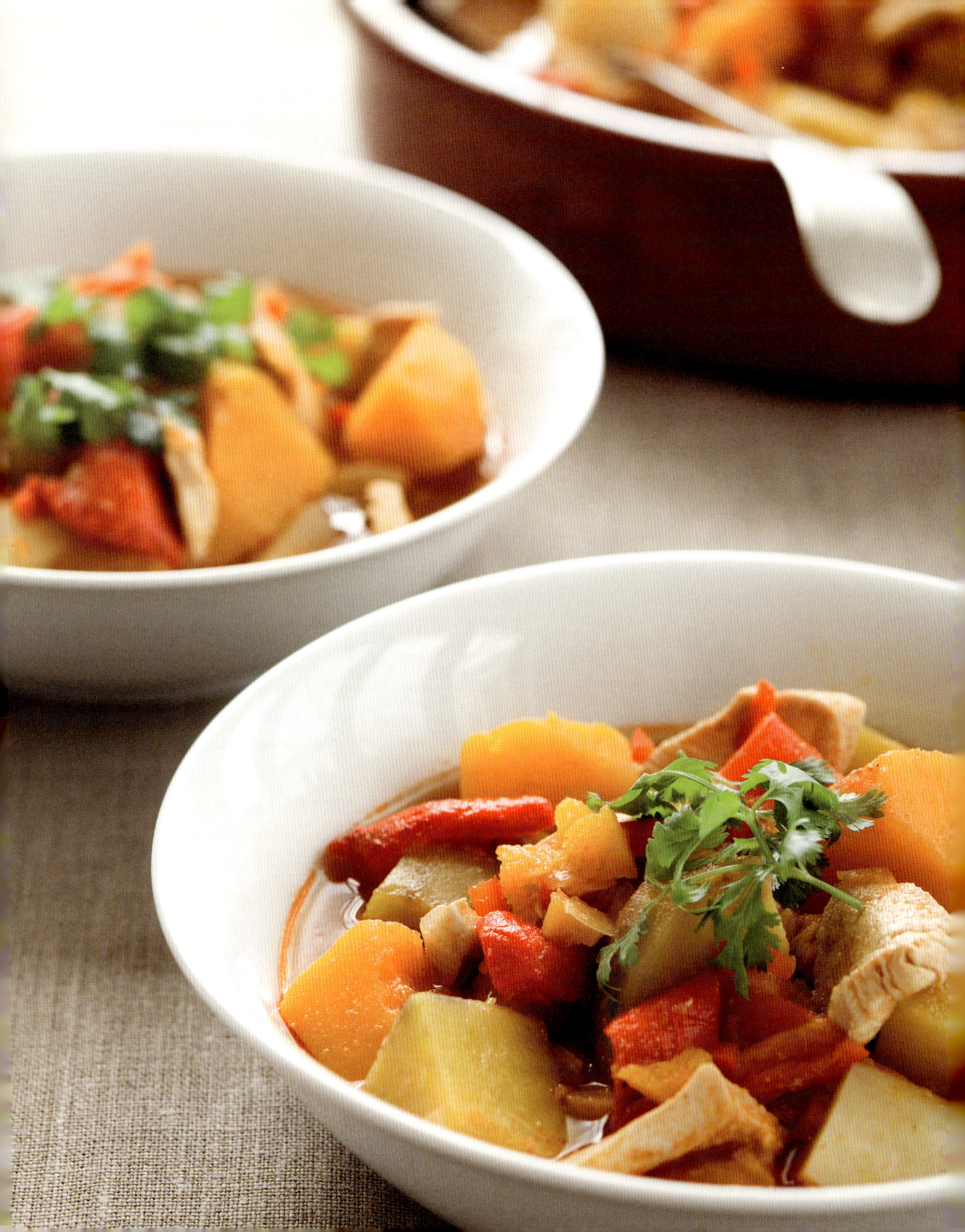

'When it was cold my mother would brew a huge vat of barley and vegetable soup to heat up when we came home freezing and starving from school. We never thought of it as nutritious – just good to eat.'

Soothing soup flavours

Mexican harvest soup

Prep 20 minutes
Cook 30 minutes

2 tbsp oil
1 large onion, diced
2 red capsicums, cut into chunks
50g tomato paste
1 tbsp ground cumin
1-2 fresh chillies, minced
600-800g pumpkin
3 potatoes
1 large kumara
optional: 2 cobs corn
4 chicken breasts, thinly sliced
4 cups chicken stock
3 cups water
1 tsp salt and grinds of pepper
Garnish: 2 spring onions, very finely chopped, ½ packed cup fresh coriander, chopped, 3 tomatoes, diced

Throughout South and Central America meal-in-one soups like this go by the name of puchero. They are often prepared using a piece of brisket or a whole chicken as the base with corn, pumpkin, potatoes, tomatoes and peppers added to the flavoursome broth. They make a great weekend lunch.

Heat oil in a large pot and gently sizzle onion with capsicums, tomato paste, cumin and chillies until softened but not browned, about 10 minutes.
Peel and chop pumpkin, potatoes, kumara and corn if using, into 2-3cm chunks. Add to pot with chicken, stock and water. Season with salt and pepper and bring to a simmer. Cook until vegetables are tender, about 15 minutes. Adjust seasoning to taste.
Just prior to serving mix in spring onions, coriander and tomato. Bring back just to a simmer before serving.

Chicken minestrone

Prep 15 minutes
Cook 1 hour

2 tbsp oil
4 rashers bacon, diced
1 large onion, finely diced
2 stalks celery, thinly sliced
2 cloves garlic, crushed
3 tbsp tomato paste
6 chicken drumsticks
1 tsp chopped rosemary leaves
2 potatoes, finely diced
2 carrots, finely diced
2 cups tomato juice
1 tsp sugar
8 cups good chicken stock
400g cooked chickpeas
1 cup dry pasta, eg macaroni
¼ cup winter pesto (pg 192)
Garnish: grated parmesan

Heat oil in a large, deep pot and cook bacon until fat runs and it starts to brown. Add onion, celery and garlic and cook over low heat until softened, 10 minutes. Add tomato paste and stir over heat for a minute or two before adding all other ingredients except pasta, pesto and parmesan. Season with salt and pepper, cover and cook at lowest simmer for 40 minutes. Add pasta and simmer until pasta is just cooked, 5-6 minutes. Mix in pesto just before serving.
To serve, place a portion of chicken in 6 deep bowls. Spoon over vegetables and ladle over broth. Garnish with parmesan.
Serves 8, pictured on page 181

Variation: The cooked chicken meat can also be shredded (discard the bones) and added back into the minestrone.

MUSHROOMS

Foraging for mushrooms is a particular autumn pleasure. The combination of cooler temperatures and humidity sends spores into procreation and the result is a raft of delicious edible fungi to collect. Care needs to be taken to identify what you harvest as a number of look-alike species are deadly and others can make you very sick. It's best to stick with a few easily recognisable species. If you are planning to eat anything unfamiliar, make sure you identify it first, preferably with an expert.
The white caps of the field mushroom (which we buy in the shops as button mushrooms), *Agaricus campestris*, pop up in grassy paddocks. They have a sweet, mushroomy smell and pink gills that turn brown.
On the farm you will also encounter *Agaricus arvensis*, the huge horse mushroom that makes great eating. In Wanaka we also get a tasty *Birch boletus* and giant puffballs, *Calvatia* which are delicious when young. The flavour of all mushrooms intensifies dramatically when dried and adds richness and depth to soups and stews. You'll find a nice recipe for mushroom bruschetta on page 188.

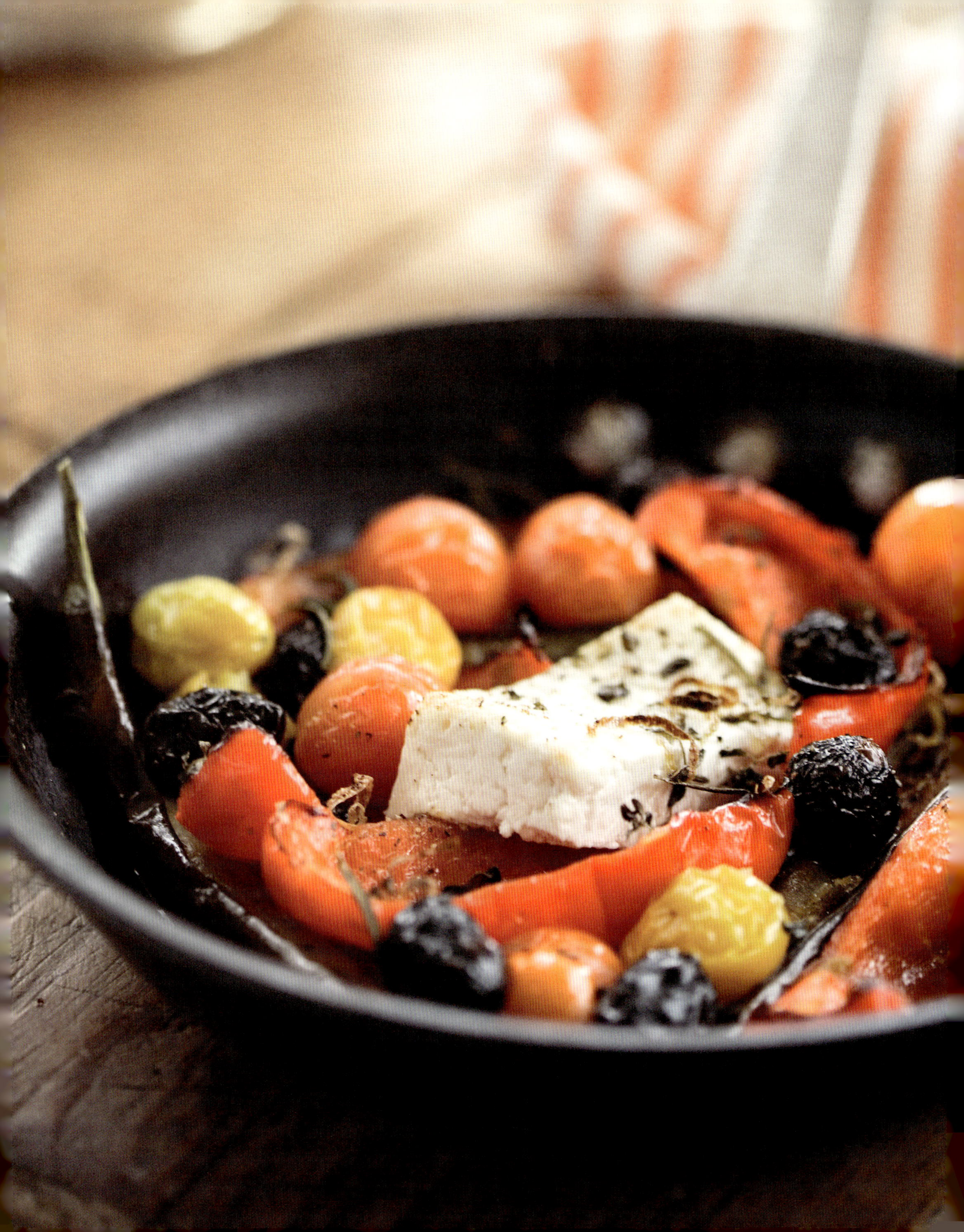

'Adding fat is one of the easiest ways to add flavour to a dish but it's also the laziest. Extra fat equals extra calories, which equals extra fat on you. Roasting delivers intense, satisfying flavours – without the fat.'

Oven-baked vegetable dishes

Grilled feta & vegetables

Prep   10 minutes
Cook 10 minutes

2 tbsp olive oil
2 capsicums, quartered
Optional: 2 long Asian eggplants, halved
200g goat's feta or chèvre
250g cherry tomatoes
½ cup kalamata or other tasty olives
1 tbsp chopped oregano (or 1 tsp dried)
1 tsp rosemary leaves
2 tbsp best-quality extra virgin olive oil
finely grated zest of 1 lemon
salt and grinds of pepper

Heat oil in a large frypan and gently fry capsicums and eggplants, if using, until softened, about 6-8 minutes. Remove from heat.
Slice feta into 4 portions and place in the centre of 4 heatproof gratin dishes or metal pans. Divide capsicums, eggplants, cherry tomatoes and olives between dishes and scatter over herbs and zest. Drizzle with olive oil and sprinkle with sea salt and pepper.
Place under a preheated grill and cook until cheese is lightly browned, 6-8 minutes.
Serves 4

Grilled eggplant & capsicum salad

Prep   15 minutes
Cook 20 minutes

2 eggplants, halved and thinly sliced
oil spray
2-3 red capsicums
1 punnet (about 200g) cherry tomatoes, halved

Basil mint dressing:
2 cloves garlic, peeled
1 packed cup basil leaves
15 mint leaves
¼ cup olive oil
¼ cup water
½ tsp salt and grinds of pepper
50g feta, crumbled
To garnish: fresh basil leaves

The smoky, sweet flavours of grilled eggplants and capsicums make a classic combination. Adding tomatoes and a herb dressing turns them into a simple salad. Even better, it can be made up to 24 hours ahead of time and chilled.
Spray eggplant slices lightly on both sides with oil and grill over medium heat until lightly charred and softened, about 5-6 minutes each side. Grill whole capsicums until blistered and charred, about 15 minutes.
Transfer cooked eggplant and capsicum to a plastic bag or sealed container to cool. Peel off skins and remove seeds and pith from capsicum. Cut flesh into thin strips. Place in a bowl with tomatoes.
Purée garlic, basil, mint, oil, water, salt and pepper until smooth. Toss through salad. Pile on to a serving platter and scatter over cheese and basil leaves.
Serves 6, pictured on page 125

DUKKAH

This wonderful dry, Egyptian spiced-nut mix is served with bread and a bowl of good olive oil. Dip bread into the oil then the dukkah. It will keep in a jar for weeks and is also useful as a coating for fish or chicken or sprinkling over salads.
Preheat oven to 160°C. Place on a large oven tray 1 cup each almonds and hazelnuts, ¼ cup sesame seeds, 1 tbsp each coriander seeds and cumin seeds and 1 tsp each ground turmeric, paprika and salt. Spread out and bake for 15 minutes. Cool for about 20 minutes then place in a food processor and pulse until crumbly. Pause between pulses to prevent overheating and making the mixture oily. Makes 2½ cups. Store in an airtight container in a cool place.

ODORI

This mixture of carrot, onion, celery and parsley is the flavour base of many Tuscan sauces and meat dishes. It can be made in bulk and stored for 2-3 days in the fridge. Heat 3 tbsp olive oil and gently cook 1 diced onion, 1 finely chopped carrot, 2 stalks celery, finely diced, and ½ cup chopped parsley until softened. To this base, add tomatoes, stock and browned meats as desired.

'Texture is such an important component on the plate. With soft, smooth dishes like polenta or a savoury souffle, serve a salad using crisp leaves and a good tangy vinaigrette. A few bitter leaves add balance.'

Baked polenta

Harvest polenta bake with rocket, capsicums & feta

Prep 10 minutes
Cook 20 minutes

4 cups water
finely grated zest of 1 lemon
1 tsp salt and grinds of pepper
1 cup quick-cooking polenta
140g rocket, spinach or silverbeet, finely chopped
2 tbsp pesto
¼ cup chopped coriander or mint
150g feta, crumbled
2 large capsicums, thinly sliced
2 cloves garlic, crushed

Preheat oven to 200°C. Place water in a medium saucepan with zest, salt and pepper and bring to the boil. Add polenta in a slow stream, stirring until fully absorbed. Cover and cook for 5 minutes (it splatters so take care not to burn yourself). Stir in rocket or other chopped greens, pesto, coriander or mint and half the feta.
Grease a 25cm shallow baking dish with a little butter or oil and spoon polenta mixture into dish. Heat oil and cook capsicums and garlic over medium heat 2-3 minutes until softened. Spoon over polenta and top with remaining feta. Bake 20 minutes or until puffed and golden.
Serves 4 as a main course

Variations: In summer I like to make a corn, mint and feta polenta. Prepare polenta as above, stirring in 2 cups corn kernels and ½ cup chopped mint in place of the rocket, pesto and herbs. Use the same amount of feta. Bake as above.
When mushrooms are in season make a mushroom and blue cheese polenta. Prepare polenta as above, using 500g cooked mushrooms and 150g crumbled blue cheese in place of the rocket, pesto, herbs and feta. Slice 500g mushrooms and fry in butter with a little garlic until browned and no longer juicy. Season well. Stir into polenta with half the cheese and scatter the other half on top of the dish with some chopped walnuts before baking as above.

PUFFY BAKED POLENTA

Polenta, like porridge, does not like to wait about once it has been cooked and sets to a gloopy mat as it cools. This is useful if you wish to cut and grill it, but if you want a soft polenta and do not want the last-minute fuss of timing it right, the best thing is to bake it.
Preheat oven to 160°C. Place 4 cups water in a medium saucepan and add 1 tsp salt and several grinds of pepper. Bring to the boil. Add 1 cup quick-cooking polenta in a slow stream, stirring until fully absorbed. Cover and cook for 5 minutes (take care splatters do not burn you). Stir in 2 tbsp chopped parsley, 2 tsp chopped rosemary, 2 tbsp grated parmesan and ½ cup cream or milk. Spoon into a 20-25cm baking dish. Bake for 30-40 minutes or until crusty and golden.
Serves 6

RECYCLING SYSTEMS

Invented in Japan, the bokashi bin is a recycling system that decomposes everything, including meat and bones. There's no smell so you can keep the bucket under your sink. It takes three to four weeks to fill. Check the web for your nearest supplier.
Worm farms are another good option for recycling food waste.

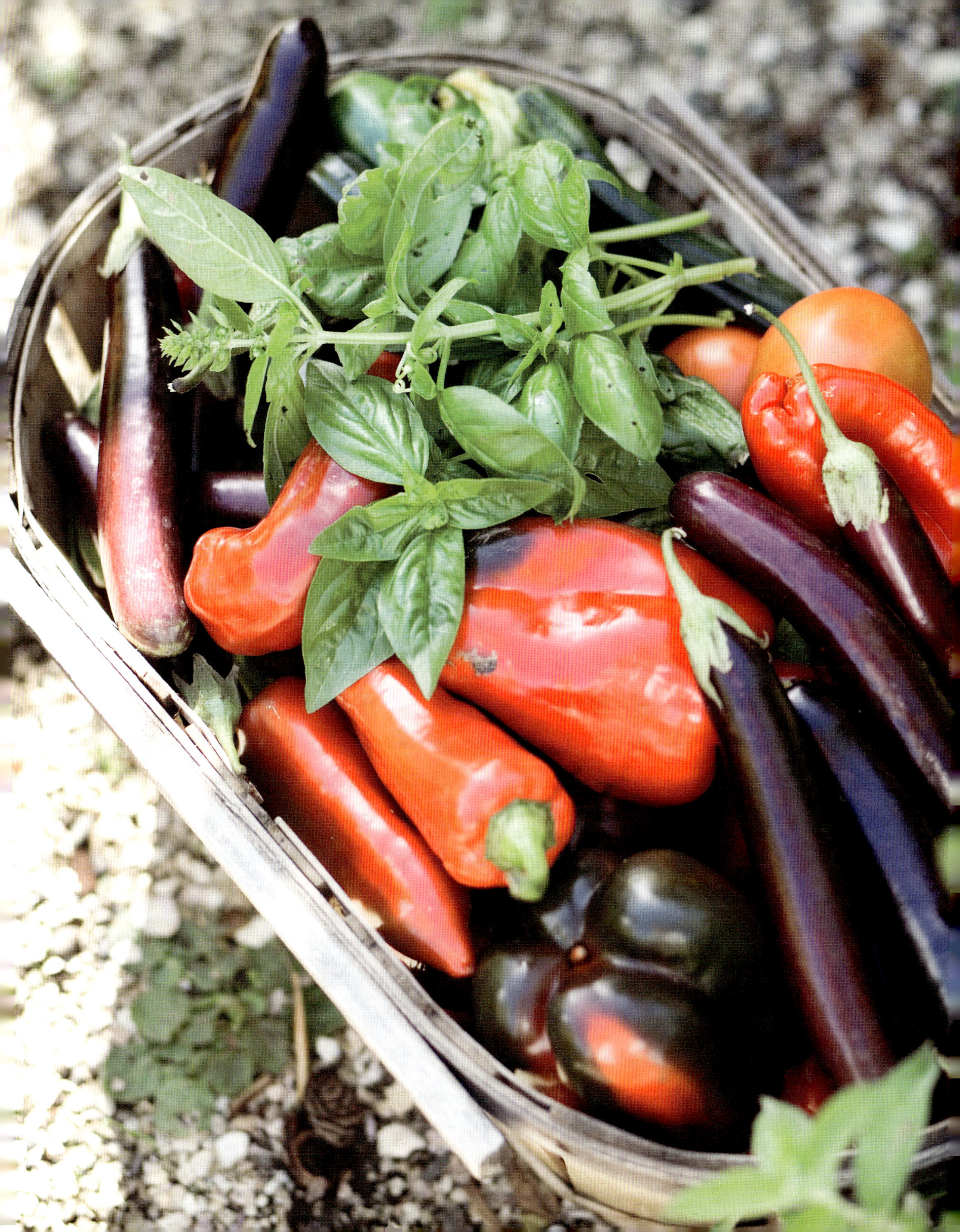

'When the kids were little we kept five chooks in our Auckland garden. On a diet of organic mash, food scraps and greens, they produced the best-tasting eggs. Such a satisfying, wholesome equation.'

Harvest chicken

Harvest chicken bake

Prep 10 -15 minutes
Cook 1 hour 15 minutes

500-600g pumpkin, peeled and cut into 4cm wedges
4-6 small red onions, unpeeled, washed and halved
2 red capsicums, quartered, seeds and pith removed
1 whole head garlic, cloves separated but not peeled
2 tbsp olive oil
1 tsp chopped fresh rosemary
finely grated zest of 1 lemon
salt and grinds of pepper
1 medium-sized fresh chicken, visible fat removed
olive oil and salt, to rub
1½ cups chicken stock
2 tbsp capers

Preheat oven to 220°C. Place pumpkin, onions, capsicums and garlic in a large, deep roasting dish. Add oil, rosemary and lemon zest, season with salt and pepper and spread out evenly in dish. Roast for 40 minutes. Reduce oven to 200°C.

Dry chicken with paper towels. Rub all over with olive oil and sprinkle with salt. Set on top of vegetables, pour over ½ cup stock and sprinkle over capers. Bake 45-55 minutes or until juices run clear, basting chicken 2-3 times with pan juices during cooking.

Lift chicken out of pan on to a serving platter with vegetables. Place pan on heat, add remaining stock, adjust seasonings to taste and simmer. If desired, thicken sauce with 2 tsp cornflour mixed with a dash of water.

Serves 4

Mediterranean chicken bake

Prep 10 minutes
Cook 1 hour 10 minutes

500g fresh tomatoes, chopped
2 onions, halved and thinly sliced
2 red capsicums, cut into chunks
2 tbsp tomato paste
2 tbsp olive oil
1 tsp sugar
1 tsp chopped rosemary
1 tsp fennel seeds
2 fat cloves garlic, crushed
1 tsp salt and grinds of pepper
6-8 chicken thigh cutlets
3-4 slices streaky bacon, cut in half
60g feta, coarsely crumbled

Preheat oven to 200°C. Place tomatoes, onions and capsicums in a large baking dish. Combine tomato paste, olive oil, sugar, herbs, garlic, salt and pepper and mix through vegetables. Roast for 40 minutes.

Wrap chicken pieces in bacon, season and place on top of vegetable sauce. Scatter feta around chicken and bake a further 30 minutes or until chicken is cooked through. Serve with roasted potatoes.

Serves 4

CAPSICUMS (BELL PEPPERS)
Capsicum annuum
Green capsicums are actually unripe red capsicums – same fruit but less time on the vine. When red they are very sweet and more easily digested. To prepare capsicums, cut them in half and remove the seeds and core. Cut away and discard the white pith. Eat raw in salads or cook in a little olive oil with onions and garlic as a starting point for sauces, stir-fries, tagines and stews. Roasting is one of the best ways to concentrate the flavour of capsicums see page 136. Halved capsicums can be stuffed with all kinds of savoury mixtures (cheese, rice and herbs and spicy mince) then baked.

FRESH CORIANDER CHUTNEY
Delicious with roasted meats and vegetables. Best made on the day it is to be served.
Place 2 whole coriander plants, washed and roots and tough stalks removed, in a bowl. Pour over boiling water then drain and cool under cold water. Drain well. Place in a blender with 1 green chilli, seeded and finely chopped, 2 cloves garlic, peeled, 1 tbsp olive oil, 1 tsp cumin seeds, 1 tsp coriander seeds, 1 tsp sugar and a pinch of salt and purée until smooth.

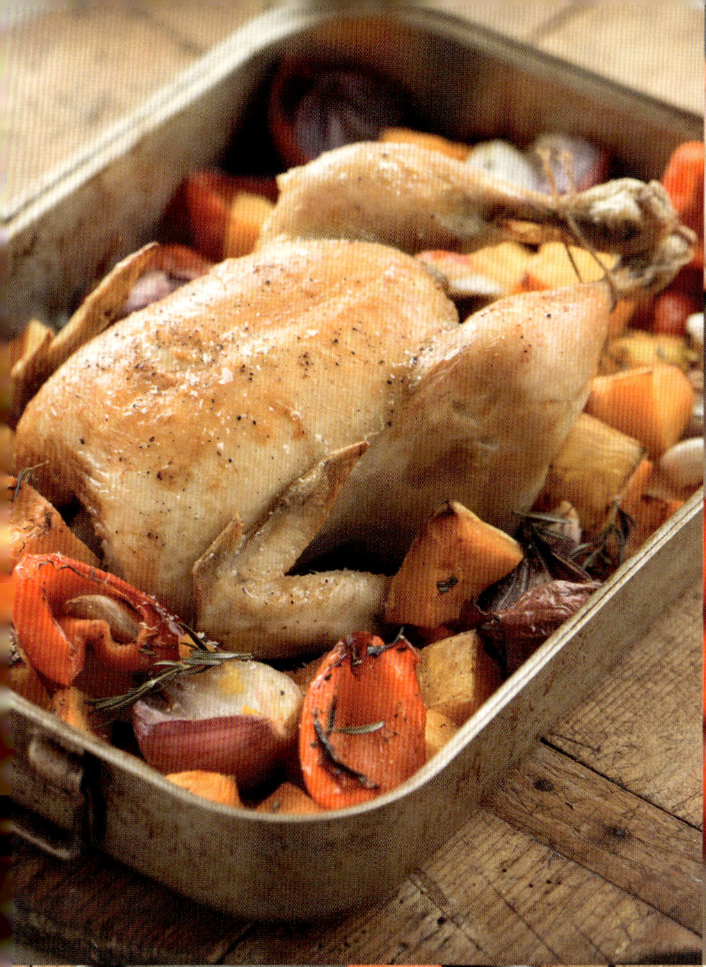
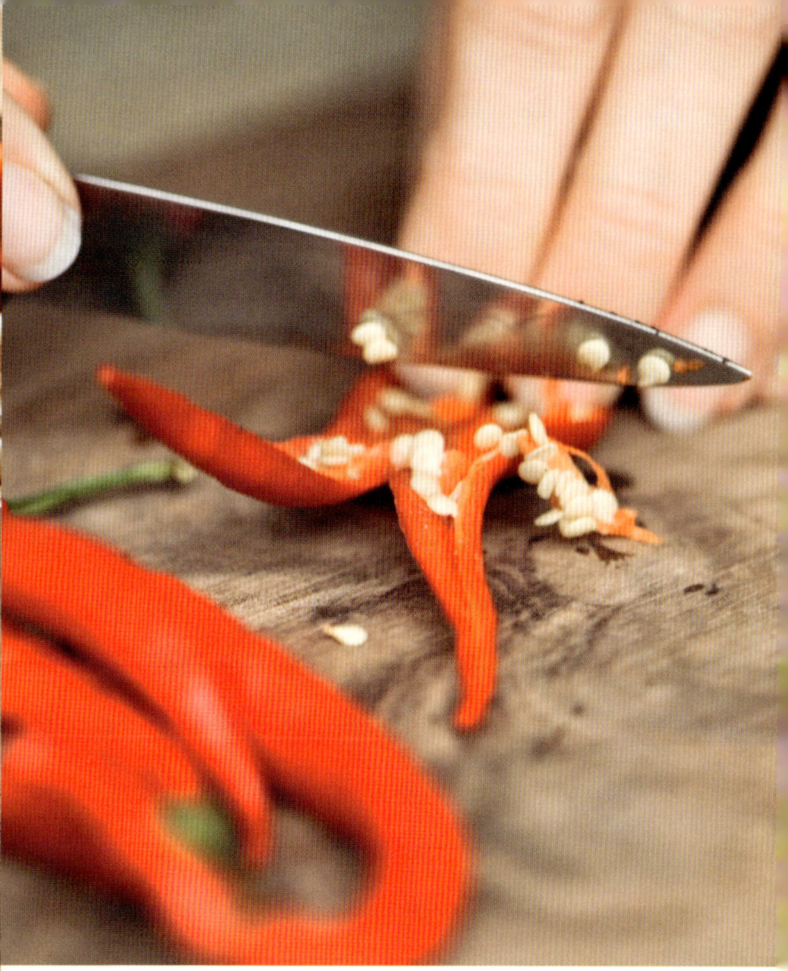
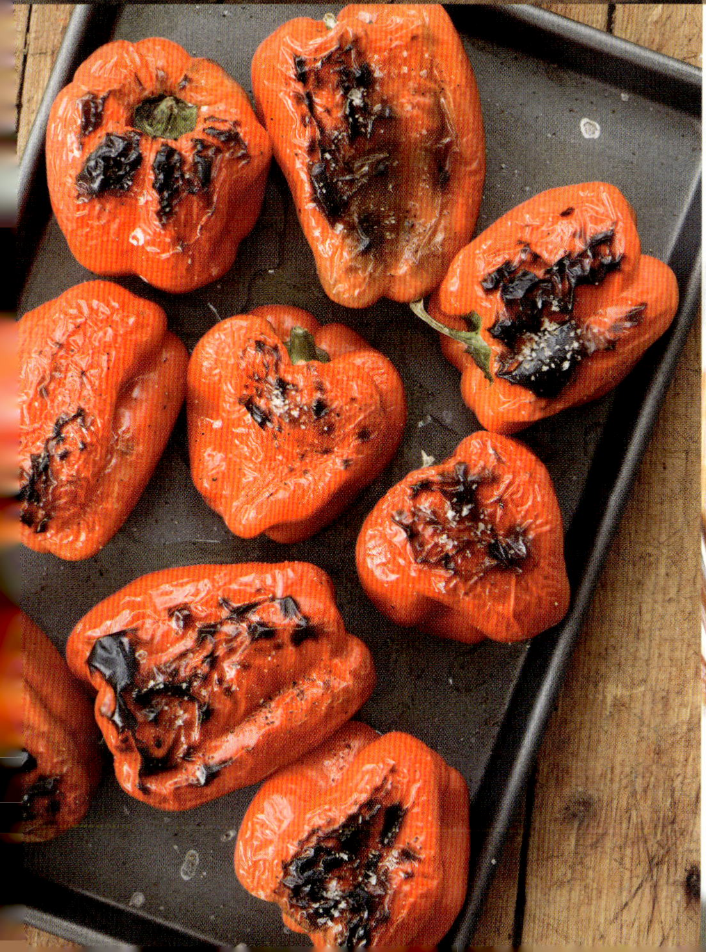
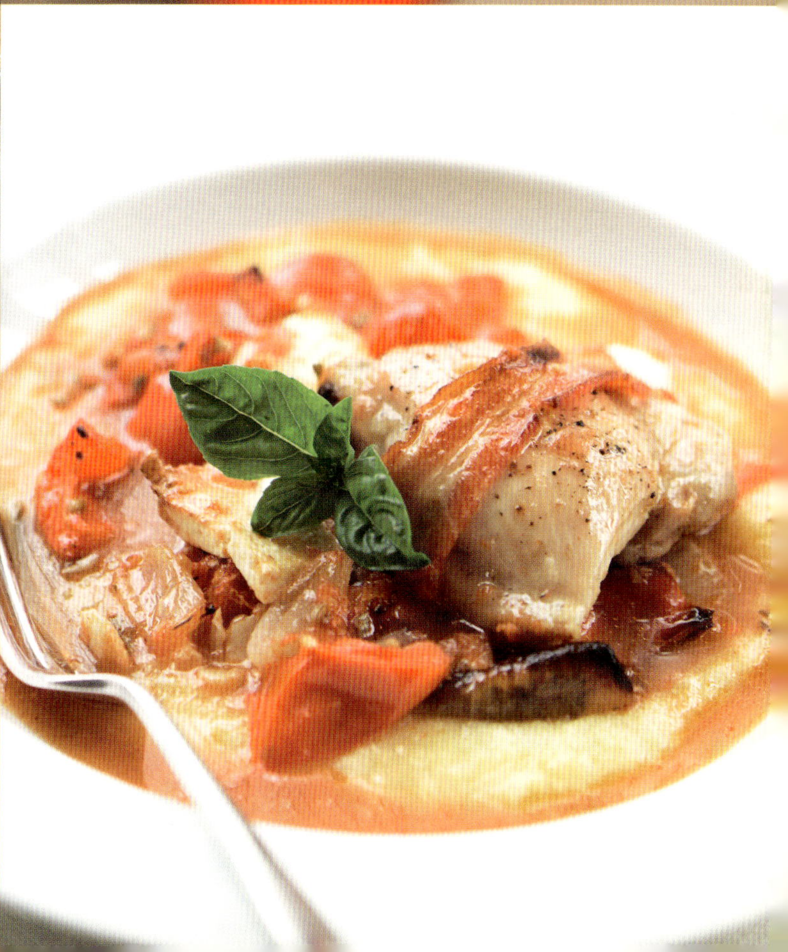

'"The gentleman who pays the rent" is an old Irish farming euphemism for a pig. Forget the rent, a pig is a damned useful and delicious animal.'

Roast pork and crackling

Fennel & rosemary braised pork with crackling

Prep 10 minutes + brining for at least 4 hours
Cook 45 minutes

1 whole pork scotch fillet, approx 1.5kg

Brine:
1 tsp fennel seeds
1 tsp chopped rosemary leaves
1 tsp whole peppercorns
⅓ cup salt
⅓ cup sugar
1 cup boiling water
3 cups cold water
1 cup fruity white wine
To serve: roast tomato sauce (page 130)

Using a sharp fork or skewer, prick the meat deeply all over in about 30-40 places.
Place fennel, rosemary, peppercorns, salt and sugar in a mixing bowl. Pour over boiling water, stir to dissolve sugar then add cold water.
Place pork in a large, clean plastic bag and pour over the brine, adding all the herbs and spices. Seal and place in the fridge for at least 4 hours or up to 10 hours.
Preheat oven to 160°C. Discard liquid from brine but save spices and herbs and place with meat in a deep oven dish. Pour over wine. Cover and bake about 1¾ hours or until meat is very tender.
Serve meat with its juices and some crackling over soft polenta. I like to serve this with roast tomato sauce, a platter of roasted kumara and lightly cooked green beans.
Serves 6

CRISPY CRACKLING
Scotch fillet is an internal cut from up near the neck so there is no skin to crackle. Get the butcher to give you a piece of pork skin. Score it on the skin side in a hatchet pattern and rub in ½ tsp salt. Place skin-side up on a roasting tray and roast at 160°C for 1 hour. Drain off fat. Just before serving place under a hot grill until crispy, 5-6 minutes.

BRINING
Brining is a useful way to add tenderness and moisture to any cut. I often brine pork chops before cooking them. Whole chickens and chicken breasts are also delicious brined using the mixture at left.

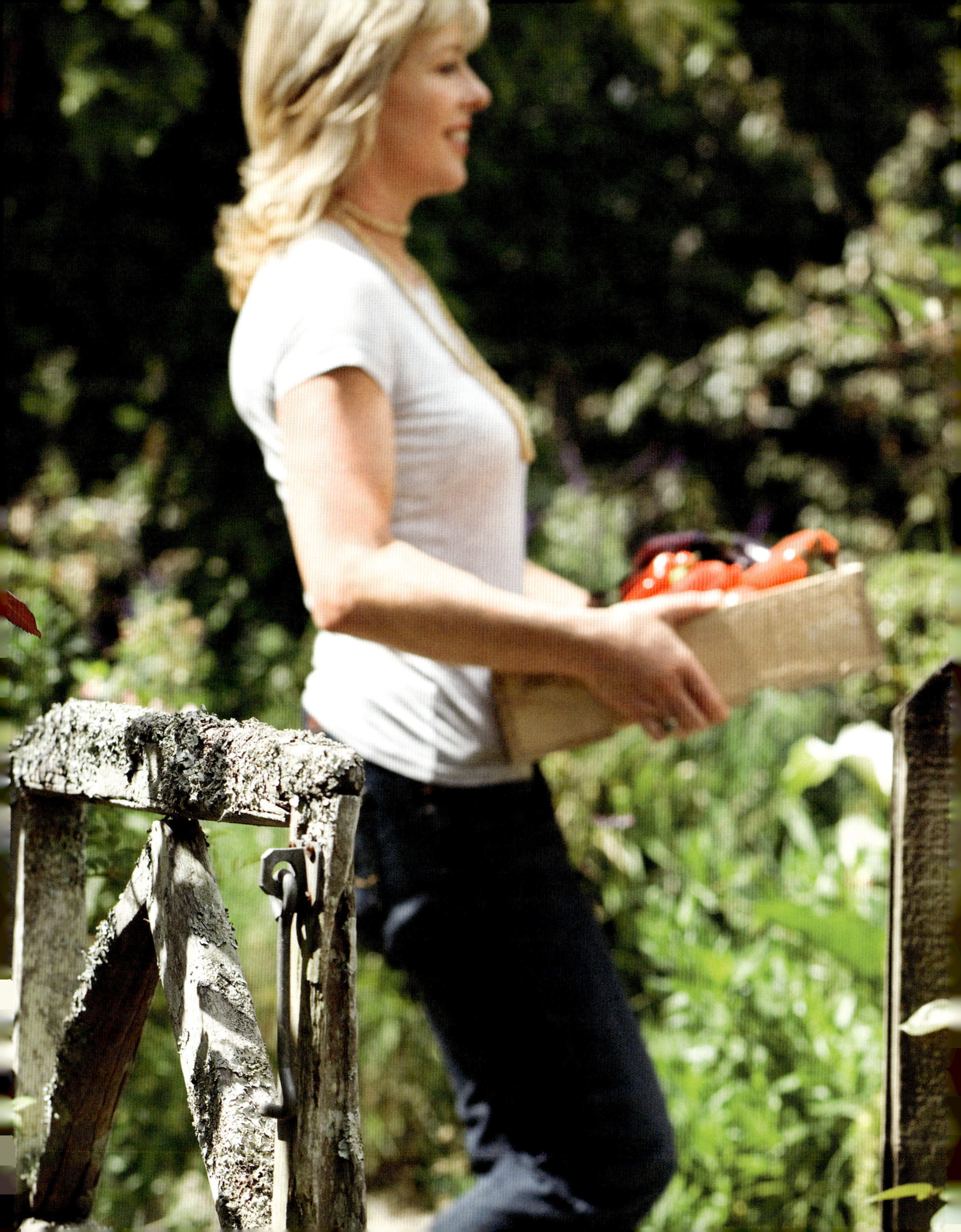

'Travelling the coast road north of Barcelona up to the French border, you'll find some delicious seafood. The fideua in Cadaques is a dish I still hanker for – noodles and seafood in a rich, dark sauce.'

One-dish noodles and rice

Fideua

Prep 10 minutes
Cook 10 minutes

¼ cup extra virgin olive oil
4 cloves garlic, crushed
2 tsp smoked sweet paprika
½-1 tsp chilli flakes
375g dried angel-hair pasta or ribbon egg noodles
½ cup white wine
4 cups fish or chicken stock
20 strands saffron
3 large tomatoes, chopped
1 tsp salt and grinds of pepper
Seafood: 300g prawns, 1.3kg fresh mussels/and or cockles in the shell, 400g boneless fish, cut into chunks
Garnish: ¼ cup finely chopped parsley, diced flesh of 2 roasted red capsicums (optional), wedges of lemon or lime

This noodle-style version of paella can be prepared using seafood, chicken or even spicy sausage. The noodles cook much more quickly than rice so take note of the cooking time for noodles or pasta before you start.

Heat oil in a large, deep pan and sizzle garlic, paprika and chilli flakes for a few seconds. Break up noodles or pasta into small pieces with your hands and add to pan. Stir over heat for a minute or two until noodles start to brown a little. Add wine, stock and saffron if using, cover and bring to a simmer.
Add tomatoes, seasoning and all the seafood, stirring to combine evenly and pushing the mussels into the mixture to submerge their bases.
Cover and cook until mussels open, 5-6 minutes. Taste for seasoning and garnish with parsley and roast capsicums if using. Accompany with wedges of lemon or lime.
Serves 6

Duck & chorizo paella

Prep 10 minutes
Cook 1½ hours

Use the ingredients for the fideua above, substituting shortgrain rice for noodles and roasted duck pieces and chorizo for seafood. Season 4 duck leg quarters with salt, pepper and a little smoked paprika. Roast on a baking tray at 220°C until ducks are golden, 50 minutes. Reserve fat for another use. Reduce oven temperature to 170°C. In a deep pot heat oil with garlic, paprika, chilli flakes and 150g sliced chorizo. Sizzle for 2-3 minutes then add 2 cups medium-grain rice, stirring for 1 minute to coat in oil. Add white wine, chicken stock, saffron and tomatoes, season with salt and pepper and bring to a simmer. Push the roasted duck pieces into the rice to fully submerge. Cover and bake for 35-40 minutes. Stand, covered, for 5-10 minutes then mix through capsicums and garnishing herbs. Squeeze over the juice of a lemon and serve.
Serves 4

*Backpacking around South America in my twenties, I encountered foods that in my own cultural context would be considered incomprehensible – boiled blood, pig-ball soup, dog sausage – all the more horrific for being revealed after the fact.
In Puno, Peru, I was robbed of my passport and all my valuables while watching a street festival. I was taken to the military tent of a squat, heavily-armed general and troops were dispatched on a recovery mission. The general and I sipped Krug and exchanged pleasantries. A few hours passed before finally my passport and most of the dosh were returned. By this stage a great deal of champagne had been consumed, the general and I had danced a kind of hip-hop in the town square and things were getting very jolly. "Delicosa," I simpered politely, munching on some sweet, tender joint. "Un animal locale?" My enthusiastic reaction prompted an unexpected response. The general dropped to his knees and, gushing compliments (a woman with such taste, a woman who could bear his heir), implored me to accept him as my husband. Even for all the Krug in the world, being married to a Bolivian dictator, especially one who ate guinea pigs, was not on my agenda.*

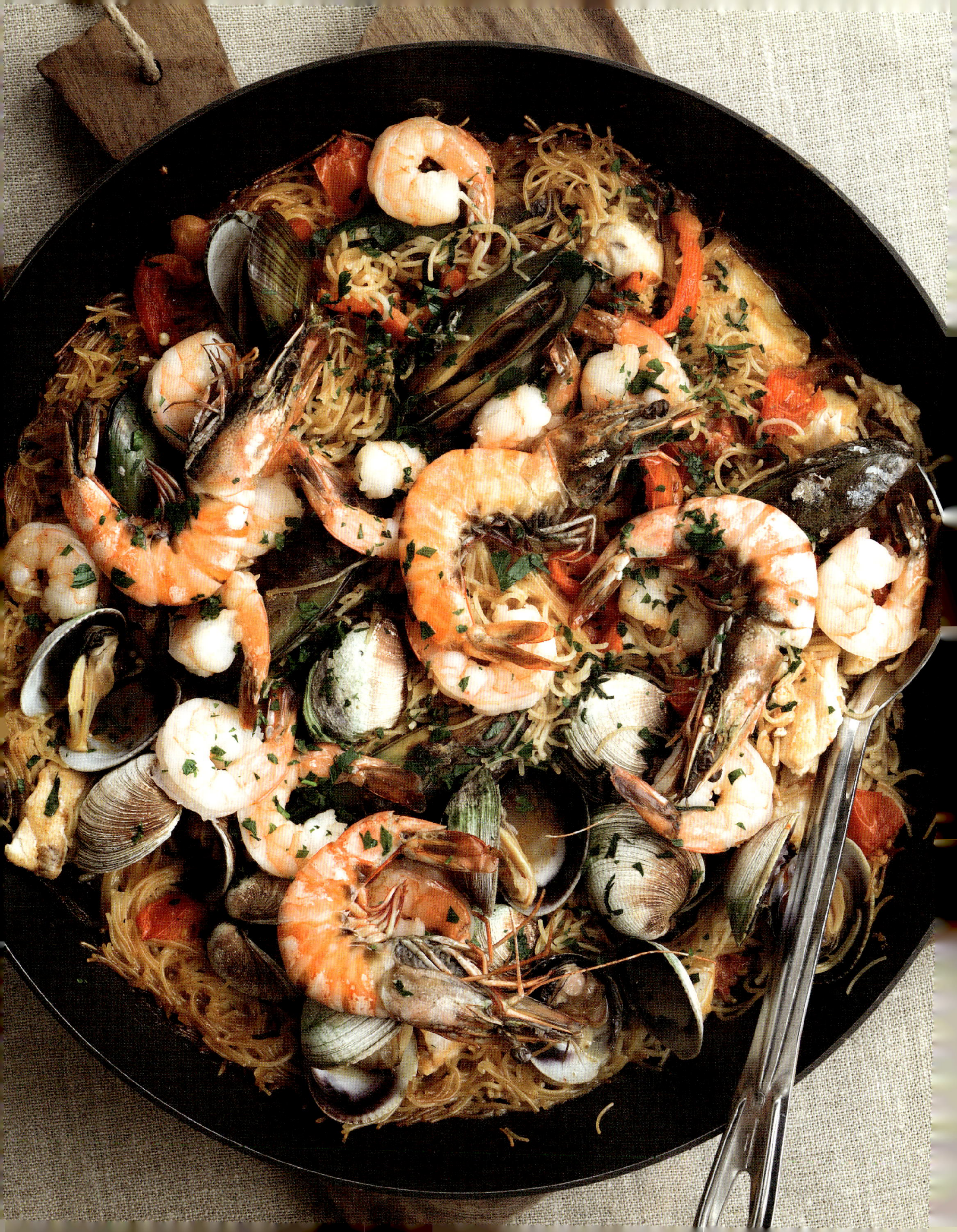

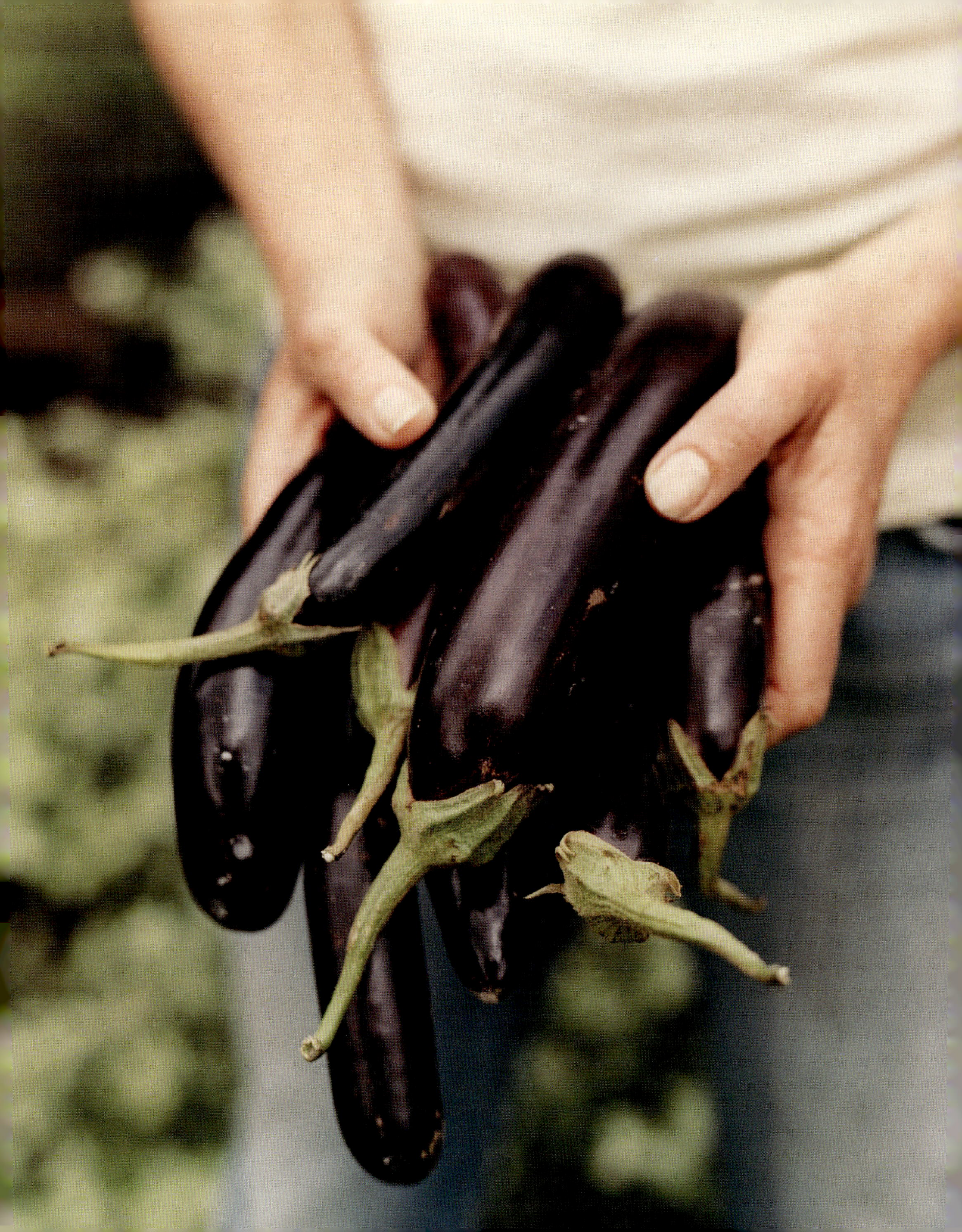

'Utilising different ethnic flavours when we cook is not authentic in any traditional culinary sense but it opens up our taste experiences and brings fresh, interesting flavours to the table.'

Harvest stir-fries

Ginger pork with beans & eggplant

Prep 5 minutes
Cook 15 minutes

5 long Asian eggplants (350g), sliced into 2cm chunks
2 tbsp neutral oil
400g lean pork mince
1 tbsp soy sauce
2 tbsp grated fresh ginger
2 cloves garlic, crushed
300g green beans, cut in 4-5cm lengths
1 cup water
¼ cup oyster sauce
1 tsp sesame oil
2 tbsp chopped coriander
Optional: ½ cup roasted peanuts

Drop sliced eggplants into a medium-sized pot of boiling water. Weight down with a smaller pot lid or plate to submerge eggplant and boil for 5 minutes. Drain thoroughly. Heat oil in a large wok or deep-sided pan over highest heat.
Add mince, soy sauce, ginger and garlic and stir-fry until meat is lightly browned. Add eggplant, beans and water. Cook, uncovered, for 5-6 minutes or until liquid has all but evaporated, stirring occasionally. Mix through oyster sauce, sesame oil, coriander and peanuts if using. Accompany with rice or noodles.
Serves 4, pictured right

Stir-fried chicken with cashews

Prep 15 minutes
Cook 10 minutes

400g boneless skinless chicken, thinly sliced
2 tbsp grated fresh ginger
2 fat cloves garlic, crushed
Optional: 1 tbsp hot chilli sauce
1 large red capsicum, thinly sliced
2 tbsp neutral oil
1 large or 2 medium heads broccoli, cut into florets
¼ cup oyster sauce
½ cup water
greens of 1 spring onion, thinly sliced
½ cup roasted cashews

Mix chicken with ginger, garlic and chilli sauce if using. Heat oil in a large wok or frypan and stir-fry chicken and sliced capsicum over high heat until chicken starts to colour, about 5 minutes. Add broccoli, oyster sauce and water, cover and simmer for 5 minutes or until broccoli is crisp-tender and chicken is cooked through.
Serve immediately garnished with spring onions and cashews.
Serves 2

CRUSHING GARLIC

There are two easy ways to remove garlic skin. Loosen it by whacking cloves with the flat blade of a heavy knife or slice bases off cloves and cover with boiling water. Like almonds, the cloves will pop out of the skin. This latter method takes away some of the flavour. I generally crush garlic by placing the peeled cloves on a board and giving them a good bash, sprinkling with a little salt and chopping finely. You can also make a garlic paste by applying pressure with the flat side of the knife in a bread-buttering motion against the board.

'Middle Eastern cooking often uses fruit in a savoury context. The juxtaposition of sweet, slightly acidic flavours with savoury sauces goes particularly well with sweet meats such as duck and pork.'

Fruit in a savoury context

Duck & quince tagine

Prep 15 minutes
Cook 2 hours; longer for wild ducks

4 duck leg quarters, or 4 whole wild ducks
1 tsp each ground ginger, cinnamon and ground cumin
salt and grinds black pepper
1 large quince, washed, cored and sliced in thin wedges
1 large brown onion, halved and cut into thin wedges
¼ cup (30g) finely chopped fresh ginger
½ cup white sugar
1 cup white wine eg riesling
1 cup chicken stock
2 tbsp wine vinegar

Preheat oven to 200°C. If using farmed ducks prick skin all over to allow fat to escape. Rub duck all over with combined spices, season with salt and pepper. Place duck on a rack in a roasting dish. Roast at 200°C for 1 hour.
While duck roasts, place sliced quince, onion, ginger sugar and 2 cups water in a pot. Cover and simmer over lowest heat for 1 hour.
Pour the cooked quince and onion mixture into the base of a casserole dish large enough to fit the duck in a single layer. Mix wine, stock and vinegar and pour over duck. Cover and bake at 200°C for a further hour or until duck is very tender.
Serves 4
Cook's notes: If quinces are unavailable prepare this dish using a can of guavas, sliced in their juices with a firm pear, cut in thin wedges.
If making this dish with wild ducks which have no fat, hot roast only for 30 minutes then bake with onions and quince for about 3 hours, or until tender.
Serve with parsnip mash (page 219) or Turkish pilaf with apricots and nuts (see right).

TURKISH PILAF WITH APRICOTS & NUTS

Preheat oven to 200°C. Heat 2 tbsp olive oil in a deep, heavy ovenproof dish (eg Le Creuset) and gently fry 1 large onion, finely diced, with 2 cloves crushed garlic and the finely grated zest of 1 lemon. Cook until tender, 7-8 minutes. Bring 6 cups salted water to the boil in a separate saucepan with 12-15 strands saffron, add 2 cups basmati rice and cook over high heat for 6 minutes. Drain thoroughly. Add rice to onion with 6-8 whole cardamom pods, coarsely crushed, 2 cinnamon quills, ½ cup chopped dried apricots, ¼ cup pine nuts and ¼ cup sliced almonds. Pour over 1 cup chicken or vegetable stock and season with pepper. Cover tightly and bake for 40 minutes until rice is tender. Mix in 2 tbsp butter and 2 tbsp lemon juice and adjust seasonings to taste.
Serves 6 as a side dish

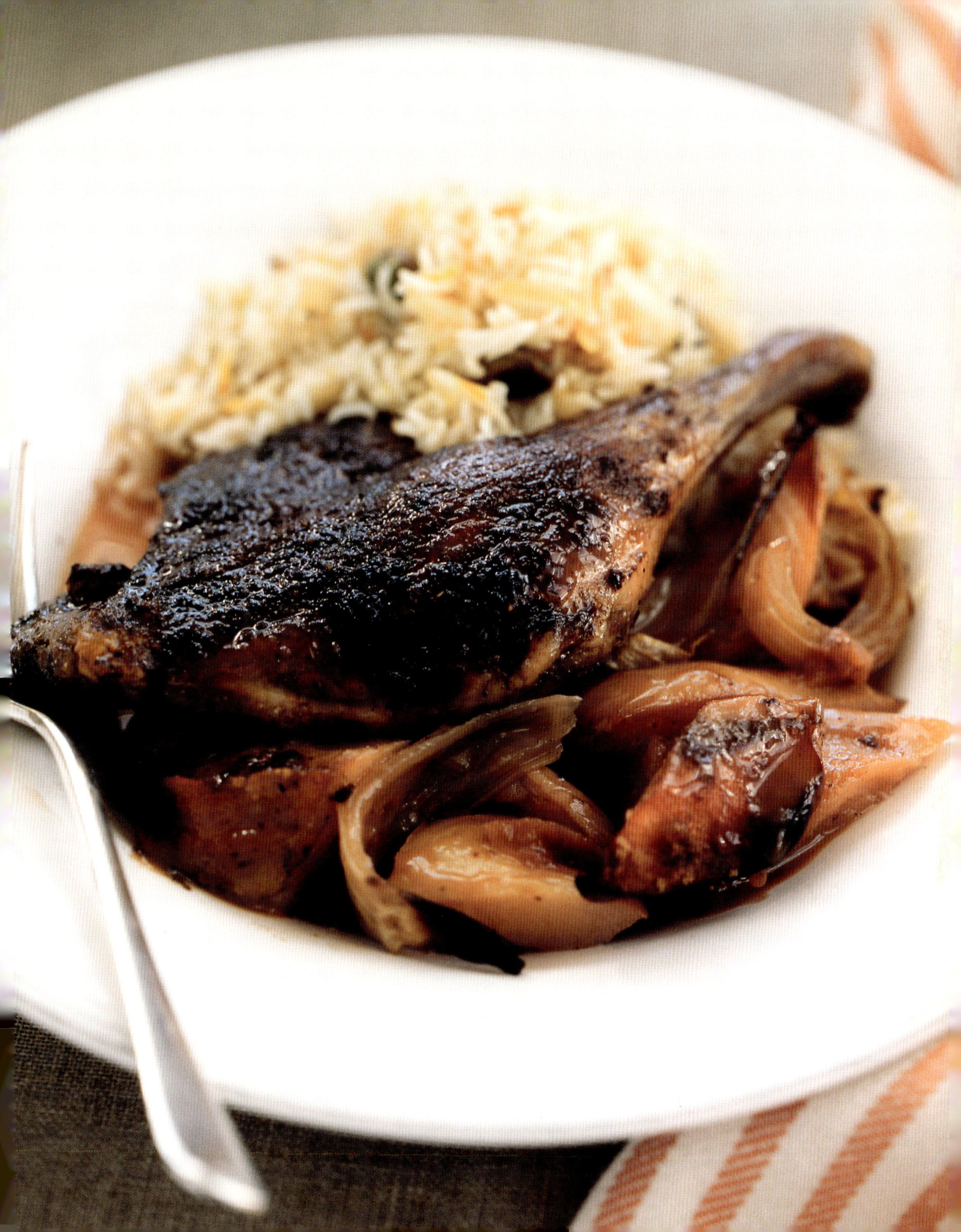

'The feel-good generosity and celebration conveyed in a big roast is incredibly simple to achieve. Everything goes into the oven and cooks itself. If you match effort against result, roasting is hard to beat.'

Pleasures of a roast

It's hard to go wrong with a piece of beef unless you overcook it, in which case it will be dry and horrid. Test for doneness using a meat thermometer (45-50°C for rare and 55-60°C for medium-rare).

Resting large cuts of meat prior to carving is crucial. I generally cover the cooked roast with a piece of tinfoil then lay clean towels on top and leave it for 15-20 minutes. While it rests gravy can be made and green vegetables cooked. The difference in texture, evenness and moisture after resting is like chalk and cheese.

It's nice to very thinly slice a fillet and roll strips of carrot and capsicum inside with a little pesto or vinaigrette.

To easily slice cooked beef super-thin, cool and wrap in plastic film and freeze for about 1½ hours until firm. Use a very sharp knife to slice thinly while meat is still semi-frozen. Bring to room temperature before serving.

I often roast a selection of vegetables with the meat. In autumn, whole peppers, zucchini, Japanese eggplant and halved tomatoes go in to roast with the meat. They take about 35-40 minutes to cook. (Pictured right.)

BENGAL PEACH CHUTNEY

Before the peach season comes to an end, make a brew of this spicy chutney. It's delicious with meats and added into casseroles and tagines.

Peel, stone and chop 3kg ripe peaches. Place in a large, heavy-bottomed pot or preserving pan along with 1kg brown sugar, 4 cups malt vinegar, 500g raisins or dates, 3 onions, finely chopped, 6 fat cloves crushed garlic, 3 tbsp grated fresh ginger, 2 tbsp salt, 1 tbsp ground cinnamon, 3-4 whole cardamom pods, 4 chillies or 1 tsp chilli powder and 1 tsp each ground cloves, allspice, ground black pepper and ground ginger. Bring to the boil then reduce heat to a low simmer and cook for about 1½-2 hours until the mixture is thick and pulpy, taking care it doesn't catch near the end of cooking. Bottle in small, sterilised, screw-top jars. Keeps for months.

Makes 8 small jars

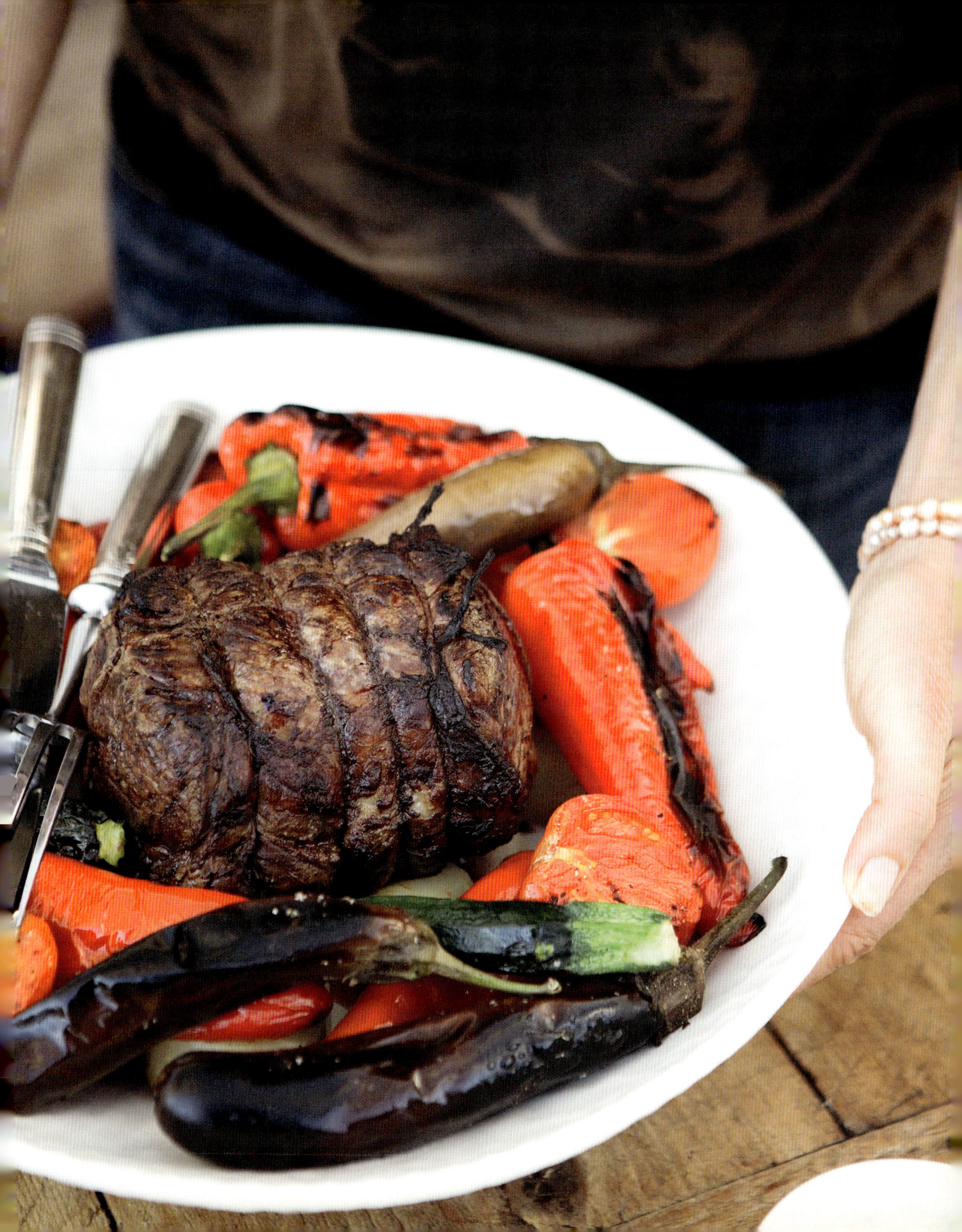

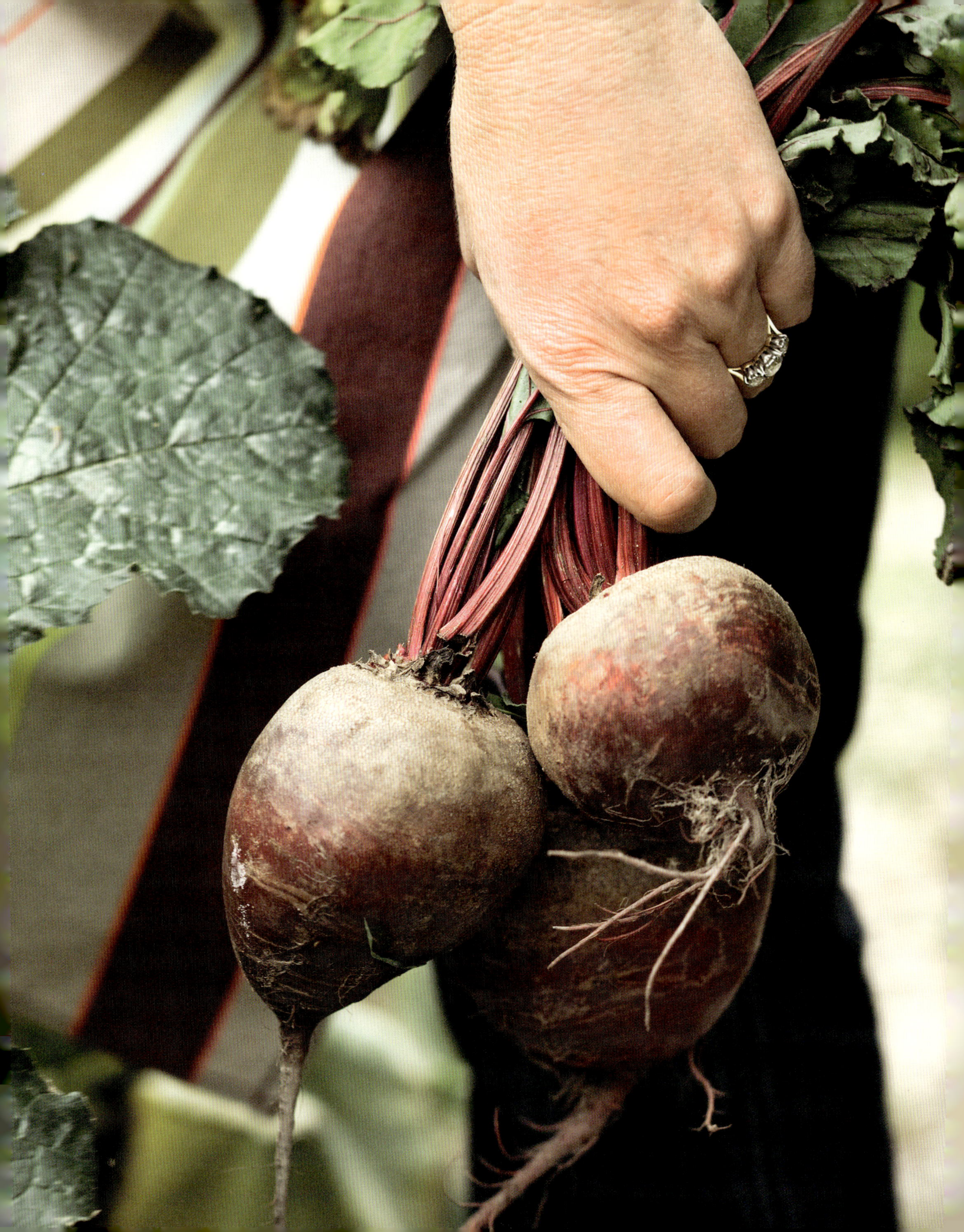

'Meat-and-three-veg dinners seem such an old-fashioned tradition, but are delicious and easy to put together. Make them interesting with a zesty salsa, sweet onion confit or a deeply layered red wine sauce.'

Perfect roast beef

Perfect roast beef with red wine sauce

Prep 10 minutes + at least 1 hour marinating
Cook 20-25 minutes

1.5kg piece beef scotch fillet, fillet or sirloin
1 tbsp balsamic vinegar
2 tsp horseradish sauce or Dijon mustard
salt and grinds of pepper
spritz of oil to brown meat

Red wine sauce:
1 tbsp butter
3 large shallots, finely diced
1 tsp fruit jelly, eg red currant or cranberry
2 cups red wine
3 cups beef stock
1 tsp sherry or red wine vinegar
salt and grinds of pepper

I find beef Scotch fillet, fillet and sirloin immensely gratifying cuts to cook in the piece – the meat holds well once cooked, is a happy chameleon to a vast array of sauces and flavourings and, provided you don't overcook it, tastes superb hot or cold. Here I have used a simple balsamic and horseradish baste but you can keep the meat plain if preferred or spread it with pesto or with 1 tablespoon soy sauce mixed with 2 teaspoons Dijon mustard.

Tie beef into a neat roll with cooking string. Combine balsamic vinegar and horseradish and rub all over meat. Cover and marinate at least 1 hour or up to 48 hours in the fridge.

Season meat with salt and pepper and brown all over in a hot, lightly oiled pan. Transfer meat to a baking tray, reserving the unwashed pan to make the sauce.

To cook beef: Preheat oven to 220°C and roast beef until cooked to your liking. (Scotch fillet will take about 40-45 minutes for medium-rare, fillet 25-30 minutes and sirloin about 30-35 minutes. Use a meat thermometer to gauge preferred doneness.) Take from oven, cover and rest at least 10 minutes before serving in thick slices with sauce.

To prepare red wine sauce: Heat butter over low heat in the frypan used to brown the meat. Add shallots and gently sizzle for 5 minutes or until softened but not browned. Add fruit jelly, wine and stock and simmer 40-45 minutes, stirring to lift pan brownings, until reduced and slightly thickened. Add vinegar and season to taste with salt and pepper. If preferred, strain sauce, discarding solids. Add any juices from the roasted meat into the sauce.

Makes 1½ cups, serves 6, pictured with roasted beets (page 136) and Yorkies (see right)

YORKIES

Traditionally served with roast beef and gravy, these can be made in muffin pans or cooked in a large roasting dish. You can also mix fresh herbs, roasted vegetables or cheese into the batter before cooking.
Whisk together ½ cup milk, 2 eggs, ¾ cup flour and ½ tsp salt until smooth. Stand 10 minutes then whisk in ½ cup cold water. Heat oven to 200°C. Drop ½ tsp oil into each pan of a 12-tin medium muffin tray. Place tray in oven to heat for 5 minutes. Pour 3 tbsp batter into each hot, oiled tin. Bake 15-20 minutes or until puffed and golden. Serve immediately.
Makes 8

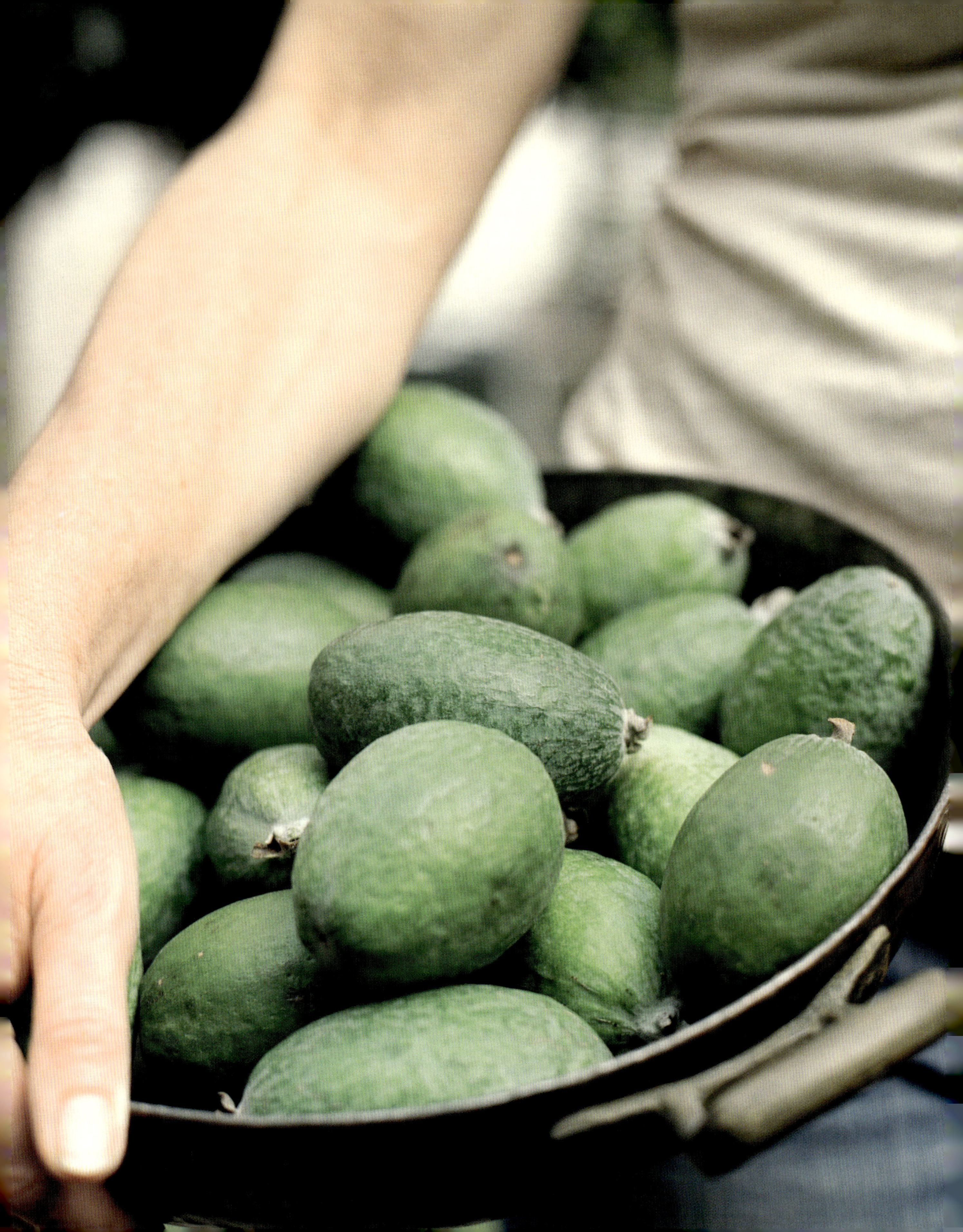

'Bananas, guavas, feijoas, cherimoyas, limes, kiwifruit, pomegranates and persimmons all ripen through autumn in our garden. Summer may be over but there is still lovely ripe fruit to be had.'

Subtropical feijoas

Apple & feijoa breton cake

Prep   25 minutes + chilling pastry
Cook   about 1 hour

Breton base:
250g butter, softened
1 cup sugar
1 tsp natural vanilla essence
1 tbsp iced water
4 egg yolks
3 cups flour
1 egg yolk for glaze

Filling:
4 large green apples and 4 feijoas or use 6 apples total
sugar to taste (about ½ cup)
¼ cup water

This rich dessert cake is reminiscent of the buttery fruit-filled cakes of France. It's good with any acidic fruit filling – in summer I like to make it with rhubarb and apples, apples and berries or apricots.

Beat butter and sugar together until very fluffy. Beat in vanilla and water and add egg yolks one at a time, beating well between each one. Stir in flour until just combined; do not beat.

Press two-thirds of the pastry into a 26cm springform tin, covering base and two-thirds up sides. Roll out remaining pastry on a sheet of greaseproof paper the same diameter as the tin. Put prepared pastry in the fridge to chill for at least 15 minutes while preparing the filling. Peel and slice apples and feijoas and place in a pot with sugar and water. Bring to a simmer over very low heat and cook for 12-15 minutes, stirring frequently, until all the liquid has evaporated. Allow to cool completely. Preheat oven to 180°C. Place fruit in pastry shell. Flip the prepared pastry lid on top, lifting off paper and pressing edges together to seal. Brush with beaten egg yolk and run the tines of a fork in a criss-cross pattern over the pastry to decorate. Bake until golden, about 40 minutes. Serve warm or cold. Cake slices well and will keep 2-3 days in the fridge.
Serves 10-12

Ginger-poached feijoas

Prep   5 minutes
Cook   5 minutes

6-8 feijoas, peeled
½ cup sugar
½ cup water
1 tsp ground ginger

This mixture is also nice puréed for a dessert sauce.

Peel feijoas, slice each one into 4-5 rounds and place in a saucepan with sugar, water and ginger. Simmer until tender, about 10 minutes. They will keep for about a week in the fridge.
Serves 2

PERSIMMONS

As autumn draws to a close, the deep orange orbs of persimmons are among the last fruits left hanging. When I lived in Brazil we would buy persimmons by the case. The old-fashioned variety, known there as kaki fruit, needs to be over-ripe to the point of becoming a deep orange jelly before it loses its mouth-puckering astringency. We would store the fragile fruit in the fridge and consume it icy cold, the coldness offsetting its bland sweetness.
The persimmons I have planted in both my Auckland and Wanaka gardens are all non-astringent Japanese varieties. They are crisp to the bite but like the old-fashioned fruit have a sweet flavour with almost no acid balance.
For a sweet crunch I like to slice persimmons into salads with rocket or slightly bitter endive, avocado and nuts, dressed with a mustard vinaigrette. They also make a great dessert sauce, chopped and puréed with a little ginger, fresh orange juice, a squeeze of lime or lemon and a little honey to taste. Or try persimmons in a fresh fruit salad combined with kiwifruit, a can of lychees, some chopped crystallised ginger and a squeeze of lemon juice.

'Home-cooked food delivers a sense of comfort that lasts a lifetime. Returning to those favourite dishes we grew up with, we find familiar tastes to recall and enjoy again.'

Passion on the plate

Coconut passion cake

Prep 10 minutes
Cook 1 hour (less if making smaller cakes)

1¾ cups sugar
180g butter, softened
4 eggs
1 tsp natural vanilla essence
2 cups desiccated coconut
2½ cups self-raising flour
1 cup milk
Optional: 1 tbsp passionfruit pulp

Preheat oven to 160°C. Line a 25cm cake tin with baking paper to cover base and sides. Alternatively, prepare 4 x 10cm tins (recycled large tuna cans are perfect) or 12-16 muffin tins (use ⅓-½ cup batter per muffin tin.)
Beat sugar and butter until creamy. Beat in eggs one at a time. Stir in vanilla. Combine coconut and flour and fold into mixture alternately with combined milk and passionfruit, if using.
Pour mixture into prepared tin and smooth top. Bake until a skewer inserted into the centre comes out clean. One large cake will take about 60 minutes, for 4 medium cakes allow about 50 minutes and for muffin-sized cakes allow about 20-25 minutes. Cool in tin.
Prepare icing (see right) while cake cooks. Spread over cooled cake. Store in a cool place.
Makes 1 x 25cm cake, 4 x 10cm cakes or 12-16 mini cakes

Passionfruit vanilla terrine

Prep 15 minutes
Cook 2-3 minutes

300ml cream
½ cup sugar
2 tsp natural vanilla essence
5 tsp powdered gelatine
½ cup unstrained passionfruit pulp (or commercial passionfruit syrup)
600ml Greek yoghurt
To serve: sliced golden kiwifruit, extra passionfruit pulp or syrup

This silky, beguiling dessert is a favourite in our house. It will keep for 3-4 days in the fridge. Enjoy it on its own, with fresh fruit, or serve with poached lemon and ginger pears (page 173) for a special occasion.
Combine cream, sugar and vanilla in a pot and bring to a low simmer. Mix gelatine with passionfruit until absorbed then stir this into hot cream until dissolved. Remove from heat and whisk in Greek yoghurt until evenly combined. Divide the mixture between 6 serving glasses or bowls or place in a large serving dish. Chill for at least 3 hours until firm.
Serve topped with sliced golden kiwifruit drizzled with a little extra passionfruit syrup.
Serves 6

PASSIONFRUIT
Passiflora edulis
Passionfruit vines are a useful and attractive plant to grow in frost-free areas. They take only 18 months to produce their first crop and the vines last about 8 years. The fruit ripens through the autumn and the pulp preserves and freezes well, adding a tropical note to dessert sauces, ice cream and pie fillings. The seeds can be sieved out if preferred.

PASSIONFRUIT SYRUP
This is a great way to preserve passionfruit – equal volumes of fruit and sugar create a rich macerating syrup that will keep for months in the fridge.
Place 1 cup passionfruit pulp in a sterilised jar and pour over 1 cup brown or white sugar. Cover and store in fridge. Shake occasionally over the first day or two until all the sugar dissolves. Syrup can be sieved to remove pips if preferred.
Makes 1½ cups

PASSIONFRUIT ICING
Beat together 50g softened butter, 3 tbsp passionfruit pulp, 3 cups icing sugar and ½ tbsp hot water until creamy.

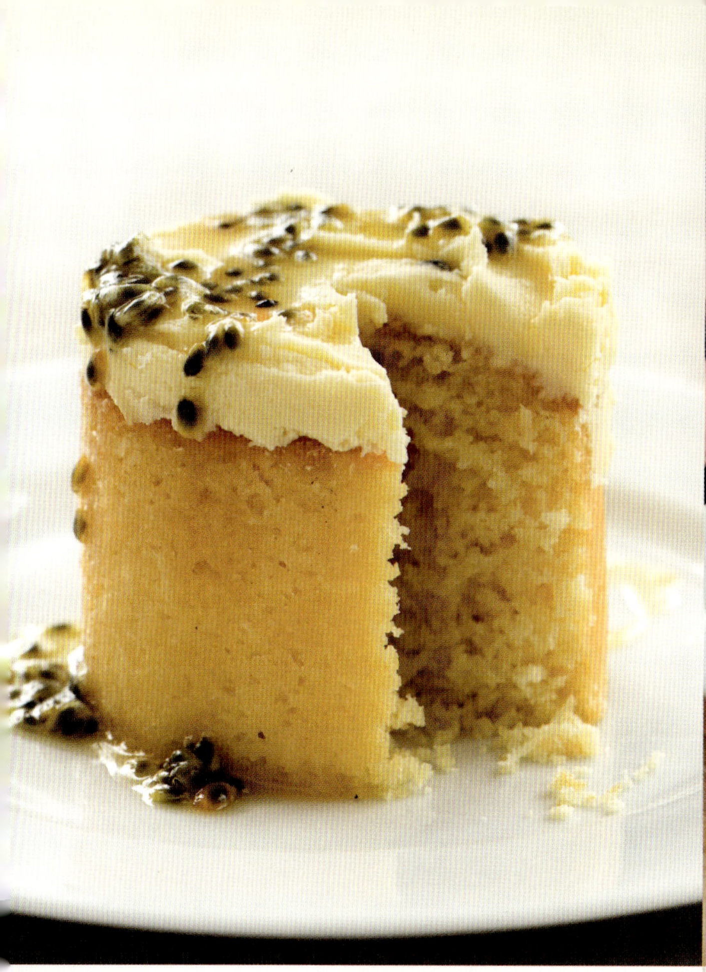
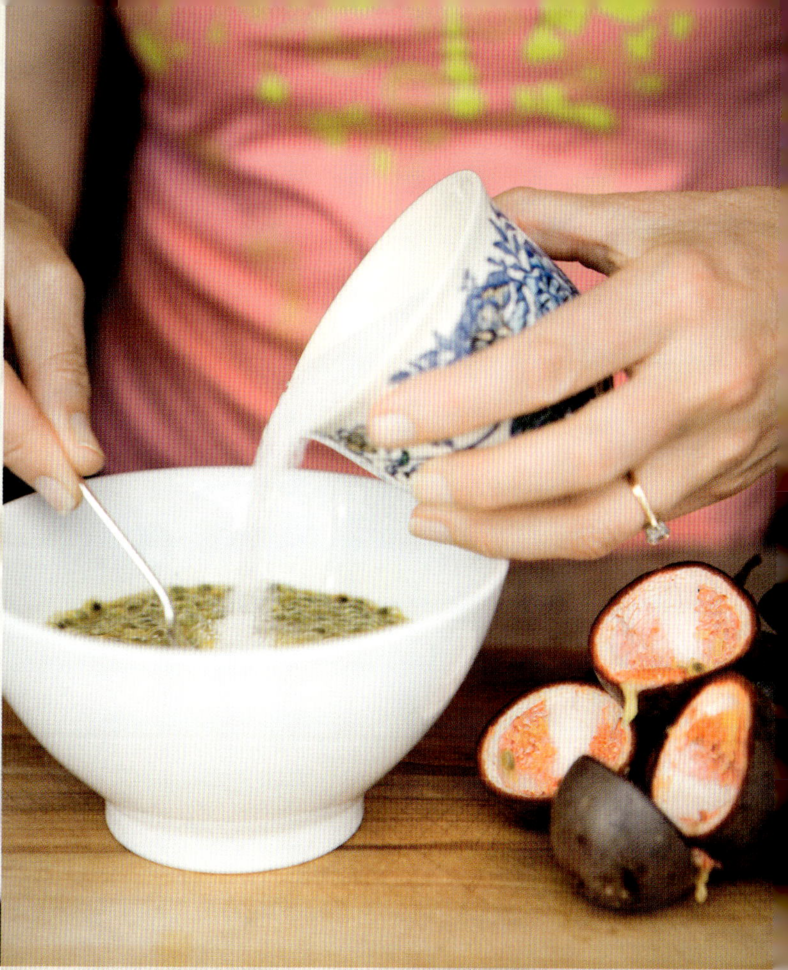
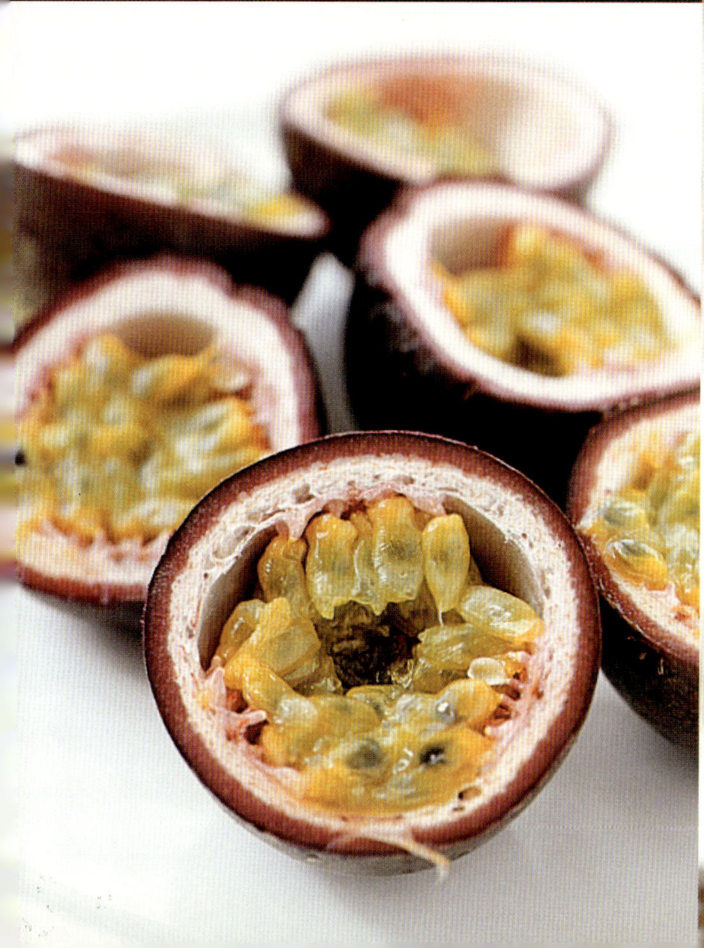
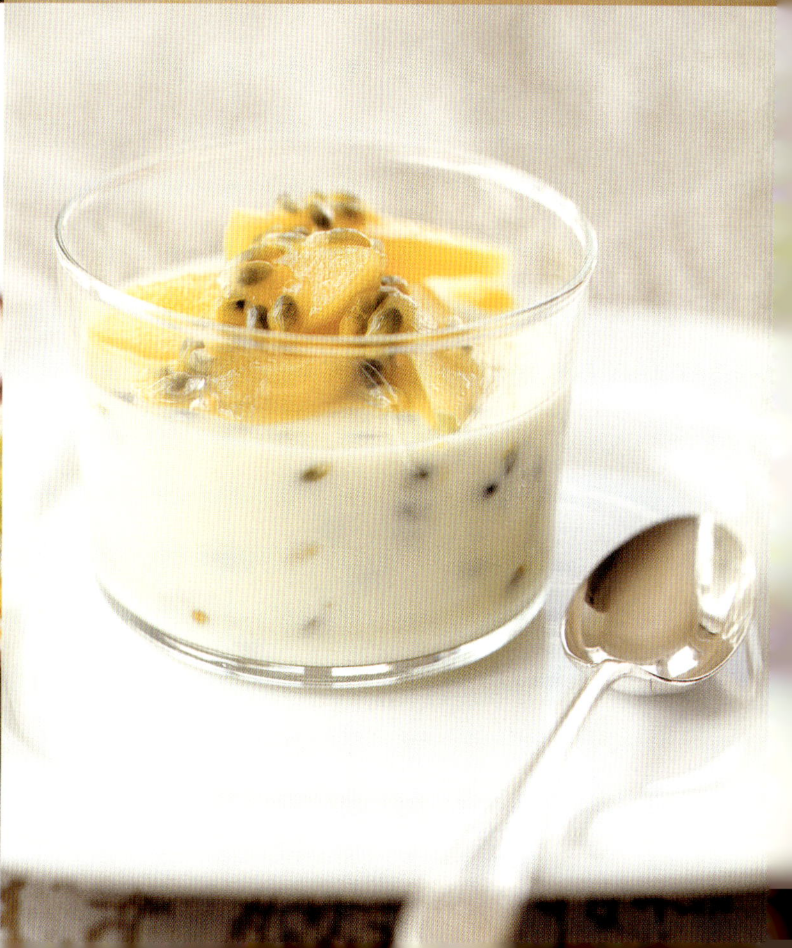

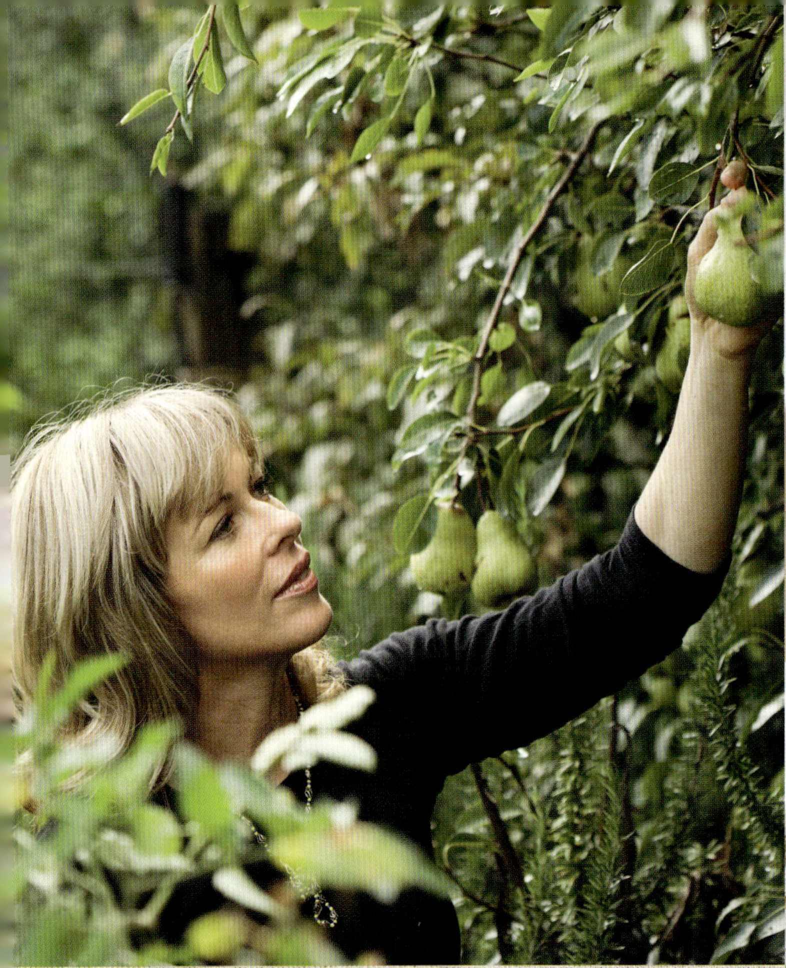
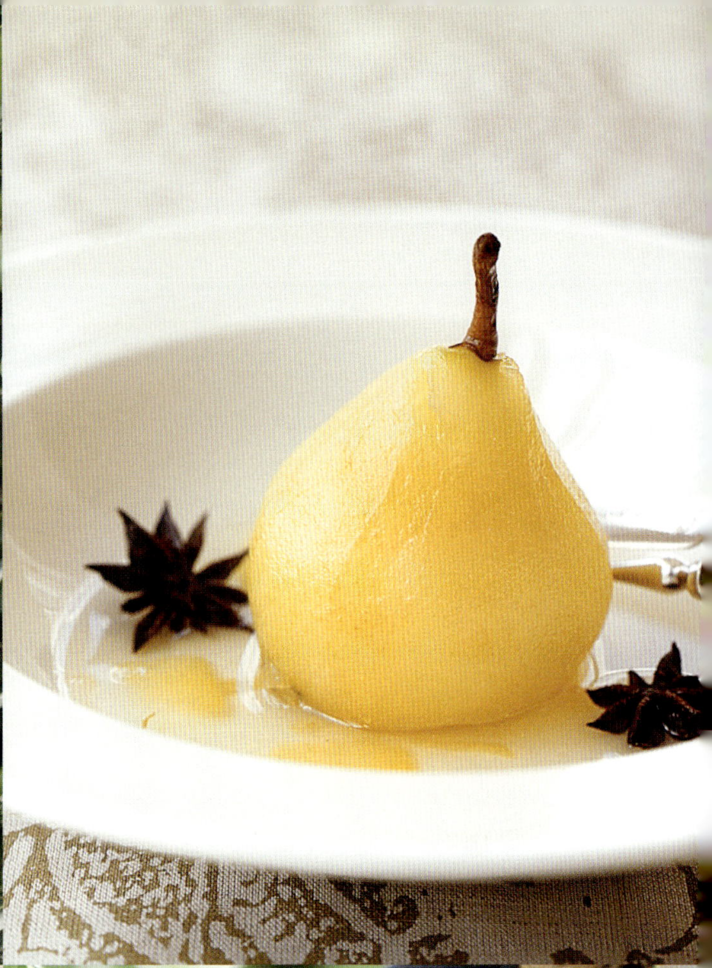
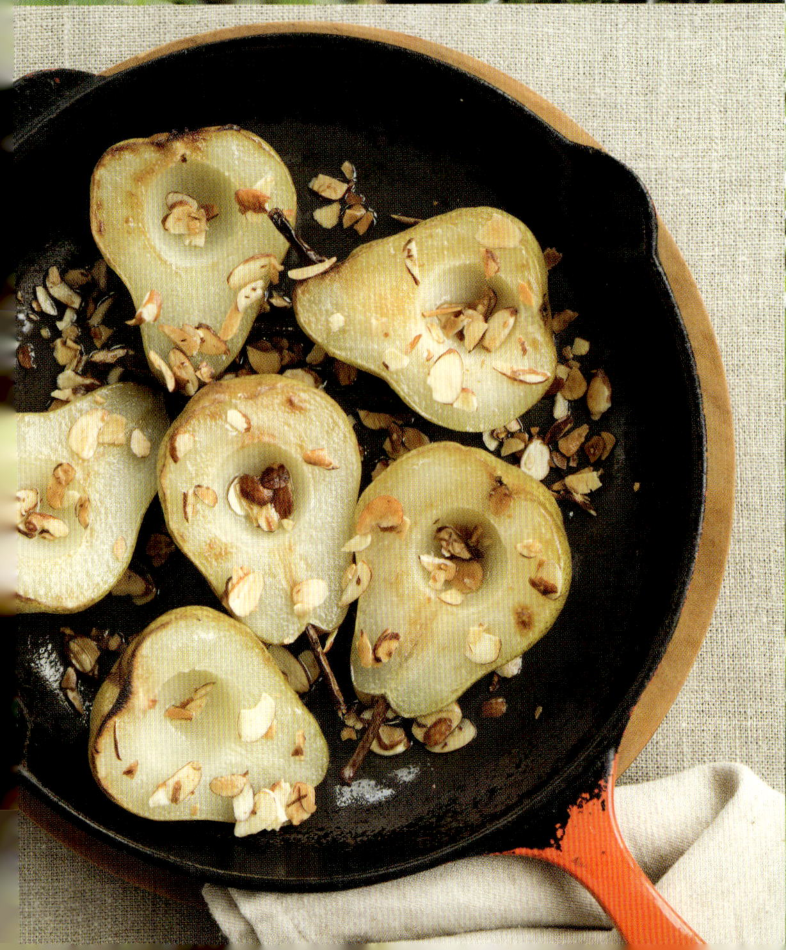
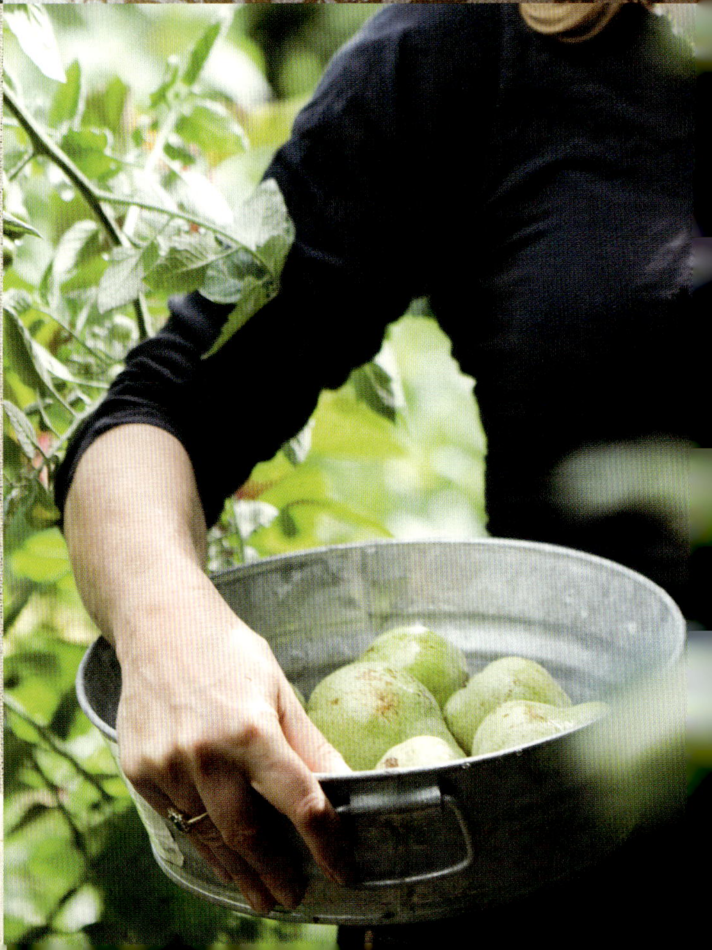

'Of all pears, it is the juicy comice that offers the greatest pleasure. Its sensuous, creamy, smooth flesh literally melts in the mouth. This is a pear to enjoy in your own company, preferably in the bath.'

Tender pear harvests

Poached lemon & ginger pears

Prep   5 minutes
Cook   50 minutes

3cm piece of fresh ginger, cut very thinly with a vegetable peeler
1 whole organic lemon, sliced very thinly
3 whole star anise
2 tbsp lemon juice
2 cups sugar
3 cups water
6-8 just-ripe pears, stems intact

These pears are best made a day or two before you plan to serve them so the flavours have time to mellow and develop.

Use a saucepan that will fit the pears snugly in a single layer. Put in all ingredients except pears and bring to a simmer, stirring to dissolve sugar. Simmer 10 minutes.

Peel pears and place in syrup. Cook at lowest simmer until just tender, about 30-35 minutes.

Lift pears out of syrup and place in a bowl. Boil syrup over high heat for a further 10 minutes to reduce.

Pour over pears. Cooked pears will keep in a covered container in the fridge for at least 2 weeks.

Serves 6-8

PORT GLAZE

This superb glaze keeps in the fridge for weeks and is terrific with any kind of fruit as well as sweet meats such as duck and pork. Make the glaze by placing together in a saucepan 1 cup red wine (eg merlot), ½ cup port, ¾ cup sugar, 6 whole cloves and 1 cinnamon quill. Bring to a simmer, stirring until sugar has dissolved. Reduce heat to low and simmer until syrupy and reduced by half, about 20-25 minutes. Serve warm or cool, spooned over fruit.
Serves 4

Roasted pears & almonds

Prep   5-10 minutes
Cook   30 minutes

½ cup sugar
1 cup water
2-4 whole cloves
2-3 strips lemon peel cut with a vegetable peeler
3 firm but ripe pears, halved and cored
2 tbsp melted butter
½ cup almond slices

Preheat oven to 220°C. In a pot or pan large enough to hold pear halves in a single layer, heat sugar, water, cloves and lemon peel, stirring to dissolve sugar. Bring to a simmer, add pear halves, cover and simmer 20 minutes. Lift pears out of syrup and place in a shallow baking dish, cut side up. Pour over syrup and bake until starting to caramelise, about 30 minutes.

Melt butter in a pan and cook almonds until golden, stirring frequently. Scatter almonds and butter over pears and serve.

Serves 6

BAKED PEARS WITH PORT GLAZE

Place 4 just-ripe pears with their stems intact in a baking dish with 2 tbsp honey and 1 cup water. Cover and bake at 180°C until tender, about 1 hour. Spoon over port glaze.
Serves 4

'The act of cooking is nourishing both for the cook and the eater. It's always a treat to have someone else cook for you, and when you cook there is a sense of care and usefulness in providing food for others to enjoy.'

Sweet autumn tarts

Fig & walnut tarts

Prep 15 minutes
Cook 16-18 minutes

1 sheet ready-rolled flaky pastry
1 cup shelled walnuts
⅓ cup icing sugar
1 teaspoon ground cinnamon
finely grated zest of ½ lemon
1 egg white
6 preserved figs
　(see right), quartered

Preheat oven to 200°C. Cut pastry in half and cut each half into 3 to make 6 rectangles. Arrange pastry on a baking sheet, allowing a little space between each piece.

Purée walnuts with icing sugar, cinnamon, lemon zest and egg white to form a coarse paste. Divide paste between pastry bases, spreading out to within 1cm of edges. Place 4 pieces of fig on top of each one. Brush with a little of the juice from the figs.

Bake for 10 minutes then reduce heat to 180°C and cook until golden and crisp, about 6-8 minutes more. Serve warm with whipped cream.

Variation: Use fresh fig quarters and sprinkle liberally with sugar before baking.

PRESERVED FIGS

As figs ripen you can keep preserving them in the same rich syrup. This mixture will cook up to 6kg of figs but I usually cook batches of 1-2kg as fruit ripens.

In a large pot, heat together 1½ litres water, 3kg sugar, 300ml malt vinegar, 100g sliced preserved ginger and 3 lemons, halved and thinly sliced. Bring to a simmer, stirring to dissolve sugar. Add figs and simmer gently for 2 hours. Bottle in sterilised preserving jars filled to overflowing with a little syrup or boiling water and sealed. Wipe jars clean and store in a cool, dark place.

Pear & almond tarts

Prep 15 minutes
Cook 25-30 minutes

1 sheet ready-rolled flaky pastry
　or 160g rolled thinly (5mm)
½ cup ground almonds
¼ cup sugar
1 tsp natural vanilla essence
½ teaspoon almond essence
1 egg white
2 just-ripe pears, cored
　and quartered
Glaze: 2 tablespoons apricot jam,
　warmed and thinned with
　1 tablespoon water

Preheat oven to 200°C. Cut 4 x 10cm rounds from pastry and place on a baking tray allowing a little space between each.

Combine ground almonds, sugar, vanilla, almond essence and egg white. Divide evenly between pastry rounds, about 2 tablespoons per tart, leaving a 1cm pastry border around the edge.

Thinly slice the pear quarters lengthways, leaving the stem end attached so they can be fanned out. Place a fan of pear on top of each tart.

Bake until pastry starts to puff, about 10 minutes, then reduce temperature to 180°C and cook until tarts are golden, fruit is tender and pastry cooked through, about 15-20 minutes. Brush tarts with apricot glaze while hot.
Serves 4

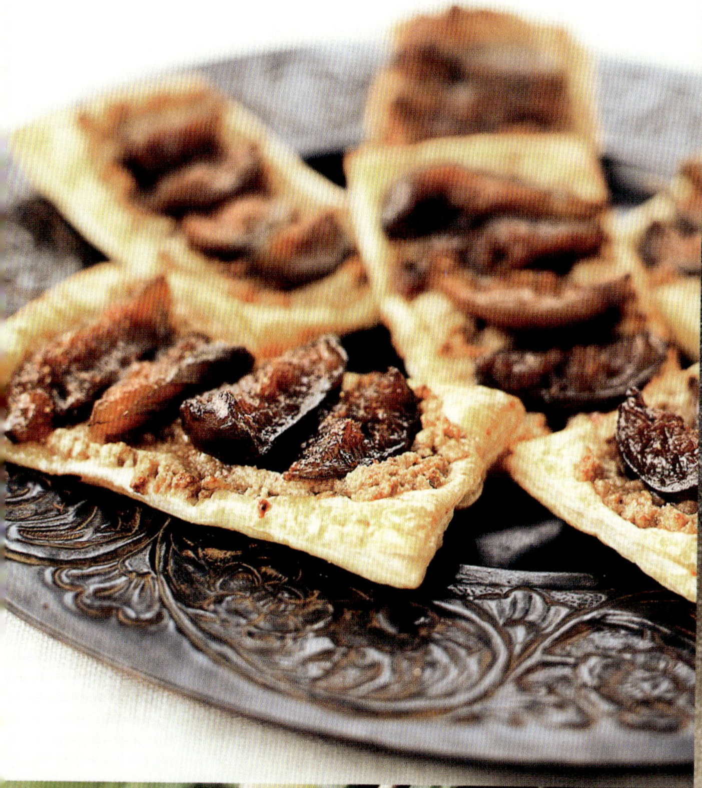
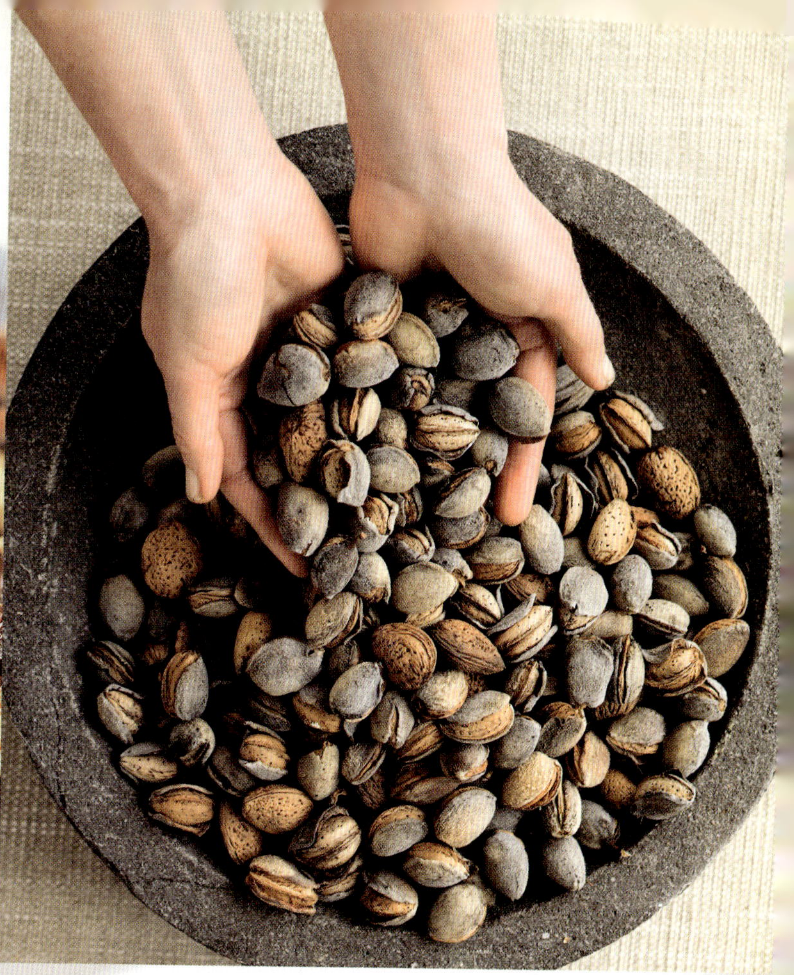
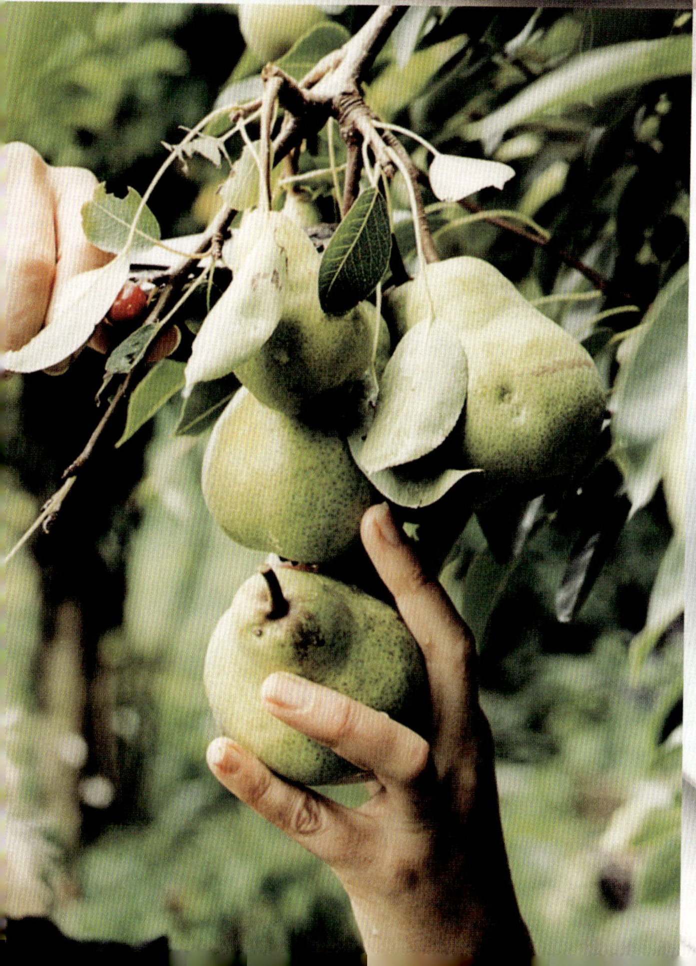
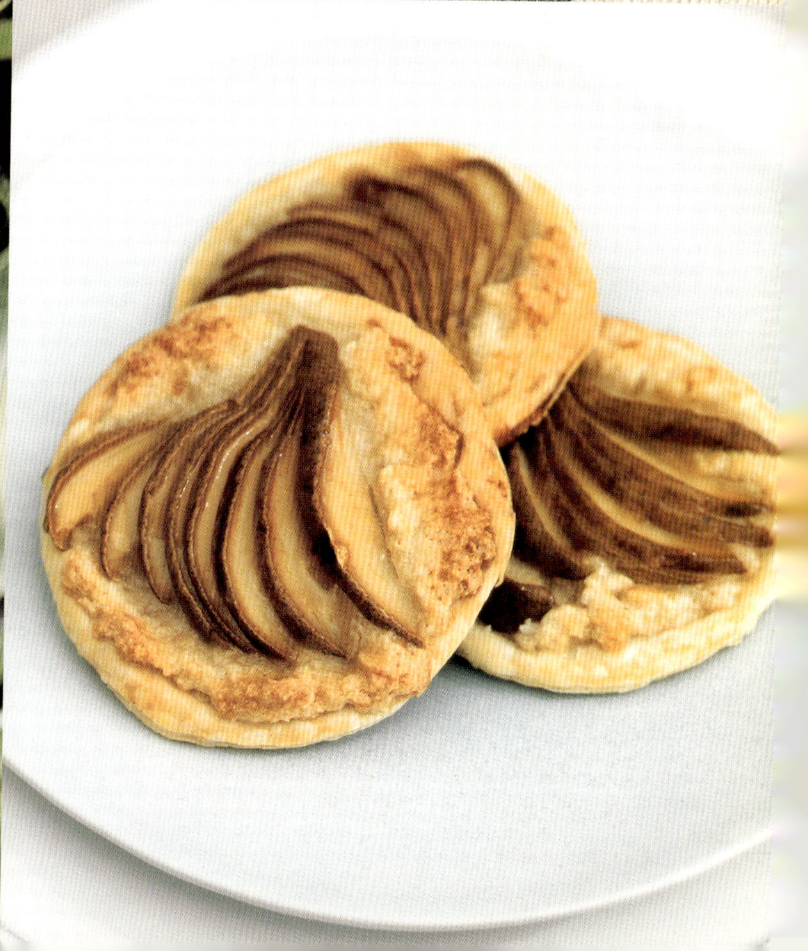

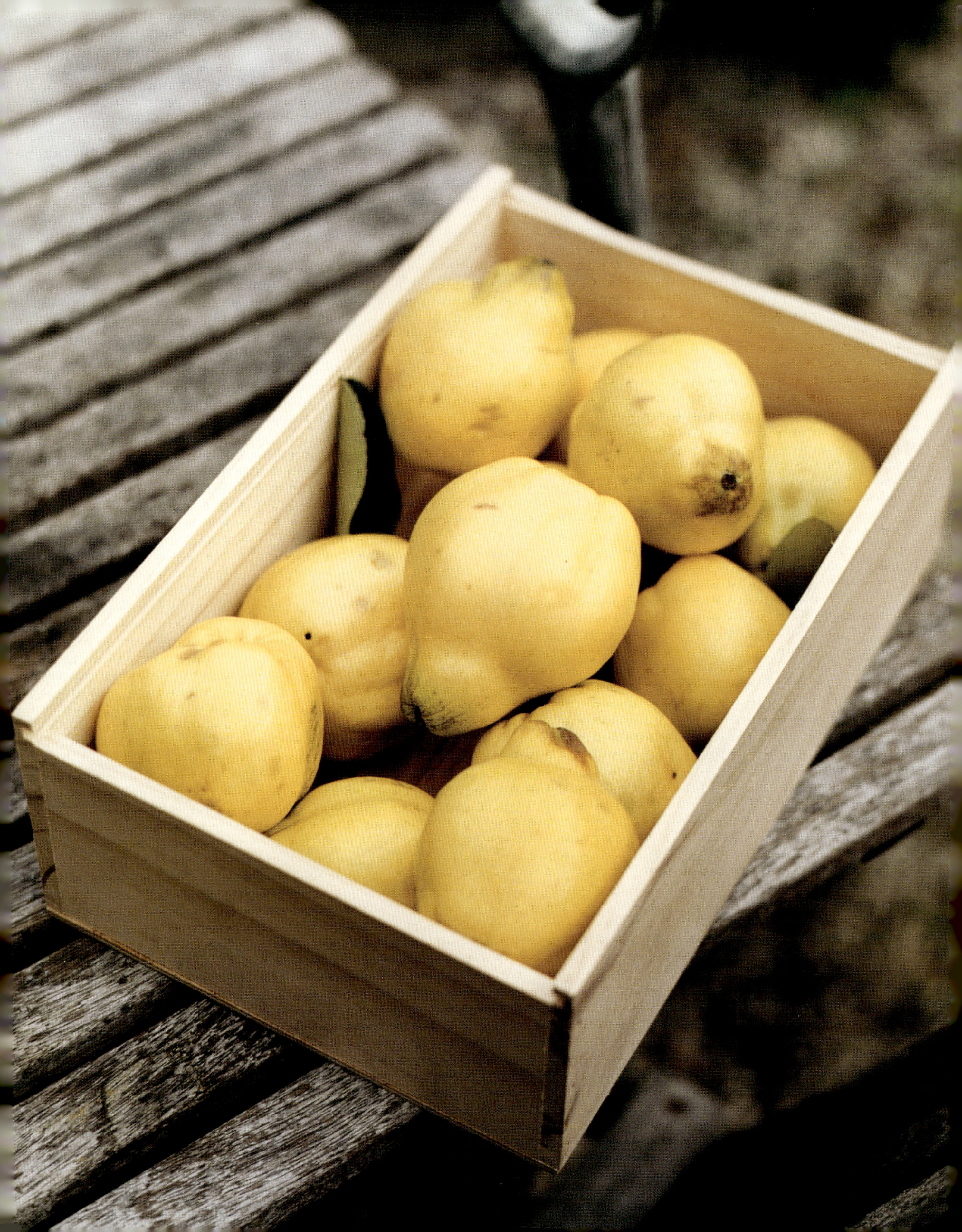

'The transformation of a gritty, hard, pale-fleshed quince into deep ruby melting softness is one of the most extraordinary changes in a fruit. Such alchemy is achieved simply with sugar and long, slow cooking.'

Old-fashioned quinces

Quince confit & ruby syrup

Prep 10 minutes
Cook 1 hour

2 large quinces (about 1kg), washed
2 cups water
3 cups sugar
½ cup lime or lemon juice

Quarter quinces, discarding cores. Heat water, sugar and lime or lemon juice, stirring to dissolve sugar. Add quinces, cover and simmer over low heat until tender and pink, about 1 hour.

Carefully lift out of syrup. Serve quinces and a little of their syrup with crème fraîche or mascarpone or use to make a ruby-red tarte tatin (see below).

Pour leftover syrup into a clean bottle and store in the fridge. Use as a drink, mixing 1 part syrup to 4 parts soda or water, as a syrup for ice cream or fruit salads, or to deglaze a pan after browning meats. It will keep for months.

Quince tarte tatin

Prep 10 minutes
Cook 15-20 minutes

1 recipe quince confit
⅓ cup syrup from cooked quinces
1 sheet flaky pastry or 160g pastry rolled thinly

Preheat oven to 200°C. Slice quince quarters lengthways into 3-4 pieces each. Pour syrup into a 20-23cm frying pan and arrange quinces on top in an overlapping ring. Simmer for 2-3 minutes.

Roll and cut the pastry to fit the pan and place on top of quinces. Bake tart until pastry is puffed and golden, 15-20 minutes. Remove from oven and invert on to a serving plate.

If tart cools too much before being inverted it will stick in the pan. Place pan over heat for a minute to soften juices then tip tart out on to plate.

Serves 6-8

HOME-MADE FRUIT ICE CREAM

Place 1 cup fresh fruit purée, eg feijoa, apricot, berry, plum, gooseberry or other tart fruit as available in a pot with ½ cup sugar, the finely grated zest of 1 lime and 2 tbsp lime juice. Simmer for 5 minutes. Put 4 egg whites in the clean bowl of an electric beater and beat to soft peaks. Add ½ cup sugar and beat until stiff, glossy peaks form when the beater is lifted. On low speed, gradually add hot fruit purée and beat until cool and very thick, about 10 minutes.

In a separate bowl, whisk 1 cup cream to soft peaks. Fold into egg white mixture using a large, flat spoon until evenly blended. Place in a freezing container, cover, and freeze until firm, about 4 hours. Keeps in freezer for several weeks.

Makes 1 litre

'Why do we love chocolate? Is it the phenylethylamine or "love chemical" in it that triggers feelings of euphoria? Whatever it is, unlike most feel-good foods, this one is fabulously good for you.'

Chocolate in disguise

Magic chocolate cake

Prep 15 minutes
Cook 50 minutes (less if making smaller cakes)

1 cup sugar
1 large egg
½ cup milk
1 packed cup (100g) grated raw pumpkin or carrot or a mix of both
⅓ cup premium-quality cocoa powder, sifted if lumpy
½ tsp mixed spice
½ tsp ground cinnamon
100g butter, softened
1 tsp baking soda
1 tsp natural vanilla essence
1 tbsp golden syrup
2 cups self-raising flour
½ cup strong, boiling-hot coffee
Garnish: chocolate ganache (see right)
Optional: melted white chocolate or silver cachou balls

If you have never made a cake before, let this be your first. It is so simple and the results are satisfyingly impressive. Everything gets whizzed in a blender and the result is a moist, dense, dark chocolate cake that cuts and keeps well and can be frozen.

Preheat oven to 160°C. Line a 23cm round cake tin with baking paper or prepare 2 x 10cm tins (recycled large tuna cans are perfect) or 10 muffin tins (using ½ cup of mixture per muffin tin).

Place all ingredients in the bowl of a food processor and mix until combined, about 30-40 seconds (or place ingredients in a mixing bowl and beat with an electric beater). Pour into prepared tin and smooth the top. Bake until risen, no longer wobbly in the middle and a skewer inserted into the centre comes out clean. One large cake will take about 50 minutes, for 2 medium cakes allow about 40 minutes and for muffin-sized cakes allow 20-25 minutes. Cool in tin and cover with ganache when cold. If desired, drizzle with melted white chocolate or sprinkle with silver cachou balls. Store in a sealed container in a cool place for 2-3 days or wrap and freeze.
Makes 1 x 23cm cake, 2 x 10cm cakes or 10 muffin-sized cakes

CHOCOLATE GANACHE
Heat ½ cup cream in a small pot. Add 150g chopped dark eating chocolate. Allow cream to simmer then remove from heat and stir until smooth. Ganache will thicken when it cools.
Makes 1 cup

CHOCOLATE CRAVINGS
So what is it about chocolate that makes women crave it once a month? Research suggests that its rich magnesium content may be the answer. Magnesium deficiency exacerbates PMT. Progesterone levels are also high at this time. Progesterone promotes fat storage, preventing its use as fuel, and high levels of progesterone produce a periodic craving for fatty foods. This affects both men and women.

CREAM CHEESE ICING
Mix 35g soft butter, 125g cream cheese (not spreadable), juice and finely grated rind of ½ lemon and 2 cups icing sugar in a food processor until smooth. Cool to a spreadable consistency then spread over cake.
Makes 1½ cups

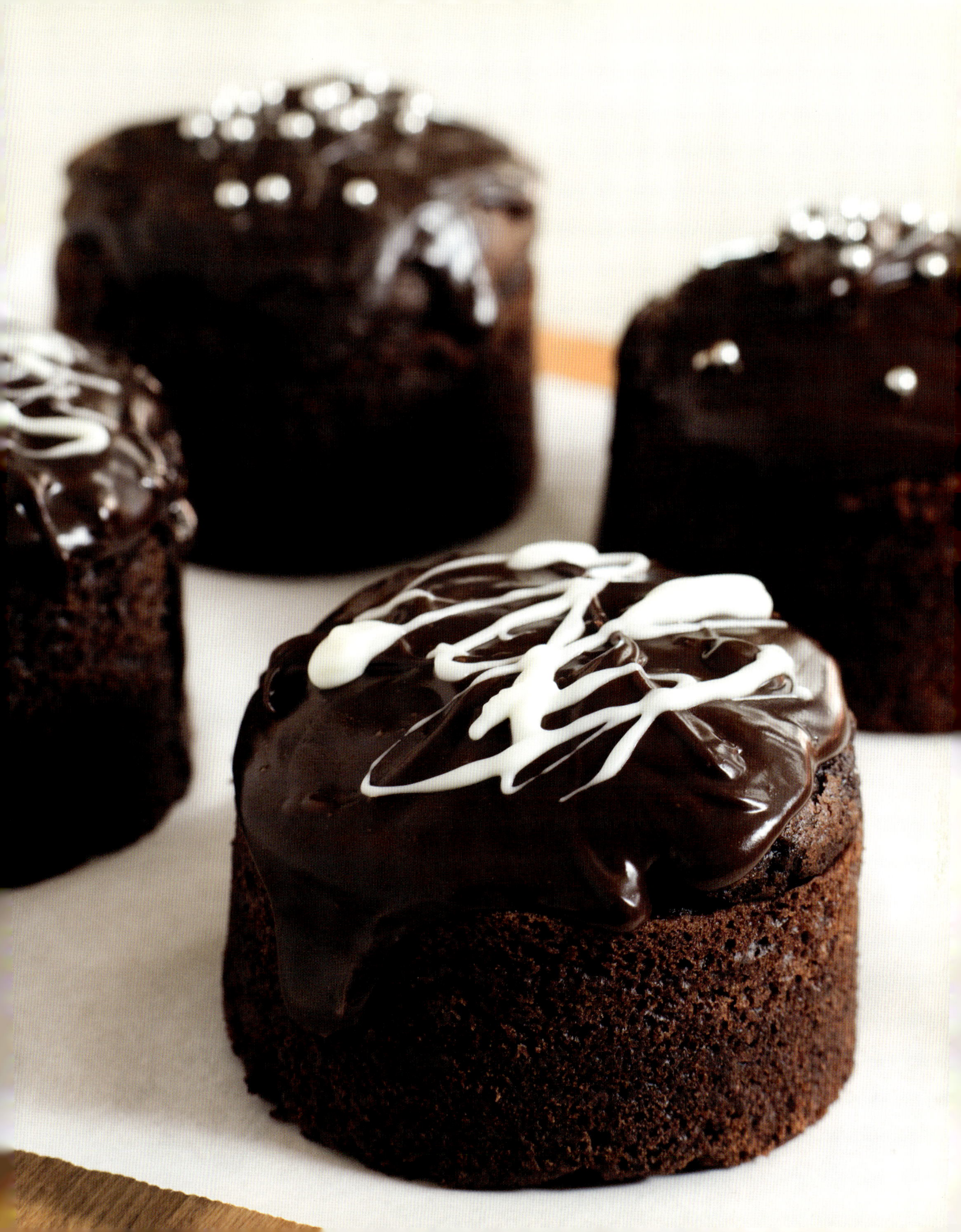

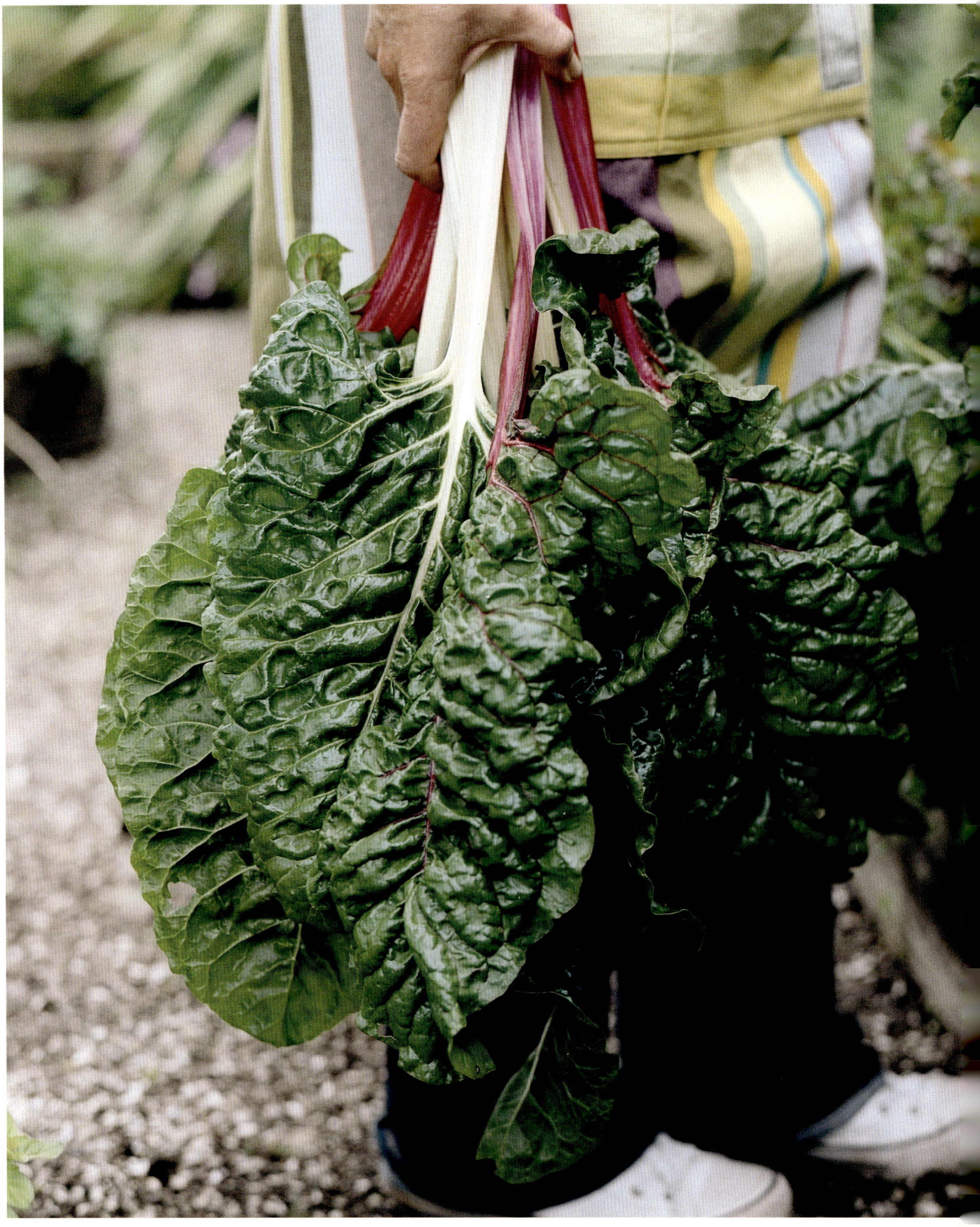

Winter

It's a primal instinct for our appetites to seek out richer, more substantial tastes over winter – a hangover in our genes from the hunter-gatherer days when packing on the fat meant surviving the cold. The instinct remains, although our lifestyles no longer demand it. Reigning in our appetites requires a sacrifice to quantity but not good taste. The inclement weather brings us indoors to potter over the stove with heart-warming concoctions. Without the outdoors to distract us we are drawn to the table, assuaging our need for sociability and good conversation over the rustic flavours of hearty soups and stews.

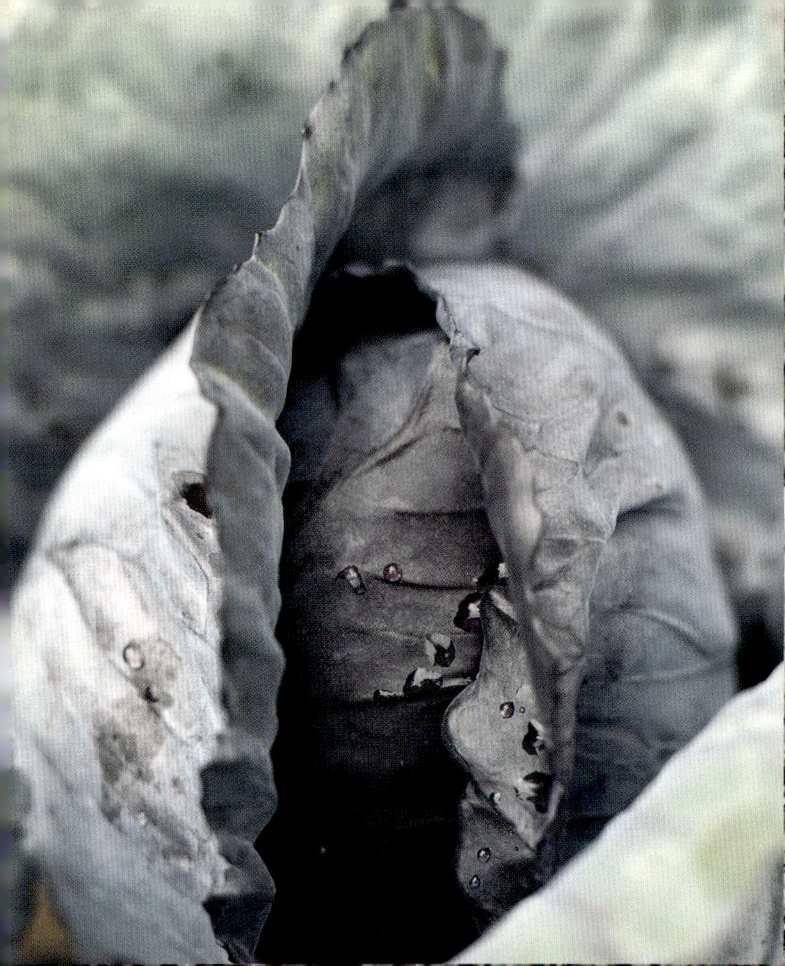
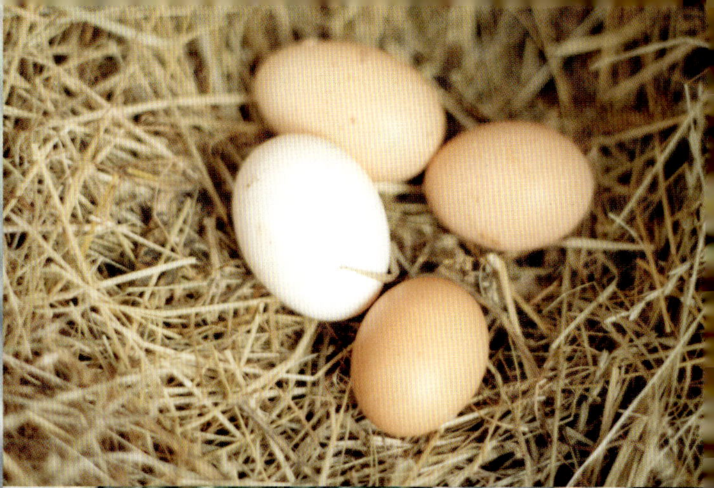
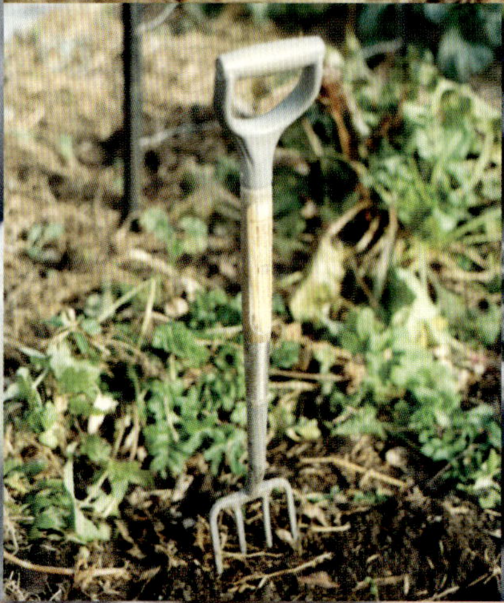
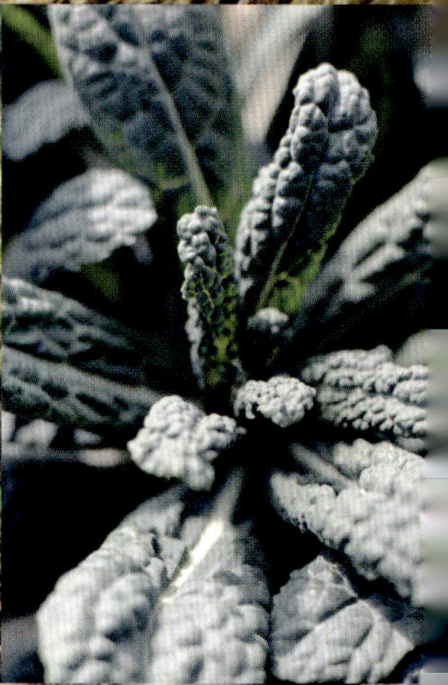
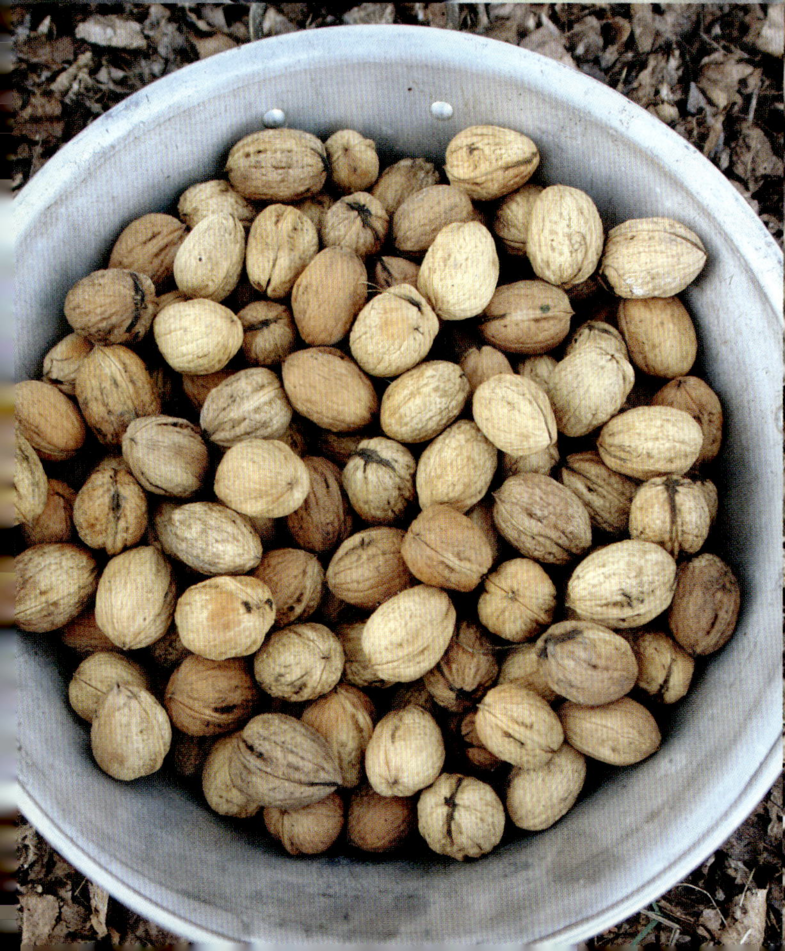
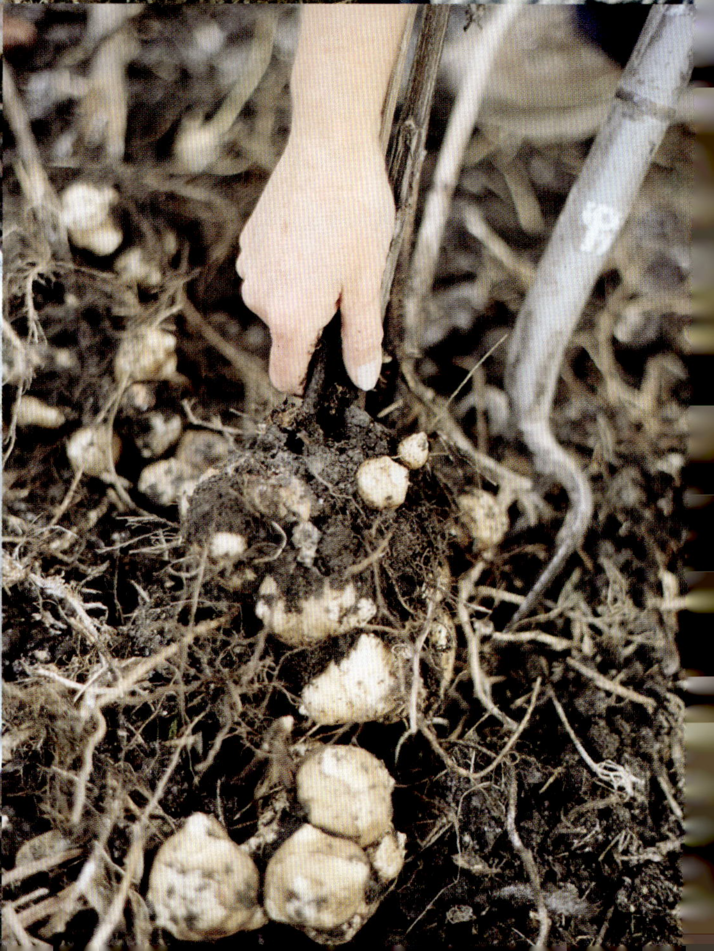

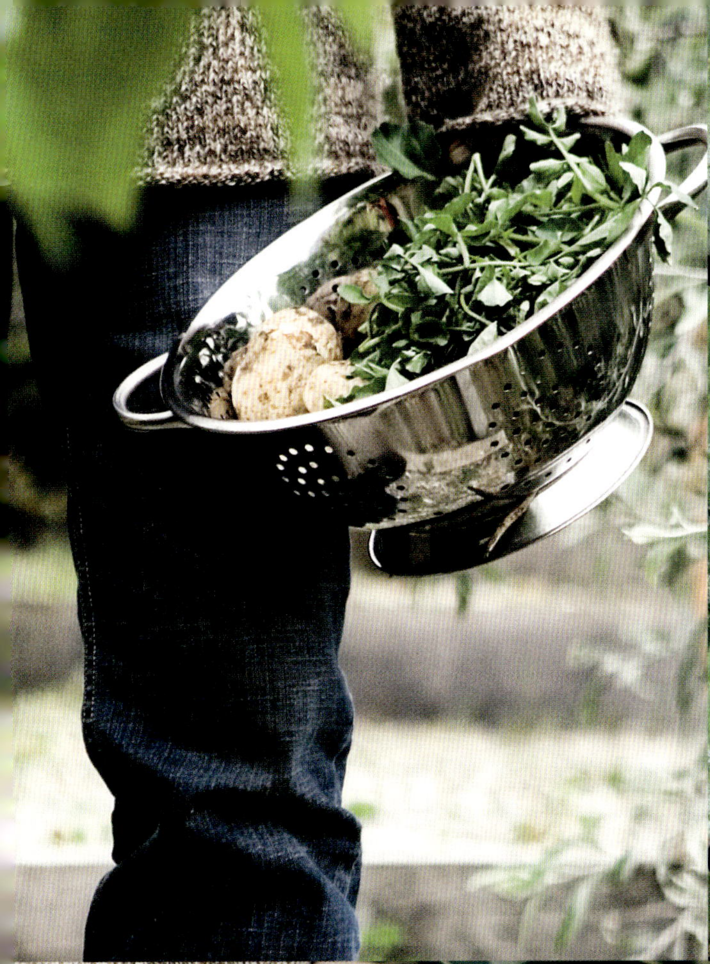
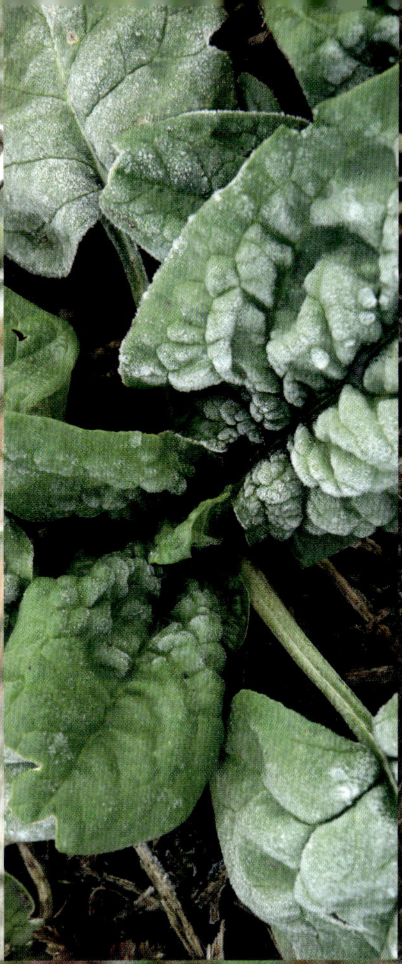
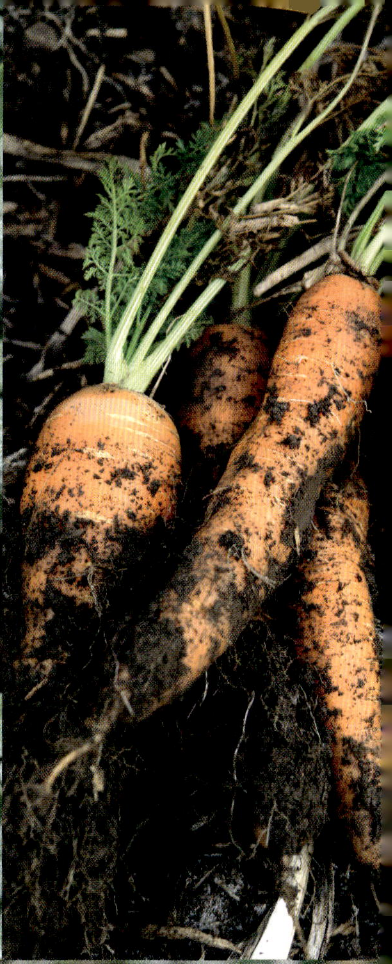
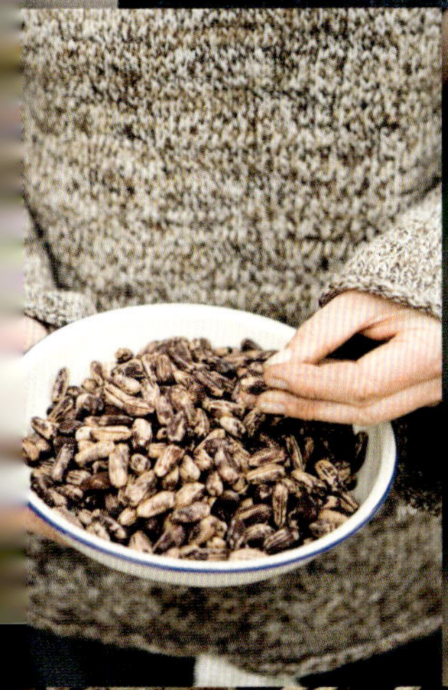
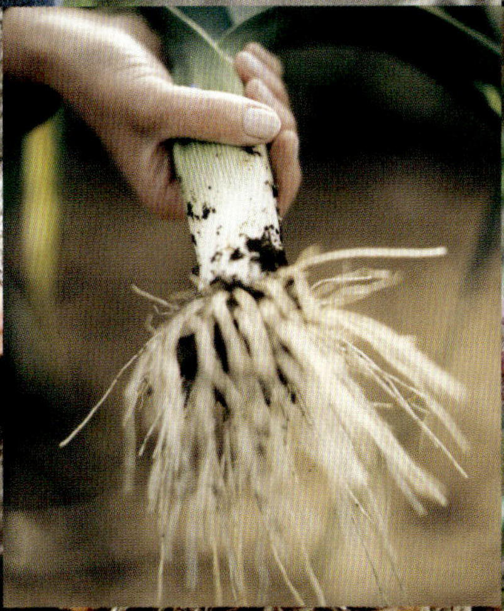
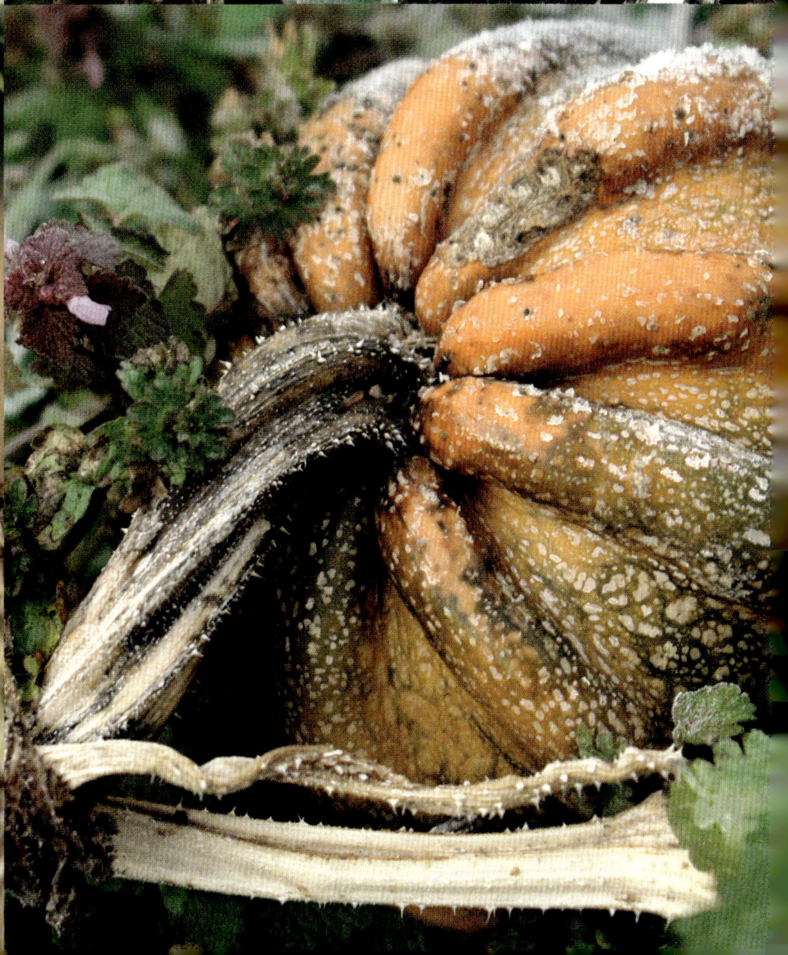
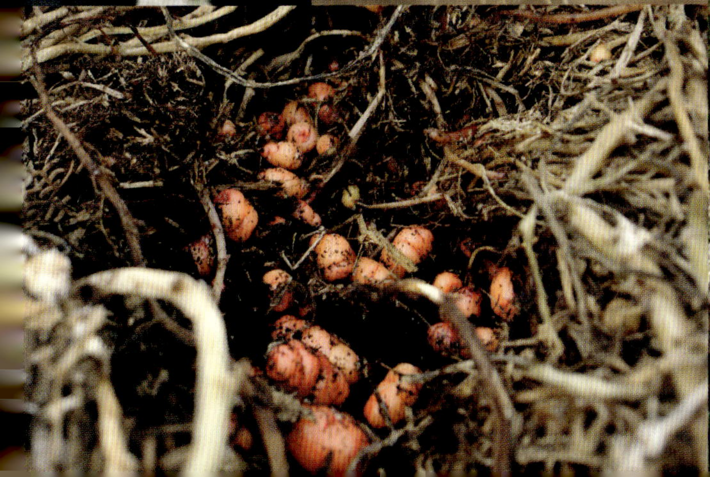

'Aromatic spices give depth to winter flavours. Buy them whole and toast before use to release their essential oils. Seed spices grind easily once toasted and their flavour is fresher and more intense.'

Spicing up winter

Fresh in winter

beetroot
brassicas including kale, brussels sprouts & cavalo nero
carrots
celeriac
cherimoya
chestnuts
citrus including limes
earth gems
fennel
kiwifruit
Jerusalem artichokes
land cress
leeks
miner's lettuce
parsnip
pomegranates
silverbeet
spinach
swedes
tamarillos
turnips
winter lettuces
witloof, chicory and endive
yams

Flavours

bay
chervil
coriander
garlic
oregano
parsley
rosemary
sage
thyme
winter mint

I enjoy spicy, aromatic food in winter and find Asian-style dishes based around lentils, grains and vegetables satisfying to eat without generating extra unwanted kilos. Cravings for hot, belly-filling food see the preparation of hearty one-dish meals – big pots of richly flavoured stews and soups that can be dipped into as the week progresses. Salads take a back seat, coming into play as light starters or side dishes to accompany a hot main course.

With many of the annuals and perennials in hibernation the choice of fresh harvests is limited, amounting to little more than hardy greens and roots and stored autumn crops. Many tender salad greens won't survive the cold but spinach, miner's lettuce, land cress and chervil are worth growing for fresh salad tastes through the winter months. The Allium family (onions, garlic, shallots and leeks) comes to the fore, adding depth and sweetness to winter dishes while the brassicas deliver clean, sometimes pungent, green tastes. Crops like brussels sprouts and swedes need the cold to really bring out their flavour and never taste better than after a good frost.

Find a good source of natural stocks or make your own in bulk and freeze to ensure hearty flavours in soups and stews. Cut down on the butter and cream and look to spices and other flavourings to give depth to winter dishes. Fresh spices such as cardamom, cloves, fennel, cumin, coriander, peppercorns, sweet smoked paprika, as well as Thai curry pastes, frozen chillies, dried mushrooms, ginger and garlic with accents of winter citrus deliver the goods when it comes to rich, satsifying winter flavours.

1. Fennel seeds
2. Turmeric
3. Smoked paprika
4. Cardamom pods
5. Cumin seeds
6. Dried chillies

CHICKEN STOCK

Pack 3-4 raw chicken frames or necks into a very large pot with 2 peeled onions, 2 carrots, 2 bay leaves and 6 peppercorns. Add cold water to come 2 finger joints above the chicken. Do not add salt. Bring to the boil and cook for 1½ hours, skimming off any surface scum. Cool and strain. Chill for up to 5 days or freeze.

VEGETABLE STOCK

Chop without peeling 1 large carrot, 2 large onions, 3 stalks celery, 1 large leek, split lengthways and cleaned, and 1 large potato. Add 2 bay leaves, 10 peppercorns and a couple of parsley sprigs. Add 12 cups water. Simmer 1 hour, skimming off any surface scum. Cool and strain. Chill for up to 5 days or freeze.

1.

2.

3.

4.

5.

6.

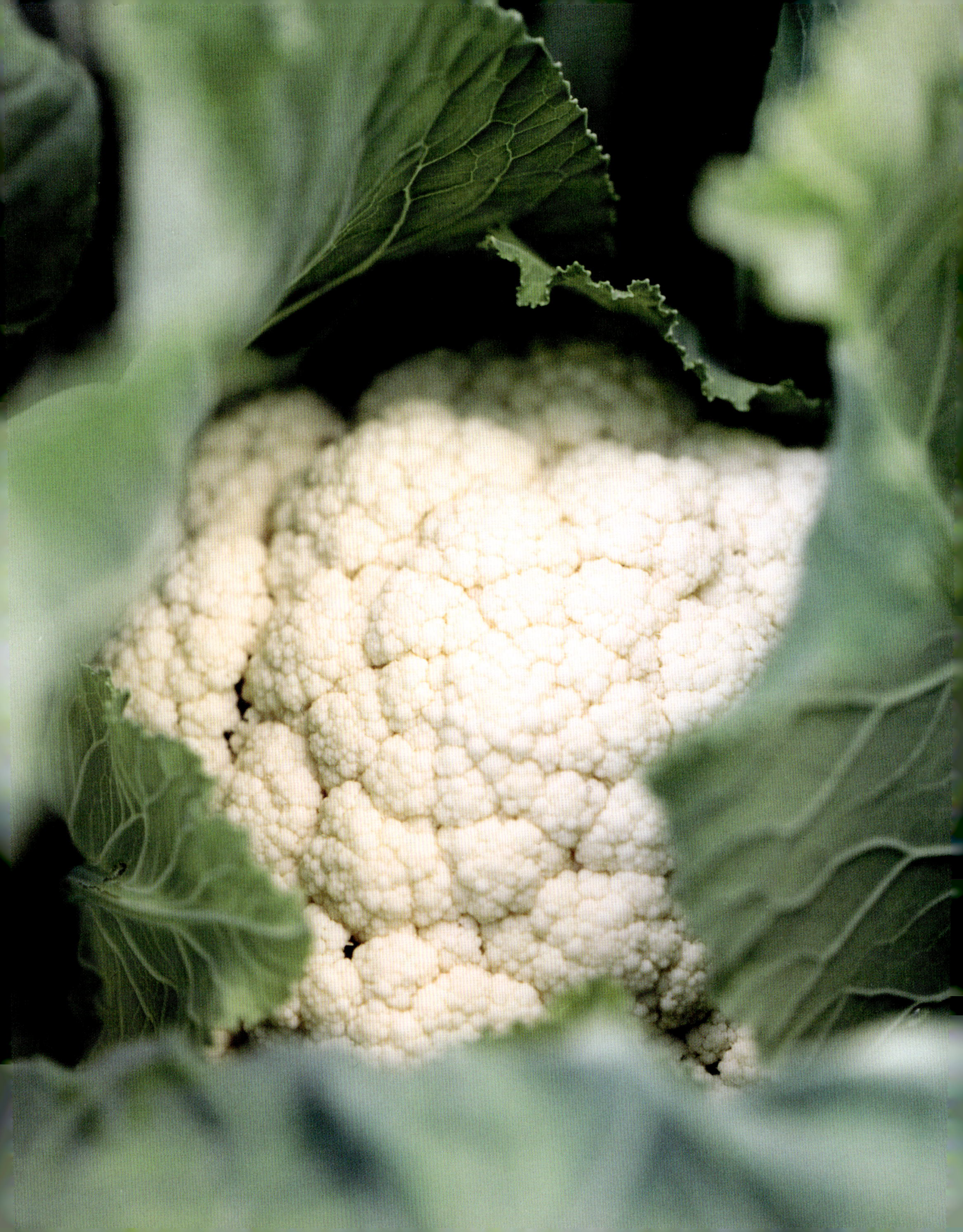

'The aroma of baking bread evokes a feel-good sense of hearth and home. A tray of roasting almonds delivers the same welcoming effect with less effort.'

Dip or spread

Anchoïade
Prep   10 minutes
Makes 1 cup

Anchovy sauce:
2 x 50g cans anchovies
3 cloves garlic, crushed
1 tbsp capers
6 kalamata olives, pitted
2 tbsp red wine vinegar
grinds of pepper
¼ cup olive oil

To serve: a selection of fresh and lightly cooked vegetables, allow about 60-80g per person

This dense, rich, Mediterranean blend is wonderful served with fresh seasonal vegetables. Lightly cook cauliflower and broccoli for 2 minutes, cool in iced water and drain before serving. Serve other vegetables such as fennel, carrots, celery and endive raw. In summer include capsicums, beans, cucumber and snowpeas as dunkers.

To prepare sauce, place all ingredients in a food processor or blender and purée until smooth.
Cover tightly and chill for at least 2 hours to allow flavours to develop. Serve with seasonal vegetables for dipping. Sauce will keep in the fridge for up to a week. To use as a dressing, thin with a little more oil.
Makes 1 cup, enough for 8-10 serves

Broccoli & blue cheese cichetti
Prep   10 minutes
Cook   30 minutes

2 heads broccoli (800-900g)
2 fat cloves garlic, crushed
finely grated zest of 1 lemon
3 tbsp olive oil
½ tsp salt and grinds of pepper
30g blue cheese, finely crumbled or grated
1 tsp chilli oil or a pinch of chilli flakes

This makes a great topping for bruschetta or pizza and is also delicious as a sauce for cooked pasta or thinned with stock for a soup.

Preheat oven to 160°C. Trim broccoli into very small florets. Peel and finely chop the stems (1-2cm). Place florets and stems in a bowl and pour over boiling water to cover. Stand for 2 minutes then drain thoroughly. Combine in a roasting dish with garlic, zest and oil. Spread out evenly, season with salt and pepper and roast for 30 minutes.
Remove from oven and sprinkle with cheese and chilli oil or flakes. Allow to cool.
Makes about 3 cups

Variation: For broccoli and blue cheese pasta, toss through 500g cooked pasta with a little olive oil or stock.
Serves 4
For broccoli and blue cheese soup, purée with 4-5 cups vegetable stock.
Serves 6

ALMOND BUTTER
Preheat oven to 180°C. Place 300g raw almonds (or cashews) in a baking dish and mix through ¼ cup neutral oil, eg grapeseed. Spread out evenly in dish and sprinkle with ¼ tsp salt. Roast until golden and aromatic, 12-15 minutes. Remove nuts from tray and allow to cool, about 30 minutes. Place cooled nuts in the bowl of a food processor and blend in bursts until they form a fine crumb. Slowly add an extra ¼ cup oil and continue blending to form a smoothish butter with a spreadable consistency – do not blend too finely. Store butter in a sealed jar in a cool place; it will keep for a couple of months.
Makes 2 cups

'While you can use soft-leaved herbs like basil or parsley with abandon, those perennials or shrubby herbs with woody stems tend to have much stronger-tasting leaves and as such should be used judiciously.'

Pre-dinner snack

I like to serve a little snack in the kitchen before we head to the table for dinner. It's a chance to relax and have a chat over a glass of nice wine and an appetite-whetting snack. A bowl of marinated olives will suffice if you don't want to go to any fuss. I make my own spicy marinated olives by baking them in a 180°C oven for about 20 minutes with a little oil, a couple of chillies, a sprig of rosemary and 2-3 cloves of garlic. They keep in the fridge for weeks.

Ready-cooked bruschetta bases spread with tasty toppings make a great stand-up starter. We tend to think of bruschetta as a summer dish topped with sweet tomatoes, basil and olive oil but over the winter I use toppings such as the mushroom mixture at right, the semi-dried tomato and olive salsa on page 192, the broccoli and blue cheese cichetti on page 187, or the winter pesto on page 192 topped with sliced pear and a little feta.

BRUSCHETTA BASES

Angle-slice a sourdough or country loaf into slices about 5mm thick. Brush with olive oil and grill or brown on a griddle, pressing down firmly as they cook to brown evenly. Bases are best made the day they are to be served. You can also make crisp bases to store by brushing with oil and baking. Brush olive oil over sliced bread and sprinkle with garlic salt or citrus salt (page 222). Bake until crisp, about 20 minutes in a 180°C oven. Cool then store in an airtight container.

MUSHROOM BRUSCHETTA

Heat a heavy frying pan, add 2 rashers diced streaky bacon and cook until starting to crisp. Add 250g thinly sliced portobello or button mushrooms, 2 cloves crushed garlic and the finely grated zest of 1 lemon and cook over medium-high heat until mushrooms are starting to brown, about 5 minutes. Remove from heat, season to taste and mix through 2 tbsp mascarpone or softened cream cheese and 1 tbsp finely chopped parsley. Divide mixture over 10 slices grilled bread. *Makes 10, serves 3-4 as a snack*

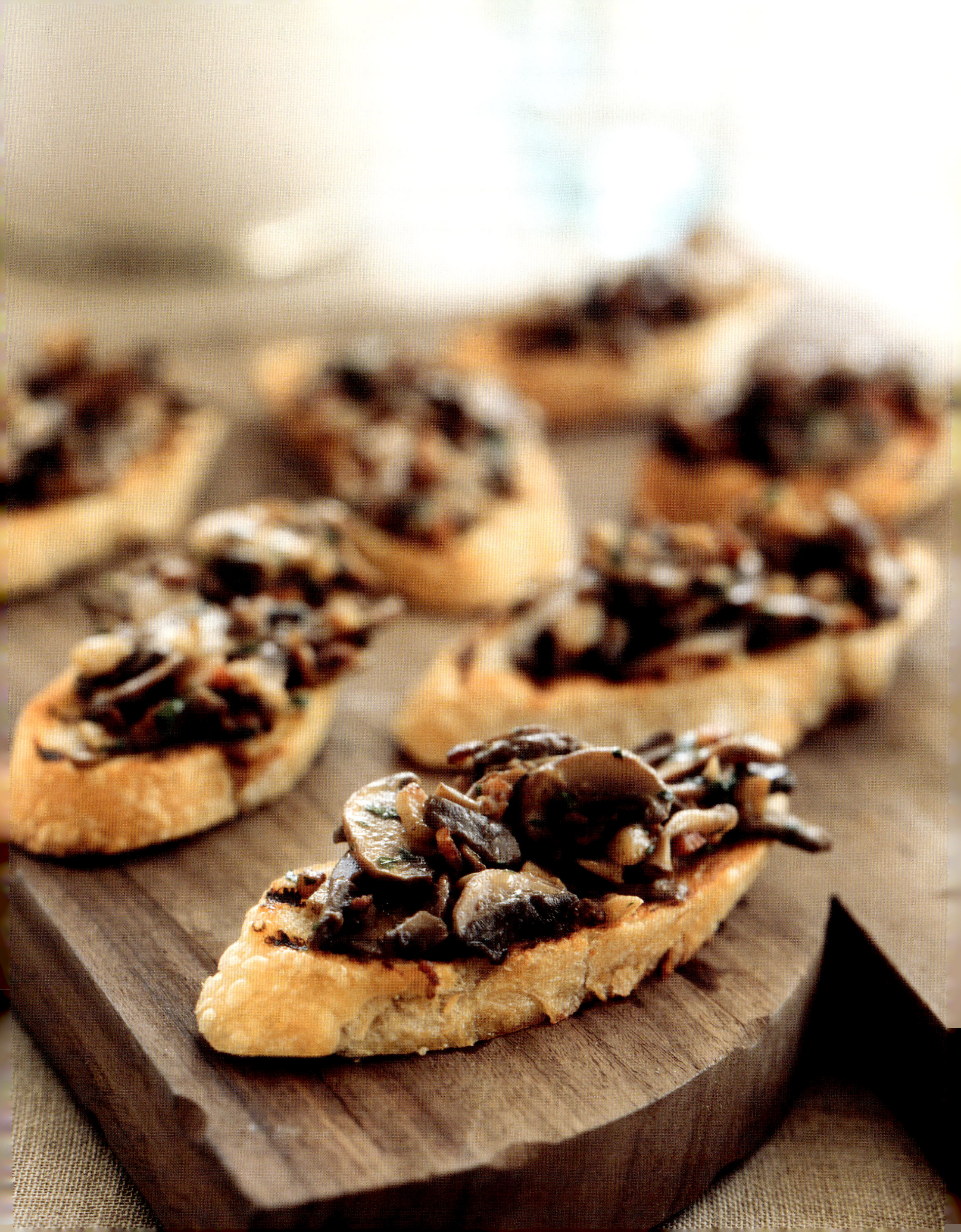

'Discovering how other cultures use everyday produce opens new worlds of cooking possibilities. It's always fascinating to learn of different ways to deal with a staple like potatoes or silverbeet.'

Spinach and silverbeet tarts

Spinach & mozzarella tarts

Prep 10 minutes
Cook 15 minutes

1 cup (250g) cooked spinach, squeezed dry
2 tbsp mascarpone
⅓ cup finely grated parmesan
¼ tsp ground nutmeg
½ tsp salt and grinds of pepper
1 sheet flaky or savoury shortcrust pastry
60-70g mozzarella, sliced into 12 pieces

Use fresh or frozen thawed spinach for these great little tarts. They can be cooked ahead of time and reheated or, if you prefer, have the topping ready mixed to assemble and bake tarts when you want to serve them.

Preheat oven to 200°C. Place spinach in a mixing bowl with mascarpone, parmesan and nutmeg and season with salt and pepper. Use a spoon to mix until evenly combined.
Cut pastry sheet into 12 rectangles and arrange on a baking tray. Place spinach topping on pastry pieces and top each one with a slice of mozzarella. Bake until golden and pastry is fully cooked, about 15-20 minutes. Serve warm or hot. Cooked pastries can be reheated in a moderate oven (180°C) for a few minutes.
Makes 12

Greek silverbeet roll

Prep 15 minutes
Cook 40 minutes

2 tbsp olive oil
1 large onion, finely chopped
250g silverbeet with half the white stalk removed, washed and chopped (or use spinach)
1 egg, lightly beaten
200g ricotta
100g feta, crumbled
½ cup grated parmesan
¼ cup chopped coriander
½ tsp ground nutmeg
finely grated zest of ½ lemon
salt and grinds of pepper
optional: ¼ cup pine nuts, toasted
8 sheets filo pastry
melted butter or oil spray

Preheat oven to 180°C. Heat oil in a deep frypan and cook onion over low heat until soft. Add silverbeet and cook until pan is dry. Take off heat and mix in all other ingredients except pastry and melted butter.
Place 2 sheets of filo on the bench, overlapping their shortest sides by 2cm to make a very long rectangle. Brush with butter or spray liberally with oil. Repeat layers, brushing or spreading with butter between, to form a long, joined, rectangular stack of pastry 4 sheets thick. Divide silverbeet mixture into a sausage shape along nearest edge of pastry, leaving a border at the sides to turn in. Roll up to fully enclose filling, forming a long cigar shape. Seal edge with oil spray and gently roll cigar into a spiral shape on a baking tray. Brush with more oil or butter. Bake until crisp and golden, 40 minutes.
Serves 4-6

SILVERBEET
Beta vulgaris var. cicla
Silverbeet might lack the tender, sweet succulence of spinach or the nutty al dente bite of broccoli, but it's one of the most reliable and unfussy vegetables in the garden. Use stainless steel to prepare and cook it rather than raw steel, which causes the leaves to oxidise and discolour. In some cultures the leaves and white ribbed stalks are cooked separately, but if you slice them thinly the stalks cook just as quickly as the leaves. Wash well before cooking – the leaves make a good hiding place for snails.
For a simple side dish of **sautéed silverbeet**, wash and slice stalks and leaves finely and cook in a little olive oil with a pinch of salt until tender and a deep green, 5-6 minutes.
The summer we lived in Sicily, the nearby agritourism (farmstay) produced the most delicious **silverbeet gratin** as a starter dish. Prepare a big pan of sautéed silverbeet as above, using about 600g, and spread in a shallow baking dish. Drizzle with a little extra virgin olive oil. Make the lemon caper crumb on page 46 and scatter over the dish, sprinkle with grated parmesan and bake at 180°C until crusty and golden, about 30 minutes.
Serves 4-6

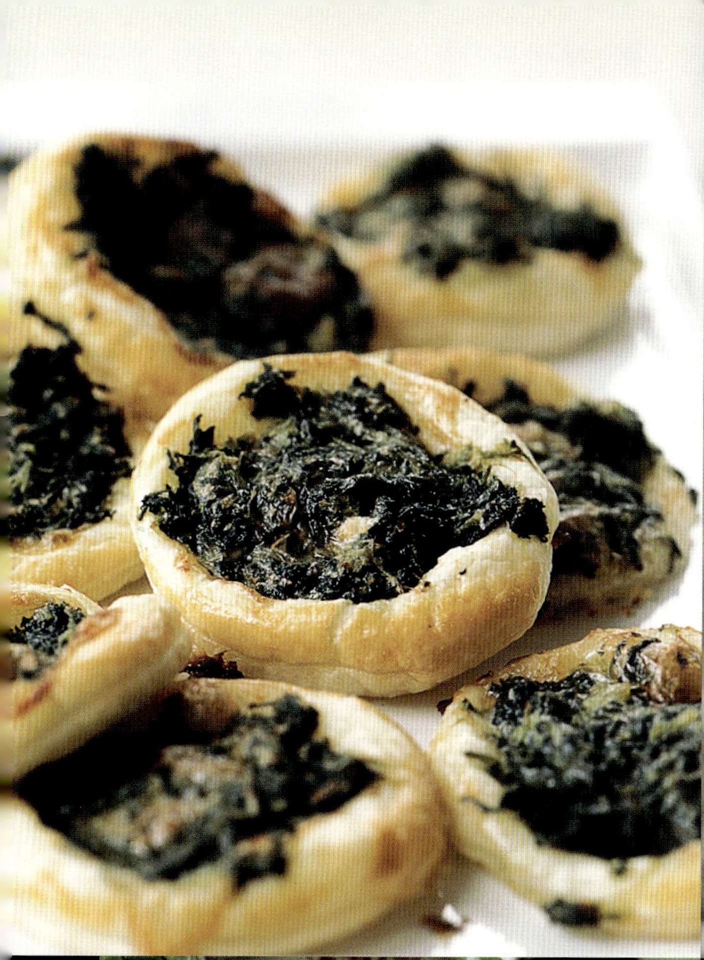
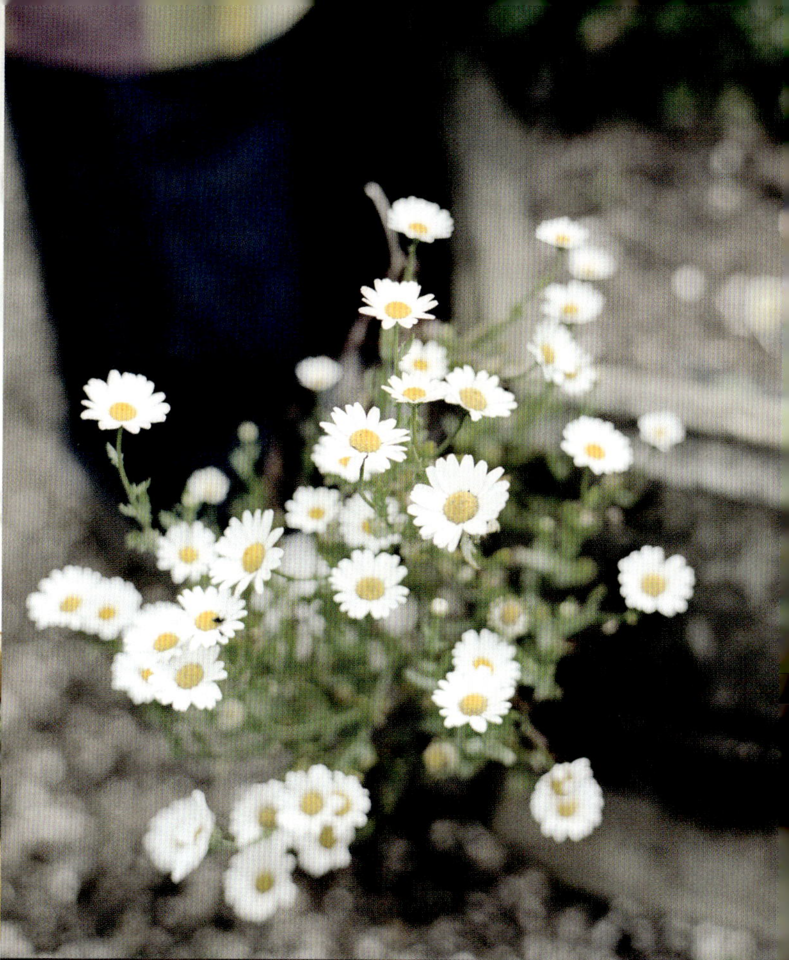
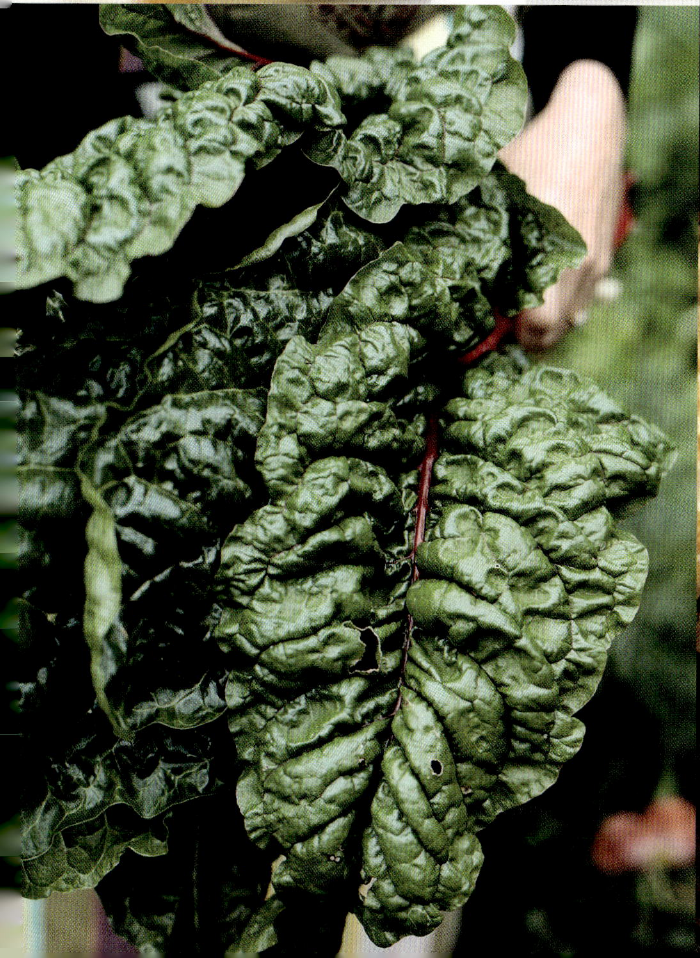
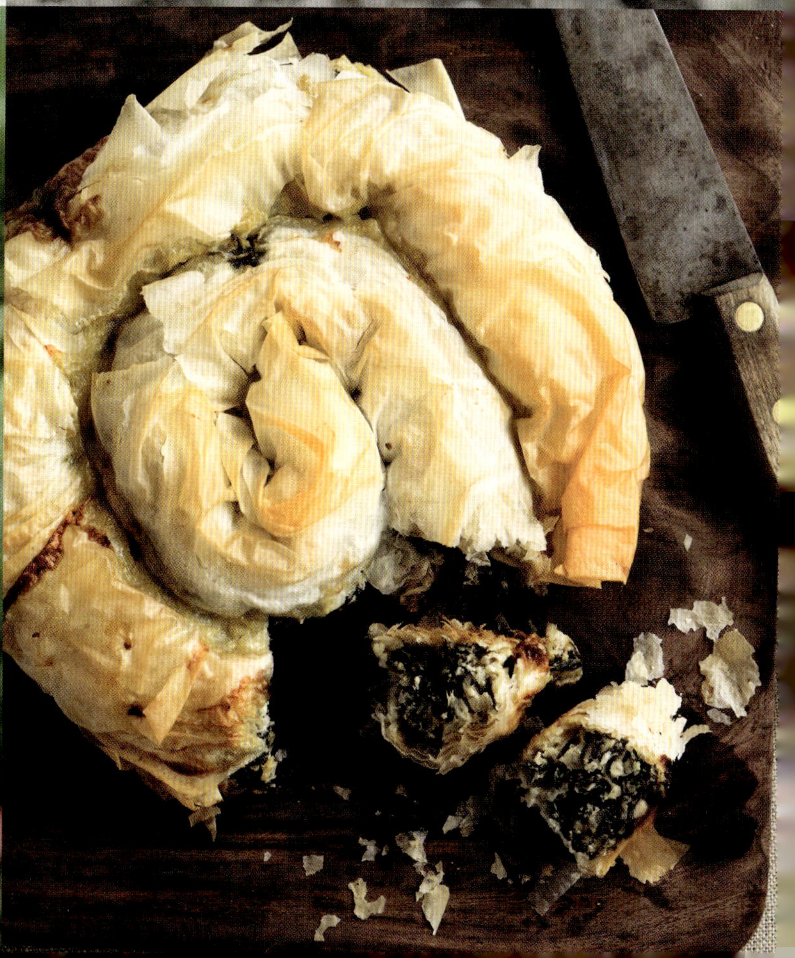

'Keeping a supply of what I call "fridge flavour boosters" on hand perks up winter food that might otherwise taste a bit ordinary. Semi-dried tomatoes, olives and roasted garlic keep for weeks in the fridge.'

Flavour boosters

Semi-dried tomato & olive salsa
Prep 10 minutes

Combine ½ cup chopped semi-dried tomatoes, 20 pitted and chopped black olives, ½ cup finely chopped flat-leaf parsley, ¼ cup toasted pine nuts, 2 tbsp chopped capers, 2 tbsp extra virgin olive oil, 2 cloves crushed garlic and the finely grated zest of 1 lemon. Keeps up to a week in the fridge.
Makes 1½ cups

Roasted garlic aioli
Prep 10 minutes

Mix 3 egg yolks, 2 tbsp lemon juice, ½ tsp salt and a few grinds of black pepper in a blender or food processor until smooth. With motor running, slowly add 1½ cups neutral oil, eg grapeseed, and process until thick. Blend in the flesh from 1 large or 2 small heads of roasted garlic (see right). Adjust seasonings to taste. Chill. Keeps up to 2 weeks in the fridge.
Makes about 2 cups

Winter pesto
Prep 10 minutes

Purée together until smooth 1 packed cup mint leaves, 1 packed cup parsley without stalks, the finely grated zest of 1 lemon, 2 cloves garlic, peeled, ¼ cup toasted walnuts or almonds, ¼ tsp salt and ¼ cup olive oil. Season with salt and freshly ground pepper to taste. Keeps up to 2 weeks in the fridge (cover the top with a layer of oil).
Makes about 1½ cups

ROASTED GARLIC
Slice 2 whole heads of garlic in half and place in a shallow roasting dish, cut side up. Pour over ½ cup olive oil. Bake at 160°C until soft, about 30 minutes. Cool then remove and discard skins (cloves should push out easily). Store garlic in cooking oil in the fridge; it will keep for weeks. Both the garlic and the oil can be used – the oil has a nice roasted-garlic flavour, good for risottos and sauces.

PRESERVED LEMONS
Wash 8 lemons, preferably organic. Cut in thick wedges, place on a tray and freeze until firm (2 hours). Remove from the freezer and sprinkle with ¼ cup salt. Stand for at least 1 hour or up to 4 hours. Pack slices into a jar, sprinkling with a little paprika and turmeric between each layer. Pour over the salty juices and cover with vegetable oil. Lemons will be ready in a few days and will keep for months. Remove the flesh and pith and use only the rind, finely chopped into couscous, salads and sauces.
Makes 1 large jar

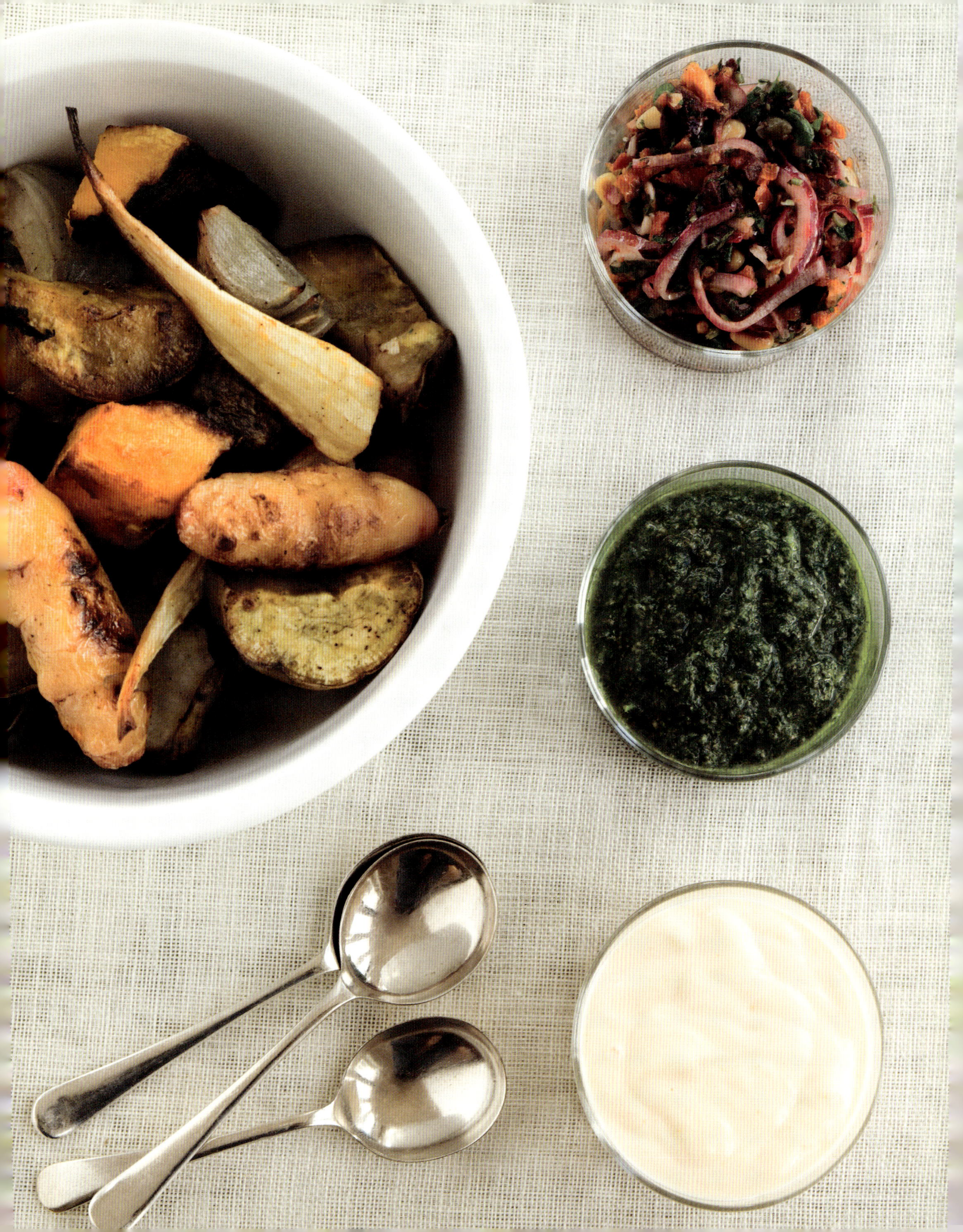

'Heading out into the garden on a frosty winter's day to dig leeks or pick spinach gets fresh air into house-bound lungs. Fresh, raw tastes alleviate that sense of cold-weather stodge.'

Winter salad combinations

Winter spinach, witloof & orange salad
Prep 10 minutes

Place 140g baby spinach or miner's lettuce in a large mixing bowl. Finely slice 2 heads witloof or a head of curly endive and add to bowl with 3 sliced oranges, 1 finely chopped spring onion, ½ cup roasted almonds and the diced flesh of 1 avocado (optional). Toss gently to combine with 2-3 tbsp chilli citrus dressing (page 26) and divide between serving plates.
Serves 4 as a side dish

Crisp cauliflower & cashew salad
Prep 5 minutes

Cut 200g fresh cauliflower into florets, discarding stems. Place in a food processor with ½ cup salted roasted cashews and pulse a few times until mixture resembles coarse crumbs. Mix in 2 tbsp chopped coriander leaves, 1 tsp grated fresh ginger, 2 tsp neutral oil, a pinch of salt and several grinds of pepper. Toss to combine evenly.
Serves 6 as a side dish

Leeks vinaigrette
Prep 5 minutes
Cook 15 minutes

Halve 10 baby leeks lengthways and wash well, removing any grit or soil. Lay leeks flat in a large, deep frypan or pot. Pour over boiling water to just cover, add ½ tsp salt and 1 tbsp extra virgin olive oil and simmer gently until tender, about 12-15 minutes. Drain leeks thoroughly. Divide between 4 serving plates and drizzle each one with 1 tbsp honey mustard dressing (page 84).
Serves 4, pictured right

PLANTING FOR YEAR-ROUND HARVESTS
By planting successively, some vegetables provide crops year-round, with different varieties preferring or tolerating the conditions relevant to each season. I try to keep a supply of broccoli, carrots, spring onions, silverbeet and salad greens in the garden to dip into at any time of the year. Most brassicas grow year-round, the exceptions being kale, cavalo nero and brussels sprouts, which not only need a frost to taste good but go to seed quickly as the days lengthen. Autumn harvests such as onions, shallots, garlic, pumpkin, potatoes and kumara will keep over winter if stored in a cool, dry place. Ensure there is no damage or rot before storing and allow space between each or wrap in paper to prevent the spread of rot.
After my sister left home to make her way in the world our father turned off the heating and made her bedroom his winter store room. Cases of apples, pears, kiwifruit and tamarillos were perched on and under the bed. It was the coldest room in our 1920s brick and stucco house and in the absence of a cellar proved the perfect place to store autumn harvests.

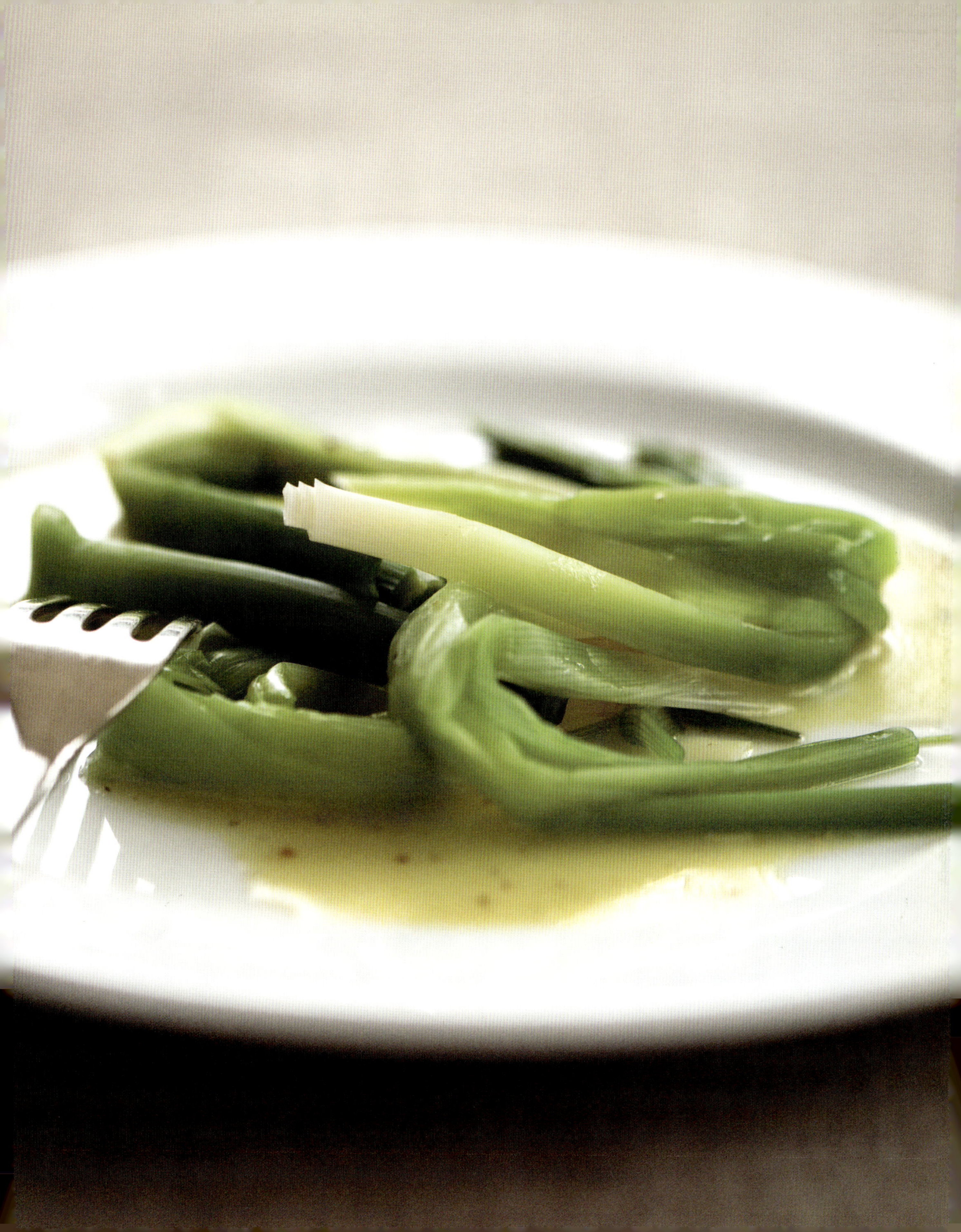

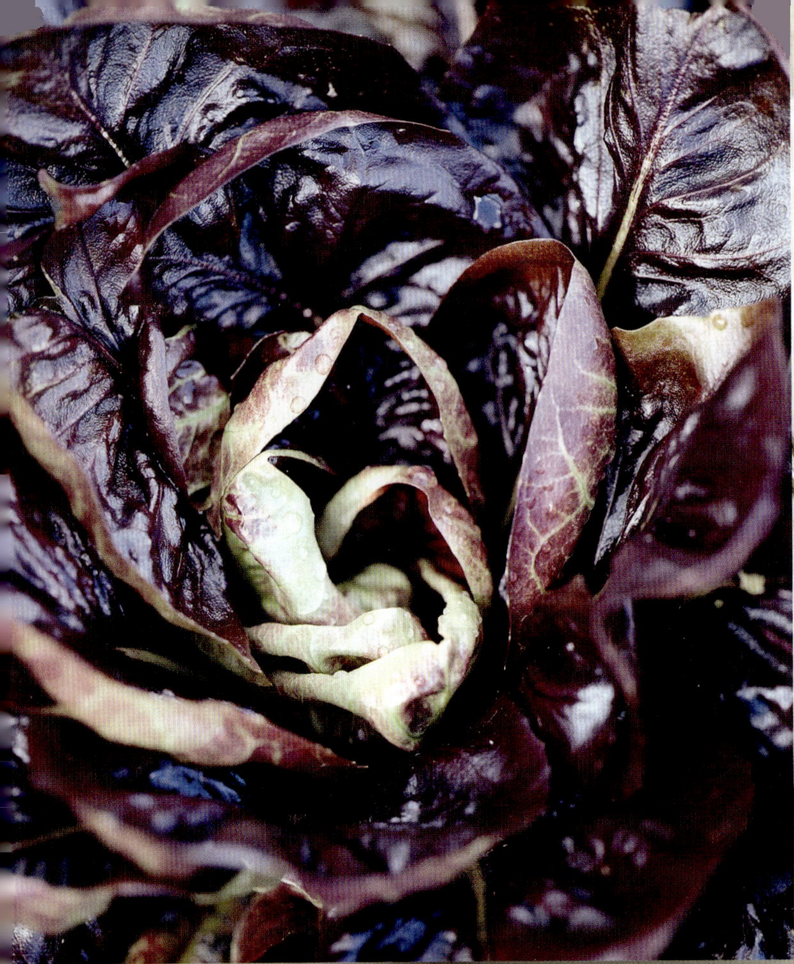
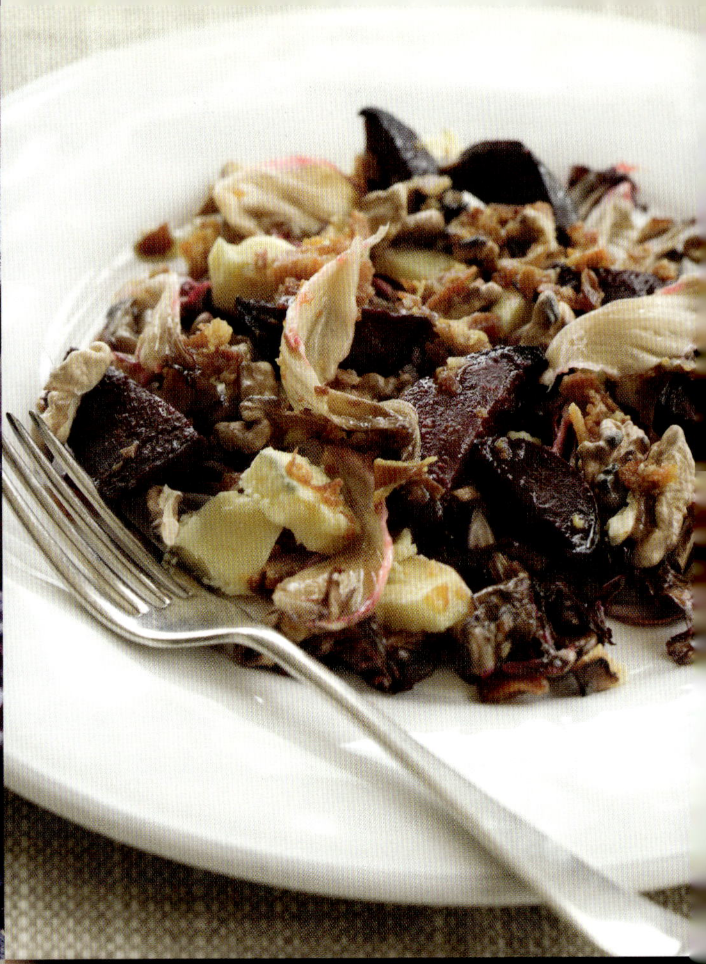
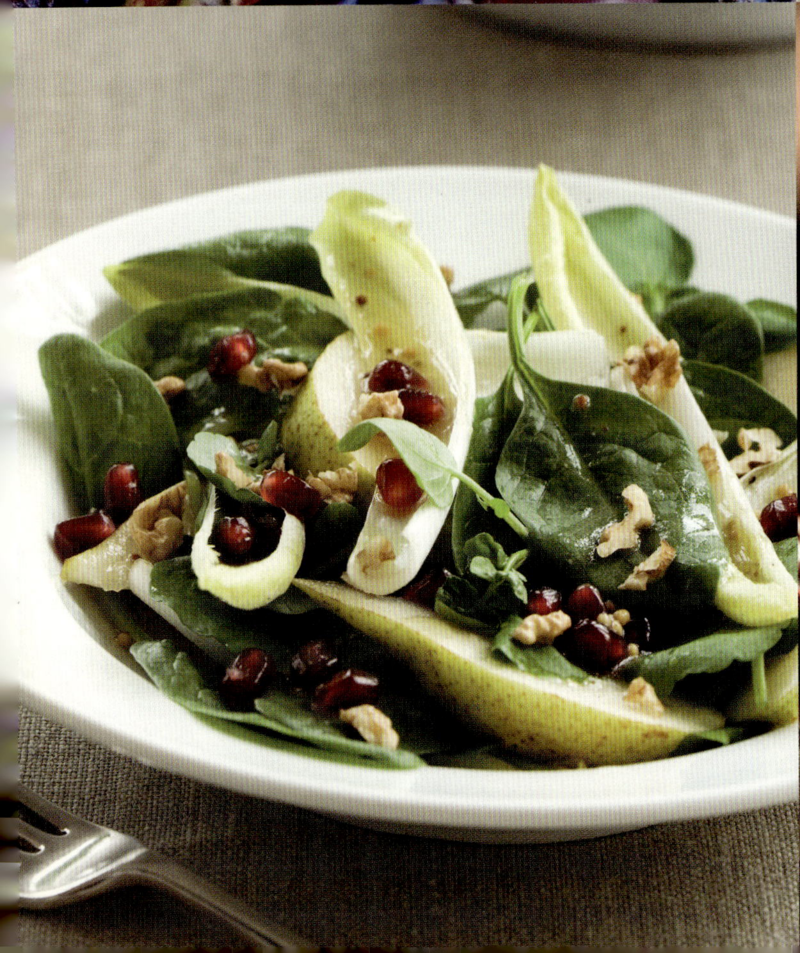
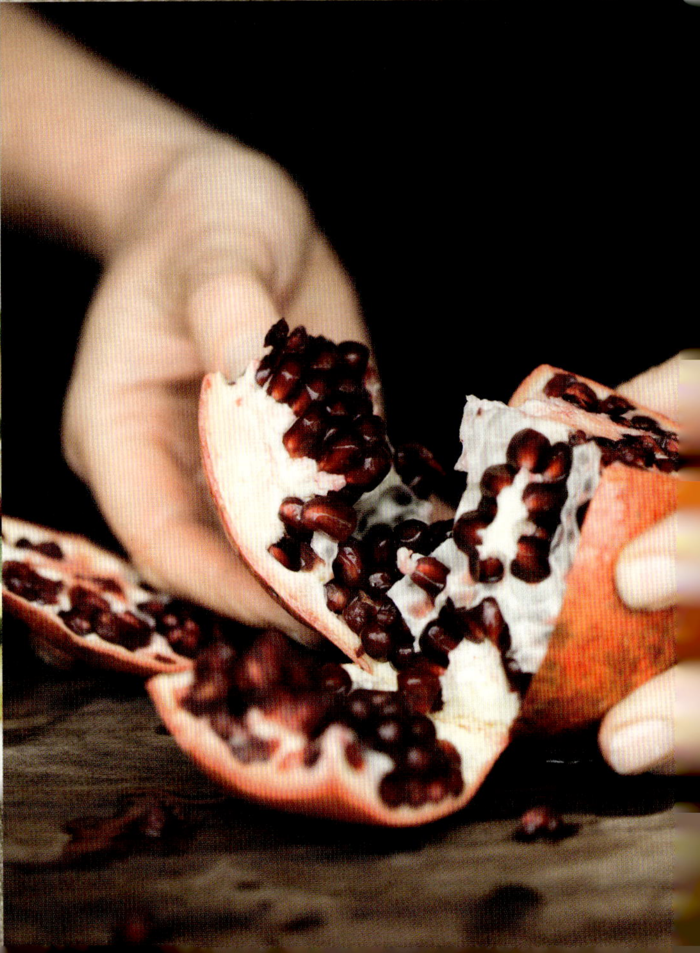

'Peasant cultures throughout Europe and Asia understand the benefits of bitter greens, using dandelions, rocket, chicory and endive as a liver tonic to help process the heavier winter diet.'

Bitter greens

Grilled radicchio with blue cheese & beetroot

Prep 10 minutes + marinating
Cook 8-10 minutes

2 firm heads radicchio, cut into quarters lengthways then into thin wedges (about 10-12 per head)
5 tbsp olive oil
1 tbsp lemon juice
1 tsp sugar
salt and grinds of pepper
2 beetroot, peeled and cut into small batons
2 tablespoons best-quality extra virgin olive oil
4 thin slices prosciutto
100g blue cheese, crumbled
100g walnut halves or pine nuts, toasted

Place radicchio in a shallow dish. Combine 2 tbsp of the oil with the lemon juice, sugar, salt and pepper. Drizzle over radicchio, turning to coat evenly. Leave to marinate for at least 30 minutes or up to 4 hours.

While the radicchio marinates, preheat oven to 200°C. Place beetroot on an oven tray, drizzle with 1 tbsp of the remaining olive oil and season with salt and pepper. Roast until tender, about 30 minutes.

Heat the 2 remaining tablespoons of oil in a frypan and cook prosciutto over low heat until very crisp. Allow to cool then break up very finely in the oil and set aside. Arrange radicchio on a shallow roasting tray and grill about 8-10cm from the heat source until wilted and starting to brown, 8-10 minutes. Toss through the prosciutto-oil mixture then divide between serving plates. Scatter over beets, cheese and nuts.
Serves 4

Pomegranate with witloof & spinach

Prep 10 minutes

140g baby spinach leaves
1 just-ripe pear, cored and thinly sliced
1 head witloof, leaves separated
seeds from ½ pomegranate
3 tbsp chopped walnuts
2-3 tbsp honey mustard dressing (page 84)

Place all ingredients In a mixing bowl and toss gently to combine.
Serves 4 as a side dish

JERUSALEM ARTICHOKES
Helianthus tuberosus
Sometimes known as a sunchoke, thanks to the leggy growing habit and golden flowers shared with its cousin the sunflower. Jerusalem artichokes have knobbly root tubers that come into harvest through autumn and winter. They have a better flavour if left in the ground until frosted. Make an excellent **Jerusalem artichoke soup** by cooking a chopped onion in butter then adding scrubbed, chopped chokes, chicken stock and a grating of nutmeg and simmering until tender. Purée the soup and flavour with parsley or a little mushroom powder.

To prepare a **Jerusalem artichoke gratin**, combine layers of scrubbed, thinly sliced chokes with a little garlic, nutmeg and enough cream to just cover. Bake for about 50 minutes in a 200°C oven.

To **roast chokes**, scrub and place in a roasting dish with a little oil (add other vegetables as preferred). Bake at 200°C until golden and tender, about 40 minutes. Drizzle over 1 teaspoon sherry vinegar before serving.

Jerusalem artichokes are very good for your gut, with useful bacteria-promoting properties. However, these health benefits come at a price: be warned, they are also known as fartichokes.

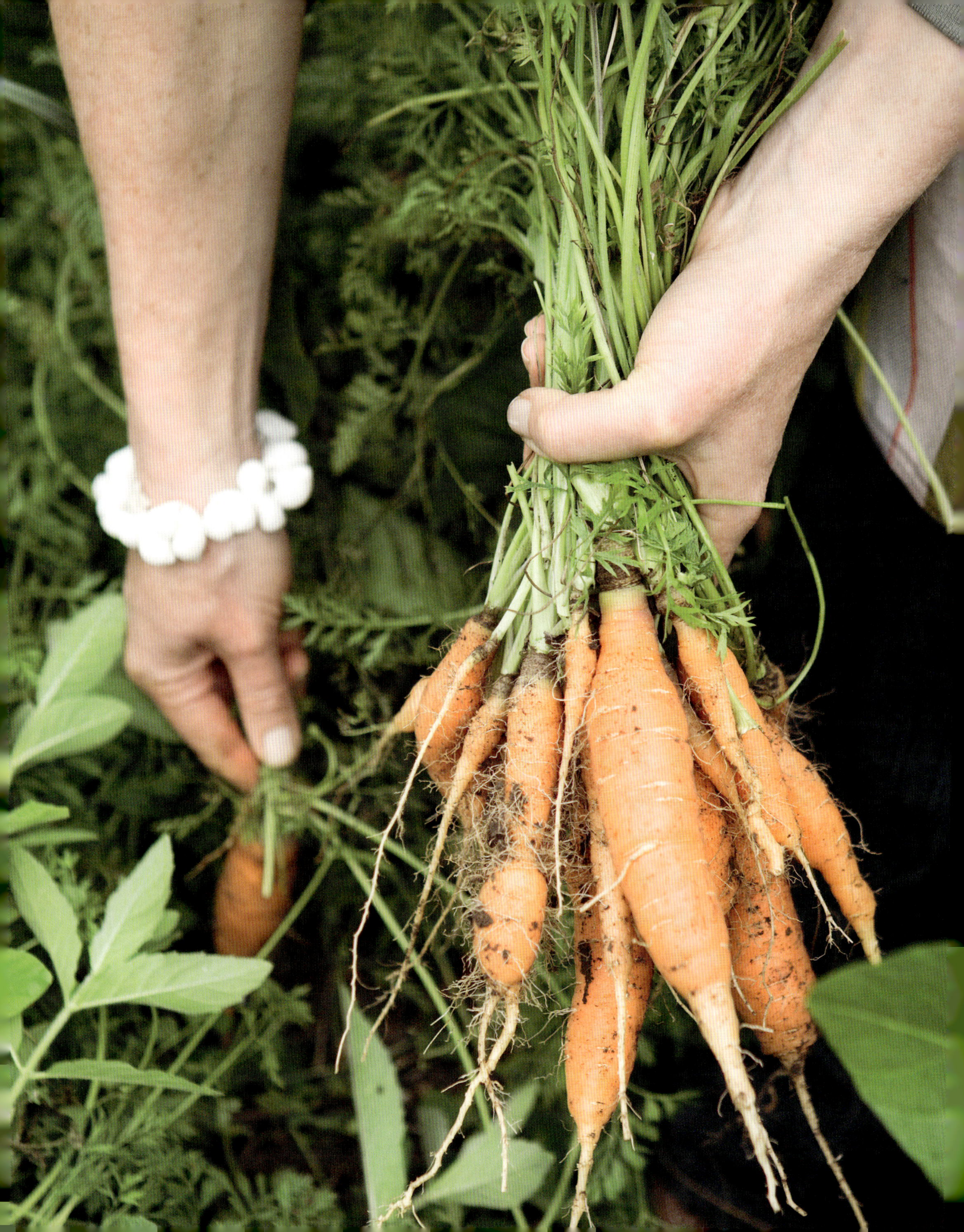

'Even in winter I like to go to the farmers' market, just to check what's in season ... a bunch of leeks and some potatoes for a nice soup or a savoy cabbage to braise with lentils. It's all good.'

Rib-stickers

Southern Italian chestnut soup

Prep 20 minutes + soaking
Cook 3½ hours

3 cups white lima beans
1 large bacon hock
2 onions, finely diced
1 large fennel bulb, thinly sliced
5 cloves garlic, chopped
150g spicy sausages,
   eg cacciatore, finely diced
2 x 400g cans tomatoes in juice,
   chopped
2 tbsp tomato paste
1 tsp chopped rosemary
1 tsp dried chilli flakes
2 cups cooked peeled chestnuts
   (see right)
To serve: juice of 1 lemon, ½ cup
   finely chopped parsley, salt and
   grinds of pepper

Soups of this kind are a feature of southern Italian country cooking. Try adding chestnuts to minestrone or any vegetable soup. This soup is also good without the chestnuts, add an extra cup and a half of cooked beans.

Place beans in a bowl, cover with cold water by 5cm and stand somewhere cool for 6-12 hours.
Place bacon hock in a large pot with 3 litres cold water. Boil 1½ hours then add drained beans, onions, fennel, garlic, sausage, tomatoes and tomato paste, rosemary, chilli flakes and chestnuts. Simmer 1½-2 hours or until beans are tender.
Lift hock out of soup and strip off meat, discarding skin. Return meat to pot along with parsley and lemon juice. Bring to a simmer, season to taste with salt and pepper and serve.
Serves 8-10

CHESTNUTS
Castanea sativa
In late autumn and early winter the prickly burrs that contain chestnuts fall to the ground, releasing 2-3 smooth brown nuts. With their high starch content (double that of potatoes), they perish quickly and are usually dried or frozen to extend their season.
To prepare fresh chestnuts for cooking or freezing, cut a cross in the flat end of each shell, spread in a roasting tray and roast at 200°C for 20 minutes then peel off shells while nuts are still warm. Freeze on a tray then free-flow into bags and seal.
Or soak whole nuts for 4 hours, then boil for one hour. Cool and remove skins.
Dried chestnuts need to be soaked in cold water overnight before cooking.

Nonna's lamb & barley soup

Prep 20 minutes
Cook 4 hours

4 lamb shanks or 1 leg lamb
12 cups water
300g barley or barley soup mix
500g pumpkin, peeled and diced
4 stalks celery, finely sliced
3 carrots, finely diced
2 large onions, finely diced
2 x 400g cans tomatoes
140g tomato paste
2 bay leaves
1 tsp salt
1 tsp finely ground black pepper
1 cup finely chopped parsley or
   ½ cup winter pesto (page 192)

Make this soup well in advance and chill to remove fat that will rise to the surface. Reheat to serve as required. It will keep in the fridge for 5-6 days and freezes well.

Place meat and water in a very large pot and simmer for 2 hours. Add all other ingredients except parsley or pesto and simmer for another 2 hours or until meat is tender. Strip meat off bones, dice and return to pot.
Cool and chill. Remove all surface fat. Store soup in the fridge and reheat as needed, or freeze and reheat as needed. Add parsley or pesto just before serving.
Serves 12-16

'In the two years I spent backpacking around South America in my 20s, there were a lot of beans and rice to be had. The weekend family lunches were memorable, though – wondrous puchero and feijoada.'

Pulse power

Moroccan lentil soup

Prep   10 minutes
Cook   1 hour

2 tbsp olive oil
1 large onion, diced
2-3 cloves garlic, chopped
1 tbsp grated fresh ginger
2 tbsp tomato paste
1 tbsp ground cumin
2 tsp ground coriander
½ tsp each ground cinnamon, smoked paprika and turmeric
1 tsp chilli flakes
pinch of saffron (optional)
2 carrots, peeled and grated
2 stalks celery, finely diced
250g pumpkin, grated
400g can tomatoes in juice
2 cups puy lentils, washed
9-10 cups water
1 tsp salt and grinds pepper
½ cup chopped fresh coriander or parsley

Heat oil in a medium-large saucepan and gently fry onion, garlic, ginger, tomato paste and spices until aromatic and onion has softened without browning. Add vegetables, lentils and water and simmer on lowest heat for 1 hour. Season to taste.
When ready to serve, mix in coriander or parsley. Delicious served with crusty bread topped with hummus. Soup reheats well – add coriander or parsley when serving.
Serves 6-8

Black bean & bacon soup

Prep   30 minutes
Cook   3½ hours

2 tbsp olive oil
1 large onion, finely diced
3 fat cloves garlic, crushed
2 stalks celery, thinly sliced
1 tbsp ground cumin
1 tsp smoked paprika
1 tsp chilli flakes
50g tomato paste
12 cups water
2 x 400g cans tomatoes
1 large smoked bacon hock
200g smoked sausage, sliced
3 cups cooked black beans
1 cup chopped coriander

Heat oil in a large pot and sizzle onion, garlic, celery and spices over low heat until softened but not browned. Add tomato paste and stir over heat for a minute then add water, tomatoes and bacon hock.
Simmer over low heat until bacon is very tender, about 2½ hours, removing any surface scum with a slotted spoon. Lift out bacon bone and, when cool enough to handle, strip off meat, discarding fat. Shred meat and return to pot with sausage and beans. Simmer for 1 hour. Adjust seasoning to taste and stir in coriander
Serves 4-6
Cook's note: If bacon bones are overly salty, cover them with boiling water and soak for 30 minutes, drain and cook as above.

LATINO SOUPS

Most cultures have evolved one-dish soup meals that are often served for weekend lunches. These nourishing dishes are made by combining a tough but tasty meat cut (or boiling fowl) with vegetables and occasionally fruit in a deeply flavoured broth that is cooked for hours. Puchero is to Central and South America what pot au feu is to France, with as many variations as it has cooks. I have prepared a version on page 149 as a Mexican harvest soup. Sometimes the dish is presented in three courses with the cooking broth eaten first, followed by the vegetables and the meat on two separate platters. There will often be chopped onions, coriander, sliced avocado and a selection of salsas to accompany the broth. In Brazil the dish of feijoada, made with black beans and pork, reigns supreme. Feijoada can be a very complex dish using different meats and garnishes but the black bean and bacon soup (at left) is a simple and great-tasting starting point. Feijoada is traditionally garnished with toasted manioc (cassava), sliced oranges and lightly cooked kale or collard greens.

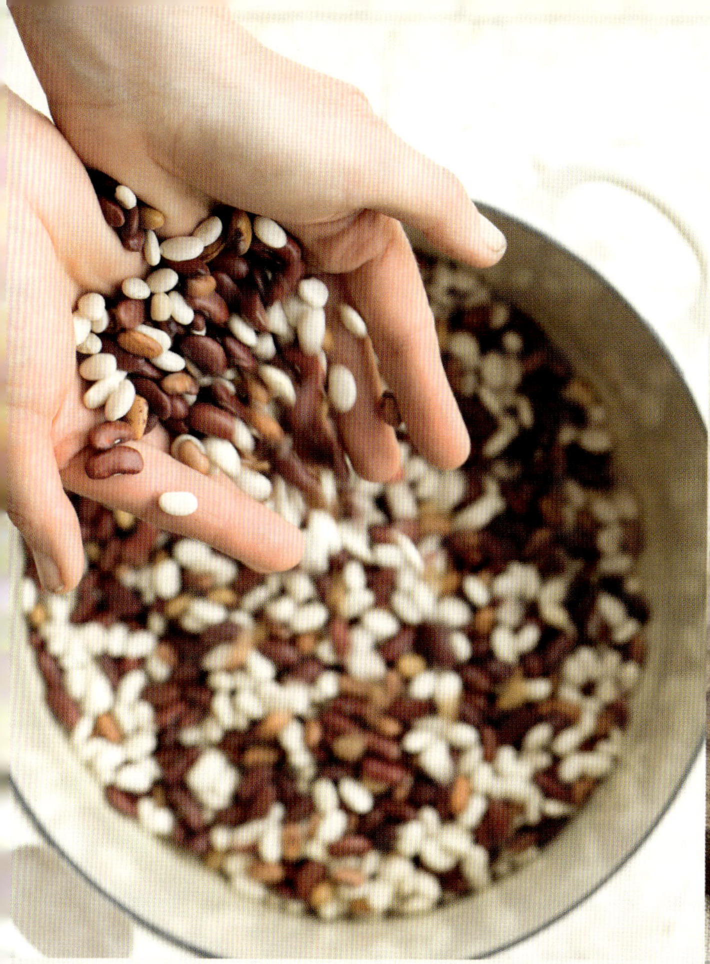
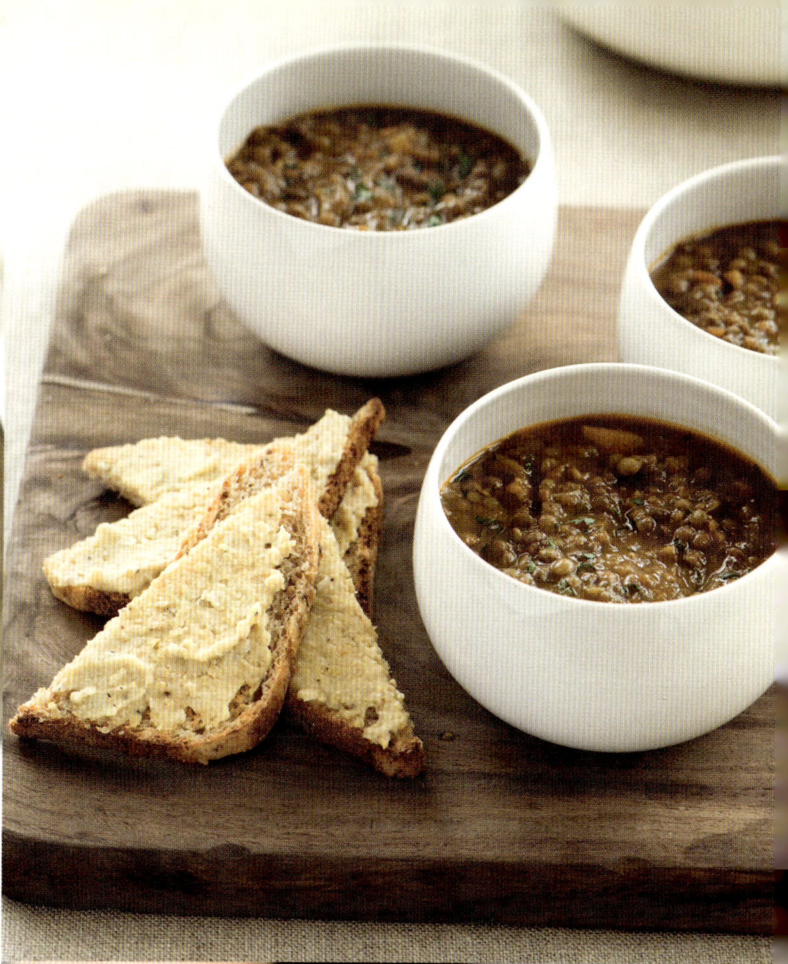
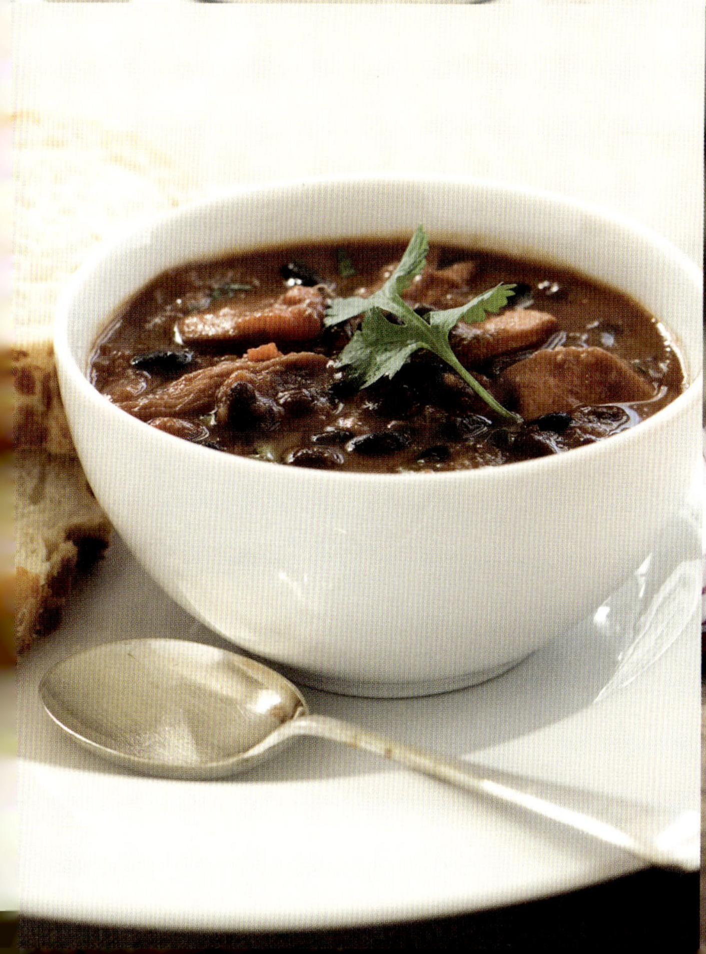
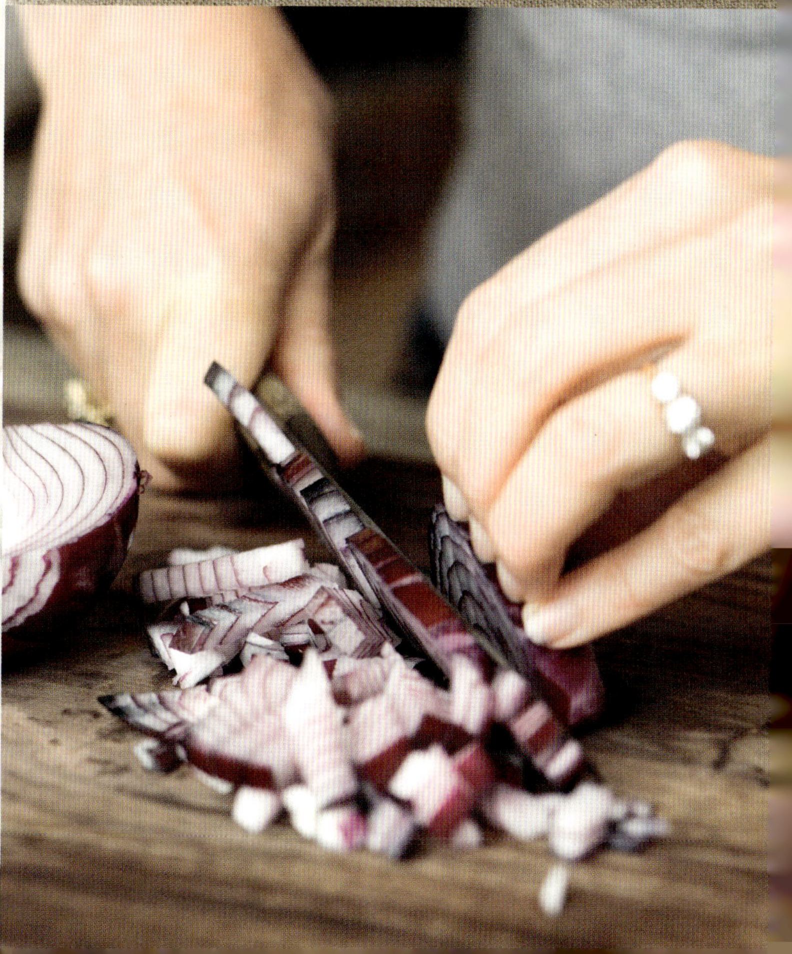

'On days when the weather rages furiously outside and you just want to curl up on the sofa by the fire with a good book, there has to be soup. Nothing else delivers quite the same comfort.'

Classic pea and ham

Pea & ham soup with crispy croûtons

Prep 10 minutes
Cook 2 hours 40 minutes

1 smoked meaty ham or bacon hock
1 pig's trotter (optional)
2 bay leaves
3½ litres water
500g dried split green peas
salt and grinds of pepper
2 cups crispy croûtons (see right)
Optional: 2-3 tbsp winter pesto (page 192) to serve

Place hock and trotter, if using, in a large pot with bay leaves and water. Bring to the boil, removing any scum that rises to the surface. Cover and simmer for 2 hours. While the meat cooks, place the dried green peas in a separate pot. Cover with 4cm water and bring to the boil. Reduce heat to a simmer and cook, uncovered, until water has almost evaporated.

Lift hock out of cooking liquid, remove and discard skin and finely dice meat. Add meat back to the cooking liquid along with the bone and partly cooked peas. Continue cooking over low heat until peas are fully broken down, another 40 minutes.

Remove bone and season soup to taste. Serve garnished with croûtons and pesto if using.

Soup will keep in the fridge for up to 5 days or can be frozen.

Makes about 10 cups, serves 6-8

CRISPY CROÛTONS

Remove the crusts from 4 thick slices of bread. Mix together ½ cup extra virgin olive oil, 1 tsp crushed garlic, 2 tbsp grated parmesan, 1 tsp dried oregano and ½ tsp salt. Brush over the bread on both sides. Dice the bread into 2cm pieces and spread out on a baking tray. Bake at 150°C until golden and crisp, about 25 minutes. Store croûtons in an airtight container. They will keep fresh for several weeks and if they become stale simply heat in a 180°C oven for 5-10 minutes to refresh.

Makes about 3 cups

ROASTING NUTS

It's very simple to roast your own nuts and the flavour is fresher than any store bought nuts. Place raw nuts on a baking tray and drizzle or spray with just a little oil, tossing to coat. Spread out and bake at 180°C until crisp and pale golden. Cooking time depends on fat content. Almonds take about 12-15 minutes while walnuts and pine nuts, which have higher levels of fat, cook more quickly – test after 10 minutes. Peanuts have slightly less fat than the rest and will take a little longer. Cool nuts before storing – they will crisp as they cool.

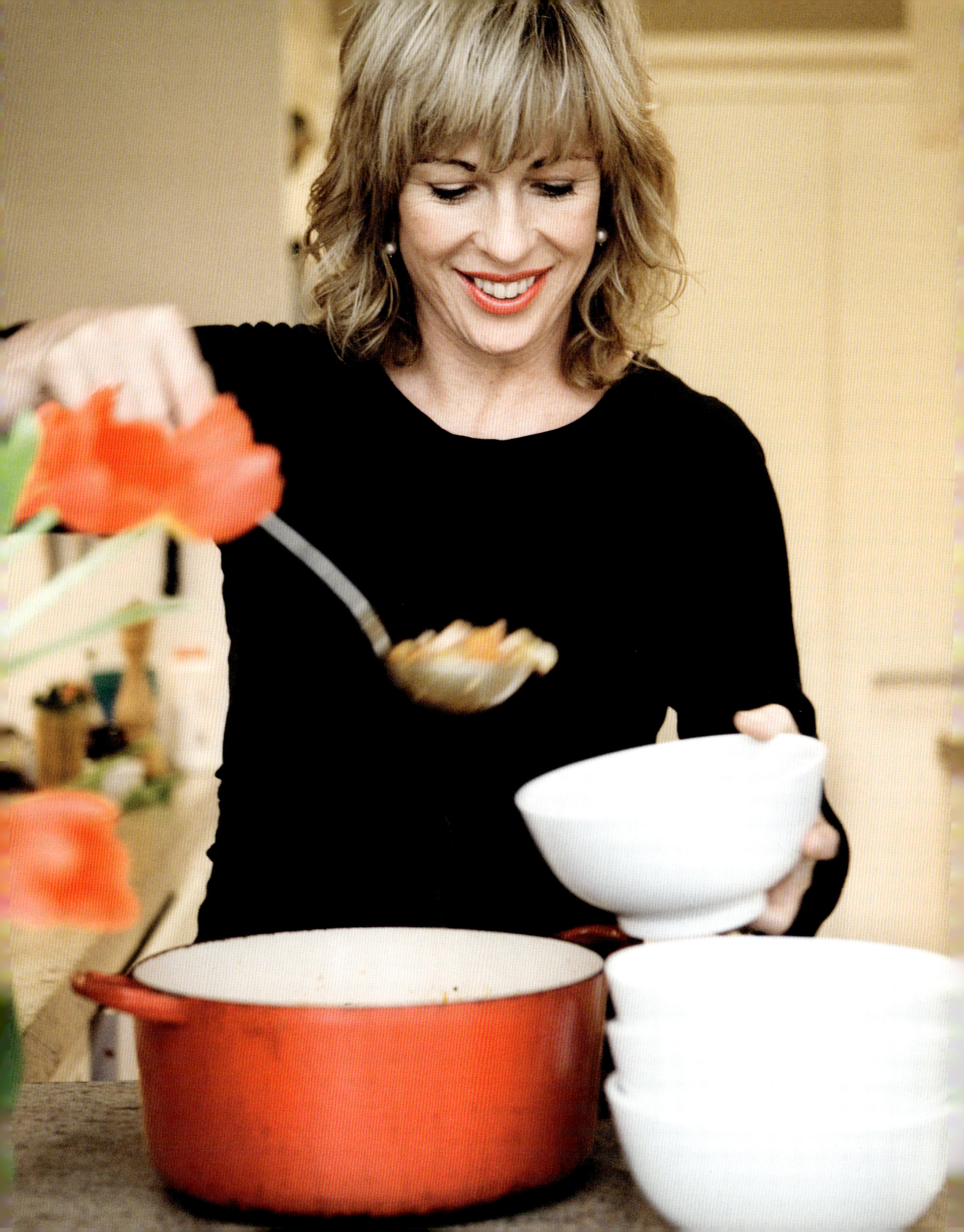

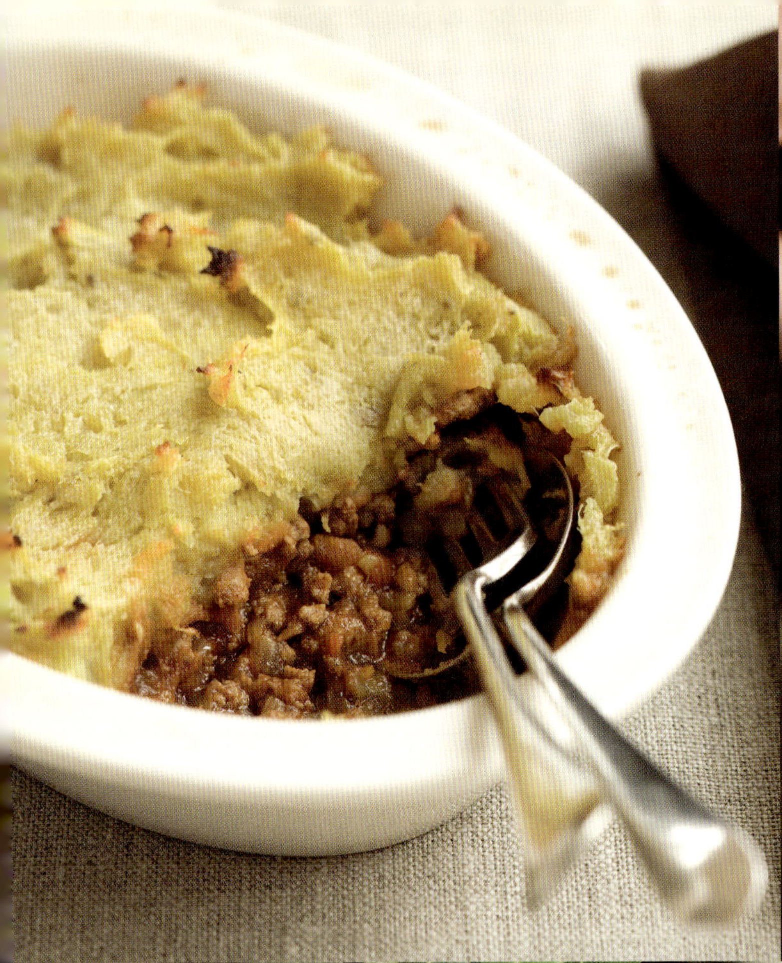
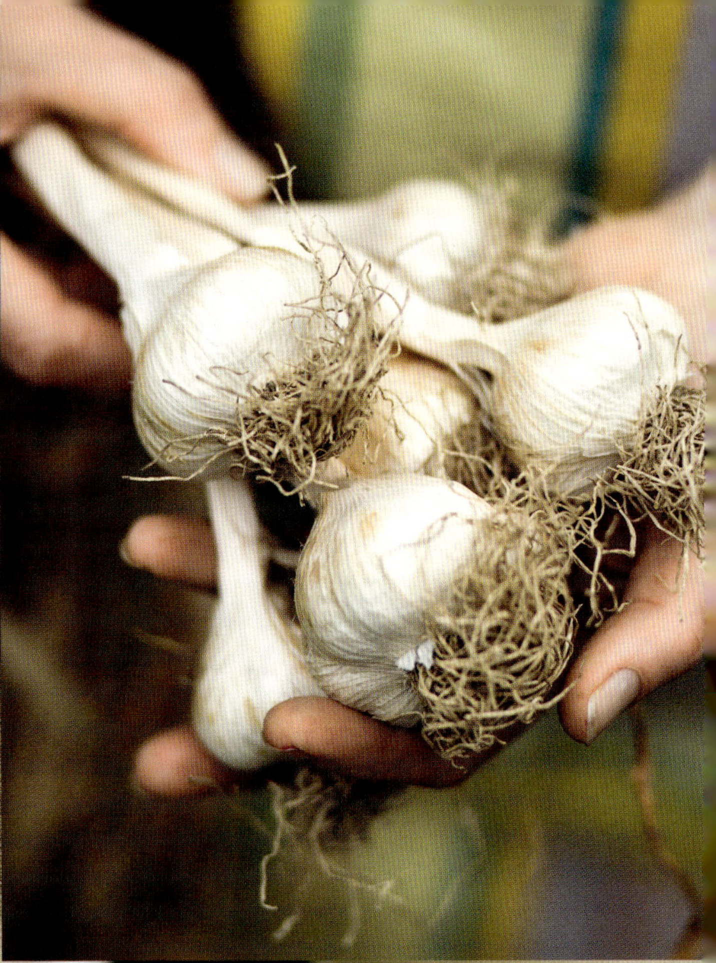
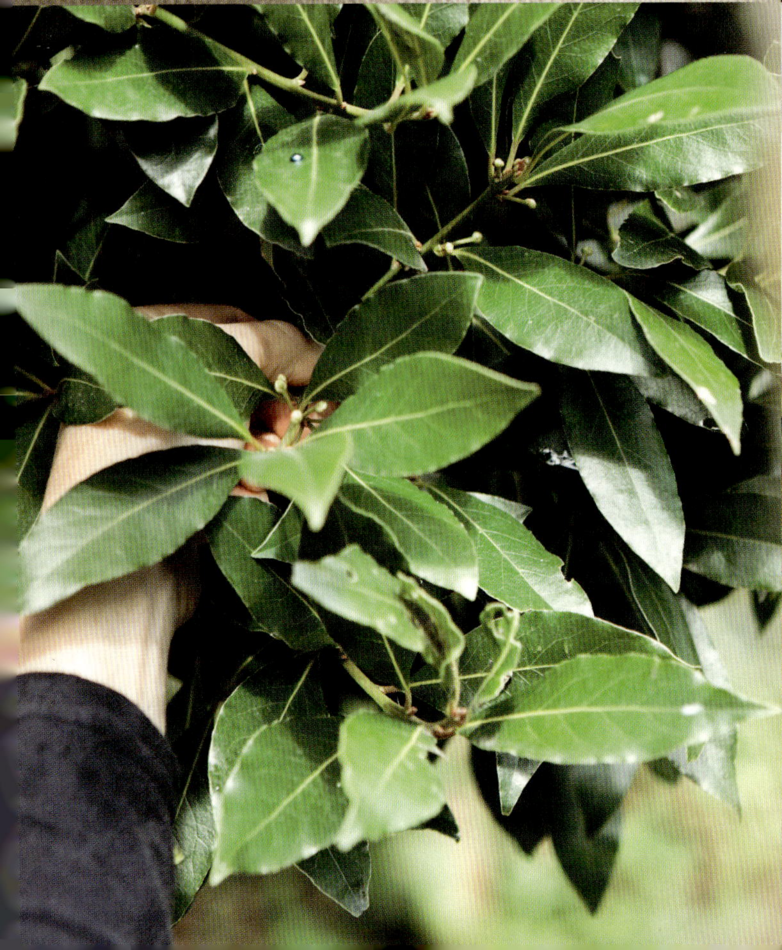
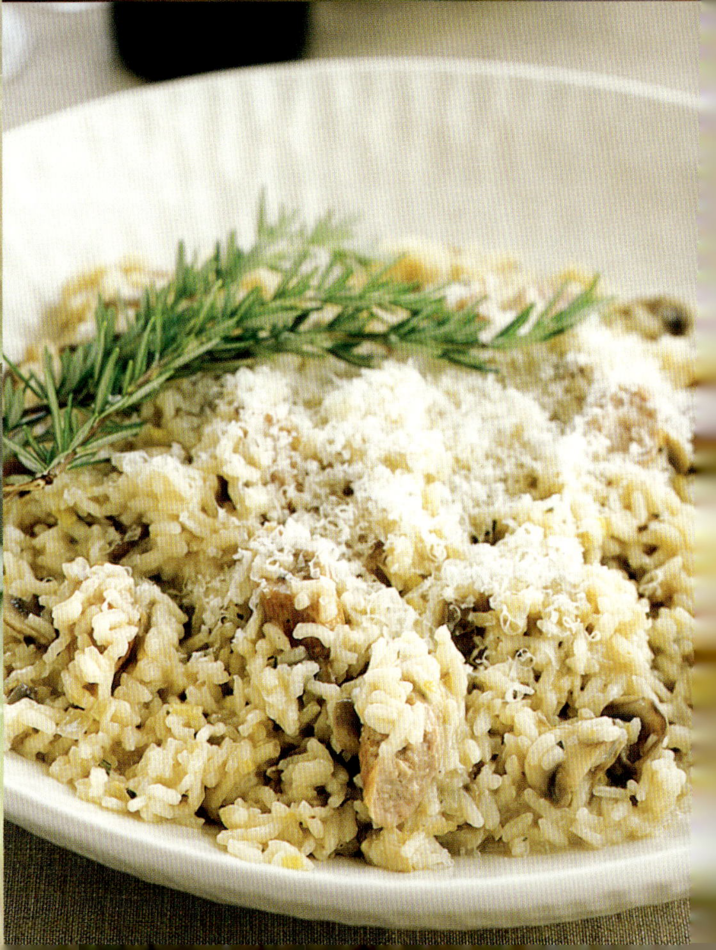

'Timing is everything when it comes to dishes like pasta and risotto. The creamy toothsomeness of perfectly cooked arborio rice is so appealing but an over-cooked gloopy slurry is not.'

Dishes to soothe

Leek, mushroom & sausage risotto

Prep 10 minutes
Cook 30 minutes

3 tbsp butter
1 large leek, white part only, finely chopped
1 onion, finely diced
250g mushrooms, thinly sliced
2 cups risotto rice
½ cup white wine
1.5 litres vegetable or chicken stock, heated to a simmer
8-10 fennel seeds, chopped
1 tbsp chopped fresh rosemary
1 tsp salt and grinds of pepper
6 Sicilian pork and fennel sausages
30g parmesan, finely grated

Heat butter in a deep, heavy pot and cook leek, onion and mushrooms over low heat until softened but not browned, 10-12 minutes.
Add rice and stir over heat for 1-2 minutes to lightly toast. Add wine and cook until evaporated then stir in hot stock, fennel seeds, rosemary, salt and pepper. Simmer gently, stirring occasionally, until rice is creamy and just tender – 17 minutes, the rice should be quite sloppy.
While rice cooks, pan-fry sausages until golden and cooked through. Remove from heat, slice into chunks and mix into cooked rice with parmesan. Adjust seasonings to taste.
Serves 4

Shepherd's pie

Prep 20 minutes
Cook 1 hour

3 tbsp oil
600g lean lamb mince
salt and grinds of pepper
1 large onion, finely diced
2 fat cloves garlic, crushed
1 tbsp grated fresh ginger
2 tsp ground cumin
½ tsp ground cinnamon
2 tbsp tomato paste
1 large carrot, coarsely grated
400g can tomatoes
3 cups vegetable stock
1 tsp chopped rosemary
½ cup finely chopped parsley
Topping:
1kg kumara or potatoes, peeled and cut into chunks
2 tbsp butter
2-3 tbsp milk
pinch of nutmeg

Heat half the oil in a large frypan over high heat. Season the lamb and fry in two batches until well browned. Set aside. Drain off any fat from the pan, add remaining oil and cook onions with garlic, ginger, cumin and cinnamon over medium heat until softened, 6-7 minutes. Add tomato paste and stir over heat for a minute or two. Add browned lamb, carrot, tomatoes, stock and rosemary and simmer for about 30 minutes, stirring to loosen pan brownings, until reduced to a thick, meaty sauce. Mix in parsley and adjust seasoning to taste. Transfer to a baking dish.
While meat cooks, boil kumara until tender. Drain and mash, mixing in butter and enough milk to make a smooth, fluffy purée. Add nutmeg and season to taste with salt and pepper. Spread over lamb mixture. If not serving at once, cover and chill. When ready to serve bake at 200°C until golden brown, 30-40 minutes.
Serves 4

CELERY
Apium graveolens dulce
Celery is not the easiest plant to grow. It likes a cool but not cold, moist season and won't tolerate frost. Without enough water it gets very tough and stringy. Having only minimal calories, celery is a hit among the weight-loss brigade.
Choose fat, heavy heads and remove the risk of stringiness by peeling the outer stalks. For a classic **celery soup**, finely chop celery and onion and cook in a little butter. Add nutmeg and chicken stock, simmer and thicken with some white sauce. For an easy celery snack, prepare the mint and chive cream on page 23 or the chèvre-stuffed vegetables on page 81.

CELERIAC
Apium graveolens var. rapaceum
Celeriac is a much hardier plant than celery and will tolerate a frost. It produces a knobbly swollen 'bulb' at the base of the stem. Peel and cook, or grate and serve raw. It makes a great mash to serve with fish cooked 50:50 with potatoes. Use raw for **celeriac remoulade**, made by mixing a spoonful of Dijon mustard and a little lemon juice through a good-quality mayonnaise and stirring it into grated raw celeriac.
For more information on this family see page 210.

'To me, the hallmark of a good cook (rather than a chef) is resourcefulness. It's easy to cook with fancy ingredients but to make something really delicious out of basic ingredients takes thought and imagination.'

Braised duck & cabbage

Duck breasts with savoy cabbage & lentils

Prep 15 minutes
Cook 1½ hours

4 duck breasts (or duck legs)
finely grated zest of ½ orange
2 tbsp red wine vinegar
salt and grinds of pepper
2 tbsp butter
4 rashers bacon, diced
1 white onion, finely diced
1 large carrot, finely diced
2 cloves garlic, crushed
1½ cups puy lentils
finely grated zest of 1 lemon
5-6 cups good-quality duck or chicken stock
To serve: ¼ savoy cabbage, finely sliced

Score duck skin with a sharp knife in a fine criss-cross pattern without cutting into flesh. Rub with orange zest and half the vinegar and season with salt and pepper. Cover and chill for at least 1 hour or up to 24 hours. Heat a heavy pan and place duck skin side down in pan. Cook on skin side only over medium heat until skin is crisp and golden and most of the fat has rendered out, about 8 minutes. Set aside. Drain fat into a container for later use (it's delicious for roasting potatoes). Leave the pan unwashed for cooking cabbage later.

While duck browns, start preparing lentil base. In a separate pot or deep-sided pan, heat butter and cook bacon until it starts to brown. Add onion, carrot and garlic and cook over medium heat until softened, 5-6 minutes. Add lentils, lemon zest and stock. Bring to a simmer and cook over low heat until tender, about 30-40 minutes, adding a little water if mixture starts to get dry – it should be quite sloppy. Season with salt and pepper and mix in the remaining tablespoon of vinegar.

Spoon lentils into a baking dish, top with the partly cooked duck breasts, skin side up, and bake at 200°C for 30 minutes (or 50 minutes for duck legs).

During the last 10 minutes of cooking, heat the unwashed frypan and stir-fry cabbage over high heat until wilted. To serve, mix cabbage through lentils and divide between 4 heated serving plates. Place duck on top.

Serves 4

Variation: Prepare this dish with 4 chicken breasts or leg quarters. Prepare as above, browning chicken pieces lightly all over before placing on top of lentil mixture and baking as for duck.

The first question my kids ask when they arrive home from school is: "What's for dinner, Mum?" In the early days my answers followed a reasonably narrow orbit of meals like spaghetti carbonara, roast chicken and vegetables, steak with potatoes and gravy, macaroni cheese, chicken teriyaki on rice, lasagne and chicken and noodle stir-fry. One liked sausages; one couldn't face them. Seafood was out, as was anything spicy. In fact small-kid food was awfully dull. And then they stopped eating anything green. But before I completely despaired, things started to change. Now mutiny is unlikely no matter which of my experiments arrives at the table (except for total abstinence from organic broccoli due to slug-laden experiences). Culinary historian Margaret Visser in her scholarly tome The Rituals of Dinner writes: "The language one first learns to speak, and the food one is accustomed to eat in childhood, are two of the fundamental preservers of an adult's social and racial identity." Kids lock into a set of expectations about food, becoming finicky from their own experiences (as in broccoli with slugs) and depending on what's "in" at the time. Which makes advertising of processed foods with little value aimed at kids so insidious.

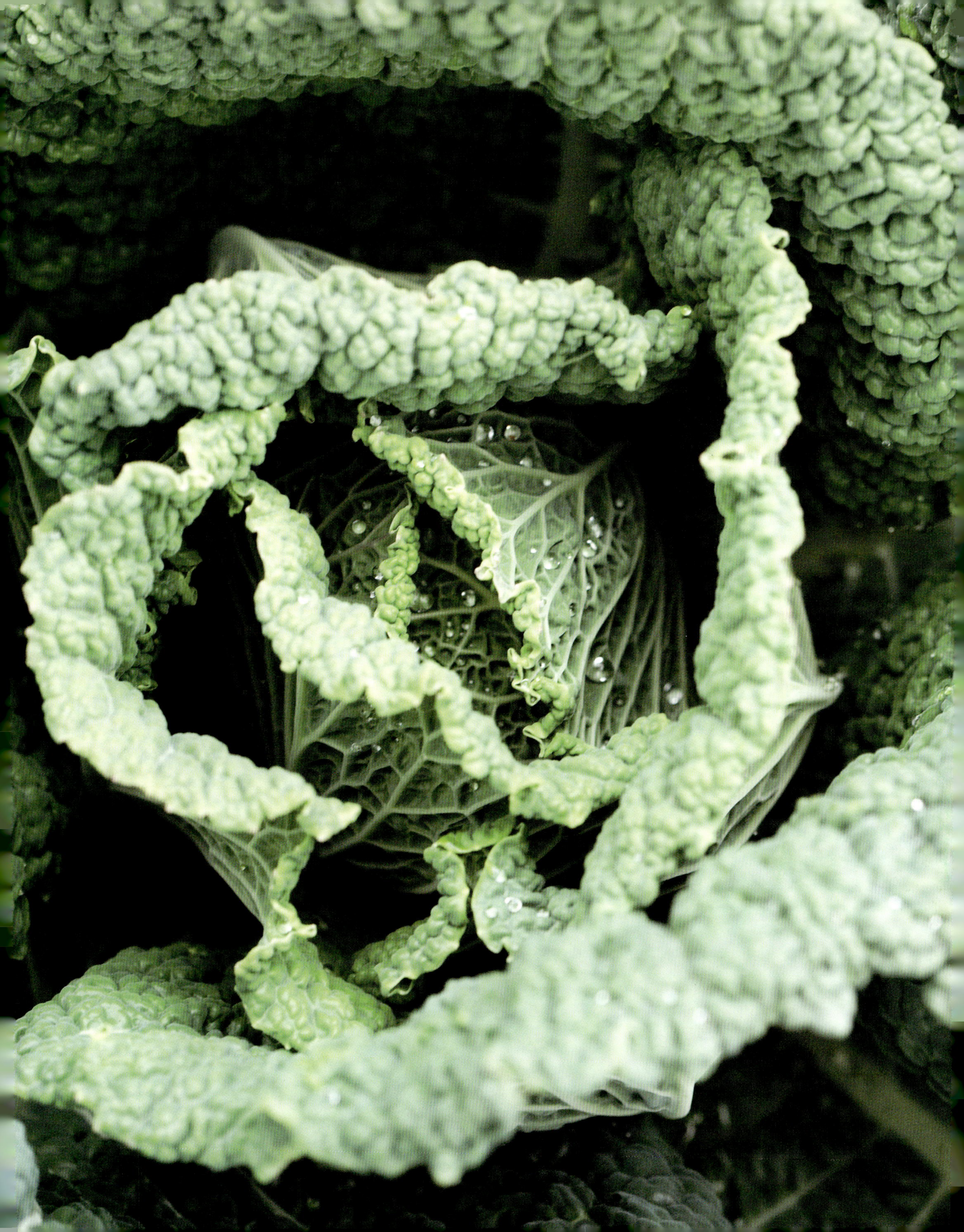

'You need look no further than India for food that is deeply satisfying yet cheap as chips. Certainly there are extravagent dishes to be had, but the spice-rich tastes of everyday fare never fail to please.'

Indian rice and lamb

Lamb biriyani

Prep 15 minutes
Cook 1 hour 20 minutes

1 cup plain yoghurt
3 tbsp grated fresh ginger
3 cloves garlic, crushed
Optional: pinch of saffron
1 tbsp ground cumin
1 tbsp garam masala
2 tsp cardamom seeds
1 tsp each ground turmeric, cinnamon and black pepper
½ tsp cayenne pepper
1 tsp salt
1 kg diced lean lamb
2 tbsp oil
2 large onions, thinly sliced
400g can tomatoes
1 tsp honey
2½ cups basmati rice
10-12 whole cloves
2 bay leaves
finely grated zest of 1 lemon
½ cup roasted cashews
⅔ cup sliced almonds
½ packed cup chopped mint

This classic dish can be far more complex, however the simple version I have given here yields an impressive and delicious result.

Mix yoghurt with ginger, garlic and all the spices (except the whole cloves) and salt and stir through the lamb to evenly coat. Cover and chill for at least 2 hours or up to 48 hours (it tastes even better after marinating for a day or two).

Heat oil in a very large, ovenproof casserole and fry onions over medium-high heat until they start to brown, 10-12 minutes. Add meat and its marinade, tomatoes and honey. Cover and simmer on lowest heat for 30 minutes. While meat cooks, boil a big pot of water with 1 teaspoon salt. Add rice and simmer for exactly 8 minutes. Drain thoroughly then mix through cloves, bay leaves, lemon zest, cashews and half the almonds and mint, reserving remainder for garnish. Spoon the rice evenly over the cooked lamb, cover tightly and bake at 180°C for 40 minutes. Sprinkle with remaining nuts and mint.

Serves 8

THE CURCUBIT FAMILY

Known for its twisting vines and vegetable fruits, the Curcubit family includes zucchini, cucumber, pumpkin and butternut, gourds and the melons – rock melon, watermelon, prince, bitter, pie and honeydew. They are all tender plants, needing warm temperatures to germinate and collapsing at the first hint of frost. All develop tougher skins as they ripen, but only pumpkins and gourds are sturdy enough to store over the winter. Nutritionally it is the pumpkin that is the powerhouse of the family, providing very high levels of beta carotene. I grate pumpkin into chocolate cakes for extra moisture and nutrition (carrot can also be used to the same effect). See the recipes on pages 178 and 232 for two great **cakes** that utilise pumpkin and carrot. **Pumpkin roasts** wonderfully, cut into wedges and drizzled with a little oil and a spash of maple syrup or golden syrup to caramelise flavours during cooking. I like to make **pumpkin risotto** with chunks of roasted pumpkin, a couple of heads of roasted garlic and chopped spinach or rocket stirred through just before serving with either parmesan or blue cheese. Follow the risotto recipe on page 205 for the cooking method.

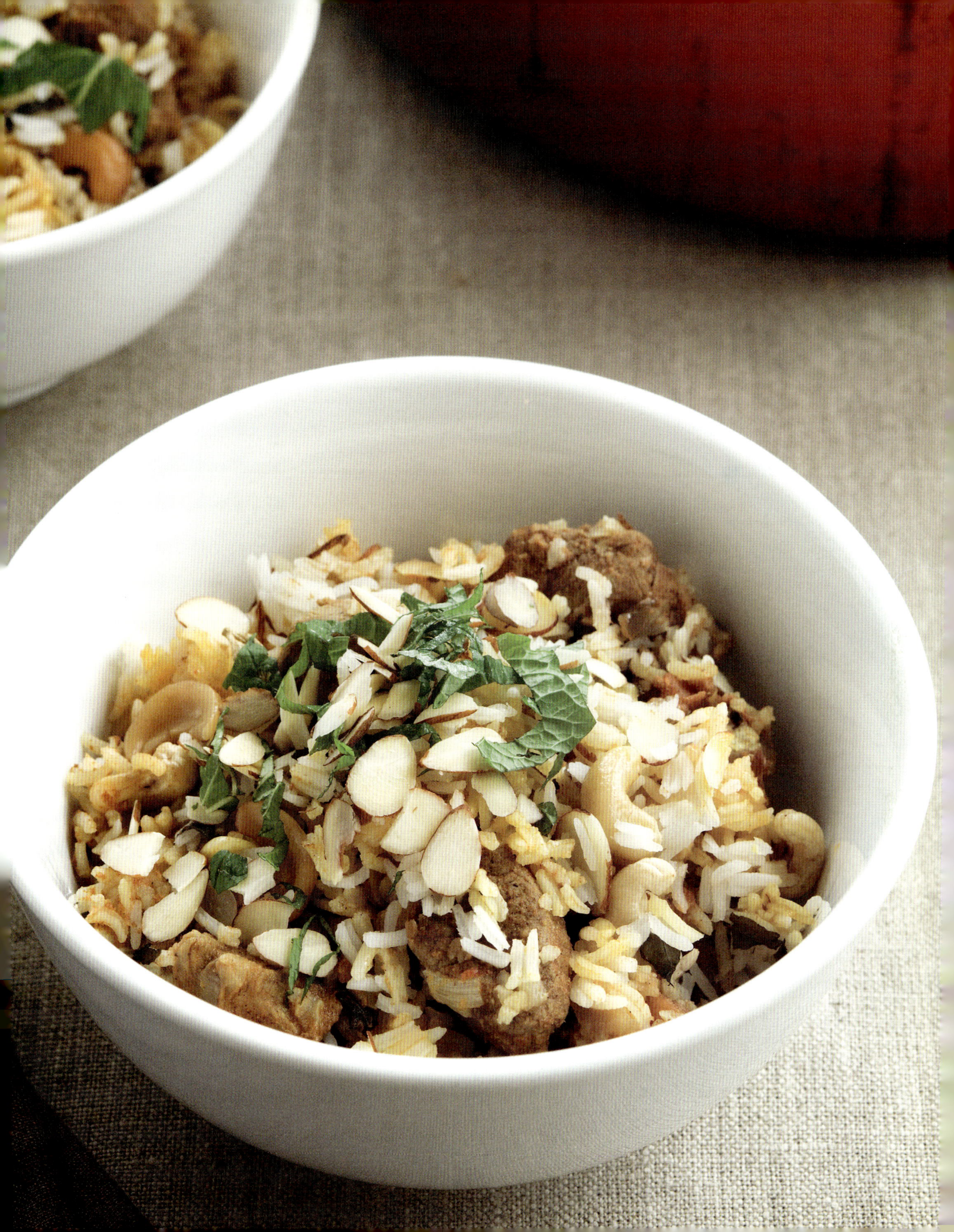

'Taste, unlike appetite, is a learnt response, dictated by tradition and cultural bias. The melting-pot of international cities brings us new tastes and expands our culinary horizons.'

Devilled chicken

Chicken & leek diablo

Prep 20 minutes + chilling
Cook 40 minutes

12 boneless chicken thighs or 6 skinless boneless breasts
diablo marinade (see right)
3 tbsp butter
2 large leeks, (600-700g trimmed weight), whites and ⅓ of the pale green tops, washed and thinly sliced
½ tsp salt and grinds of pepper
½ cup cream
1½ cups chicken stock

Parsley crumb topping:
2½ cups crumbled stale sourdough or other rustic bread
2 tbsp chopped parsley
1 tsp fresh thyme leaves or ½ tsp dried thyme
3 tbsp neutral oil

An easy dish to assemble in advance then finish in the oven at serving time.

Place chicken in a sealable plastic bag or a mixing bowl. Stir diablo marinade evenly through chicken. Chill for at least 30 minutes or up to 4 hours.
Heat butter in a heavy pan, add leeks and season with salt and pepper. Cover and cook over low heat until softened, about 15 minutes. Remove from heat and mix in chicken stock and cream. Divide mixture between 6 shallow baking dishes or ramekins or spread in the base of a large, shallow baking dish. Arrange chicken on top (if using thighs, fold each side under to form small rolls).
Blend bread to coarse crumbs in a food processor. Add parsley, thyme and oil and pulse just enough to coat evenly. Sprinkle crumbs over chicken. Chill until ready to cook, it will hold for several hours.
Preheat oven to 200°C. Bake chicken 35-40 minutes or until fully cooked and crumbs are golden.
Serves 6

DIABLO MARINADE

Mix together 2 tsp Dijon mustard, 2 tbsp Worcestershire sauce, ½ tsp salt, ½ tsp cayenne and 1 tsp fresh thyme leaves. Good to rub over chicken or pork before baking.
Makes enough for 4-6 serves

UMBELLIFERAE FAMILY

Along with the Alliums, vegetables from the Umbelliferae family are stalwarts in the kitchen with their aromatic sweetness. Carrots and celery are the starting point for many dishes. Add onion at a ratio of 2 to 1 each of carrot and celery for a mirepoix which, either raw, roasted or gently cooked in butter, is the flavour base for a wide number of French dishes such as soups, stews and sauces. Fennel and parsnip also belong to this family along with herbs such as parsley, chervil, cumin and coriander. The umbrella-like flower heads make for easy identification in the garden but take care not to confuse chervil with the poisonous hemlock, which I often find growing wild in my Wanaka garden. Do not let hemlock go to seed.

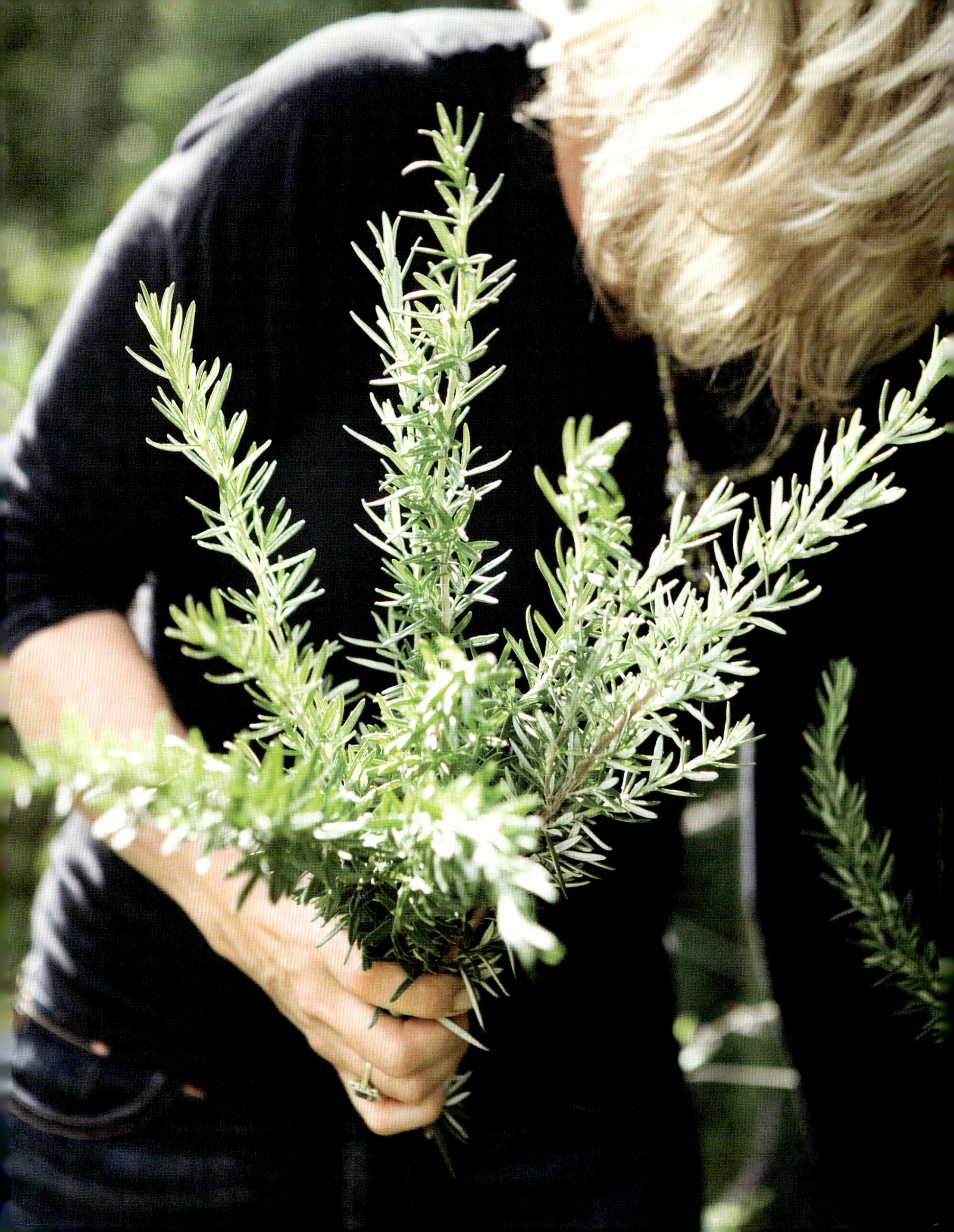

'In the pill-popping, quick-fix culture we currently inhabit, it's easy to forget that communities once flourished using only what was found naturally around them to keep them strong and healthy.'

Slow-cooked Asian flavours

Crisp pork belly with Asian spices & bok choy

Prep 15 minutes
Cook 1½ hours

1-1.3kg whole boned pork belly, rind on
2 tsp salt
1 tsp five-spice powder
2 cups water
¼ cup light soy sauce
1 tbsp liquid honey
4 whole star anise
10-12 thin slices fresh ginger
1 tsp rice vinegar or cider vinegar

4 heads bok choy
1 tsp sesame oil
To serve: cooked rice

Preheat oven to 240°C. Dry the pork rind and rub in the salt and five-spice powder. Place pork skin side up on an oven rack and roast for 30 minutes.

Place water, soy sauce, honey, star anise, ginger and vinegar in a shallow baking dish. Transfer browned pork, skin side up, to this dish. Reduce oven temperature to 180°C and cook a further hour until pork is tender.

While pork cooks, bring a pot of lightly salted water to the boil. Halve or quarter bok choy lengthways and drop into boiling water for 1 minute. Drain in a colander and cool under running water to prevent further cooking. When ready to serve, heat sesame oil in a frypan and stir-fry bok choy for 1-2 minutes to just heat through.

Slice pork and accompany with bok choy and rice.

Serves 4-6

Kashmiri-style lamb knuckles

Prep 10 minutes + marinating
Cook 3-3½ hours

1 cup plain unsweetened yoghurt
½ cup lemon juice
¼ cup (60g) grated fresh ginger
4 cloves garlic, crushed
1 tbsp ground cumin
1 tbsp garam masala
2 tsp cardamom seeds
2 tsp ground turmeric
½ tsp cayenne pepper, or to taste
¼ cup brown sugar
1 tsp salt
½ tsp black pepper
6-8 lamb knuckles
Garnish: a little coriander or mint

This dish gets better with a couple of days marinating. It's also a terrific treatment for a leg of lamb, in which case I cook it at 150°C for 5-6 hours.

Combine yoghurt, lemon juice, ginger, garlic, all the spices, sugar, salt and pepper in a bowl or plastic bag. Add lamb and mix to coat evenly. Chill for at last 4 hours or up to 48 hours (or 3-4 days for a whole lamb leg). Preheat oven to 170°C. Spread meat out in a deep casserole and pour over all the liquids. Cover tightly and bake until very tender, 3-3½ hours. Drain off cooking juices and remove fat. Pour de-fatted liquid back over meat and garnish with coriander or mint.

If making a day ahead, cook for 3 hours then cool, chill and remove fat. Reheat at 180°C for 45 minutes.

Serve with parsnip mash (page 219) or rice and flatbreads brushed with garlic butter and heated in a 200°C oven for 5 minutes.

Serves 6-8

SOLANACAEA FAMILY

Otherwise known as the nightshades, this family of plants contains some of our most important food crops, including potatoes, eggplants, tomatoes, capsicums and chillies as well as tomatillos, cape gooseberries and that old devil, tobacco. A number of plants in this family, like deadly nightshade and belladonna, have toxic fruits and leaves. In the case of potatoes, the fruits that hang from the plant above ground are poisonous. The plants in this family are easily distinguished by their tubular five-petalled star or saucer-shaped flowers. Flavours in the edible fruits of this family tend to be acidic, ranging from piquant through to sweet. Tomatoes and cape gooseberries provide the sweetest flavours while the green fruits of tomatillos, like green capsicums, offer a sweet-sour taste. Ripe capsicums and chillies have a sweet taste that is carried through degrees of hotness. Eggplant is the astringent member of the pack. It carries a bitterness that comes to the fore if it is not fully cooked. Potatoes, being tubers rather than fruit, belie their origins with a mildly sweet gentle taste and starchy texture and none of the acidity of the fruiting crops.

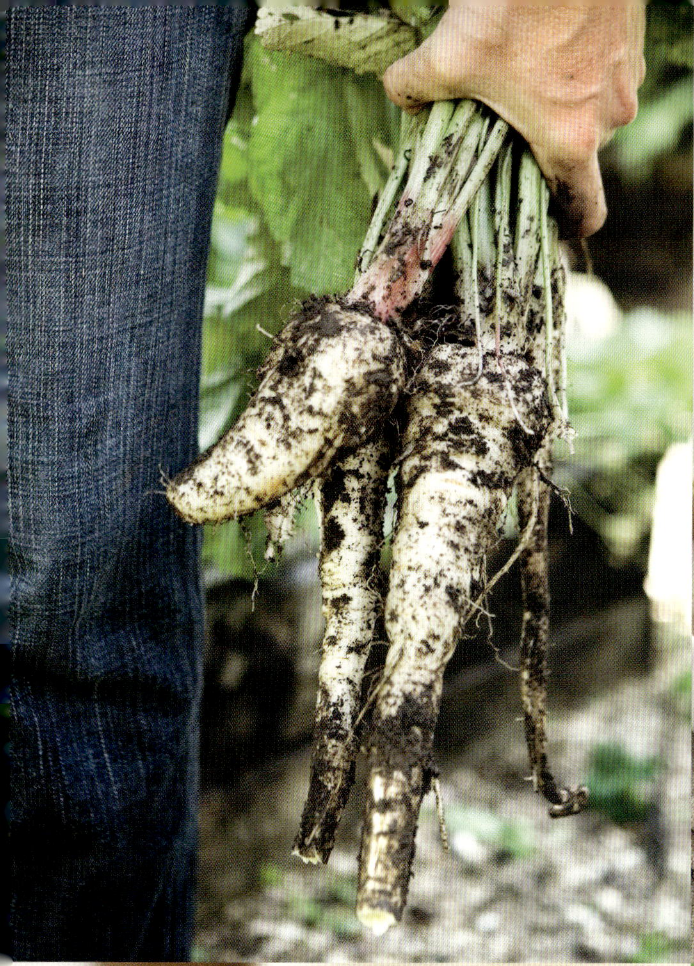
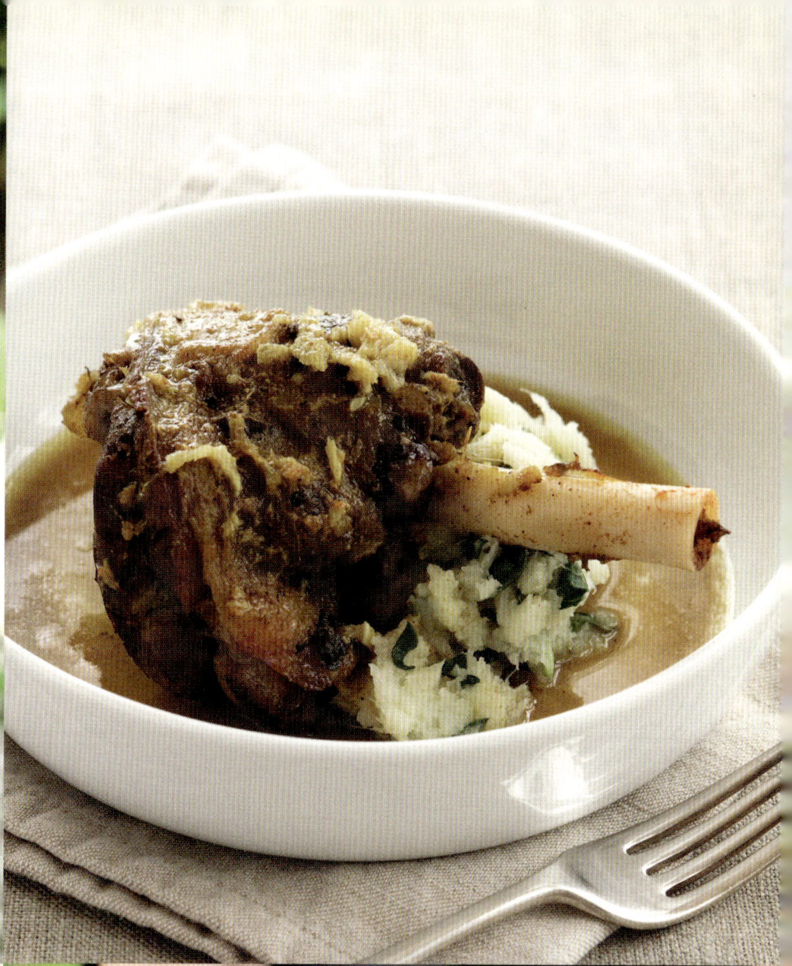
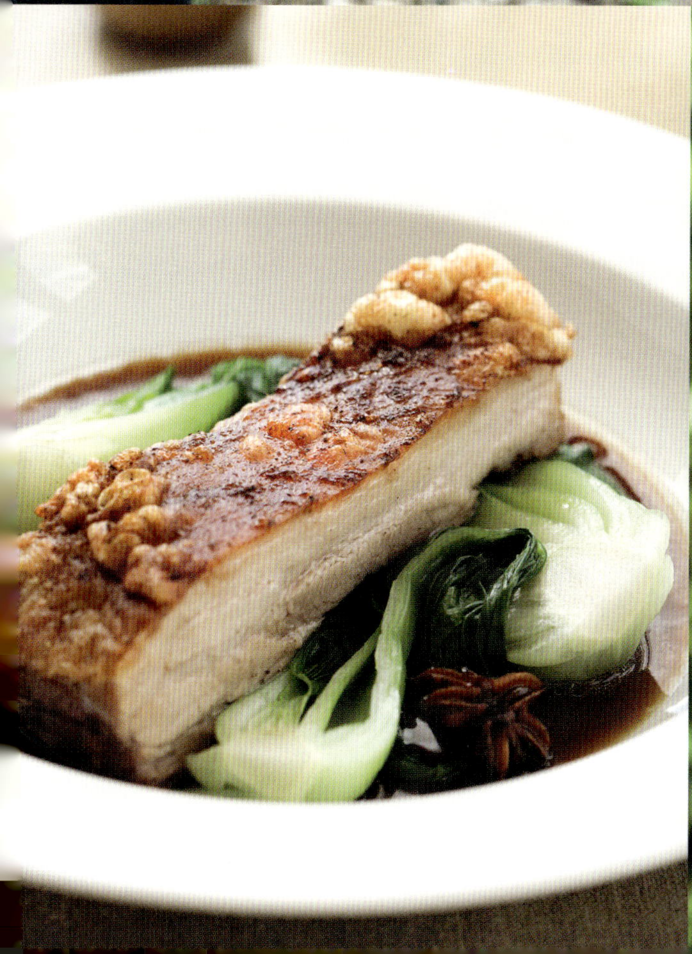
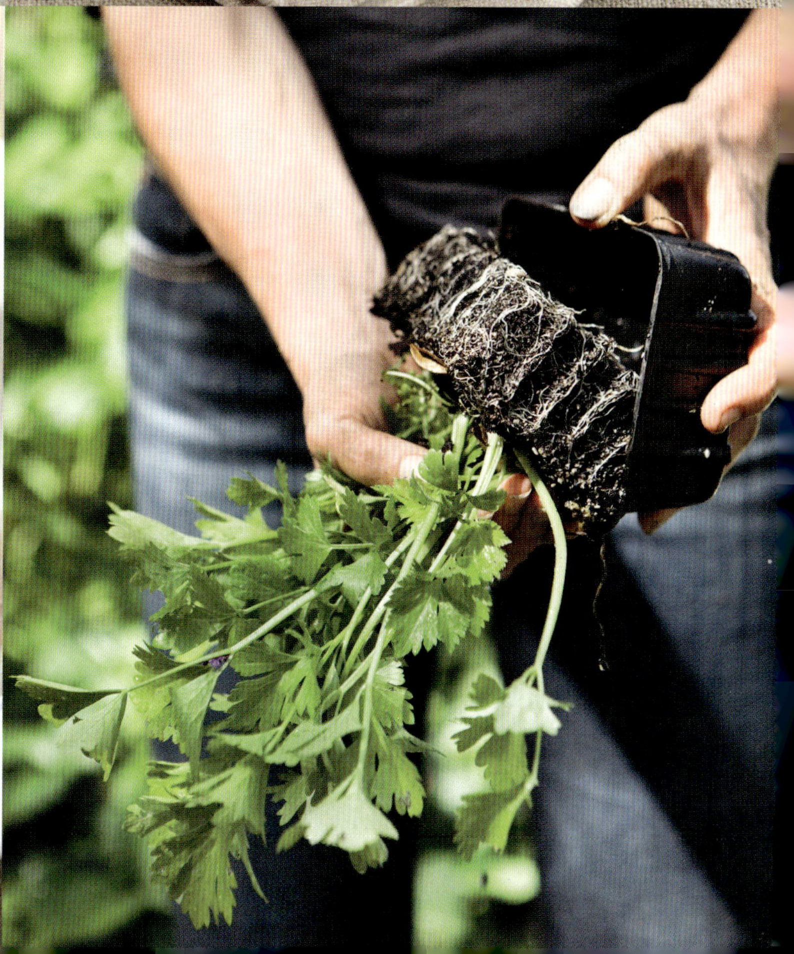

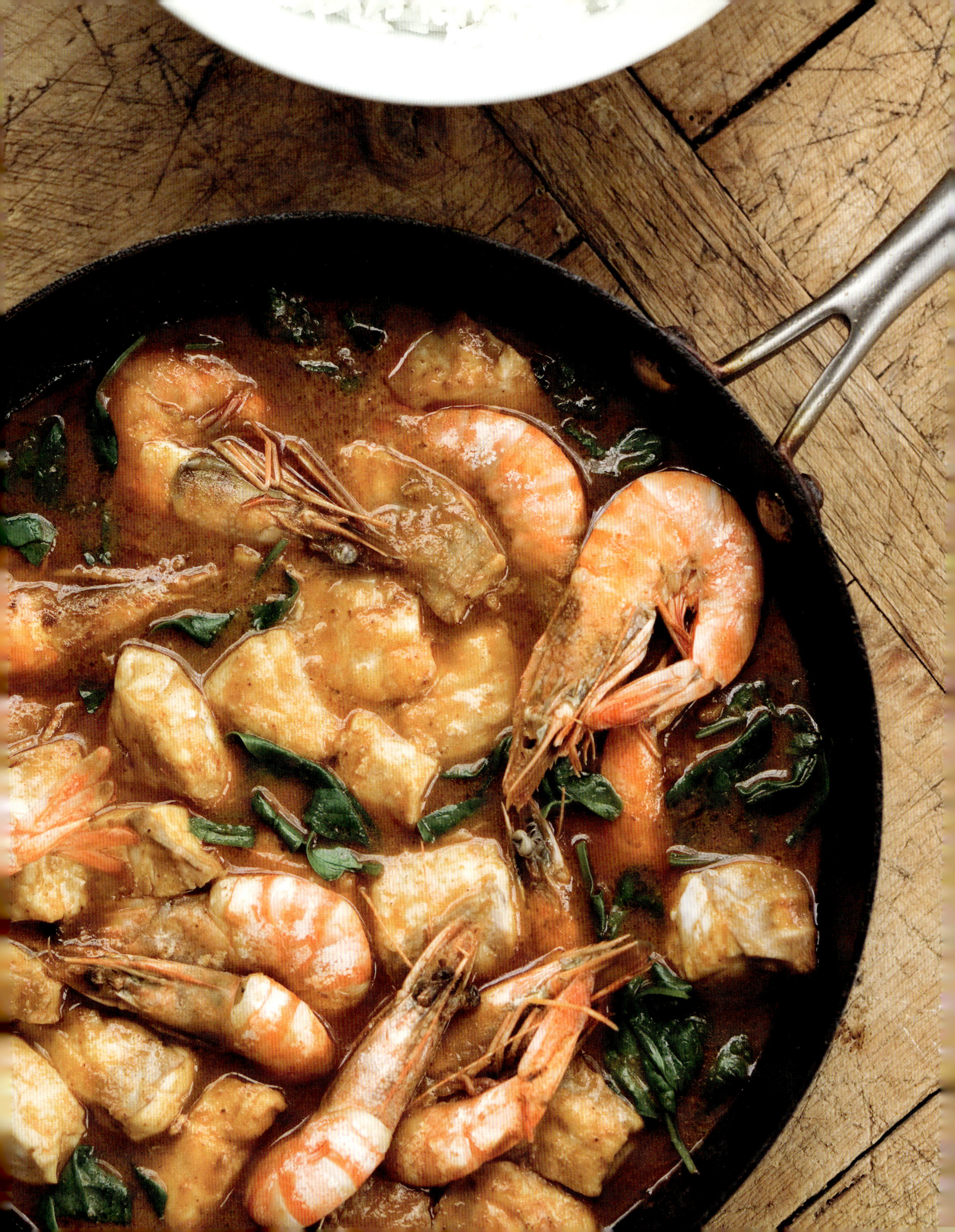

'The livelihoods of millions of people are supported by fishing. Add technology and it's no surprise that 70 per cent of the world's oceans are over-fished. When you buy seafood check it's from sustainable sources.'

Currying flavour

Seafood curry

Prep 5 minutes
Cook 20 minutes

2 tbsp oil
1-2 tbsp Thai red curry paste
3 tbsp tomato paste
1 fat clove garlic, crushed
½ tsp curry powder
1 tsp cumin seeds
1 tbsp brown sugar
2 cups fish or chicken stock
1 tbsp fish sauce
½ cup coconut cream
Optional: 2 kaffir lime leaves
500-600g fresh boneless fish, diced into 3cm chunks
12-16 large prawns
140g spinach
Garnish: ½ cup fresh coriander

Good curries start with flavoursome sauces. This simple base is excellent with any kind of seafood.
    Heat oil in a large pot and sizzle curry paste, tomato paste, garlic, curry powder and cumin seeds for 2-3 minutes or until aromatic. Add brown sugar, stock, fish sauce, coconut cream and kaffir lime leaves if using and simmer for 15 minutes. (Curry can be prepared ahead up to this point.)
Five minutes before serving, add fish, prawns and spinach to sauce. Stir to coat in sauce, cover and cook without stirring for 5 minutes. Garnish with coriander. Accompany with rice.
Serves 4, pictured left

Mixed seafood laksa

Prep 15 minutes
Cook 10 minutes

1 recipe laksa sauce base (see right) or 5 cups of your favourite laksa base
12 raw prawn tails
16 fresh mussels
400g fresh fish, finely sliced
Optional: 200g baby octopus or thinly sliced squid
500g cooked rice noodles or rinsed and drained udon noodles
Garnish:
3 hard-boiled eggs, quartered
1 cup bean sprouts
½ cup coriander leaves

Bring laksa sauce base to a simmer and add mussels. When mussels start to open, add all the other seafood. (If using octopus or squid, add in the last minute of cooking so as not to overcook and toughen.) Simmer for 2-3 minutes until seafood is cooked through.
Divide noodles between 4 heated serving bowls. Top with cooked seafood and pour over broth. Divide garnishes over top and serve.
Serves 4

Variation: In summer add 3 chopped tomatoes with the seafood and include a sliced Lebanese cucumber in the garnish.

SEEDS AND SPROUTS

Seeds can be saved from most vegetables and flowers unless they are sterile hybrid plants. Allow one or two plants to go to seed and when they start to brown and dry collect the seeds.
Store in labelled, dated brown paper bags in a cool place.
I like to sprout my own seeds to enjoy as edible sprouts. Organically grown peas, radishes, red orach and broccoli make really nutritious sprouts. Do not try to sprout commercial seed unless it is labelled organic as most commercial seeds are treated with chemicals to prevent disease or fungus.

LAKSA SAUCE BASE

Heat 2 tbsp neutral oil and cook 1 tbsp minced fresh ginger, 1 tsp ground turmeric, 1-2 tsp Thai curry paste (to taste), ½ tsp chilli flakes and 1 tsp tomato paste for a few seconds. Add 1 cup coconut cream, 4 cups fish or chicken stock, 2 tbsp fish sauce, 2 tsp brown sugar, 1 tsp ground cumin, 2 fresh kaffir lime leaves or the finely grated zest of 1 lime and 4 cardamom pods and simmer for 10 minutes. Season to taste with salt and pepper. Remove kaffir leaves if using. Sauce can be prepared to this point and chilled for up to 2 days, or frozen.
Makes 5 cups

'The rituals and elegance of the Japanese kitchen are so appealing. Attention to detail shows in the simplest things, imparting a sense of caring. The result is inevitably a nourishing experience.'

Japanese-style steak

Beef sirloin with Asian greens & ponzu sauce

Prep 10 minutes
Cook 10 minutes

1 recipe ponzu sauce (see right)
2 large thick-cut (3cm) pieces aged steak, preferably sirloin (600-700g)
a little neutral oil for frying
150g Asian greens, eg gai lan or bok choy, washed and trimmed
½ cup water
1 teaspoon sesame oil
pinch of salt

Mix 2 tablespoons ponzu sauce through steaks and leave until ready to cook (up to 4-5 hours in the fridge). Preheat oven to 200°C. Heat a little oil in a heavy frying pan and cook steaks over medium-high heat for 3 minutes each side. If you prefer steaks cooked a little more, transfer them to the oven and cook a further 3-4 minutes or until done to your liking (steak is best served rare to medium-rare). Rest for 3-5 minutes before slicing on an angle.

While steaks cook, place greens in a pot with water, sesame oil and salt. Cover and cook over high heat for 4-6 minutes until just tender but still green (all the water should have evaporated).

Divide greens between 4 serving plates, top with sliced steak and spoon over remaining ponzu sauce.

I like this dish accompanied with cooked pumpkin mashed with a little butter and seasoned to taste with salt, pepper and a few sesame seeds.

Serves 4

PONZU SAUCE

This is a terrific dipping sauce for tempura, meat and vegetables. Once prepared, it will keep in the fridge for at least a week. Chilli flakes can also be added. Traditionally it is made with yuzu, a Japanese citrus that looks like a grapefruit. In its absence I use lime juice. A teaspoon of bonito flakes is often added too. Using a blender or food processor, blitz together ¼ cup fresh lime juice, 1 tbsp rice vinegar, 1 tsp minced fresh ginger, 1 tsp prepared wasabi, 2 tbsp Japanese-brand soy sauce, eg Yamasa, 1 tbsp sake or mirin, 1 tsp sesame oil and 1 tbsp brown sugar. With the motor running, add 100ml neutral oil in a slow, steady stream until mixture thickens slightly. Spoon into a jar and chill until ready to use. If mixture separates, shake before using.

Makes ¾ cup, serves 6-8

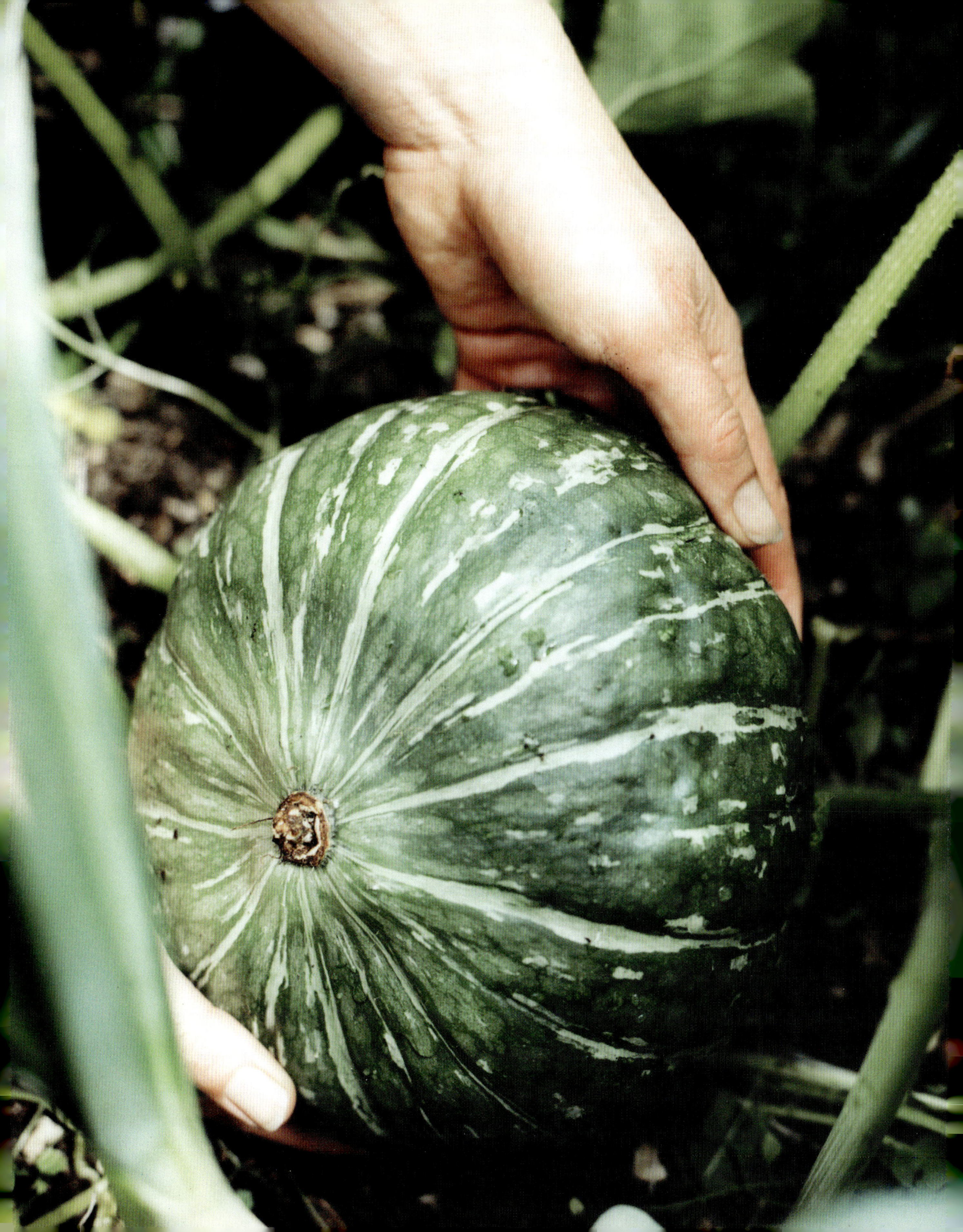

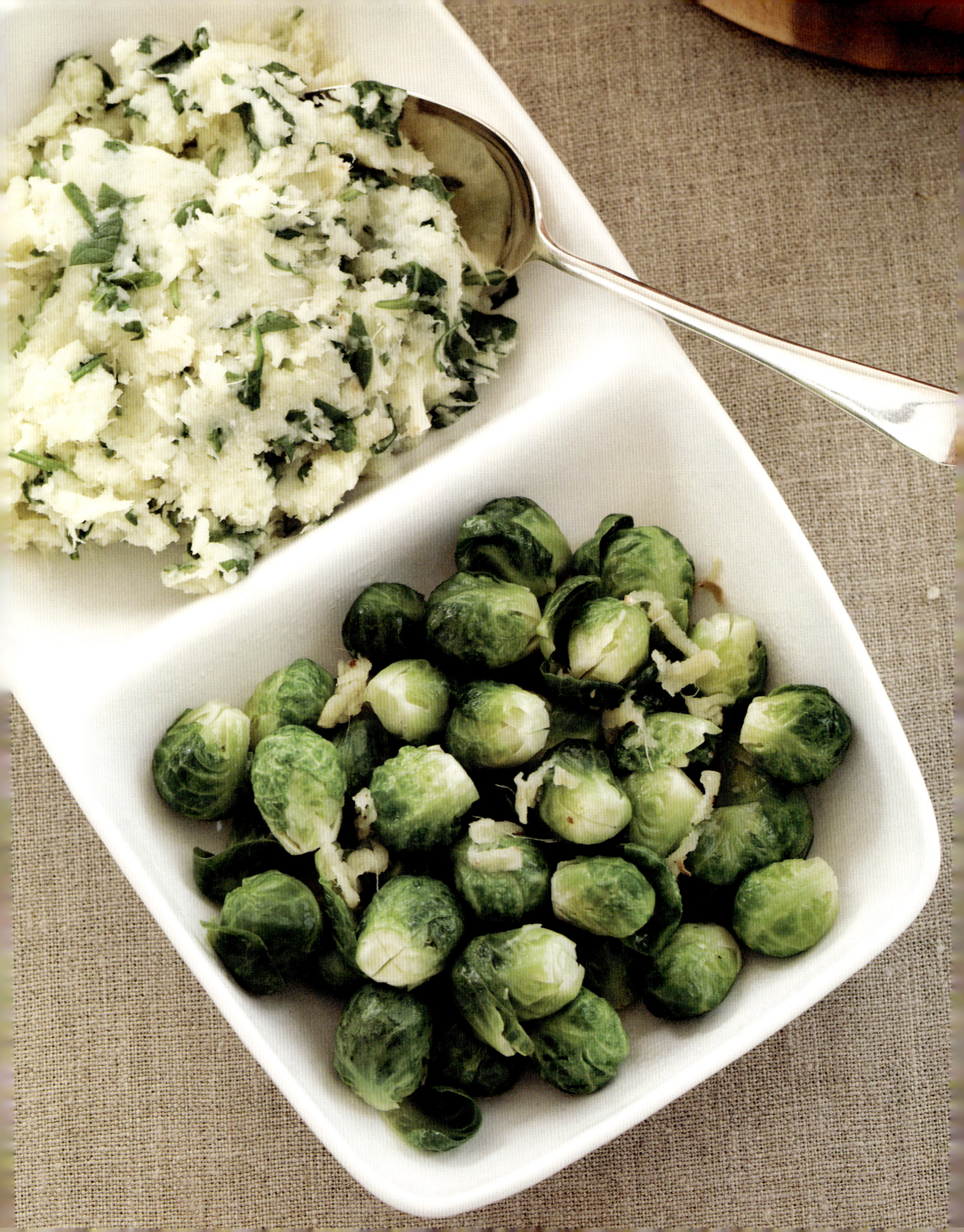

'Poor old brussels sprouts and parsnips – despised and unloved. But with a little spicing-up they take on a new life. Bubble-and-squeak made by frying up the mashed leftovers is a breakfast made in heaven.'

Winter sides

Brussels sprouts
Prep   5 minutes
Cook   6 minutes

Place in a pot 400g brussels sprouts, trimmed and with a cross cut in the ends, ½ cup water, 1 tbsp grated fresh ginger, 1 tbsp butter, ½ tsp salt and ½ tsp sesame oil (optional). Cover and cook for 6 minutes. Drain if necessary and serve.
Serves 4 as a side dish

Parsnip & rocket mash
Prep   10 minutes
Cook   30 minutes

Peel 4 medium-large parsnips and chop into small chunks. Place in a pot and cover with cold water. Bring to the boil then reduce heat and simmer until tender, about 30 minutes. Drain well and place in a bowl. Mash thoroughly with a potato masher until no big chunks remain. Mix in 3 tbsp milk, 2 tbsp butter, ½ tsp salt, ⅛ tsp ground white pepper, a pinch of nutmeg and 1 packed cup baby spinach or rocket, coarsely chopped, and serve.
Serves 6 as a side dish

Wilted spinach
Prep   5 minutes
Cook   5 minutes

Wash 150g spinach and leave wet. Heat 1 tbsp olive oil in a frypan, add spinach and cook until wilted. Mix in a grating of nutmeg and season with salt and pepper.
Serves 2 as a side dish

Orange buttered yams
Prep   5 minutes
Cook   12 minutes

Boil 300g scrubbed yams in lightly salted water for 10 minutes. Drain. Add 1 tbsp very thinly sliced ginger, the juice of an orange, 1 tbsp butter and a little salt and pepper. Cover and cook another minute or two for flavours to absorb.
Serves 4 as a side dish

MAKING SUBSTITUTIONS
When you get into the kitchen to start cooking, you may not always have all the right ingredients at hand. A recipe might call for celery and you have only leeks, or pumpkin and you have only a kumara. This isn't a problem and shouldn't stop you from making the dish. However, there are a couple of things to consider when making substitutions. What you want are things with a similar texture and/or flavour. A salad that calls for spinach can easily be prepared using watercress, rocket, soft salad greens or mâche. In each case the flavour will differ but texturally the dish will be the same. When it comes to cooking mixtures of onions, celery, leeks and the like, you can vary the mix. If you don't have fennel, add celery or leeks. Replace onions with shallots or spring onions or leeks (for a much milder flavour) or some garlic. Leafy green vegetables like silverbeet, cavalo nero, kale or collard greens are all reasonably interchangeable.
If it's thickening power you are after and you don't have any potatoes, try pumpkin or kumara. Cabbage can be swapped with bok choy, chinese cabbage or even bean sprouts, while the denser brassicas like broccoli, cauliflower and gai lan all cook in a similar way.

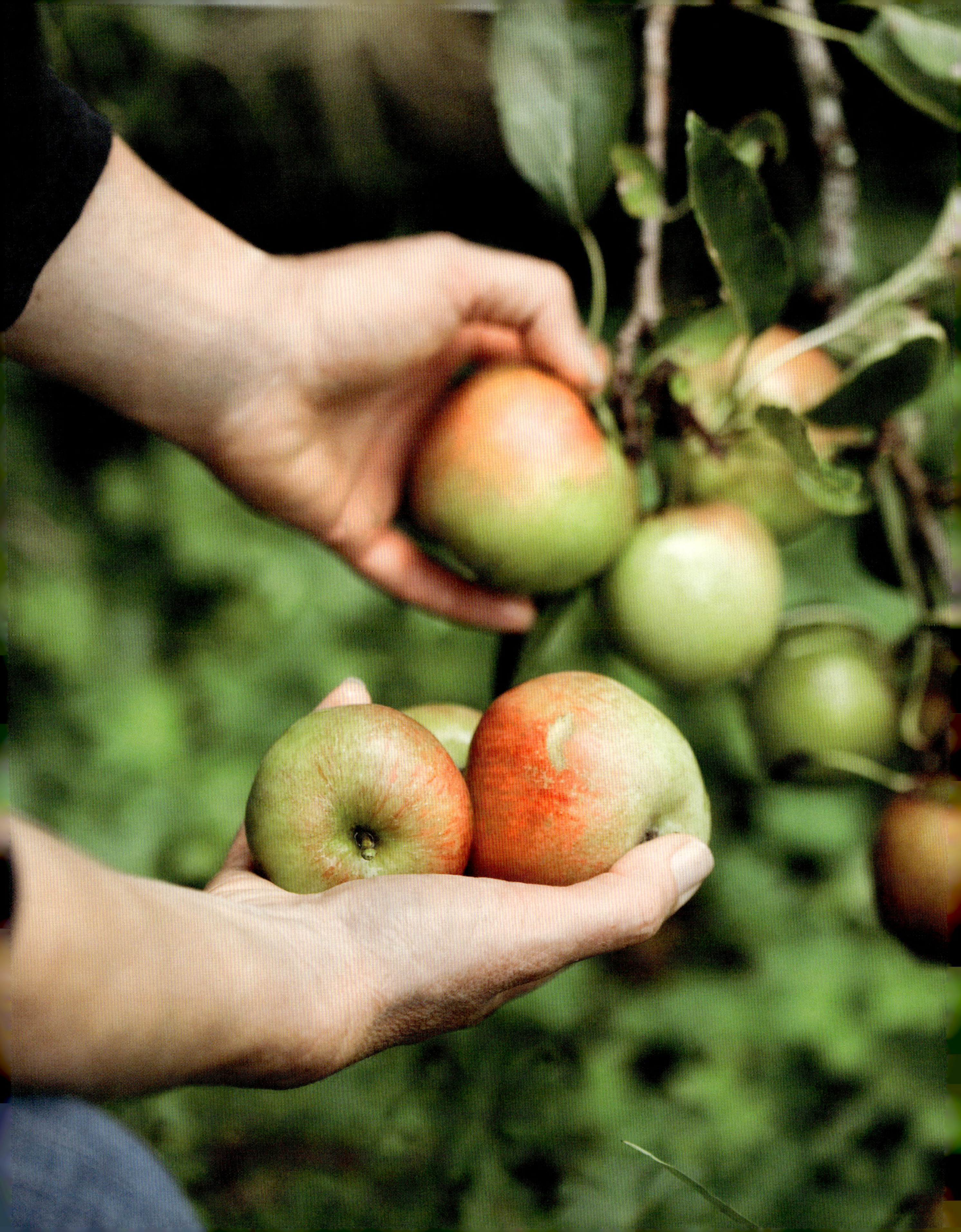

'The language of a food culture is handed down through families with a twist here and a pinch there. Drawing on the season's harvests and the staples at hand, each cook in each household produces something slightly different.'

Cold-weather puddings

Lemon-ginger sponge pudding

Prep   15 minutes
Cook   45 minutes

¼ cup flour, sifted
½ cup sugar
1 tsp ground ginger
2 eggs, separated
1 cup milk
⅓ cup lemon juice
finely grated zest of 1 lemon
2 tbsp butter, melted
Optional: 4 tsp finely chopped glacé ginger

It's always surprising the way this pudding makes its own sauce at the base. I like to add some chopped glacé ginger but you can leave it out if you prefer. You need to eat the puddings as soon as they are cooked, as the sauce absorbs into the mixture as they cool.

Preheat oven to 180°C. Combine flour, sugar, ginger and egg yolks. Mix in milk, lemon juice, zest and butter. Beat egg whites to stiff but not dry peaks and gently fold into mixture.

If using glacé ginger, sprinkle it over the base of a 23cm square baking dish (or for individual puddings into 4-6 small ramekins or cups). Spread batter in dish and place the dish in a larger baking dish or roasting pan. Fill outer pan with hot water to come halfway up the sides of the pudding dish. Place in oven and bake until risen and spongy, 45 minutes. Individual ramekins will take 5-10 minutes less. Lift puddings out on to small plates, taking care not to burn yourself when removing them from the water bath.
Serves 4-6

Spicy berry puddings

Prepare pudding mixture as above, substituting 1tsp of mixed spice for the ginger and zest and ⅓ cup of orange juice for the lemon zest and juice.

Sprinkle 100g of frozen berries over the base of a buttered baking dish or between 4-6 small ramekins or cups. Spread batter in dish and place the dish in a larger baking dish or roasting pan. Fill outer pan with hot water to come halfway up the sides of the pudding dish and cook as above.
Serves 4-6

ZEST

The outer, coloured skin of citrus known as the zest contains the fruit's aromatic oils. Each type of citrus zest has its own distinct flavour and aroma. To my mind the zest encapsulates the essence of the fruit. I use lemon zest throughout my savoury cooking – it gives a neutral freshness. Lime zest is more floral with tropical tones, while the zest from oranges has a distinctly orange citrus taste. Use a zesting tool or microplane to remove zest – both are shallow enough to just take off the skin without the bitter white pith that lies directly underneath.
For a nice citrus salt see page 222.

'I use lemons more than any other flavour in my food. Their juice provides a gentle acid balance, neither too biting nor too fragrant, that brightens a dish, while the zest delivers depth and a piquant lemony flavour.'

Refreshing lemon flavours

Lemon curd

Prep   10 minutes
Cook 6 minutes

340g caster sugar
220g butter
finely grated zest of 1 lemon
300ml lemon juice (about 6 juicy lemons), strained
6 eggs, beaten lightly with a whisk

A jar of lemon curd on hand makes for the speedy construction of some sensational desserts. A thermometer is the best means of gauging the correct degree of cooking and avoids the need for a double boiler.

    Place sugar, butter, lemon zest and juice in a pot (use a double boiler if you don't have a thermometer). Heat over medium-low heat until butter has melted. Take off heat and strain eggs into mixture.
Return to heat with a thermometer attached and cook, stirring constantly, until temperature reaches 75°C. (If using a double boiler, cook until mixture thickens enough to coat the back of a spoon.) Remove at once from heat and stir a little to prevent mixture overheating at base and egg from curdling.
Pour into hot sterilised jars while still hot and seal with pop-top lids or store in a sealed container in the fridge. Chilled, it will keep for several weeks. Preserved lemon curd will keep indefinitely as long as seal is unbroken.
Makes just over 1 litre

Lemon kiwi syllabub parfait

Prep   10 minutes

600ml chilled cream
½ cup icing sugar
2 tbsp brandy
½ cup lemon juice
finely grated zest of 1 lemon
3-4 meringues, coarsely crushed
3 kiwifruit, peeled and diced
¾ cup lemon curd, chilled
Garnish: ¼ cup thread coconut, toasted

This luxurious dessert is a quick assembly using lemon curd and meringues.

    Whip cream to soft peaks and fold in icing sugar, brandy, lemon juice and zest. Gently mix in meringues and kiwifruit.
Divide two-thirds of the mixture between 6 serving glasses. Top each one with a tablespoon of lemon curd. Spoon over remaining cream mixture and swirl another spoon of lemon curd on top. Garnish with coconut. Chill until ready to serve.
Serves 6

THE RUTACEAE FAMILY

The family of citrus fruits covers the range of sweet, sour and bitter flavours. Oranges, mandarins and tangelos offer sweet flavours, lemons are sour (the exception being Meyer lemons, which err on the sweet-sour side), while grapefruit and limes, also have sweet-sour tones.
Kumquats and bitter oranges are bitter-sweet, which makes them especially useful for preserves such as marmalade.
Lemons are in season for most of the year, with a down time in the late summer and early autumn. I grow Yen Ben for an early-season lemon and the soft-skinned, sweeter Meyer for harvests through to early summer. Preserved lemons or limes are useful for salads and fish dishes. I have included a recipe for these on page 192. Citrus-based dressings are always refreshing. The citrus chilli dressing on page 26 is one of my favourites for seafood, chicken and light green salads.
Make **citrus salt** by mixing 1 tbsp each finely grated lemon zest and lime zest with ¼ cup salt. Spread on a baking tray and dry in a 120°C oven for 2 hours. Cool and blitz in a food processor. It will keep in a jar for months. Use to season anything savoury before cooking.

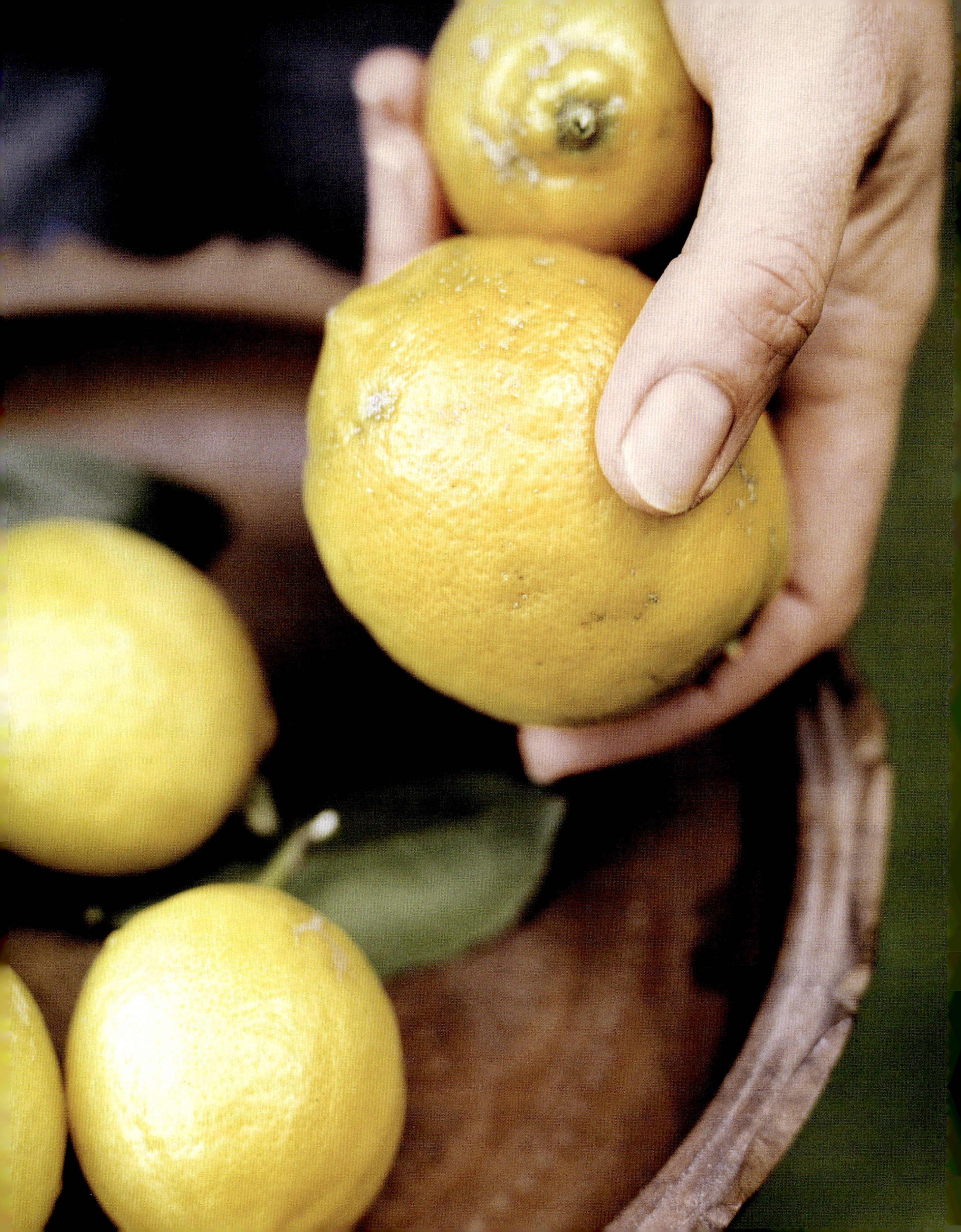

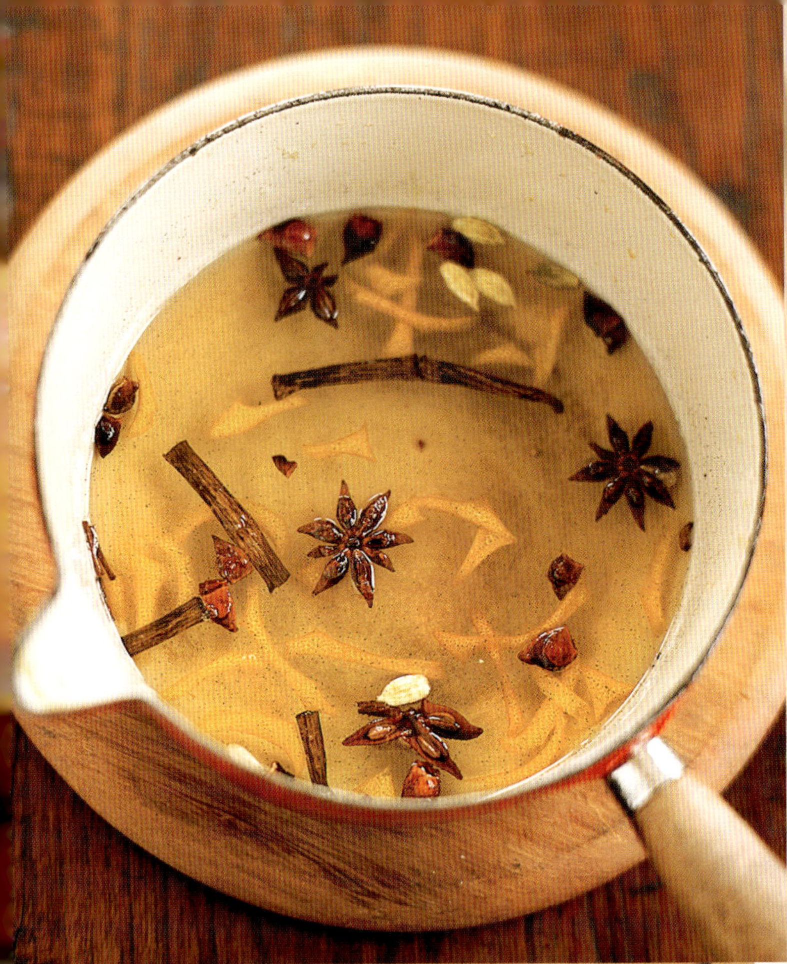
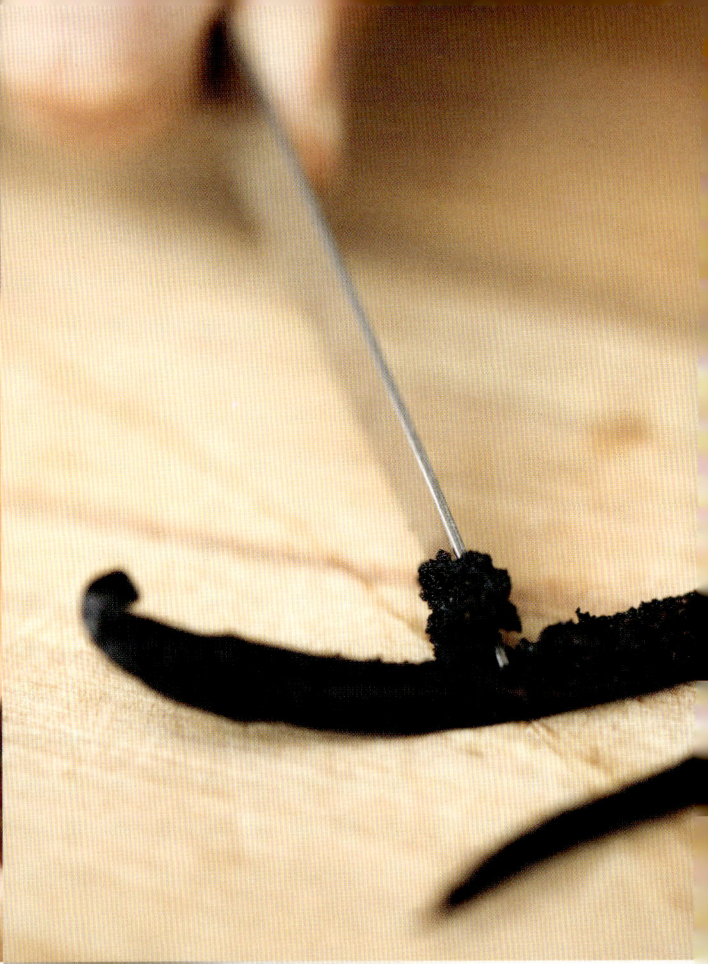
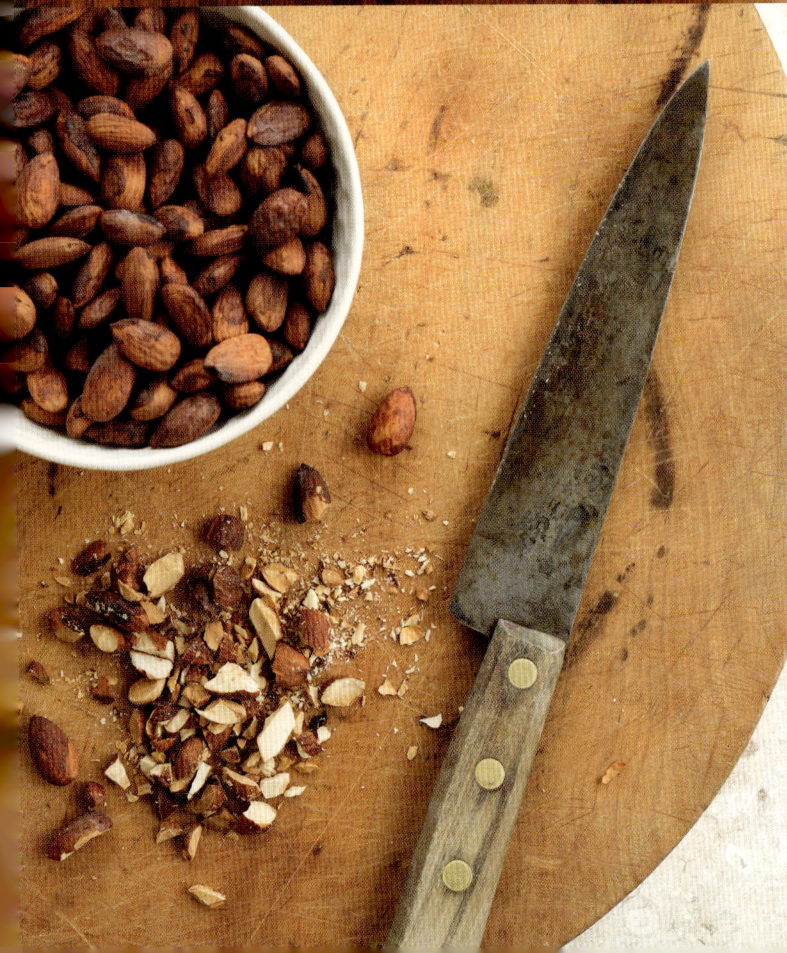
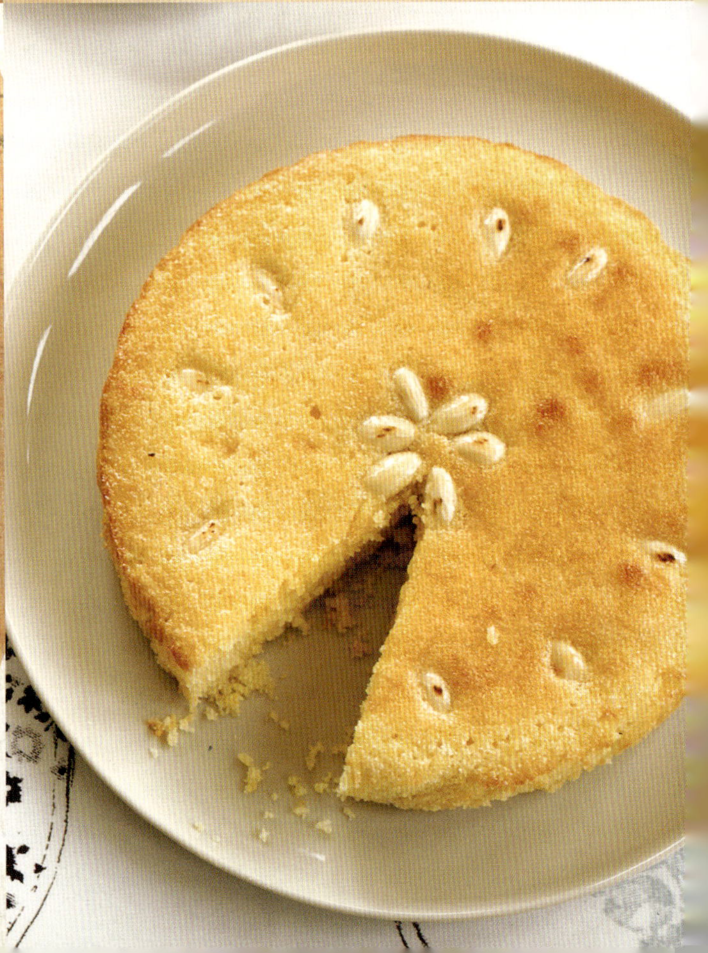

'Take care when buying vanilla from Mexico as it is often mixed with a tonka bean extract that contains coumarin. This has been shown to cause liver damage and is a known carcinogen.'

Syrup cake

Greek almond citrus cake

Prep 10 minutes
Cook 30-35 minutes

¾ cup self-raising flour
1 tsp baking powder
½ cup semolina
1 cup ground almonds
125g unsalted butter
1 cup caster sugar
finely grated zest of 1 lemon and ½ orange
1 tsp natural vanilla essence
3 eggs, at room temperature
60ml lemon juice
12-16 whole peeled almonds, to garnish
¼ cup lemon anise syrup (see below)

Preheat oven to 180°C. Grease a 23cm spring-form cake tin. Combine flour, baking powder, semolina and ground almonds in a mixing bowl. In another bowl beat butter and sugar together until creamy. Beat in zests and vanilla. Add eggs one at a time, beating well after each addition.
Stir in half the flour mixture then the lemon juice. Stir in the remaining flour mixture until evenly combined.
Pour mixture into the prepared tin, top with almonds and bake for 30-35 minutes until a skewer comes out clean. Brush lemon anise syrup over hot cake. Serve with crème fraîche or whipped cream on the side.
Serves 8-10

Lemon anise syrup

Prep 5 minutes
Cook 15 minutes

1½ cups water
2 cups sugar
peeled rind of 3 lemons, no pith
6 cardamom pods
1 vanilla pod
3 whole star anise

This useful syrup keeps for months in the fridge and makes a great garnish for a wedge of cake or tart. It can also be poured over ice cream or brushed hot over Greek-style cakes such as the Greek almond citrus cake above.
Place all ingredients in a pot and bring to a simmer, stirring to dissolve sugar. Boil until syrupy, about 10 minutes. Cool and strain into a clean jar or bottle.
Makes 1 cup

TYPES OF VANILLA

VANILLA BEANS
Choose supple, moist beans. Split and scrape out the seeds, which carry the bulk of the flavour. Infuse beans in milk for custards and sauces. Once used they can be rinsed and stored in sugar and will impart a light vanilla flavour. Or blitz the chopped beans with raw sugar in a food processor and use this as a flavouring – 1-2 tbsp will add a rich vanilla taste to sauces and cakes.

NATURAL VANILLA ESSENCE OR EXTRACT
Beans are soaked in alcohol to release the essential vanilla flavour.

PURE VANILLA EXTRACT
You should be getting the real thing. A minimum of 35% alcohol is required for an extract and sugar and other substances may be added. Nielsen Massey is a premium brand.

NATURAL VANILLA FLAVOURING
Derived from vanilla beans with little or no alcohol.

ARTIFICIAL VANILLA FLAVOURING
A byproduct of the paper industry, chemically treated to mimic the flavour of vanilla.

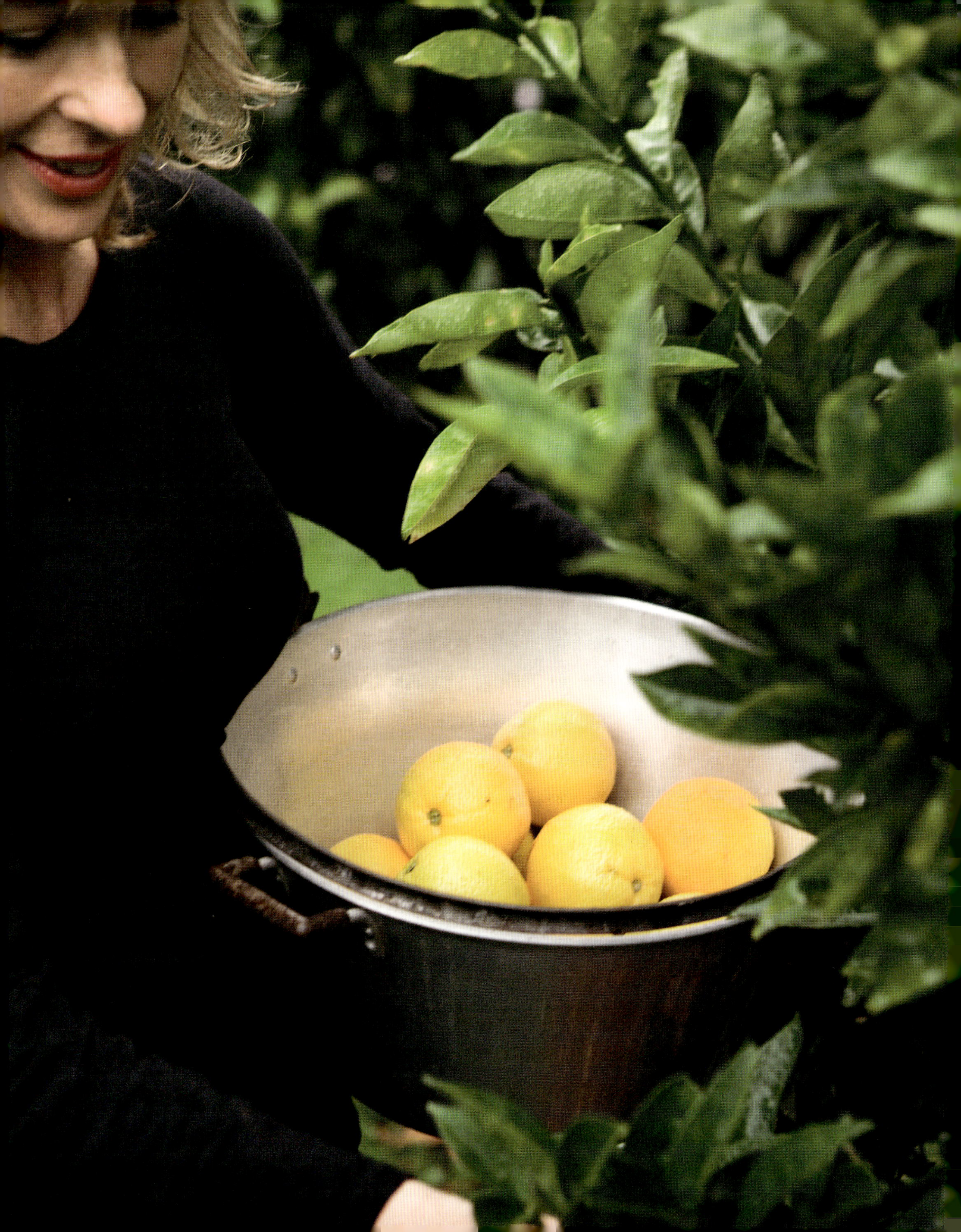

'When you are planning a menu, aim to create a balance of tastes and textures. There's a sense of unity in a set of dishes that share a style and some flavours – much better than trying to globe-hop in one meal.'

Caramelised fruit

Rum sabayon with winter fruits

Prep 10 minutes
Cook 10 minutes

Sabayon:
2 egg yolks
⅓ cup sugar
¼ cup rum (I use Appeltons)
½ cup cream

Fruit:
2-3 oranges, peeled and segmented
4-6 kiwifruit, peeled and sliced (use gold or green)
½ pineapple, peeled and sliced in thin wedges

The light custard base for the sabayon mixture can be made ahead of time and chilled. All kinds of fruit go well with this rich, creamy mixture.

Beat egg yolks and sugar in a heatproof bowl until very pale and thick. Whisk in rum. Set bowl over a saucepan with 4-5cm of simmering water (water should not touch base of bowl) and continue whisking vigorously until sauce thickens and coats the back of a spoon, about 8 minutes.

Remove from heat and place bowl immediately into cold water to prevent further cooking.

Mix cream into cooled sabayon. If not using at once, cover and chill; sabayon will keep up to 24 hours in the fridge.

To serve, place prepared fruit in heat-proof shallow bowls. Whisk sabayon before pouring 2-3 tablespoons over each serving. Place under preheated grill until sabayon just starts to turn golden, 2-3 minutes.
Serve at once.
Serves 4-6

ADJUSTING BALANCE IN A DISH

Sometimes you get to the end of preparing a dish only to find that it's too sweet or too salty. (It doesn't help when someone puts icing sugar in the cornflour container!) There are a few tricks you can pull if a dish is too salty. The first, which works only if you have enough liquid to soak it up, is to add a potato or some other starchy food. Failing that, try a little sugar. Sugar added to a dish makes our taste buds perceive it as less salty. Sugar also works if a dish is bitter – think of coffee. Adding fat is another means of disguise. The fat in cream or butter coats the tongue and blocks some salt from reaching the taste buds. Conversely, if you are using an ingredient like endive which is bitter, use a little salt to hide the bitterness. Warming the dish also helps as heat hides bitter flavours – hence warm salads made with bitter greens. If you have over-sweetened a dish, add a pinch of salt or an acid balance such as lemon to create a sweet-sour effect.

'Place settings, napkins and water glasses create a welcoming ambience that invites people to sit and relax at your table. Dim overhead lights and soften the room with candles.'

Winter fruit salads

Fruit bowl with lime syrup

Prep 5 minutes
Cook 5 minutes

¼ cup sugar
½ cup water
1 vanilla pod or 1 tsp natural vanilla essence
finely grated zest of 1 lime
2 tbsp lime juice
1kg assorted fruit, eg ½ peeled pineapple, 2 persimmons, 4 peeled feijoas or kiwifruit

Make a syrup by heating together sugar, water, vanilla, zest and juice. Slice the fruit, place in a serving bowl and pour over the cooled syrup. Chill for at least 30 minutes or up to an hour before serving.
Serves 4-6

Kiwi-pineapple sorbet

Prep 30 minutes + freezing
Cook 5 minutes

1½ cups sugar
2 cups water
5 large kiwifruit (500g) peeled and puréed
500g pineapple, peeled and puréed
½ cup lime juice
zest of 1 lime
1 large egg white

Combine sugar and water in a saucepan and bring to the boil, stirring to dissolve sugar. Simmer 5 minutes then cool and chill.
Mix kiwifruit and pineapple purées with lime juice, zest and cold syrup. Place in a shallow container and freeze until semi-frozen, about 4 hours. Remove from freezer and blitz in a food processor or beat until smooth. Add egg white and process until mixture fluffs up.
Serve immediately or refreeze until firm then beat again. Pack back into a container and freeze completely.
Serve on chilled plates or glasses.
Serves 6-8

Tamarillos in port

Prep 10 minutes + at least 4 hours standing

12 ripe tamarillos
½ packed cup sugar
½ cup port or orange juice

Prick tamarillos in several places with a sharp fork, put in a bowl and pour over boiling water to cover. Leave to cool then peel off skins and discard.
Halve or slice each fruit and place in a bowl. Sprinkle with sugar and pour over port or orange juice. Leave for at least 4 hours or cover and chill for up to 48 hours. Accompany with crème fraîche or Greek yoghurt.
Serves 4-5

POMEGRANATES
Punica granatum

I planted a pomegranate in our garden about 7 years ago, not really knowing if it would fruit. It started producing last year, small fruits that tend to split as they ripen. The climate here in Auckland is a bit wet; their natural habitat is the Mediterranean and northern India. But their loose evergreen form and pretty red flowers look good in the garden. Pomegranates ripen through autumn and early winter. The juice is incredibly good for you and the jewel-like ruby seeds (the part you eat) add a sweet-sour crunch to savoury salads and desserts. The best way to get to the juicy seeds is to cut a slice off the top of the fruit then score through the skin in sections between the membrane. Open out fruit and loosen seeds into a bowl. The juice stains badly and the membrane is bitter.
Grenadine is a gorgeous sweet pomegranate syrup often used in cocktails. To prepare grenadine, add 1 part sugar to 3 parts of seeds, mashing together lightly. Let the mixture stand for a day then boil for 5 minutes. Strain out the seeds, bottle and refrigerate.

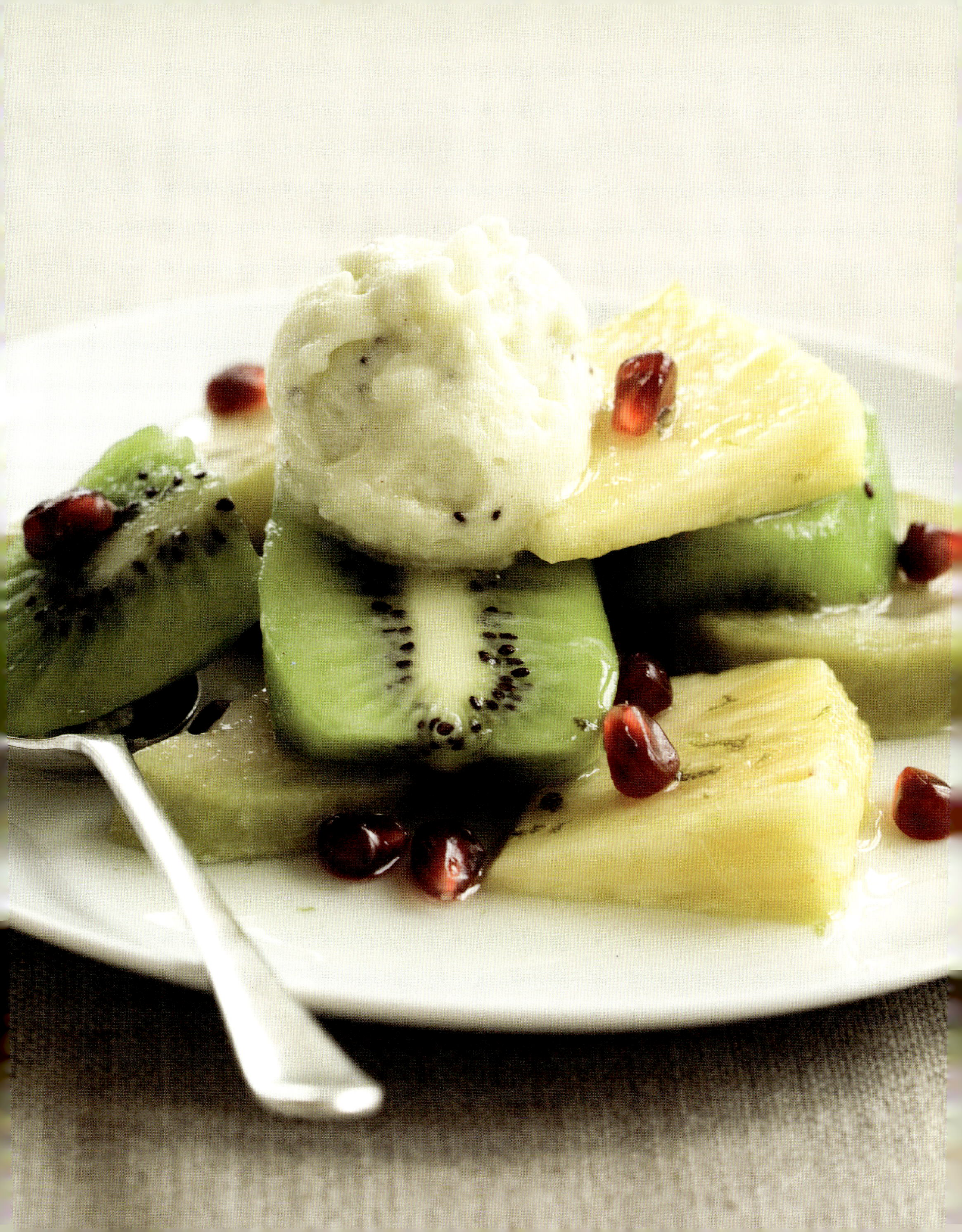

'Having a bowl of stewed fruit in the fridge makes a great start for breakfast. Stewed apple with Greek yoghurt and muesli, or in the spring a compote of rhubarb and berries, are gentle tastes to start the day.'

Poaching and stewing fruits

Poached feijoas or pears

Prep 10 minutes
Cook 10-30 minutes depending on size and ripeness

Make a syrup by heating together two parts of water to one part of sugar, stirring until sugar has dissolved. (For 1kg of fruit I use about 3 cups water and 1½ cups sugar.) Peel fruit and leave whole, halve or slice into wedges as preferred. Add fruit to the simmering syrup and cook at a low simmer until just tender. Sliced fruit will take about 10-15 minutes, halved fruit 15-20 minutes and whole fruit 20-30 minutes, depending on size and ripeness.
Vary the flavour of the syrup by adding spices such as cinnamon quills or a few star anise, slices of fresh ginger or sliced lemons or limes.

Poached & roasted pears

Prep 10 minutes
Cook 30-60 minutes

8 pears
1 cup sugar
3 cups water

Follow the above method for poaching. Carefully remove cooked pears from syrup and place on a baking tray lined with baking paper. Roast at 220°C for 20-25 minutes, basting with syrup, until just starting to caramelise.
Accompany with Greek yoghurt.
Serves 8

Apple purée

Prep: 5 minutes
Cook: 15 minutes

5-6 large tart cooking apples, peeled, cored and cut in thin wedges
½ cup water
10 whole cloves
¼-½ cup sugar, to taste

Place apples, water and cloves in a saucepan. Cover and cook over medium heat until apples start to collapse, about 10 minutes. Add sugar and continue cooking until apples are cooked through, taking care they don't catch. Cool and store in the fridge for up to a week, or freeze.
Serves 4

BREAKFAST FIX

Few people like to be challenged at breakfast. We want simple, familiar tastes, nothing too quirky. I am a fan of fresh fruit – paw paw with passionfruit and lime juice is my current habit, followed by soft-boiled eggs and soldiers of wholegrain buttered toast. Bircher muesli is also delicious if you remember to soak the oats the night before.

BIRCHER MUESLI

Combine in a mixing bowl 2 cups rolled oats, 1 cup apple juice, optional ¼ cup dried cranberries and 2 tbsp lemon juice. Mix to combine, cover and leave to stand on the bench overnight. In the morning add 2 grated green apples, 1 cup plain yoghurt, 3-4 tsp honey (to taste), ½ cup chopped roasted hazelnuts or almonds and a pinch of ground cloves. Other fruits such as chopped pineapple or banana can be added just before serving.
Serves 4

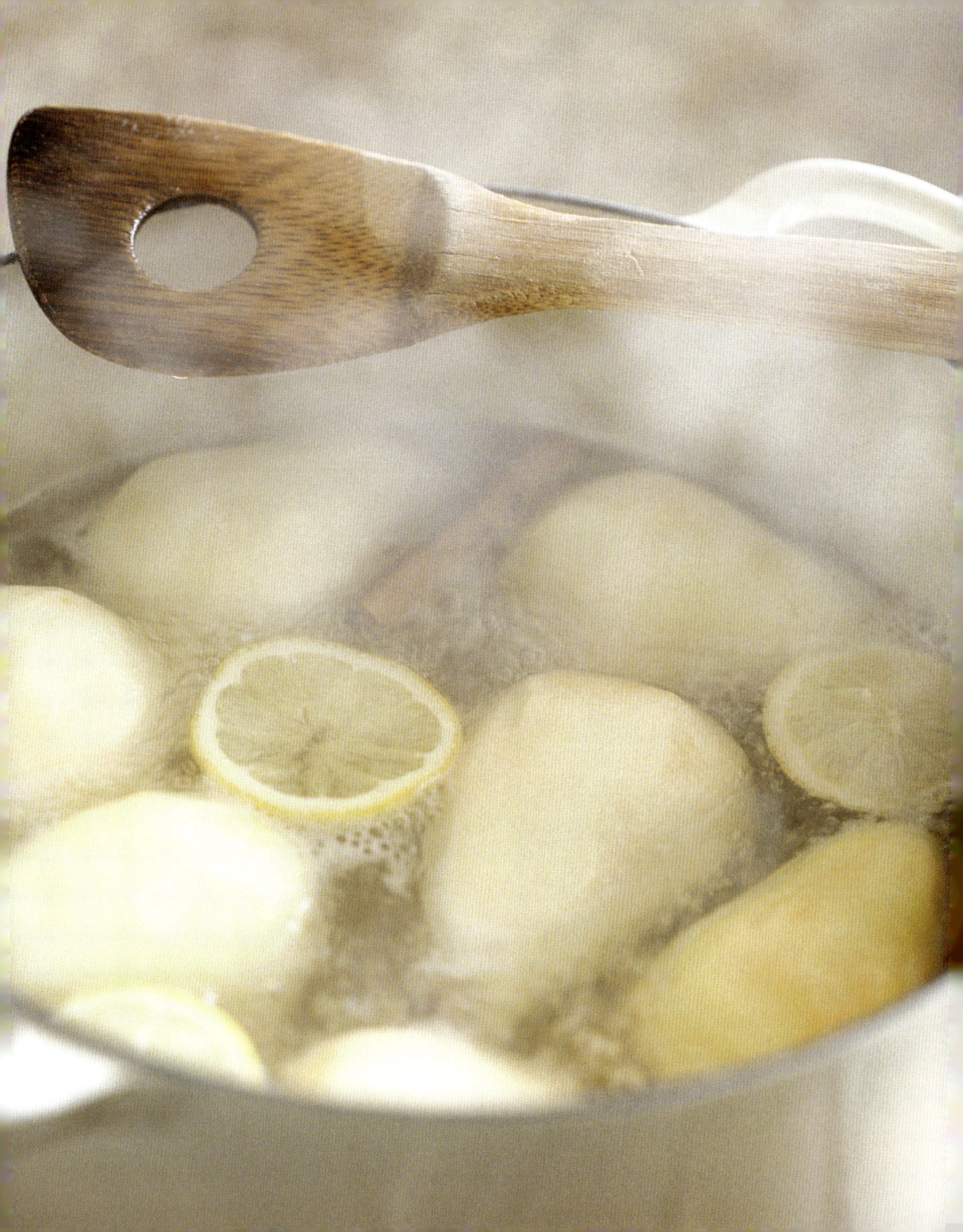

'Recently I have taken to baking my cake mixtures in 3 or 4 small tins and freezing the results to eat later. They make great gifts. Wash and recycle large tuna cans for the baking tins.'

Moist cakes that keep

Banana cake

Prep 15 minutes
Cook 1 hour (less if making smaller cakes)

250g butter, softened
1½ cups sugar
4 eggs
2 tsp natural vanilla essence
4 very ripe bananas, peeled and mashed (about 2 cups)
2 tsp baking soda
½ cup hot milk
3 cups flour
2 tsp baking powder

Icing: use recipe for passionfruit icing on page 170, using lemon juice instead of passionfruit

Preheat oven to 170°C. Line a 23cm round cake tin with baking paper or prepare 4 x 10cm tins (recycled large 425g tuna cans are perfect) or 12 muffin tins.
Beat butter and sugar until creamy. Beat in eggs and vanilla then bananas. Dissolve baking soda in hot milk and add to mixture. Sift over flour and baking powder and fold in.
Spoon mixture into prepared tin(s) and smooth top. Bake until a skewer inserted in the centre comes out clean and the top is springy to the touch. One large cake will take 50-60 minutes, allow 45-55 minutes for 4 medium cakes and about 20 minutes for muffin sized cakes.
Cool in tin and ice when cool. Store in a sealed container in a cool place for 2-3 days or wrap and freeze.
Makes 1 x 23cm cake, 4 x 10cm cakes or 12 muffin-sized cakes

Carrot cake

Prep 15 minutes
Cook 1 hour (less if making smaller cakes)

1 cup neutral oil
2 cups raw sugar
2 tbsp golden syrup
4 eggs
1 cup wholemeal flour
1 cup plain flour
pinch salt
2 tsp cinnamon
1 tsp mixed spice
1 tsp ground ginger
3 cups grated carrot or pumpkin
2 tsp baking soda
1 tbsp orange juice

Icing: use recipe for cream cheese icing on page 178

Preheat oven to 160°C. Line a 23cm round cake tin with baking paper or prepare 4 x 10cm tins (recycled large 425g tuna cans are perfect) or 15 muffin tins.
In a food processor place oil, sugar, golden syrup and eggs. Blitz to combine. Add flours, salt, spices and grated carrot. Blitz just to combine. Fold in baking soda dissolved in orange juice. Spoon mixture into prepared tin(s) and smooth top. Bake until a skewer inserted in the centre comes out clean and the top is springy to the touch. One large cake will take 50-60 minutes, allow 45-55 minutes for 4 medium cakes and about 20-25 minutes for muffin-sized cakes.
Cool in tin and ice when cool. Store in a sealed container in a cool place for 2-3 days or wrap and freeze.
Makes 1 x 23cm cake, 4 x 10cm cakes or 15 muffin-sized cakes

KIWIFRUIT
Actinidia chinensis

For some strange reason I always think of the green dragon tile in mahjong when I think of kiwifruit. Even after growing up with kiwis, there's still something foreign and lushly exotic about them. When we were kids every house had a kiwi vine growing rampantly in the backyard. They were huge, taking over sheds and lattice walls. We called them Chinese gooseberries. Commerically-grown kiwis are often sold very green and hard and need a couple of days in a paper bag with an apple to ripen. But better like this than squishy and over-ripe, when they develop a horrible fermented flavour. Check you don't put any squishy ones in the bag – the taste will put you off forever. Kiwifruit are a powerhouse of good nutrition, offering a potent cocktail of nutrients and phytochemicals which provide protective nutrition. Kiwifruit contain an enzyme (like papaya) that has an inhibiting effect on gelatine, so don't try to make jellies or mousses with them as they won't set.

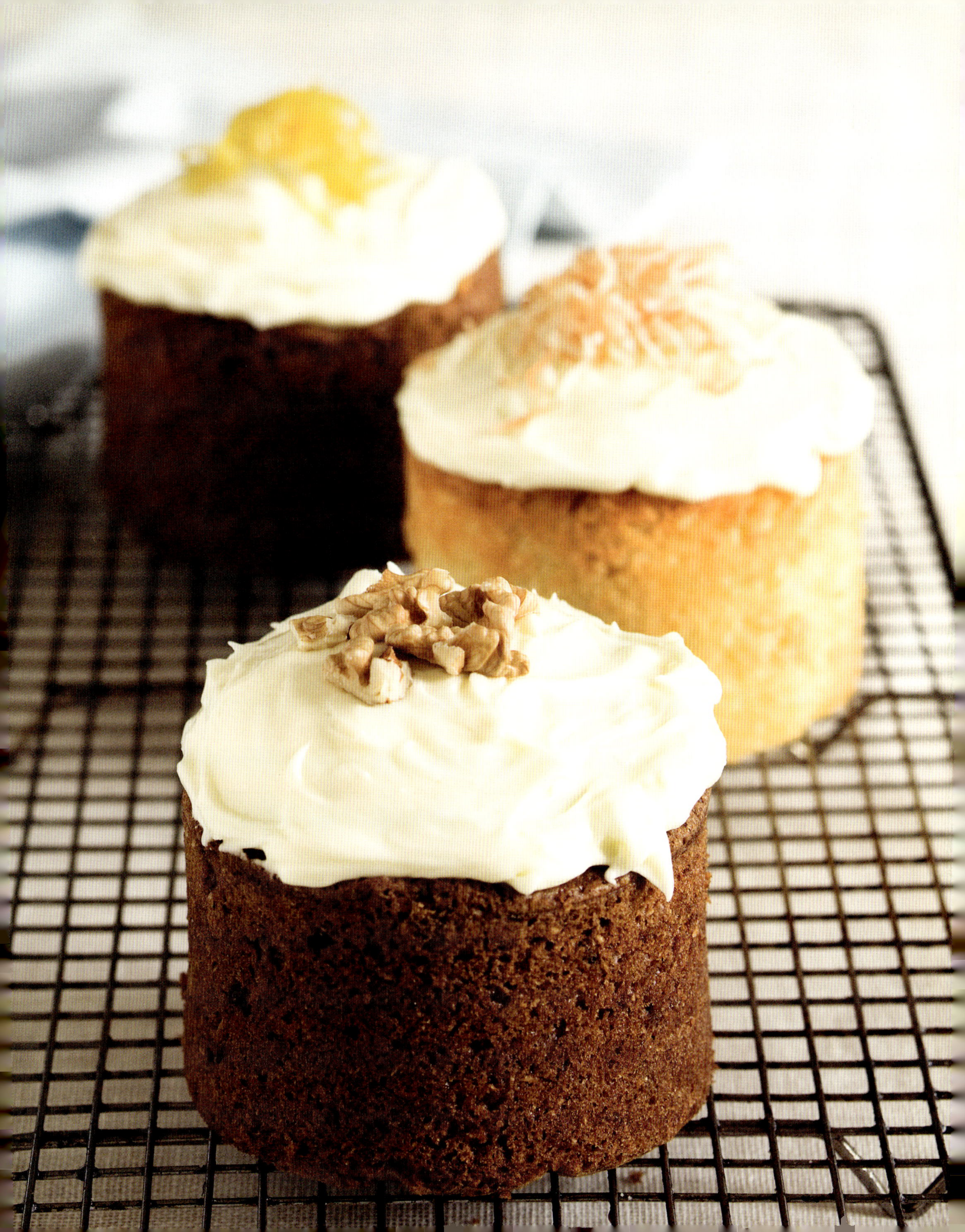

Kitchen essentials & glossary

Shopping This is probably the single most important part of the whole deal. If you start with stale or limp ingredients your job will always be hard. Support your local fresh-food suppliers and tell them what you need. A good butcher will be happy to bone, stuff and trim or try to get special items in for you. It's the same with fruit and vegetables. You want really fresh produce, ideally organically grown, from suppliers whose systems you trust. Smell, touch and gently feel before you buy. Get to know when foods are in their natural season (hopefully this book will help to that end).

Oven heat From brand to brand and kitchen to kitchen, ovens cook differently. For this reason, and also because ingredients differ in their moisture content and ability to absorb liquid etc, you do need to use your judgement and treat the cooking times in recipes as a guide. I prefer to cook with a gas cooktop and an electric fan-forced oven. Check 10-15% before the specified recipe cook time to see how things are proceeding. As you cook more you will see where your oven sits in relation to this book and will be able to judge how to amend cooking times accordingly. Remember, too, to preheat the oven to the temperature specified before you start cooking and that if you overload a domestic oven, the temperature will often drop and things will take longer to cook. All the recipes in this book have been tested with a fan-forced oven. This heats up more quickly and tends to cook food more evenly than a conventional oven. Fan-forced ovens deliver about 15% more heat than conventional ovens so if you use a non-fan oven you may need to add about 10% to the cooking time or increase the heat by 5-10°C.

Measures used in this book
1 cup equals 250ml
1 tbsp (tablespoon) equals 15ml
1 tsp (teaspoon) equals 5ml

Pantry Having a well-organised pantry is key to making good food without a lot of planning. Stocking your cupboard with ethnic ingredients allows you to be creative with very little forethought and ensures you will never be short of a flavour boost. For example, curry spices, poppadoms, lentils and rice have an Indian theme; extra virgin olive oil, balsamic and wine vinegars, anchovies, garlic, capers, tomato paste, polenta, oregano, canned tomatoes and pesto provide Mediterranean flavours; short grain rice, soy sauce, wasabi, dashi stock, miso, rice vinegar and seaweeds offer Japanese tangents; fish sauce, sesame oil, oyster sauce, ginger and kaffir lime leaves allow you to create Asian tones in your food. For browning, frying and general cooking use a commercial extra virgin olive oil and a neutral oil such as grapeseed. Avocado oil is also a good all-purpose oil with a high burn temperature. Treat the very best estate virgin olive oil like gold and use it judiciously to add flavour and garnish where it will count. Sesame oil is very useful and walnut oil is divine but only when it's fresh – it goes rancid very quickly.

GLOSSARY

Angel hair pasta finer than spaghetti. Substitutes include fine dried egg noodles.

Baking paper is incredibly useful as a liner when roasting and baking to stop sticking and save on washing up. I use it wherever I can in oven cooking to line pans before pie making, grilling or roasting – unless I want the caramelisation created by juices in a roasting pan for gravy.

Blitz pulse in food processor at high speed.

Bruschetta and crostini bases see page 188

Canned beans a 400g can of beans yields about 1½ cups cooked beans. Freshly cooked beans can also be frozen. Spread well-drained beans on to a tray to freeze, then free flow into sealed bags or containers, label and store in the freezer.

Cooking new potatoes adding a knob of butter to new potatoes as they boil helps keep them waxy.

Coring tomatoes use a sharp knife to cut the stem cores out of tomatoes; they are always tough and horrid.

Crushing garlic see page 161

Dice cut into 1cm cubes.

Double boiler used when cooking heat-sensitive mixtures like custards that will curdle if overheated. The mixture is cooked in a bowl or pot set over a pot of simmering water.

Fish sauce a strong-smelling Asian condiment; use like soy sauce.

Flat leaf parsley has a flat leaf. Regular curly-leaf parsley can be substituted.

Fold very gently combine mixtures with a large, scooping motion, using a large, flat spoon.

Glass noodles or bean thread noodles, made from mung beans, these tough, brittle noodles must be soaked to soften and then boiled for a minute so they turn clear and fully soften. They can be boiled for long periods without breaking down.

Horseradish invasive perennial from the Brassica family that has a pungent root. The root should be mixed with an acid such as vinegar or lemon juice as soon as it is grated or it turns brown and bitter.

Japanese 7 spice Shichimi is a Japanese 7-spice mix that includes hot peppers, mustard, sansho (prickly ash berries), black sesame, poppy seeds and citrus peel. It's good to sprinkle over Asian soups and stir- fries.

Kaffir lime leaves very thorny citrus with aromatic leaves that are widely used in Thai and Southeast Asian cooking. The leaves freeze well.

Lemon grass *Cymbopogon*, a coarse-stalked grass with a soft inner core at the base of each leaf. Peel off outer leaves and use a microplane to grate the inner core for a lemony flavour. The source of citronella.

Neutral oil oil with a neutral flavour, eg grapeseed, rice bran, safflower. Use cold pressed oils where possible.

Non-corrosive bowl acid ingredients should never be put into aluminium or other corrosive metal bowls. Use a plastic or glass container.

Olive oil spray buy one or put olive oil into a spritzer.

Parmesan cheese best bought in the block and grated to order. Grana padano is cheaper and makes an acceptable substitute. Do not buy ready grated.

Pepper black and white pepper all come from the same plant, *Piper Nigrum*. Black pepper is the unripe fruit and white is the ripe seed without the fruit. Black pepper is fruitier and less spicy than white. White pepper is hotter and good for sauces and mashed potatoes.

Purée blend until smooth.

Pre-cooked pastry crust and baking blind see page 32

Salting water allow about 1 teaspoon salt per 6 cups water when boiling vegetables.

Sea salt is usually coarser than fine salt and weighs less per spoonful.

Seasoning add salt and pepper to taste. Salt and pepper are primary condiments that add flavour and depth to your cooking.

Sesame oil very useful to add flavour, especially in Asian cooking.

Shanghai bok choy squatter, wider plant than regular bok choy with sweeter flavour. Regular bok choy has white stems, Shanghai has pale green stems.

Slicing oranges the pith of all citrus is bitter and should be removed before eating. The best way to slice an orange (also the most time consuming) is to first peel and remove all pith then cut down between segments with a sharp knife to release clean sections of fruit.

Star anise star-shaped spice with anise flavour, used in Chinese cooking and as a major component of garam masala. Useful in both sweet and savoury applications.

Sushi rice a sticky, short-grain rice with toothsome texture, good steamed and for rice puddings. For a sweet nutty taste, mix a little soy sauce and butter into cooked sushi rice and serve with stir-fries and other Asian dishes.

Smoked paprika regular paprika has a very mild flavour while the smoked varieties are intense. Choose sweet or hot – the sweet offers a rich smokiness without the heat.

Tamari wheat-free soy sauce. Regular soy sauce can be substituted.

Thai sweet chilli sauce red seeded sauce with sweet hot flavour. Useful flavour base for a wide range of dishes. Not as hot as the thicker sauces from Asia.

Vanilla see page 225

Zest the thin, aromatic, oily outer skin of citrus fruits. Take care not to include the white pith underneath which is bitter.

Index

Adjusting balance in a dish 227
Aioli, Roasted Garlic 192
Almonds
   Almond Butter 187
   Couscous with Beets & Almonds 110
   Greek Almond Citrus Cake 225
   Pear & Almond Tarts 174
   Roasted Pears & Almonds 173
   Tamari-almond & Basil Pesto 18
   Tamari-roasted Almonds 138
Anchoïade 187
Anchovy Sauce 187
Angel hair pasta 234
Anise, Star *see* Star anise
Appetizers & snacks
   Broccoli & Blue Cheese Chichetti 187
   Bruschetta Bases 188
   Chevre-filled summer vegetables 81
   Chicken & Mint Salad Rolls 78
   Cumin Grilled Kumara Slices 134
   Duck Finger Rolls 89
   Figs with Port Glaze 145
   Fresh Figs & Prosciutto 145
   Gravlax Crêpe Rolls 25
   Mushroom Bruschetta 188
   Potatoes with Sauce 77
   Prawn Salad Rolls 78
   Prawn-stuffed Snowpeas 25
   Roasted Asparagus Wraps 32
   Spicy Ginger Pork/Chicken Salad Cups 89
   Spicy Kumara & Prawn Fritters 134
   Spinach and Mozzarella Tarts 190
   Summer Salsas 74
   Vegetarian Salad Rolls 78
   Vegetarian Spiced Egg Snowpeas 25
   Zucchini & Basil Bruschetta 82
Apples
   Apple & Feijoa Breton Cake 169
   Apple Purée 230
   Pork with Fennel & Apples 98
Apricots & Nuts, Turkish Pilaf with 162
Artichokes
   fresh artichokes 54
   Preserved Artichokes in Olive Oil 54
   Sicilian Artichokes, Potatoes & Olives 54
Artichokes, Jerusalem 197
Arugula 140
Asian flavours for poaching 96
Asian Pesto 18
Asian Slaw 95

Asparagus
   Asparagus & Goat's Cheese Tarts 32
   Fettucini with Prawns, Asparagus & Mascarpone 38
   Fresh Asparagus & Cashew Slaw 23
   growing asparagus 32
   handling of asparagus 46
   Lemon Carbonara with Spring Greens 37
   Roasted Asparagus Wraps 32
The Autumn Palate 128
Avocados 23
   Avocado Salsa 74
   Kerala Potato & Avocado Salad 35

Bacon
   Black Bean & Bacon Soup 200
   Fusilli with Peas, Zucchini, Bacon & Parmesan 38
Baking paper 234
Balsamic vinegar 104
   Balsamic Glaze 143
   Balsamic-glazed Duck Salad 143
   Balsamic Red Onion Confit 53
   Raspberry Balsamic Dressing 26
Banana Cake 232
Barley Soup, Nonna's Lamb & 149
Basil
   purple basil 17*ill.*
   sweet leaf basil 17*ill.*
   Tamari-almond & Basil Pesto 18
   Zucchini & Basil Bruschetta 82
Bean thread noodles 235
Beans *see also* Broad beans; Green beans
   Black Bean & Bacon Soup 200
   canned beans 234
   Chilli Bean & Corn Salad 86
   as power food 138
Beef
   Beef Sirloin with Asian Greens & Ponzu Sauce 216
   Grilled Steak on Rocket Salad with Balsamic Glaze 104
   Perfect Roast Beef with Red Wine Sauce 167
   pleasures of a roast 164
   Spicy Beef & Noodle Bowl 41
   Steak and Gravy 53
   Three Sauces for Steak 53
Beetroot
   Couscous with Beets & Almonds 110
   Fresh Beets with Coriander Seeds 23
   Grilled Radicchio with Blue Cheese & Beetroot 197

   roasted beetroot 136
   Sweet & Sour Beets and Onions 136
Bell peppers *see* Capsicums
Bengal Peach Chutney 164
Berries *see also* Raspberries; Strawberries
   Berry Brûlée 56
   Berry Smoothie 56
   Berry Soufflés 59
   Five-berry Confit 122
   Spicy Berry Puddings 221
   Summer Berry Coulis 122
Bircher Muesli 230
Biriyani, Lamb 208
Blanching 37
Blitz 234
Blue cheese
   Broccoli & Blue Cheese Cichetti 187
   Grilled Radicchio with Blue Cheese & Beetroot 197
Bok choy 235
   Crisp Pork Belly with Asian Spices & Bok Choy 212
Bread *see also* Bruschetta 82, 187, 188
   Best, chicken sandwiches the 96
   Lemon-caper crumb 46
   Parsley crumb topping 210
Breakfast fix 230
Breton Cake, Apple & Feijoa 169
Brining 156
Broad beans 29
   Bean & Pecorino Salad 50
   Fresh Broad Beans with Parmesan & Olive Oil 23
   Ligurian Bean Pesto 18
   Spanish Broad Beans with Eggs & Ham 29
Broccoli
   Broccoli & Blue Cheese Cichetti 187
   Thai Chicken & Broccoli Stir-fry 44
Broths *see* Soups
Brûlée, Berry 56
Bruschetta
   Broccoli & blue cheese chichetti 187
   Bruschetta Bases 188
   Mushroom Bruschetta 188
   Zucchini & Basil Bruschetta 82
Brussels Sprouts 219
Butters, Flavoured *see* Flavoured butters

Cabbage & Lentils, Duck Breasts with Savoy 206
Cakes
   Apple & Feijoa Breton Cake 169

Banana Cake 232
Carrot Cake 232
Coconut Passion Cake 170
Greek Almond Citrus Cake 225
Magic Chocolate Cake 178
Rhubarb & Yoghurt Crumble Cake 64
Capers
   Mint & Caper Sauce 77
   Roasted Fish with Lemon-caper Crumb 46
   Salted capers 74
Capsicums 154
   Grilled Eggplant & Capsicum Salad 151
   Harvest Polenta Bake with Rocket, Capsicums & Feta 152
   Roast Capsicum & Coriander Sauce 130
   Roasted Red Capsicums 136
   Stir-fried Scallops with Capsicums & Spinach 132
Caramel Sauce 117
Carbonara with Spring Greens, Lemon 37
Carrot Cake 232
Cashews
   Crisp Cauliflower & Cashew Salad 194
   Fresh Asparagus & Cashew Slaw 23
   Stir-fried Chicken with Cashews 161
Cauliflower & Cashew Salad, Crisp 194
Celeriac 205
Celery 205
Champagne Vinegar Dressing 98
Cheese *see also* Blue cheese; Feta; Goat's cheese; Mascarpone; Parmesan cheese
   Lamb Cutlets with Bean & Pecorino Salad 50
   marinating soft cheeses 81
   Spinach & Mozzarella Tarts 190
Chermoula
   Chermoula Butter 101
   Chermoula Grilled Crayfish 109
   Chermoula Marinade 101
   Chermoula Paste 101
Cherries, Pickling 114
Chervil 20
Chestnuts 199
   Southern Italian Chestnut Soup 199
Chèvre-filled Summer Vegetables 81
Chicken
   Chicken & Leek Diablo 210
   Chicken & Mint Salad Rolls 78

Chicken Minestrone 149
Chicken Sandwiches 96
Chicken Stock 184
Chinese Chicken Noodle Bowl 41
Grilled Chicken with Israeli
   Couscous Salad 102
Grilled Lime & Coriander Chicken
   104
Harvest Chicken Bake 154
Lemon Chicken & Fennel Salad
   98
Mediterranean Chicken Bake 154
Mediterranean Chicken Salad 96
Mexican Harvest Soup 149
Moroccan Chicken & Chickpea
   Salad 98
Spicy Ginger Chicken Salad Cups
   89
Stir-fried Chicken with Cashews
   161
Tender Poached Chicken Breasts
   96
Thai Chicken & Broccoli Stir-fry 44
Chickpeas
   Moroccan Chicken & Chickpea
      Salad 98
   as power food 138
   Spicy Chickpea Salad 110
Chillies
   bird's eye chilli 73*ill*.
   cayenne chilli 73*ill*.
   Chilli Bean & Corn Salad 86
   Chilli Citrus Dressing 26
   Chilli Lime & Cockle Noodle Bowl
      42
   Chilli Lime Dressing 84
   dried chillies 185*ill*.
   hot stuff 72
   jalapeno chilli 73*ill*.
   Peanut Chilli Dipping Sauce 78
   Scotch bonnet chilli 73*ill*.
   Sweet Chilli & Coriander-roasted
      Fish 49
   Thai sweet chilli sauce 235
   Ultimate Chilli Sauce 72
Chinese Chicken Noodle Bowl 41
Chinese-styled cooked greens 41
Chives
   garlic chives 17*ill*.
   Radishes with Mint & Chive Cream
      23
Chocolate 178
   Chocolate Ganache 178
   Chocolate Raspberry Pavlovas
      118
   Magic Chocolate Cake 178
Chorizo Paella, Duck & 158
Chutney
   Bengal Peach Chutney 164
   Fresh Coriander Chutney 154
Citrus fruit *see also* Lemons; Limes;
   Oranges
   Chilli Citrus Dressing 26
   Greek Almond Citrus Cake 225
   Rutaceae family 222
   zest 221, 235
Clove-spiced Mascarpone Cream
   117
Cockle Noodle Bowl, Chilli
   Lime & 42
Coconut Passion Cake 170
Confit
   Balsamic Red Onion Confit 53
   Five-berry Confit 122
   Quince Confit & Ruby Syrup 177
Cooking Hints & Techniques
   adjusting balance in a dish 227
   baking paper 234
   blanching to set colour 37
   blitz 234
   brining 156
   choosing olive oil 84

   cooking new potatoes 234
   cool before chilling 146
   coring tomatoes 234
   crushing garlic 161
   dice 234
   flavouring soups & vegetables
      146
   fold 234
   fritter cooking tips 134
   handling fresh scallops & other
      shellfish 132
   handling roasted vegetables 146
   handling soft greens 84
   home-cooked convenience 138
   how to dress a green salad 84
   making flavoured butters 109
   making substitutions 219
   meringue know-how 118
   non-corrosive bowl 235
   pre-cooking a pastry crust 32
   purée 235
   salting water 235
   seasoning 235
   seeds & sprouts 215
   slicing oranges 235
   storing stone fruit 114
   the chemistry of baking 64
   tips to better grills 106
   toasting sesame seeds 49
   whipping cream 66
   zest 221, 235
Coriander 17*ill*.
   Fresh Beets with Coriander Seeds
      23
   Fresh Coriander Chutney 154
   as garnish 20
   Grilled Lime & Coriander Chicken
      104
   Roast Capsicum & Coriander
      Sauce 130
   Sweet Chilli & Coriander-roasted
      Fish 49
Corn
   Chilli Bean & Corn Salad 86
   cooking corn 86
   Corn, Mint & Feta Polenta *(recipe*
      variation) 152
   cutting corn from the cob 86
   Summer Cob Salad 86
   sweetcorn 86
   Corn salad *(salad green)* 140
   Coulis, Summer Berry 122
Couscous
   Couscous with Beets & Almonds
      110
   Grilled Chicken with Israeli
      Couscous Salad 102
Crab Apples, Pickling 114
Crackling, Fennel & Rosemary
   Braised Pork with 156
Cream
   Clove-spiced Mascarpone Cream
      117
   crème fraîche 66
   Rhubarb Cream 60
   whipping, thickened & clotted
      cream 66
   Cream Cheese Icing 178
   Crema, Balsamic 104
   Crêpe Rolls, Gravlax 25
   Crostini Bases 188
   Croûtons, Crispy 202
   Crumbles *see* Toppings & crumbles
   Cumin Grilled Kumara Slices 134
   Curd, Lemon 222
Curries
   Kashmiri-style Lamb Knuckles 212
   Lamb Biriyani 208
   Mixed Seafood Laksa 215
   Seafood Curry 215
   Curry Dressing, Kerala 35

Desserts
   Apple & Feijoa Breton Cake 169
   Apple Purée 230
   Baked Pears with Port Glaze 173
   Baked Rhubarb 63
   Berry Brûlée 56
   Berry Soufflés 59
   Chocolate Raspberry Pavlovas
      118
   Coconut Passion Cake 170
   Fig & Walnut Tarts 174
   Five-berry Confit 122
   Flambéed Fruit 117
   Fruit Bowl with Lime Syrup 228
   Ginger-Poached Feijoas 169
   Gooseberry Fool 66
   Greek Almond Citrus Cake 225
   Grilled Summer Stone Fruit 117
   Home-made Fruit Ice Cream 177
   Kiwi-pineapple Sorbet 228
   Lemon-ginger Sponge Puddings
      221
   Lemon Kiwi Syllabub Parfait 222
   Meringues 60
   Nectarine Compote & Semi-dried
      Nectarines 112
   Passionfruit Vanilla Terrine 170
   Pear & Almond Tarts 174
   Poached & Roasted Pears 230
   Poached Feijoas or Pears 230
   Poached Lemon & Ginger Pears
      173
   Prune & Orange Soufflés 59
   Quince Tarte Tatin 177
   Rhubarb & Strawberry Fool 66
   Roasted Pears & Almonds 173
   Rum Sabayon with Winter Fruits
      227
   Scarlet Strawberry Jellies 63
   Slow-roasted Late-season Peaches
      114
   Spicy Berry Puddings 221
   Stewed Rhubarb 60
   Strawberries in Pinot Noir 56
   Summer Berry Coulis 122
   Summer Harvest Fruit Tart 120
   Tamarillos in Port 228
   Turkish Dried Fruit Compote 60
   Vanilla-lime Panna Cotta 114
Diablo Marinade 210
Dice 234
Dipping sauces & salsas *see also*
   Pesto
   Anchoïade 187
   Avocado Salsa 74
   Fresh Coriander Chutney 154
   Fresh Nectarine or Mango Salsa
      74
   Horseradish Cream 53
   Mexican Fresh Tomato Salsa 74
   Mint & Caper Sauce 77
   Nuoc Cham (Vietnamese Dipping
      Sauce) 78
   Olive Paste 128
   Peanut Chilli Dipping Sauce 78
   Ponzu Sauce 216
   Salsa Verde 53
   Semi-dried Tomato & Olive Salsa
      192
   South-of-the-border Sour Cream
      77
   The Ultimate Chilli Sauce 72
Double-boiler 235
Dressings
   Balsamic Glaze 143
   Basil Mint Dressing 151
   Caper Marinade & Dressing 50
   Champagne Vinegar Dressing 98
   Chilli Citrus Dressing 26
   Chilli Lime Dressing 84
   Creamy Moroccan Dressing 92
   Honey Mustard Dressing 84

   how to dress a green salad 82
   Kerala Curry Dressing 35
   Mustard Red Wine Vinaigrette 84
   Nuoc Cham (Vietnamese Dipping
      Sauce) 78
   Ponzu Sauce 216
   Raspberry Balsamic Dressing 26
   Riviera Dressing 26
   Roasted Garlic Aioli 192
   Soy Mirin Dressing 49
   Spiced Oil Dressing 84
   Tuscan Herb Oil 96
Drinks
   Berry Smoothie 56
   Grenadine Syrup 228
   Home-made Lemonade 63
Duck
   Balsamic-glazed Duck Salad 143
   Duck & Chorizo Paella 158
   Duck & Quince Tagine 162
   Duck Breasts with Savoy Cabbage
      & Lentils 206
   Duck Finger Rolls 89
Dukkah 151

Eggplants
   Ginger Pork with Beans &
      Eggplants 161
   Grilled Eggplant & Capsicum
      Salad 151
   Roasted Eggplant Slices 136
Eggs
   Potato Salad with Gherkins & Eggs
      35
   Spanish Broad Beans with Eggs &
      Ham 29
   Vegetarian Spiced Egg Snowpeas
      25

Favas *see* Broad beans
Feijoas
   Apple & Feijoa Breton Cake 169
   Ginger-poached Feijoas 169
   Poached Feijoas 230
Fennel 129*ill*.
   Fennel & Rosemary Braised Pork
      with Crackling 156
   fennel & walnut slaw 98
   Lemon Chicken & Fennel Salad
      98
   Pork with Fennel & Apples 98
   versatile fennel 98
Feta
   Grilled Feta & Vegetables 151
   Harvest Polenta Bake with Rocket,
      Capsicums & Feta 152
Fideua 158
Figs
   Fig & Walnut Tarts 174
   Figs with Port Glaze 145
   Fresh Figs & Prosciutto 145
   Grilled Goat's Cheese & Fig Salad
      145
   preserved figs 174
Fish
   Flash-roasted Fish with Asian
      Dressing 49
   Roasted Fish with Lemon-caper
      Crumb 46
   Sweet Chilli & Coriander-roasted
      Fish 49
Fish sauce 235
Flavoured butters
   Almond Butter 187
   Chermoula Butter 101
   making flavoured butters 109
Flavoured oils
   Spiced Oil Dressing 84
   Tuscan Herb Oil 96
Fold 235
Friands, Plum 120
Frittata Cakes, Spring Vegetable 29

Fritters, Spicy Kumara & Prawn 134
Fruit see also Berries; and specific fruits
   Flambéed Fruit 117
   fruit nutrition 63
   Grilled Summer Stone Fruit 117
   Home-made Fruit Ice Cream 177
   from the Rose family 122
   storing stone fruit 114
   Summer Harvest Fruit Tart 120
   Turkish Dried Fruit Compote 60

Ganache, Chocolate 178
Garlic
   crushing garlic 161
   garlic chives 17*ill.*
   Roasted Garlic 192
   Roasted Garlic Aioli 192
Gherkins & Eggs, Potato Salad with 35
Ginger 89
   Ginger-poached Feijoas 169
   Ginger Pork with Beans & Eggplants 161
   Lemon-ginger Sponge Puddings 221
   Poached Lemon & Ginger Pears 173
   Spicy Ginger Pork/Chicken Salad Cups 89
Glass noodles 95, 235
   Spicy Prawn & Glass Noodle Salad 95
Glazes
   Balsamic Glaze 104, 143
   Port Glaze 173
GMO debate 38
Goat's cheese
   Asparagus & Goat's Cheese Tarts 32
   Chèvre-filled Summer Vegetables 81
   Double-baked Goat's Cheese Soufflés 30
   Grilled Goat's Cheese & Fig Salad 145
Gooseberry Fool 66
Gratin
   Jerusalem artichoke gratin 197
   Silverbeet gratin 190
Gravlax Crêpe Rolls 25
Gravy, Steak and 53
Greek Almond Citrus Cake 225
Greek Lemon & Herb Marinade 101
Greek Silverbeet Roll 190
Green beans 92
   Bean & Pecorino Salad 50
   Ginger Pork with Beans & Eggplants 161
Grenadine Syrup 228
Grilling, Tips to better 106

Ham
   Pea & Ham Soup with Crispy Croûtons 202
   Spanish Broad Beans with Eggs & Ham 29
   Harvest Chicken Bake 154
   Harvest Polenta Bake with Rocket, Capsicums & Feta 152
Health & Nutrition
   avoid green potatoes 35
   avoiding trans fats 44
   chocolate cravings 178
   fruit & vegetable nutrition 63
   protect your body with crucifers 41
Herbs see also specific herbs
   as garnish 20
   basil 16*ill.*
   coriander 16*ill.*
   fennel 129*ill.*
   garlic chives 17*ill.*
   Greek Lemon & Herb Marinade 101
   lemon grass 16*ill.*, 72*ill.*
   mint 16*ill.*, 72*ill.*
   oregano 129*ill.*
   parsley 129*ill.*
   rosemary 129*ill.*
   sage 129*ill.*
   thyme 129*ill.*
   Tuscan Herb Oil 96
Home-made Fruit Ice Cream 177
Home-made Lemonade 63
Honey Mustard Dressing 84
Horseradish 235
   Horseradish & Wasabi Cream 77
   Horseradish Cream 53

Ice Cream, Home-made Fruit 177
Icing
   Chocolate Ganache 178
   Cream Cheese 178
   Passionfruit Icing 170
Italian Chestnut Soup, Southern 199

Jellies, Scarlet Strawberry 63
Jerusalem artichokes 197
   Jerusalem artichoke gratin 197
   Jerusalem artichoke soup 197
   roast chokes 197

Kaffir lime leaves 73*ill.*, 235
Kashmiri-style Lamb Knuckles 212
Kerala Curry Dressing 35
Kerala Potato & Avocado Salad 35
Kerala Potato Salad 35
Kitchen essentials 234
Kiwifruit 232
   Kiwi-pineapple Sorbet 228
   Lemon Kiwi Syllabub Parfait 222
Kohlrabi 110
Kumara
   Cumin Grilled Kumara Slices 134
   Spicy Kumara & Prawn Fritters 134

Laksa, Mixed Seafood 215
Laksa Sauce Base 215
Lamb
   flash-roasting lamb racks 50
   Grilled Butterflied Leg of Lamb 106
   Kashmiri-style Lamb Knuckles 212
   Lamb Biriyani 208
   Lamb Cutlets with Bean & Pecorino Salad 50
   Nonna's Lamb & Barley Soup 199
   roasting a leg of lamb 50
   Shepherd's Pie 205
Lamb's lettuce 140
Latino soups 200
Leeks
   Chicken & Leek Diablo 210
   Leek, Mushroom & Sausage Risotto 205
   Leeks Vinaigrette 194
Lemon grass 17*ill.*, 73*ill.*, 235
Lemons
   Greek Lemon & Herb Marinade 101
   Home-made Lemonade 63
   Lemon Anise Syrup 225
   Lemon Carbonara with Spring Greens 37
   Lemon Chicken & Fennel Salad 98
   Lemon Curd 222
   Lemon-ginger Sponge Puddings 221
   Lemon Kiwi Syllabub Parfait 222
   Poached Lemon & Ginger Pears 173
   Preserved Lemons 192
   Roasted Fish with Lemon-caper Crumb 46
Lentils
   Duck Breasts with Savoy Cabbage & Lentils 206
   Lentil & Feta Salad 138
   Moroccan Lentil Soup 200
   as power food 138
   Spicy Lentils 138
   Vegan Lentil Salad 138
Lettuces 140
Ligurian Bean Pesto 18
Limes
   Chilli Lime & Cockle Noodle Bowl 42
   Chilli Lime Dressing 84
   Fruit Bowl with Lime Syrup 228
   Grilled Lime & Coriander Chicken 104
   Lime & Coriander Marinade 104
   kaffir lime leaves 73*ill.*, 235
   Tahitian or Persian lime 73*ill.*
   Vanilla-lime Panna Cotta 114

Mâche 140
Mangos
   Fresh Mango Salsa 74
   Grilled Prawn & Mango Salad 92
Marinades
   Caper Marinade & Dressing 50
   Chermoula Marinade 101
   Diablo Marinade 210
   Greek Lemon & Herb Marinade 101
   Lime & Coriander Marinade 104
   marinating soft cheeses 81
   Spice Trail Marinade 101
Mas Masumoto 112
Mascarpone
   Clove-spiced Mascarpone Cream 117
   Fettucini with Prawns, Asparagus & Mascarpone 38
Measures used in this book 234
Mediterranean Chicken Bake 154
Mediterranean Chicken Salad 96
Meringues 60
   meringues know-how 118
Mexican Fresh Tomato Salsa 74
Mexican Harvest Soup 149
Mexican Tomato Soup, chilled 90
Miner's lettuce 140
Minestrone, Chicken 149
Mint 73*ill.*
   apple mint 17*ill.*
   Chicken & Mint Salad Rolls 78
   as garnish 20
   Mint & Caper Sauce 77
   Radishes with Mint & Chive Cream 23
   winter mint 17*ill.*
Mirin Dressing, Soy 49
Mizuna 140
Moroccan Chicken & Chickpea Salad 98
Moroccan Dressing, creamy 92
Moroccan Lentil Soup 200
Moroccan Potato Salad 109
Moroccan Seafood Salad 92
Mozzarella Tarts, Spinach & 190
Muesli, Bircher 230
Mushrooms 149
   Leek, Mushroom & Sausage Risotto 205
   Mushroom and blue cheese polenta *(recipe variation)* 152
   Mushroom Bruschetta 188
Mustard
   Honey Mustard Dressing 84
   Mustard Red Wine Vinaigrette 84

Nectarines
   Fresh Nectarine Salsa 74
   Nectarine Compote & Semi-dried Nectarines 112
Non-corrosive bowl 235
Nonna's Lamb & Barley Soup 199
Noodles see also Glass noodles
   Chilli Lime & Cockle Noodle Bowl 42
   Chinese Chicken Noodle Bowl 41
   Fideua 158
   Spicy Beef & Noodle Bowl 41
   Nuoc Cham (Vietnamese Dipping Sauce) 78
Nuts see also Cashews; Walnuts
   Peanut Chilli Dipping Sauce 78
   roasting nuts 202
   Turkish Pilaf with Apricots & Nuts 162

Odori 151
Oils
   avoiding trans fats 44
   flavoured see Flavoured oils
   neutral oil 235
   sesame oil 235
Olive oil
   choosing olive oil 84
   Fresh Broad Beans with Parmesan & Olive Oil 23
   olive oil spray 235
   Preserved Artichokes in Olive Oil 54
Olives
   Olive Paste 128
   Semi-dried Tomato & Olive Salsa 192
   Sicilian Artichokes, Potatoes & Olives 54
Onions
   Balsamic Red Onion Confit 53
   Sweet & Sour Beets and Onions 136
Oranges
   Orange Buttered Yams 219
   Prune & Orange Soufflés 59
   slicing oranges 59
   Winter Spinach, Witlof & Orange Salad 194
Oven heat 234

Paella, Duck & Chorizo 158
Panna Cotta, Vanilla-lime 114
Pantry 234
Paprika 235
Parmesan cheese 235
   Fresh Broad Beans with Parmesan & Olive Oil 23
   Fusilli with Peas, Zucchini, Bacon & Parmesan 38
Parsley 129*ill.*
   flat leaf parsley 235
   as garnish 20
   Parsley Crumb Topping 210
Parsnip & Rocket Mash 219
Passionfruit 170
   Coconut Passion Cake 170
   Passionfruit Icing 170
   Passionfruit Syrup 170
   Passionfruit Vanilla Terrine 170
Pasta see also Glass noodles; Noodles
   angel hair pasta 234
   Fettucini with Prawns, Asparagus & Mascarpone 38
   Fusilli with Peas, Zucchini, Bacon & Parmesan 38
   Lemon Carbonara with Spring Greens 37
   Summer Orzo Salad 110
Pastes, rubs & blends 101
   Chermoula Paste 101

Olive Paste 128
Pastry, Pies and Tarts, Savoury
   Asparagus & Goat's Cheese Tarts 32
   Greek Silverbeet Roll 190
   pre-cooked pastry crust and baking blind 32
   Spinach & Mozzarella Tarts 190
Pastry, Pies and Tarts, Sweet
   Apple & Feijoa Breton Cake 169
   Fig & Walnut Tarts 174
   Pear & Almond Tarts 174
   Quince Tarte Tatin 177
   Summer Harvest Fruit Tart 120
Pavlovas, Chocolate Raspberry 118
Peaches
   Bengal Peach Chutney 78
   Slow-roasted Late-season Peaches 114
Peanut Chilli Dipping Sauce 78
Pears
   Baked Pears with Port Glaze 173
   Pear & Almond Tarts 174
   Poached & Roasted Pears 230
   Poached Lemon & Ginger Pears 173
   Poached Pears 230
   Roasted Pear & Walnut Salad 140
   Roasted Pears & Almonds 173
Peas
   Fusilli with Peas, Zucchini, Bacon & Parmesan 38
   handling 46
   Pea & Ham Soup with Crispy Croûtons 202
   pea pleasures 30
Pecorino Salad, Lamb Cutlets with Bean & 50
Pepper 235
Persimmons 169
Pesto
   Asian Pesto 18
   Ligurian Bean Pesto 18
   Rocket Pesto 18
   Tamari-almond & Basil Pesto 18
   Winter Pesto 192
Pickling Cherries & Crab Apples 114
Pie, Shepherd's 205
Pilaf with Apricots & Nuts, Turkish 162
Pineapple Sorbet, Kiwi- 228
Plant families
   Cruciferae family 41
   Curcubit family 208
   Lily family 130
   Rosasceae family 122
   Rutaceae family 222
   Solanacaea family 212
   Umbelliferae family 210
Plum Friands 120
Polenta
   Corn, Mint & Feta *(recipe variation)* 152
   Harvest Polenta Bake with Rocket, Capsicums & Feta 152
   Mushroom & Blue Cheese *(recipe variation)* 152
   puffy baked 152
Pomegranate with Witloof & Spinach 197
Ponzu Sauce 216
Pork *see also* Bacon; Ham
   brining 156
   Crisp Pork Belly with Asian Spices & Bok Choy 212
   crisping crackling 156
   Fennel & Rosemary Braised Pork with Crackling 156
   Ginger Pork with Beans & Eggplants 161
   Pork with Fennel & Apples 98

Spicy Ginger Pork Salad Cups 89
Port
   Port Glaze 173
   Tamarillos in Port 228
Potatoes
   avoid green potatoes 35
   Baby Potatoes with Three Sauces 77
   cooking new potatoes 234
   growing potatoes 77
   Kerala Potato & Avocado Salad 35
   Kerala Potato Salad 35
   Moroccan Potato Salad 109
   new & old potatoes and old potatoes 77
   Potato Salad with Gherkins & Eggs 35
   Sicilian Artichokes, Potatoes & Olives 54
Prawns
   Fettucini with Prawns, Asparagus & Mascarpone 38
   Grilled Prawn & Mango Salad 92
   Prawn Salad Rolls 78
   Prawn-stuffed Snowpeas 25
   Spicy Kumara & Prawn Fritters 134
   Spicy Prawn & Glass Noodle Salad 95
   Warm Zucchini & Prawn Salad 82
Preserves *see also* Chutney
   Lemon Curd 222
   pickling cherries & crab apples 114
   Preserved Artichokes in Olive Oil 54
   preserved figs 174
   Preserved Lemons 192
Prosciutto, Fresh Figs & 145
Prune & Orange Soufflés 59
Pumpkin 208
Purée 235
   Apple Purée 230

Quinces
   Duck & Quince Tagine 162
   Quince Confit & Ruby Syrup 177
   Quince Tarte Tatin 177

Radicchio 140
   Grilled Radicchio with Blue Cheese & Beetroot 197
   Radishes with Mint & Chive Cream 23
Raspberries
   Chocolate Raspberry Pavlovas 118
   Raspberry Balsamic Dressing 26
Recycling systems 152
Rhubarb
   Baked Rhubarb 63
   Rhubarb & Strawberry Fool 66
   Rhubarb & Yoghurt Crumble Cake 64
   Rhubarb Cream 60
   Stewed Rhubarb 60
Rice
   Duck & Chorizo Paella 158
   Lamb Biriyani 208
   Leek, Mushroom & Sausage Risotto 205
   pumpkin risotto 208
   sushi rice 235
   Turkish Pilaf with Apricots & Nuts 162
Risotto
   Leek, Mushroom & Sausage 205
   pumpkin 208
Riviera Dressing 26
Roasts (meat) 164

Rocket 140
   Grilled Steak on Rocket Salad with Balsamic Glaze 104
   Harvest Polenta Bake with Rocket, Capsicums & Feta 152
   Rocket Pesto 18
Rosemary Braised Pork with Crackling, Fennel & 156
Rubs & blends *see* Pastes, rubs & blends

Sabayon with Winter Fruits, Rum 227
Salads *see also* Dressings
   Asian Slaw 95
   Balsamic-glazed Duck Salad 143
   Bean & Pecorino Salad 50
   Chicken & Mint Salad Rolls 78
   Chilli Bean & Corn Salad 86
   Crisp Cauliflower & Cashew Salad 194
   Duck Finger Rolls 89
   Grilled Chicken with Israeli Couscous Salad 102
   Grilled Eggplant & Capsicum Salad 151
   Grilled Goat's Cheese & Fig Salad 145
   Grilled Prawn & Mango Salad 92
   Grilled Radicchio with Blue Cheese & Beetroot 197
   Grilled Steak on Rocket Salad with Balsamic Glaze 104
   handling soft greens 84
   how to dress a green salad 84
   Kerala Potato & Avocado Salad 35
   Kerala Potato Salad 35
   Lemon Chicken & Fennel Salad 98
   Lentil & Feta Salad 138
   Mediterranean Chicken Salad 96
   Moroccan Chicken & Chickpea Salad 98
   Moroccan Potato Salad 109
   Moroccan Seafood Salad 92
   Pomegranate with Witloof & Spinach 197
   Potato Salad with Gherkins & Eggs 35
   Prawn Salad Rolls 78
   Roasted Pear & Walnut Salad 140
   Roasted Tomato Salad with Tamari-almond & Basil Pesto 90
   salad greens 140
   Spicy Chickpea Salad 110
   Spicy Ginger Pork/Chicken Salad Cups 89
   Spicy Prawn & Glass Noodle Salad 95
   Summer Cob Salad 86
   Summer Orzo Salad 110
   Summer Tomato Salad 90
   tossed salads 26
   Vegan Lentil Salad 138
   Vegetarian Salad Rolls 78
   Warm Zucchini & Prawn Salad 82
   Winter Spinach, Witloof & Orange Salad 194
Salsas *see* Dipping sauces & salsas
Salt
   salting water 235
   sea salt 235
Sandwiches, Chicken 96
Sauces, Savoury *see also* Dipping sauces & salsas, pesto
   Anchovy Sauce 187
   Balsamic Glaze 143
   Balsamic Red Onion Confit 53
   Broccoli & Blue Cheese Cichetti 187
   Horseradish & Wasabi Cream 77

Horseradish Cream 53
Laksa Sauce Base 215
Mint & Caper Sauce 77
Olive Paste 128
Ponzu Sauce 216
Red Wine Sauce 167
Roast Capsicum & Coriander Sauce 130
Roast Tomato Sauce 130
Salsa Verde 53
South-of-the-Border Sour Cream 77
Thai sweet chilli sauce 235
Ultimate Chilli Sauce 72
Sauces/Syrups, Sweet
   Brandied Berry Confit 122
   Caramel Sauce 117
   Clove-spiced Mascarpone Cream 117
   Five-berry Confit 122
   Ginger-poached Feijoas 169
   Lemon Anise Syrup 225
   Quince Confit & Ruby Syrup 177
   Summer Berry Coulis 122
Sausages
   Duck & Chorizo Paella 158
   Leek, Mushroom & Sausage Risotto 205
   Savoy Cabbage & Lentils, Duck Breasts with 206
Seafood *see also* Fish; Prawns
   Anchoïade 187
   Chermoula Grilled Crayfish 109
   Chilli Lime & Cockle Noodle Bowl 42
   Fideua 158
   Gravlax Crêpe Rolls 25
   handling of fresh scallops and other shellfish 132
   Mixed Seafood Laksa 215
   Moroccan Seafood Salad 92
   Seafood Curry 215
   Spicy Scallops in the Half Shell 132
   Stir-fried Scallops with Capsicums & Spinach 132
Seasoning 235
Seeds and sprouts 215
Sesame seeds
   sesame oil 235
   toasting sesame seeds 49
Shanghai bok choy 235
Shepherd's Pie 205
Shopping 234
Sicilian Artichokes, Potatoes & Olives 54
Silverbeet 190
   Greek Silverbeet Roll 190
   sautéed silverbeet 190
   silverbeet gratin 190
Slaws
   Asian Slaw 95
   Fennel & Walnut Slaw 98
Smoked paprika 235
Smoothie, Berry 56
Snacks *see* Appetizers & snacks
Snowpeas
   Lemon Carbonara with Spring Greens 37
   Prawn-stuffed Snowpeas 25
   Spiced Egg Snowpeas 25
Solanacaea family 212
Sorbet, Kiwi-pineapple 228
Soufflés
   Berry Soufflés 59
   Double-baked Goat's Cheese Soufflés 30
   Prune & Orange Soufflés 59
Soups
   Black Bean & Bacon Soup 200
   Chicken Minestrone 149
   Chilled Mexican Tomato Soup 90

Chilli Lime & Cockle Noodle Bowl 42
Crispy Croûtons 202
flavouring soups & vegetables 146
Jerusalem artichoke soup 197
Latino soups 200
Mexican Harvest Soup 149
Moroccan Lentil Soup 200
Nonna's Lamb & Barley Soup 199
Pea & Ham Soup with Crispy Croûtons 202
Seasonal Vege Soups 146
Southern Italian Chestnut Soup 199
Sour Cream, South-of-the-Border 77
Soy sauce *see also* Tamari
Soy Mirin Dressing 49
Spanish Broad Beans with Eggs & Ham 29
Spices *see also* Chillies; Mustard
cardamom pods 185*ill.*
Crisp Pork Belly with Asian Spices & Bok Choy 212
cumin seeds 185*ill.*
fennel seeds 185*ill.*
Japanese 7 spice 235
pepper 235
smoked paprika 235, 185*ill.*
Spice pastes, rubs & blends *see* Pastes, rubs & blends
Spice Trail Marinade 101
Spiced Oil Dressing 84
toasting sesame seeds 49
turmeric 185*ill.*
Spicy Berry Puddings 221
Spinach
Pomegranate with Witloof & Spinach 197
Spinach & Mozzarella Tarts 190
Stir-fried Scallops with Capsicums & Spinach 132
Wilted Spinach 219
Winter Spinach, Witloof & Orange Salad 194
Spring
Platter of Spring Tastes 20
The Spring Palate 16
Spring Vegetable Frittata Cakes 29
Sprouts 215
Star anise 235
Lemon Anise Syrup 225
Stir-fries
Stir-fried Chicken with Cashews 161
Stir-fried Scallops with Capsicums & Spinach 132
Thai Chicken & Broccoli Stir-fry 44
Tofu & Spring Vegetable Stir-fry 44
Stock
Chicken Stock 184
Vegetable Stock 184
Strawberries
Rhubarb & Strawberry Fool 66
Scarlet Strawberry Jellies 63
Strawberries in Pinot Noir 56
Summer
Grilled Summer Stone Fruit 117
Summer Berry Coulis 122
Summer Cob Salad 86
Summer Harvest Fruit Tart 120
Summer Orzo Salad 110
The Summer Palate 72
Summer Tomato Salad 90
Sustainability council 38
Sushi rice 235
Sweet & Sour Beets and Onions 136
Syllabub Parfait, Lemon Kiwi 222
Syrups *see* Sauces/Syrups, Sweet

Tagine, Duck & Quince 162
Tamari 235
Tamari-almond & Basil Pesto 18
Tamari-roasted Almonds 138
Tamarillos in Port 228
Thai dishes
Thai Chicken & Broccoli Stir-fry 44
Thai sweet chilli sauce 235
Tofu & Spring Vegetable Stir-fry 44
Tomatillos 74
Tomatoes
Chilled Mexican Tomato Soup 90
coring tomatoes 234
Mexican Fresh Tomato Salsa 74
Roast Tomato Sauce 130
Roasted Tomato Salad with Tamari-almond & Basil Pesto 90
Semi-dried Tomato & Olive Salsa 192
Slow-roasted Tomatoes 90
Summer Tomato Salad 90
Toppings & crumbles *see also* Pesto
Broccoli & Blue Cheese Cichetti 187
Olive Paste 128
Parsley Crumb Topping 210
Rhubarb & Yoghurt Crumble Cake 64
Roasted Fish with Lemon-caper Crumb 46
Turkish Dried Fruit Compote 60
Turkish Pilaf with Apricots & Nuts 162
Tuscan Herb Oil 96

Vanilla
Passionfruit Vanilla Terrine 170
types of vanilla 225
Vanilla-lime Panna Cotta 114
Vegan Lentil Salad 138
Vegetables *see also specific vegetables*
blanching 37
Chèvre-filled Summer Vegetables 81
Chinese-styled cooked greens 41
Cruciferae family 41
Curcubit family 208
flavouring soups & vegetables 146
Grilled Feta & Vegetables 151
Grilled Vegetables 106
handling roasted vegetables 136
Lemon Carbonara with Spring Greens 37
Lily family 130
making substitutions 219
planting for year round harvests 194
protect your body with Crucifers 41
roasted starchy vegetables 136
salad greens 140
Seasonal Vege Soups 146
seeds and sprouts 215
spring plantings 42
Spring Vegetable Frittata Cakes 29
Tofu & Spring Vegetable Stir-fry 44
Umbelliferae family 210
vegetable nutrition 63
Vegetable Stock 184
Vegetarian dishes
Asian Slaw 95
Asparagus & Goat's Cheese Tarts 32
Brussels Sprouts 219
Chèvre-filled Summer Vegetables 81
Chilled Mexican Tomato Soup 90

Chilli Bean & Corn Salad 86
Corn, Mint & Feta Polenta *(recipe variation)* 152
Couscous with Beets & Almonds 110
Crisp Cauliflower & Cashew Salad 194
Cumin Grilled Kumara Slices 134
Double-baked Goat's Cheese Soufflés 30
Figs with Port Glaze 145
Greek Silverbeet Roll 190
Grilled Eggplant & Capsicum Salad 151
Grilled Feta & Vegetables 151
Grilled Goat's Cheese & Fig Salad 145
Grilled Radicchio with Blue Cheese & Beetroot 197
Harvest Polenta Bake with Rocket, Capsicums & Feta 152
Jerusalem artichoke soup 197
Kerala Potato & Avocado Salad 35
Kerala Potato Salad 35
Leeks Vinaigrette 194
Lemon Carbonara with Spring Greens 37
Lentil & Feta Salad 138
Moroccan Lentil Soup 200
Moroccan Potato Salad 109
Mushroom & Blue Cheese polenta *(recipe variation)* 152
Mushroom Bruschetta 188
Orange Buttered Yams 219
Parsnip & Rocket Mash 219
Pomegranate with Witloof & Spinach 197
Potato Salad with Gherkins & Eggs 35
pumpkin risotto 208
Roasted Eggplant Slices 136
Roasted Pear & Walnut Salad 140
Roasted Red Capsicums 136
Roasted Tomato Salad with Tamari-almond & Basil Pesto 90
sautéed silverbeet 190
Sicilian Artichokes, Potatoes & Olives 54
silverbeet gratin 190
Spiced Egg Snowpeas 25
Spicy Chickpea Salad 110
Spicy Lentils 138
Spinach & Mozzarella Tarts 190
Spring Vegetable Frittata Cakes 29
Summer Cob Salad 86
Summer Orzo Salad 110
Summer Tomato Salad 90
Sweet & Sour Beets and Onions 136
Tofu & Spring Vegetable Stir-fry 44
Turkish Pilaf with Apricots & Nuts 162
Vegan Lentil Salad 138
Vegetarian Salad Rolls 78
Wilted Spinach 219
Winter Spinach, Witloof & Orange Salad 194
Yorkies 167
Zucchini & Basil Bruschetta 82
Vietnamese Dipping Sauce (Nuoc Cham) 78
Vinaigrettes *see* Dressings

Walnuts
Fennel & Walnut Slaw 98
Fig & Walnut Tarts 174
Roasted Pear & Walnut Salad 140
Wasabi Cream, Horseradish & 77

Winter
Rum Sabayon with Winter Fruits 227
The Winter Palate 184
Winter Pesto 192
Winter purslane 140
Winter Spinach, Witloof & Orange Salad 194
Witloof
Pomegranate with Witloof & Spinach 197
Winter Spinach, Witloof & Orange Salad 194
Yams, Orange Buttered 219
Yoghurt Crumble Cake, Rhubarb 64
Yorkies 167

Zest 221, 235
Zucchini
Crispy Fried Zucchini Flowers 82
Fusilli with Peas, Zucchini, Bacon & Parmesan 38
Warm Zucchini & Prawn Salad 82
Zucchini & Basil Bruschetta 82
zucchini flowers 82

Photographers
All photographs taken by Aaron McLean except for the following:

Mark Smith ©, page 182 (eggs on hay, spade in garden, picking Jerusalem artichokes).

ICIP ©, pages: 14 (asparagus shoots), 48, 139 (garden images), 182 (walnuts in bucket) and 183 (spinach, carrots, yams and pumpkin).